McGraw-Hill
Mathematics

Transition
Handbook

Bridge the Gaps!

What Do I Need to Know?

Skill Builder

Challenge

Teacher Guide

3

**McGraw-Hill
School Division**

New York   Farmington

McGraw-Hill School Division 🜚

A Division of The McGraw-Hill Companies

Copyright © McGraw-Hill School Division,
a Division of the Educational and Professional Publishing Group of The McGraw-Hill Companies, Inc.
All rights reserved. Permission granted to reproduce for use with McGraw-Hill MATHEMATICS.

McGraw-Hill School Division
Two Penn Plaza
New York, New York 10121-2298

Printed in the United States of America

ISBN 0-02-100205-3 / 3

1 2 3 4 5 6 7 8 9 066 05 04 03 02 01 00

GRADE 3
Contents

To the Teacher...viii

Chapter 1
Place Value and Money

Inventory Test Blackline Masters.....................................1A
Inventory Test Prerequisite Skills Chart.......................1C
Hundreds, Tens, and Ones...2
Compare Numbers 4
Order Numbers 6
Round to the Nearest Ten 8
Counting On 10
Skip Counting 11
Counting Coins 12
Challenge: Make Your Own Numbers............................14
Challenge: Money Riddles..16

Chapter 2
Add Whole Numbers

Inventory Test Blackline Masters...................................17A
Inventory Test Prerequisite Skills Chart.....................17C
Addition Facts to 20..18
Add 2-Digit Numbers 20
Regroup Ones 22
Hundreds and Tens 24
Count Money 25
Round to Tens, Hundreds, and Thousands 26
Challenge: Equal Lines..28
Challenge: Palindrome Numbers....................................30

Chapter 3
Subtract Whole Numbers

Inventory Test Blackline Masters..............................31A
Inventory Test Prerequisite Skills Chart.......................31C
Count Back..32
Basic Addition Facts 33
Subtraction Facts to 20 34
Addition Patterns 35
Subtract 2-Digit Numbers 36
Rename Tens and Ones...38
Round to the Nearest Ten, Hundred, or Thousand 39
Challenge: Guess and Check Shapes 40
Challenge: Missing Digits 42

Chapter 4
Time, Data, and Graphs

Inventory Test Blackline Masters..............................43A
Inventory Test Prerequisite Skills Chart.......................43C
Time to the Hour, Half Hour, and Quarter Hour 44
Skip Counting by 5s 46
Ordinal Numbers 47
Tally Marks and Charts..48
Addition Patterns 49
Read Pictographs 50
Read Bar Graphs 52
Challenge: Hands Only!..54
Challenge: Make Your Own Chart and Graph 56

Chapter 5
Multiplication Concepts

Inventory Test Blackline Masters..............................57A
Inventory Test Prerequisite Skills Chart.......................57C
Equal Groups 58
Add 3 or More Numbers..60
Skip Counting 61
Commutative Property of Addition 62
Doubles to Add..63
Challenge: Logical Thinking: Missing Factors 64
Challenge: Number Sense: Choose the Greater Set 66

Chapter 6
Multiplication Facts

Inventory Test Blackline Masters.................................67A
Inventory Test Prerequisite Skills Chart......................67C
Use Arrays to Multiply 68
Equal Groups 70
Repeated Addition..72
Multiply by 3 and 4 73
Multiplication Facts Through 5...................................74
Place Value..75
Use a Multiplication Table..76
Associative Property of Addition 77
Challenge: Reading Timetable 78
Challenge: Find Factors: Multiplication Riddles..............80

Chapter 7
Division Concepts

Inventory Test Blackline Masters.................................81A
Inventory Test Prerequisite Skills Chart......................81C
Equal Groups 82
Subtraction 84
Skip Count Backwards 86
Missing Factors 87
Multiplication Facts Through 9...................................88
Multiply with 0 and 1..90
Challenge: Multiplication and Division Sentences...........92
Challenge: Logical Thinking: Use the Rules!.................94

Chapter 8
Division Facts

Inventory Test Blackline Masters.................................95A
Inventory Test Prerequisite Skills Chart......................95C
Meaning of Division 96
Skip Count Backwards by 6 and 7 98
Skip Count Backwards by 8 and 9 99
Function Tables...100
Multiplication Patterns 102
Using an Addition Facts Table 103
Fact Families 104
Challenge: Dividing — Plus One 106
Challenge: Dividing in Half 108

Chapter 9
Multiply by 1-Digit Numbers

Inventory Test Blackline Masters.................................109A
Inventory Test Prerequisite Skills Chart......................109C
Multiplication Facts 110
Patterns 111
Place Value..112
Rounding 114
Expanded Form 116
Multiplication Properties 117
Column Addition 118
Challenge: Factors and Primes 120
Challenge: Squares and Cubes 122

Chapter 10
Divide by 1-Digit Numbers

Inventory Test Blackline Masters.................................123A
Inventory Test Prerequisite Skills Chart......................123C
Multiplying with Multiples of 10, 100, or 1,000 124
Division with Remainders 126
Subtraction 128
Closest Multiple 129
Division Facts 130
Multiplying a 2-Digit Number by a 1-Digit Number........132
Multiplying a 3-Digit Number by a 1-Digit Number.......134
Challenge: Using Parentheses 136
Challenge: Distance, Speed, and Time 138

Chapter 11
Measurement

Inventory Test Blackline Masters.................................139A
Inventory Test Prerequisite Skills Chart......................139C
Measuring Length...140
Ordering Whole Numbers...142
Multiplication and Division Facts 144
Capacity...146
Multiply and Divide by 10, 100, and 1,000 148
Comparing Numbers 150
Challenge: Addition Riddles 152
Challenge: Subtraction Puzzle 154

Chapter 12
Geometry

Inventory Test Blackline Masters.................................155A
Inventory Test Prerequisite Skills Chart.......................155C
Classify Objects..156
Identify Sides and Angles.......................................158
Comparing Angles...160
Measuring Line Segments.....................................162
Add 3 or More Addends 164
Challenge: Circle Math...166
Challenge: Odds and Evens.................................168

Chapter 13
Fractions and Probability

Inventory Test Blackline Masters.................................169A
Inventory Test Prerequisite Skills Chart.......................169C
Identify Equal Parts..170
Patterns 172
Equivalent Names 174
Addition and Subtraction Facts 176
Frequency Tables..178
Challenge: Quilt Patterns......................................180
Challenge: Coin Tosses 182

Chapter 14
Relate Fractions and Decimals

Inventory Test Blackline Masters.................................183A
Inventory Test Prerequisite Skills Chart.......................183C
Meaning of Fractions 184
Money Amounts...186
Mixed Numbers 188
Addition..190
Subtraction 192
Challenge: Game of Mixed Numbers 194
Challenge: Input/Output Tables 196

To the Teacher

Welcome to *McGraw-Hill Mathematics Transition Handbook: Bridge the Gaps!* The goal of these materials is to provide assessment and instruction in the prerequisite skills that some of your students need to be successful in math at this grade level.

For each chapter of the *McGraw-Hill Mathematics* student text, there is a 2-page inventory test called *What Do I Need To Know?* You will find these inventory tests as blackline masters on the A and B pages in this Teacher Guide. The results of the tests will help you diagnose any gaps in student knowledge. You can then provide students with materials needed to reteach or challenge them as appropriate.

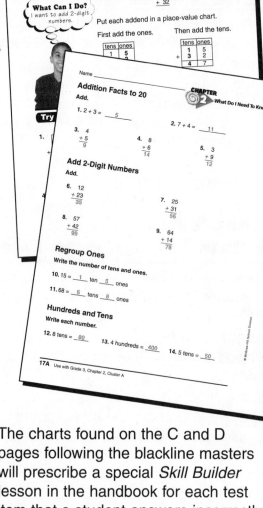

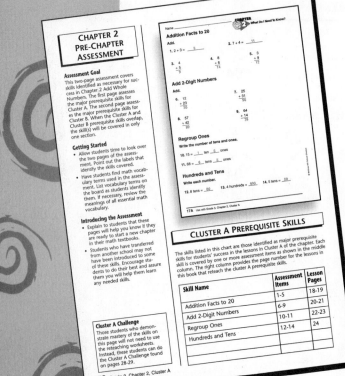

The charts found on the C and D pages following the blackline masters will prescribe a special *Skill Builder* lesson in the handbook for each test item that a student answers incorrectly.

The *Skill Builder* lessons are presented in language that is simple and direct. The lessons are highly visual and have been designed to keep reading to a minimum.

The Learn section begins with a student asking *What Can I Do?* This section provides stepped-out models and one or more strategies to help bridge any gaps in the student's knowledge. Following this is *Try It*, a section of guided practice, and *Power Practice*, a section containing exercises to ensure that your students acquire the math power they need to be successful in each chapter of their mathematics textbook.

At least one *Skill Builder* in each chapter has a feature called *Learn with Partners & Parents*. This activity is intended for students to use at home with parents or siblings or at school with a classmate-partner to practice a math skill in a game-like setting.

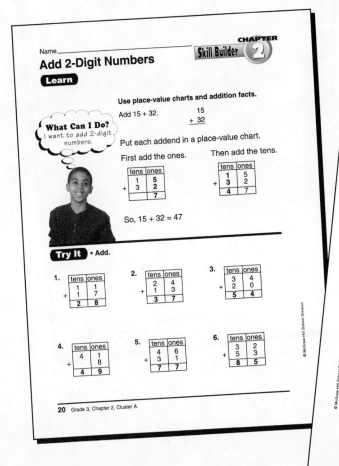

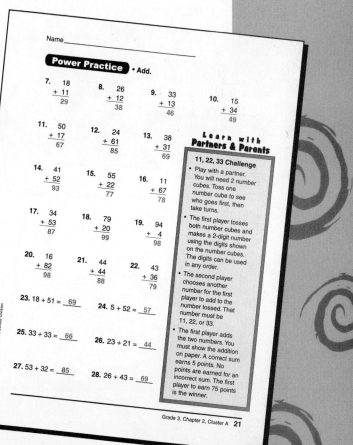

Two *Challenge* activities appear at the end of each chapter in the handbook. These provide a variety of math experiences for students who had no difficulty with the inventory test. Students will enjoy working on the puzzles, riddles, codes, and other more challenging formats. The *Challenge* activities will provide an opportunity for your more advanced students to work independently, allowing you to focus attention on those who need additional instruction before they work on the lessons in their math text.

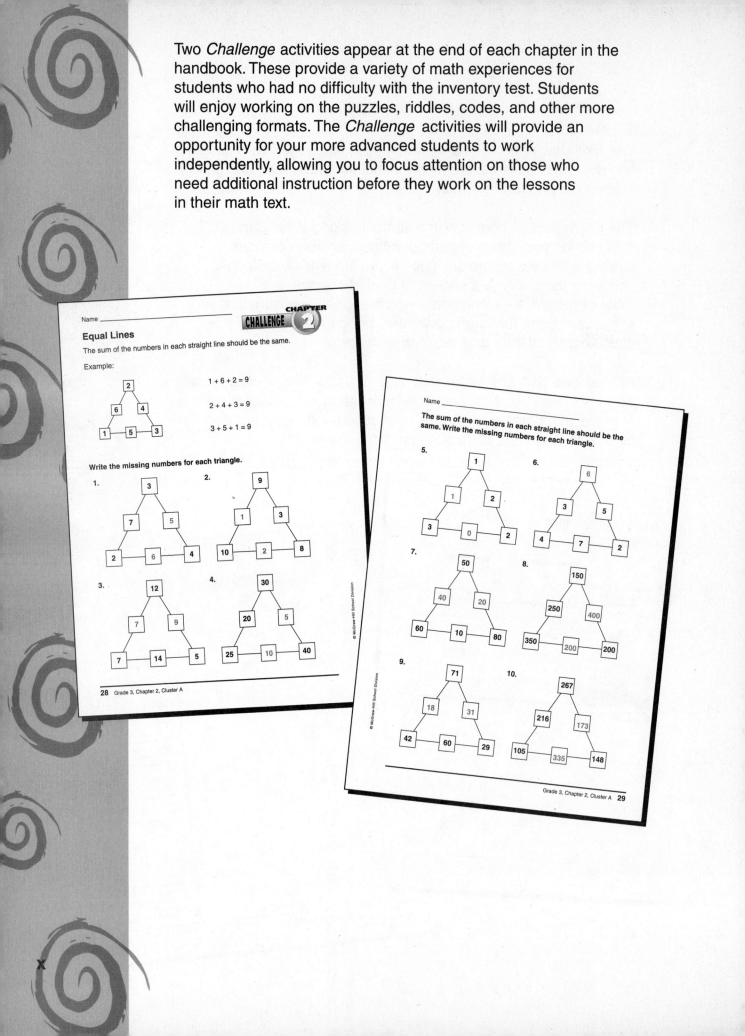

Name _____

Equal Lines

The sum of the numbers in each straight line should be the same.

Example:

$$1 + 6 + 2 = 9$$

$$2 + 4 + 3 = 9$$

$$3 + 5 + 1 = 9$$

Write the missing numbers for each triangle.

1.
2.
3.
4.

Name _____

The sum of the numbers in each straight line should be the same. Write the missing numbers for each triangle.

5.
6.
7.
8.
9.
10.

The Teacher Guide provides a complete lesson plan for each *Skill Builder* and *Challenge*. Each *Skill Builder* lesson plan includes a lesson objective, *Getting Started* activities, teaching suggestions, and questions to check the student's understanding. There is also a section called *What If the Student Can't*, which offers additional activities in case a student needs more support in mastering an essential prerequisite skill or lacks the understanding needed to complete the *Skill Builder* exercises successfully.

The lesson plan for each *Challenge* includes a lesson objective along with suggestions for introducing and using the *Challenge*.

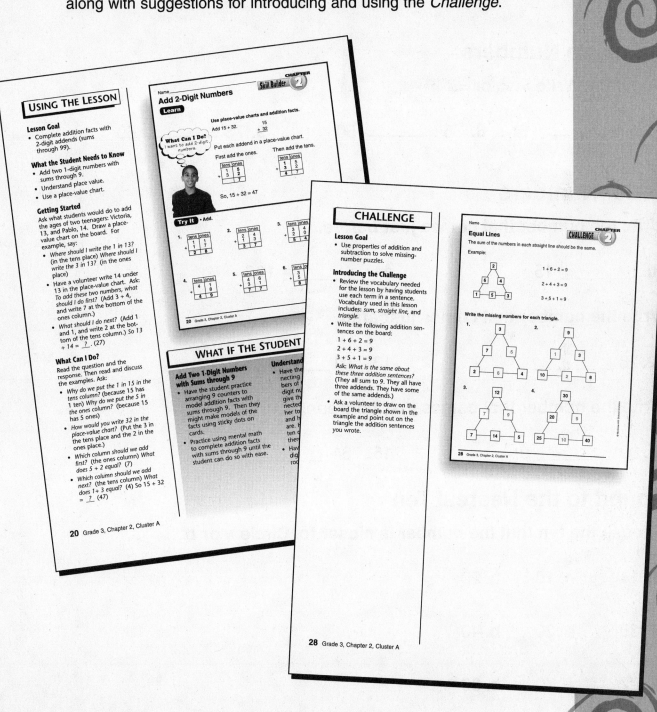

Hundreds, Tens, and Ones

Write each missing number.

1. 8 = _____ ones   **2.** 30 = _____ tens   **3.** 200 = _____ hundreds

4. 70 = _____ tens   **5.** 900 = _____ hundreds   **6.** 4 = _____ ones

Compare Numbers

Compare. Write >, <, or =.

7. 11 _____ 14   **8.** 36 _____ 50   **9.** 73 _____ 69

Order Numbers

Write the number that comes just *before.*

10. _____ 15   **11.** _____ 120

Write the number that comes just *after.*

12. 78 _____   **13.** 501 _____

Write the number that comes just *between.*

14. 89 _____ 91   **15.** 764 _____ 766

Round to the Nearest Ten

Choose the ten that the number is closer to. Circle *a* or *b.*

16. 14   **a.** 10   **b.** 20

17. 39   **a.** 30   **b.** 40

18. 77   **a.** 70   **b.** 80

Counting On and Skip Counting

Complete each addition pattern.

19. 3, 4, 5, 6, _____, _____

20. 236, 237, 238, 239, _____, _____

21. 10, 20, 30, 40, _____, _____

22. 34, 36, 38, 40, _____, _____

Counting Coins

Write each amount.

23.

_____ ¢

24.

_____ ¢

25.

_____ ¢

CHAPTER 1 PRE-CHAPTER ASSESSMENT

Assessment Goal

This two-page assessment covers skills identified as necessary for success in Chapter 1 Place Value and Money. The first page assesses the major prerequisite skills for Cluster A. The second page assesses the major prerequisite skills for Cluster B. When the Cluster A and Cluster B prerequisite skills overlap, the skill(s) will be covered in only one section.

Getting Started

- Allow students time to look over the two pages of the assessment. Point out the labels that identify the skills covered.

- Have students find math vocabulary terms used in the assessment. List vocabulary terms on the board as students identify them. If necessary, review the meanings of all essential math vocabulary.

Introducing the Assessment

- Explain to students that these pages will help you know if they are ready to start a new chapter in their math textbooks.

- Students who have transferred from another school may not have been introduced to some of these skills. Encourage students to do their best and assure them you will help them learn any needed skills.

Cluster A Challenge

Those students who demonstrate mastery of the skills on this page will not need to use the reteaching worksheets. Instead, these students can do the Cluster A Challenge found on pages 14–15.

Name_____

Hundreds, Tens, and Ones

Write each missing number.

1. 8 = __8__ ones   2. 30 = __3__ tens   3. 200 = __2__ hundreds

4. 70 = __7__ tens   5. 900 = __9__ hundreds   6. 4 = __4__ ones

Compare Numbers

Compare. Write >, <, or =.

7. 11 __<__ 14   8. 36 __<__ 50   9. 73 __>__ 69

Order Numbers

Write the number that comes just *before*.

10. __14__ 15   11. __119__ 120

Write the number that comes just *after*.

12. 78 __79__   13. 501 __502__

Write the number that comes just *between*.

14. 89 __90__ 91   15. 764 __765__ 766

Round to the Nearest Ten

Choose the ten that the number is closer to. Circle *a* or *b*.

16. 14   (a. 10)   b. 20

17. 39   a. 30   (b. 40)

18. 77   a. 70   (b. 80)

1A   Use with Grade 3, Chapter 1, Cluster A

CLUSTER A PREREQUISITE SKILLS

The skills listed in this chart are those identified as major prerequisite skills for students' success in the lessons in Cluster A of the chapter. Each skill is covered by one or more assessment items as shown in the middle column. The right column provides the page number for the lessons in this book that reteach the cluster A prerequisite skills.

Skill Name	Assessment Items	Lesson Pages
Hundreds, Tens, and Ones	1-6	2-3
Compare Numbers	7-9	4-5
Order Numbers	10-15	6-7
Round to the Nearest Ten	16-18	8-9

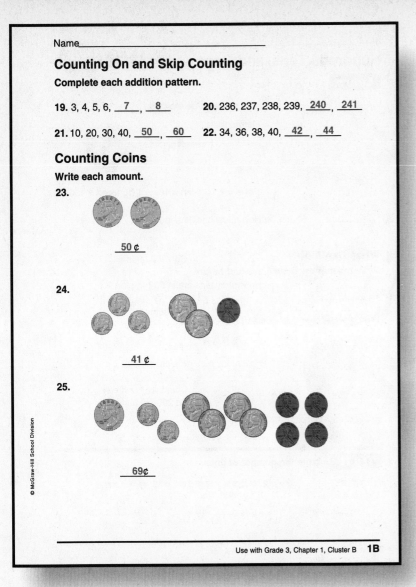

Name_____

Counting On and Skip Counting
Complete each addition pattern.

19. 3, 4, 5, 6, __7__, __8__   **20.** 236, 237, 238, 239, __240__, __241__

21. 10, 20, 30, 40, __50__, __60__   **22.** 34, 36, 38, 40, __42__, __44__

Counting Coins
Write each amount.

23.

__50 ¢__

24.

__41 ¢__

25.

__69¢__

© McGraw-Hill School Division

Use with Grade 3, Chapter 1, Cluster B **1B**

CLUSTER B PREREQUISITE SKILLS

The skills listed in this chart are those identified as major prerequisite skills for students' success in the lessons in Cluster B of the chapter. Each skill is covered by one or more assessment items as shown in the middle column. The right column provides the page number for the lessons in this book that reteach the Cluster B prerequisite skills

Skill Name	Assessment Items	Lesson Pages
Counting On	19-20	10
Skip Counting	21-22	11
Counting Coins	23-25	12-13

Alternative Assessment Strategies

- Oral administration of the assessment is appropriate for younger students or those whose native language is not English. Read the skills title and directions one section at a time. Check students' understanding by asking them to tell you how they will do the first exercise in the group.

- For some skill types you may wish to use group administration. In this technique, a small group or pair of students complete the assessment together. Through their discussion, you will be able to decide if supplementary reteaching materials are needed.

Intervention Materials

If students are not successful with the prerequisite skills assessed on these pages, reteaching lessons have been created to help them make the transition into the chapter.

Item correlation charts showing the skills lessons suitable for reteaching the prerequisite skills are found beneath the reproductions of each page of the assessment.

Cluster B Challenge
Those students who demonstrate mastery of the skills on this page will not need to use the reteaching worksheets. Instead, these students can do the Cluster B Challenge found on pages 16–17.

USING THE LESSON

Lesson Goal

- Find the number of ones, tens, and hundreds in whole numbers.

What the Student Needs To Know

- Use place-value models to identify the place value of digits.
- Recognize the place value of digits in 2- and 3-digit numbers.

Getting Started

Find out what students know about using place-value models. Display 1 ones model, 1 tens model, and 1 hundreds model in scrambled order. Call on volunteers to count and read the models and order them from largest to smallest. Say:

- *How many hundreds are in 1 hundreds model?* (1 hundred in all)
- *How many tens are in 1 tens model?* (1 ten in all)
- *How many ones are in 1 ones model?* (1 one in all)

What Can I Do?

- Read the question and the response. Then read and discuss the examples. Ask:
- *How can you figure out how many ones are in a whole number?* (Use the ones models, then count the ones.)
- *How can you figure out how many tens are in a whole number?* (Use the tens models, then count the tens.)
- *How can you figure out how many hundreds are in a whole number?* (Use the hundreds models, then count the hundreds.)
- Display 5 tens models. Say: *Count the tens.* (5 tens) *What whole number equals 5 tens?* (50)
- Display 7 ones models. Say: *Count the ones.* (7 ones) *What whole number equals 7 ones?* (7)
- Display 2 hundreds models. Say: *Count the hundreds.* (2 hundreds) *What whole number equals 2 hundreds?* (200)

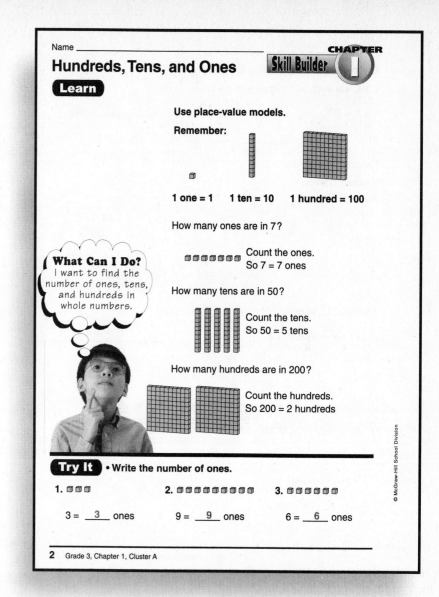

Learn

Use place-value models.

Remember:

1 one = 1   1 ten = 10   1 hundred = 100

How many ones are in 7?

Count the ones.
So 7 = 7 ones

What Can I Do?
I want to find the number of ones, tens, and hundreds in whole numbers.

How many tens are in 50?

Count the tens.
So 50 = 5 tens

How many hundreds are in 200?

Count the hundreds.
So 200 = 2 hundreds

Try It • Write the number of ones.

1. 3 = __3__ ones

2. 9 = __9__ ones

3. 6 = __6__ ones

2   Grade 3, Chapter 1, Cluster A

© McGraw-Hill School Division

WHAT IF THE STUDENT CAN'T

Use Place-Value Models to Identify the Place Value of Digits

- Have students use place-value charts to write the digits for numbers shown by hundreds, tens, and ones models. Have them point to each group of ones, tens, or hundreds as they count the models and write the appropriate digit.

- Have the student draw in a math journal a ones, tens, and hundreds model and label each model.

- Put 7 tens on a place-value mat. Help the student determine the number by counting the tens models first, then the ones. (7 tens, 0 ones, so there are 7 tens in 70)

- Ask the student to draw place-value models for 4, 30, and 600. Then have him or her tell the numbers of ones, tens, or hundreds in each.

Name _____

Write the number of tens.

4. 40 = _4_ tens

5. 70 = _7_ tens

6. 30 = _3_ tens

Write the number of hundreds.

7. 100 = _1_ hundred

8. 800 = _8_ hundreds

Power Practice • Write each missing number.

9. 2 = _2_ ones

10. 50 = _5_ tens

11. 300 = _3_ hundreds

12. 60 = _6_ tens

13. 500 = _5_ hundreds

14. 80 = _8_ tens

15. 900 = _9_ hundreds

16. 20 = _2_ tens

17. 5 = _5_ ones

18. 90 = _9_ tens

19. 400 = _4_ hundreds

20. 10 = _1_ ten

© McGraw-Hill School Division

Try It

• Have students read their answers aloud. Remind them to say "ones," "tens," or "hundreds," as appropriate.

• Ask students to show their answers on place-value charts. Have them work in pairs to reorder the numbers from least to greatest so they can see the models increase in size.

Power Practice

• Select several of the exercises and have volunteers show the numbers on place-value charts.

WHAT IF THE STUDENT CAN'T

Recognize the Place Value of Digits in 2- and 3-Digit Numbers

• Show the student a 2- or 3-digit number. Point to a digit and have the student tell the value of the digit as so many ones, tens, or hundreds. Include some examples where the answer will be 0 ones, 0 tens, or 0 hundreds.

Complete the Power Practice

• Discuss each incorrect answer. Have the student model any exercise he or she missed using a place-value chart or drawing. Then ask the student to write the correct answer.

Lesson Goal

- Compare one-digit numbers and two-digit numbers using >, <, and =.

What the Student Needs To Know

- Recognize the symbols >, <, and =.
- Use place-value models to compare two numbers.
- Identify the digit in the tens place and ones place.

Getting Started

Find out what students know about comparing two numbers. Say:

- *Let's compare 10 and 20. I'll start: There is 1 ten in 10, and 2 tens in 20. 1 ten is less than 2 tens, so 10 is less than 20.*
- *Now, you compare 70 and 70.*

What Can I Do?

- Read the question and the response. Then read and discuss the examples. Ask students to write and label the symbols >, <, and = on separate pieces of paper. Ask:
- *What are three ways to compare one number to another?* (See if it is greater than, less than, or equal to another.) *Hold up each symbol after I say its meaning: "greater than," "equal to," "less than."*
- *How can you use place-value models to compare two-digit numbers?* (Use tens models to compare the tens first. If the tens are the same, compare the ones.)
- *Compare 43 and 51. What is in the tens place in 43?* (4 tens) *What is in the tens place in 51?* (5 tens) *Are these numbers the same?* (no) *How are they different?* (4 tens is less than 5 tens) *So, how can you compare 43 and 51?* (43 is less than 51) *Hold up the "less than" symbol.*
- *Compare 64 and 62. What is in the tens place in 64?* (6 tens) *What is in the tens place in 62?* (6 tens) *These digits are the same. What is in the ones place in*

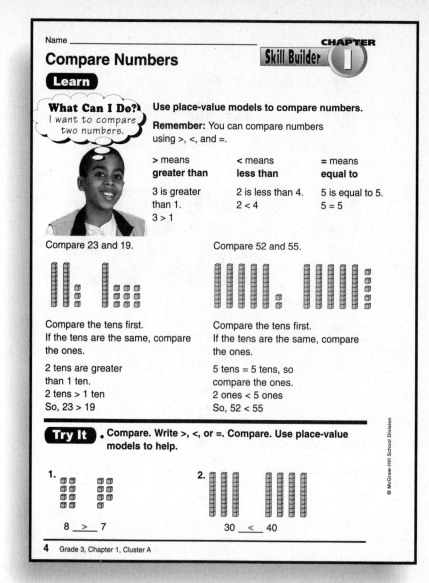

WHAT IF THE STUDENT CAN'T

Recognize the Symbols >, <, and =

- Help the student remember the difference between > and < by explaining that the open end of each symbol faces the number that is greater. Have the student choose pairs of numbers and use the symbols correctly to compare the numbers.
- Have the student write >, <, and = and the definition of each symbol in a math journal.

Use Place-Value Models to Compare Two Numbers

- Put tens blocks and ones blocks equal to 47 in a place-value mat. Help the student determine the number by counting the tens blocks first, then the ones.
- Ask the student to draw place-value models for 21 and 34. Then have them compare the numbers.

Name _____

Compare. Write >, <, or =. Use place-value models to help.

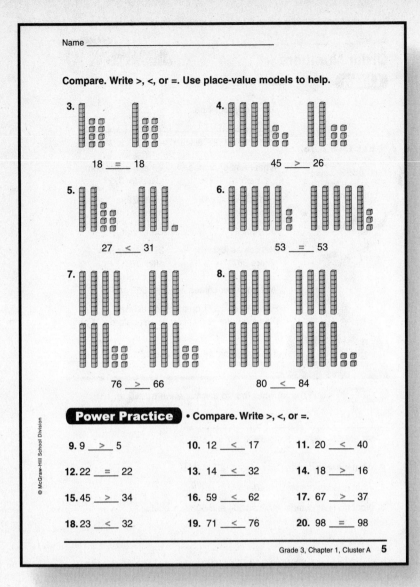

3. 18 __=__ 18

4. 45 __>__ 26

5. 27 __<__ 31

6. 53 __=__ 53

7. 76 __>__ 66

8. 80 __<__ 84

Power Practice • Compare. Write >, <, or =.

9. 9 __>__ 5

10. 12 __<__ 17

11. 20 __<__ 40

12. 22 __=__ 22

13. 14 __<__ 32

14. 18 __>__ 16

15. 45 __>__ 34

16. 59 __<__ 62

17. 67 __>__ 37

18. 23 __<__ 32

19. 71 __<__ 76

20. 98 __=__ 98

Grade 3, Chapter 1, Cluster A   **5**

WHAT IF THE STUDENT CAN'T

Identify the Digit in the Tens Place and Ones Place

- Stress that in a two-digit whole number, the digit on the left is in the tens place, and the digit on the right is in the ones place.

- Have the student read each number in the Power Practice and identify the digit in the tens place and in the ones place.

Complete the Power Practice

- Discuss each incorrect answer. Have the student use a place-value mat or make a drawing to illustrate the comparison. Then ask the student to write the correct answer.

- Have the student identify the correct symbol that compares the two numbers.

64? (4 ones) *What is in the ones place in 62?* (2 ones) *Are these digits the same?* (no) *How are they different?* (4 ones is greater than 2 ones) *So, how can you compare 64 and 62?* (64 is greater than 62) Hold up the "greater than" symbol.

- *Compare 78 and 78. What is in the tens place in 78?* (7 tens) *What is in the tens place in 78?* (7 tens) *These digits are the same. What is in the ones place in 78?* (8 ones) *What is in the ones place in 78?* (8 ones) *Are these digits the same?* (yes) *So, how can you compare 78 and 78?* (78 is equal to 78) Hold up the "equal to" symbol.

Try It

Have students say each number to be compared and explain the corresponding place-value model. Ask them to identify whether the number on the left is greater than, less than, or equal to the number on the right. Have them write the appropriate symbol. Say:

- *If the numbers have a tens place, compare the tens first. If not, compare the ones. Use the place-value models to help you.*

Power Practice

- Select several of the exercises and have volunteers model their comparisons on place-value mats.

- Ask students to review the steps to compare 2-digit numbers: compare the tens first; if the tens are the same, compare the ones.

Grade 3, Chapter 1, Cluster A   **5**

Lesson Goal
- Find which numbers come before, after, and between other numbers.

What the Student Needs To Know
- Read a number line.
- Use place value in 1-, 2-, and 3-digit numbers to find numbers on a number line.
- Recognize numbers before, after, and between other numbers on a number line.

Getting Started
Ask each student to create a number line from 60 to 65. Ask:
- *What number comes just before 61?* (60)
- *What number comes just after 63?* (64)
- *What number comes between 61 and 63?* (62)

What Can I Do?
- Read the question and the response. Then read and discuss the examples. Display a number line from 365 to 375. Ask:
- *Why is a number line a helpful tool to find number order?* (It can help you see which number is before, after, or between other numbers.)
- *How can you use a number line to figure out the number that comes just before 367?* (Find 367 on the number line. Go back 1. 366 comes just before 367.)
- *When you go back 1 from 367, are you going back in the ones place, tens place, or hundreds place?* (ones place)
- *How can you use a number line to figure out the number that comes just after 372?* (Find 372 on the number line. Go forward 1. 373 comes just after 372.)
- *When you go forward 1 from 372, are you going forward in the ones place, tens place, or hundreds place?* (ones place)
- *How can you use a number line to figure out the number that comes between 370 and 372?* (Find 370

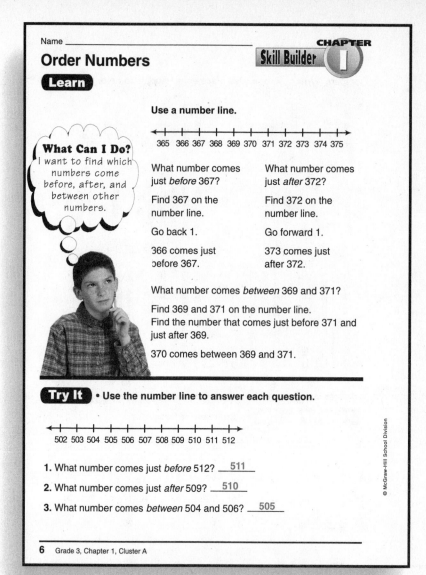

Name _____

Order Numbers

Skill Builder

CHAPTER 1

Learn

Use a number line.

```
365 366 367 368 369 370 371 372 373 374 375
```

What number comes just *before* 367?

Find 367 on the number line.

Go back 1.

366 comes just before 367.

What number comes just *after* 372?

Find 372 on the number line.

Go forward 1.

373 comes just after 372.

What number comes *between* 369 and 371?

Find 369 and 371 on the number line.
Find the number that comes just before 371 and just after 369.

370 comes between 369 and 371.

Try It • Use the number line to answer each question.

```
502 503 504 505 506 507 508 509 510 511 512
```

1. What number comes just *before* 512? __511__

2. What number comes just *after* 509? __510__

3. What number comes *between* 504 and 506? __505__

WHAT IF THE STUDENT CAN'T

Read a Number Line
- Remind the student that a number line can start and end on any number. Discuss the number line from 502 to 512 in Try It, page 6.
- Have the student copy that number line and use it to answer other number order questions. For example, say: *What number comes between 506 and 508?* (507)

Use Place Value in 1-, 2-, and 3-Digit Numbers to Find Numbers on a Number Line
- Use place-value models to stress that in a 2-digit number like 51, the 5 is in the tens place and the 1 is in the ones place. Explain that to find the number just after 51, go forward 1 in the ones place. Say: *What number is after 51?* (52)
- Follow a similar procedure for a 3-digit number like 260. Say: *What number is before 260?* (259)

Recognize Numbers Before, After, and Between Other Numbers on a Number Line
- Remind the student that on a number line, the number just *before* another number is 1 to the left of it. The number just *after* another number is 1 to

Name _____

Power Practice • Write the number that comes just *before*. You may draw a number line to help.

4. __13__ 14   5. __26__ 27   6. __59__ 60

7. __94__ 95   8. __131__ 132   9. __417__ 418

10. __520__ 521   11. __788__ 789   12. __655__ 656

Write the number that comes just *after*. You may draw a number line to help.

13. 17 __18__   14. 55 __56__

15. 113 __114__   16. 309 __310__

17. 667 __668__   18. 800 __801__

Write the number that comes *between*. You may draw a number line to help.

19. 4 __5__ 6   20. 28 __29__ 30

21. 99 __100__ 101   22. 310 __311__ 312

23. 492 __493__ 494   24. 944 __945__ 946

Learn with Partners & Parents

I Spy a Number

• Take turns. One player spies a 3-digit number in a store, on a license plate, or on a sign. The player must say, "I spy the number _____," and read the number aloud.

• The second player earns 1 point for telling the number that comes just *before* and another point for telling the number that comes just *after* the spied number.

• Write down all the numbers. The first player to get 25 points is the winner.

© McGraw-Hill School Division

---

and 372 on the number line. Go back 1 from 372. Go forward 1 from 370. 371 comes between 370 and 372.)

• Have students read their answers aloud. Ask them to point to their answers on the number line.

• For each incorrect answer, have students draw a number line, write and circle the correct answer, and draw arrows going forward, back, or between.

Power Practice

• Call on volunteers to model their answers on number lines for several of the answers.

• Have students explain how to use a number line to order numbers just before, after, or between other numbers.

Learn with Partners & Parents

• If players disagree about which number comes before or after a given number, they can sketch a number line to help them confirm the correct sequence.

WHAT IF THE STUDENT CAN'T

the right of it. The number just *between* two numbers is 1 to the left of the greater number and 1 to the right of the lesser number.

• Use number lines to illustrate these concepts daily until the student can name numbers just before, after, and between other numbers automatically.

Complete the Power Practice

• Discuss each incorrect answer. Have the student create a number line for any exercise he or she missed. Then ask the student to write the correct answer and read it aloud as a sentence. For example: *945 comes between 944 and 946.*

Lesson Goal
- Find the closest ten.

What the Student Needs To Know
- Count by tens.
- Read a number line.
- Identify which of two whole numbers is less.

Getting Started
Determine what students know about finding the closest ten. Display a number line from 20 to 30, with 23 circled. Say:

- Which two tens is the number 23 between? (20 and 30)
- *Which ten is 23 closer to, 20 or 30? (20)*
- *How can you tell?* (23 is 7 spaces from 30 but only 3 spaces from 20. 3 is less than 7, so 23 is closer to 20 than 30.)
- Display a number line from 60 to 70 with 68 circled. Say: *What two tens is 68 between?* (60 and 70) *Count the number of spaces from 60 to 68.* (8) *Count the number of spaces from 68 to 70.* (2) *Which ten is 68 closer to, 60 or 70?* (70) *Explain your answer.* (2 is less than 8, so 68 is closer to 70 than 60.)

What Can I Do?
- Read the question and the response. Then read and discuss the examples. Ask:
- *How is a number line useful for rounding to the closest ten?* (It shows the two tens a number is between and helps you count the spaces to each ten.)
- *What are the steps to figure out which ten a number is closer to?* (Circle the number on the number line. Count the spaces from the lesser ten to the number. Count the spaces from the number to the greater ten. Compare the amount of spaces. The lesser amount tells you which ten is closer.)

Name _____

Round to the Nearest Ten

Learn

Use a number line.

Find the ten that 12 is closer to.

Circle 12 on the number line.

10 11 12 13 14 15 16 17 18 19 20

The number 12 is between two tens on the number line. It is between 10 and 20.

Count the number of spaces from 10 to 12. There are 2 spaces.

Count the number of spaces from 12 to 20. There are 8 spaces.

So, 12 is closer to 10.

Find the ten that 27 is closer to.

20 21 22 23 24 25 26 27 28 29 30

The number 27 is between the tens 20 and 30.

It is 7 spaces away from 20. It is 3 spaces away from 30.

So, 27 is closer to 30.

What Can I Do?
I want to find the closest ten.

Try It • Choose the closer ten. Circle a or b.

1. Which ten is closer to 19?

10 11 12 13 14 15 16 17 18 **19** 20

a. 10   **b.** 20

2. Which ten is closer to 43?

40 41 42 **43** 44 45 46 47 48 49 50

a. 40   **b.** 50

WHAT IF THE STUDENT CAN'T

Count by Tens
- Have the student practice counting by tens from 10 to 100 a few times a day until the student can do so easily.

Read a Number Line
- Read with the student all the numbers on a number line on page 8. Say a number and have the student point to it.
- Help the student draw a number line showing all the numbers between two consecutive tens. Have the student count the spaces from one ten to the next.

Identify Which of Two Numbers is Less
- Write a number line from 0 to 9. Remind the student that in a pair of whole numbers, the number closer to 0 is less than the other. Circle two numbers on the line. Have the student tell which number is closer to 0. Repeat daily until the student can quickly name the lesser whole number in a pair.

Name _____

Choose the closer ten. Circle a or b.

3. Which ten is closer to 21?

20 **21** 22 23 24 25 26 27 28 29 30

(a. 20)   b. 30

4. Which ten is closer to 64?

60 61 62 63 **64** 65 66 67 68 69 70

(a. 60)   b. 70

5. Which ten is closer to 58?

50 51 52 53 54 55 56 57 **58** 59 60

a. 50   (b. 60)

6. Which ten is closer to 86?

80 81 82 83 84 85 **86** 87 88 89 90

a. 80   (b. 90)

Power Practice • Choose the ten the number is closer to. Circle a or b. You may draw a number line to help.

7. 11
(a. 10)   b. 20

8. 37
a. 30   (b. 40)

9. 26
a. 20   (b. 30)

10. 53
(a. 50)   b. 60

11. 22
(a. 20)   b. 30

12. 79
a. 70   (b. 80)

13. 88
a. 80   (b. 90)

14. 74
(a. 70)   b. 80

15. 62
(a. 60)   b. 70

WHAT IF THE STUDENT CAN'T

Complete the Power Practice
- Discuss each incorrect answer. Have the student say the two tens that the number falls between and show on a number line which ten is closer.
- Select several exercises and have volunteers show their work on place-value charts. Compare this method with using number lines to round to the nearest ten. Encourage the student to explain which method he or she prefers.

USING THE LESSON

Try It
- Call on volunteers to say the number in exercise 1 and in exercise 2 and then find it on the number line. Have students identify the two tens on the number line. Ask:
- *Which ten is the number closer to? How can you tell?* (Answers will vary.)
- For each incorrect answer, have students copy the corresponding number line, draw curved arrows while counting the spaces, and explain the correct answer. For example: *19 is 1 space away from 20 and 9 spaces away from 10. 1 is less than 9, so 19 is closer to 20. 43 is 3 spaces away from 40 and 7 spaces away from 50. 3 is less than 7 so 43 is closer to 40.*

Power Practice
- Call on volunteers to model their answers on number lines for several of the answers.
- Have students summarize what they learned by telling what finding the closer ten to a number means. (to go up or down to the ten closer to the number on the number line)

USING THE LESSON

Lesson Goal
- Use a number line to complete an addition pattern that goes up by ones.

What the Student Needs To Know
- Count on by ones.
- Read a pattern on a number line.

Getting Started
Find out what students know about completing an addition pattern. Say:
- *Let's start with the numbers in the pattern 1, 2, 3. Each number goes up by 1. Start at 3. What number comes just after 3?* (4)
- *Now, you continue the pattern up to 10. Start at 5.* (5, 6, 7, 8, 9, 10)

What Can I Do?
- Read the question and the response. Then read and discuss the examples. Ask:
- *What do the dark arrows on the number line from 0 to 12 mean?* (They show the direction in the number pattern.)
- *How can you figure out the missing numbers in the pattern?* (Each number goes up by 1, so count on by ones from 7 to find the missing numbers.)
- *Is the addition pattern going up or down?* (up)
- Do the same for the number line in the second example.

Try It
Have students say each number in the pattern and point to it on the number line. Have them count on by ones to complete each pattern. Ask:
- *Is the addition pattern going up on the number line or down on the number line?* (up)

Power Practice
- Have the student complete the practice items. Then review each answer.

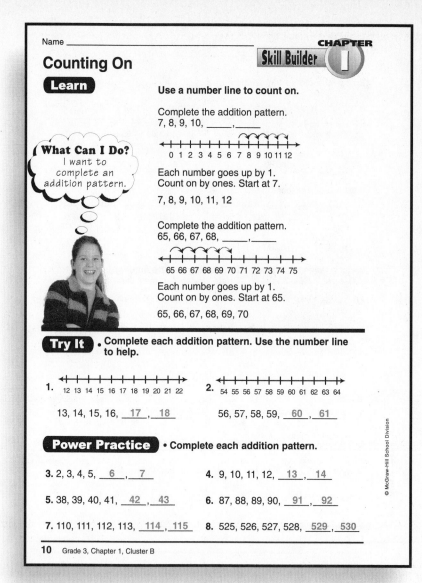

Counting On

Learn

Use a number line to count on.

Complete the addition pattern.
7, 8, 9, 10, _____, _____

What Can I Do?
I want to complete an addition pattern.

0 1 2 3 4 5 6 7 8 9 10 11 12

Each number goes up by 1.
Count on by ones. Start at 7.

7, 8, 9, 10, 11, 12

Complete the addition pattern.
65, 66, 67, 68, _____, _____

65 66 67 68 69 70 71 72 73 74 75

Each number goes up by 1.
Count on by ones. Start at 65.

65, 66, 67, 68, 69, 70

Try It • Complete each addition pattern. Use the number line to help.

1.
12 13 14 15 16 17 18 19 20 21 22

13, 14, 15, 16, __17__, __18__

2.
54 55 56 57 58 59 60 61 62 63 64

56, 57, 58, 59, __60__, __61__

Power Practice • Complete each addition pattern.

3. 2, 3, 4, 5, __6__, __7__

4. 9, 10, 11, 12, __13__, __14__

5. 38, 39, 40, 41, __42__, __43__

6. 87, 88, 89, 90, __91__, __92__

7. 110, 111, 112, 113, __114__, __115__

8. 525, 526, 527, 528, __529__, __530__

WHAT IF THE STUDENT CAN'T

Count on By Ones
- Have the student practice counting on by ones, starting with different two-digit numbers, a few times a day until he or she can do so easily.
- Have students use counters to help them count on by ones.

Read a Number Line
- Read all the numbers on a number line. Say a number and have the student point to it. Ask the student to name the next number.
- Have the student draw a number line showing all the numbers between two con-

secutive tens. Ask the student to read each number aloud.

Complete the Power Practice
- Discuss each incorrect answer. Have the student count on by ones to complete the pattern correctly.
- Remind students to proofread their work to make sure each number is in the correct place in the pattern.

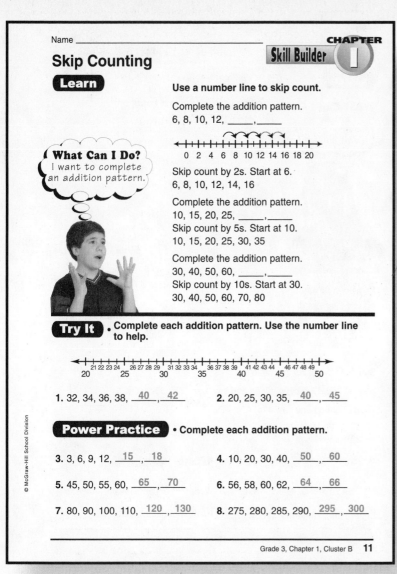

Name _____

Skip Counting

Learn

What Can I Do?
I want to complete an addition pattern.

Use a number line to skip count.

Complete the addition pattern.
6, 8, 10, 12, _____, _____

Skip count by 2s. Start at 6.
6, 8, 10, 12, 14, 16

Complete the addition pattern.
10, 15, 20, 25, _____, _____
Skip count by 5s. Start at 10.
10, 15, 20, 25, 30, 35

Complete the addition pattern.
30, 40, 50, 60, _____, _____
Skip count by 10s. Start at 30.
30, 40, 50, 60, 70, 80

Try It • Complete each addition pattern. Use the number line to help.

20 21 22 23 24 25 26 27 28 29 30 31 32 33 34 35 36 37 38 39 40 41 42 43 44 45 46 47 48 49 50

1. 32, 34, 36, 38, _40_ , _42_   **2.** 20, 25, 30, 35, _40_ , _45_

Power Practice • Complete each addition pattern.

3. 3, 6, 9, 12, _15_ , _18_   **4.** 10, 20, 30, 40, _50_ , _60_

5. 45, 50, 55, 60, _65_ , _70_   **6.** 56, 58, 60, 62, _64_ , _66_

7. 80, 90, 100, 110, _120_ , _130_   **8.** 275, 280, 285, 290, _295_ , _300_

© McGraw-Hill School Division

WHAT IF THE STUDENT CAN'T

Skip Count by 2s, 5s, and 10s
• Have the student practice skip counting by 2s, 5s, and 10s a few times a day until he or she can do so easily.

Read a Number Line
• Ask the student to read all the numbers on a number line. Say a number and have the student point to it. Ask the student to read the next few numbers, using the arrows as a guide.

• Have the student draw a number line showing all the numbers between two consecutive tens. Ask the student to read each number aloud.

Identify Place Value in Patterns
• Help students use a place-value chart to model what happens to the ones, tens, and hundreds places, if applicable, in the patterns they missed.

Complete the Power Practice
• Discuss each incorrect answer. Have the student count on by 2s, 5s, or 10s to complete the pattern correctly.

• Have students create number lines for the patterns they missed.

USING THE LESSON

Lesson Goal
• Complete an addition pattern.

What the Student Needs To Know
• Skip-count by 2s, 5s, and 10s.
• Read a pattern on a number line.
• Identify place value in patterns.

Getting Started
Find out what students know about completing an addition pattern. Say:
• *Think about the numbers in the pattern 2, 4, 6. Each number goes up by 2. Start at 6. What number comes just after 6?* (8)
• *Let's count to 20 by 2s. I'll start. 8, 10, 12….*

What Can I Do?
• Read the question and the response. Then read and discuss the examples. Ask:
• *How can using a number line help you complete an addition pattern?* (You can count the spaces between two numbers, then skip count by that amount.)
• *Do patterns that skip in 2s end in odd numbers or even numbers?* (even numbers)
• *What digit is in the ones place in patterns that skip in 10s?* (0) *What digits are in the ones place in patterns that skip in 5s?* (5 or 0)

Try It
Ask students to say each number in the pattern and point to it on the number line. Have them count the spaces on the number line to determine what each pattern is. Ask:
• *What does the first pattern go up by?* (2s)
• *What does the second pattern go up by?* (5s)

Power Practice
• Have students complete the practice items. Then review each answer.

Lesson Goal
- Find the value of a set of coins.

What the Student Needs To Know
- Identify the value of a quarter, dime, nickel, and penny.
- Skip count by 5s, 10s, and 25s.
- Keep track of the coins counted.

Getting Started
Determine what students know about the value of a set of coins. Display this set of play coins: 1 quarter, 1 nickel, and 2 pennies. Say:

- *Let's find the total amount. Start with the quarter. (25¢). Now skip count by 1 five. (30¢) Count on by 2 ones. (31¢, 32¢) What is the total amount? (32¢)*

What Can I Do?
- Read the question and the response. Then read and discuss the examples. Ask:
- By *what amount do you skip count with dimes? (by 10s)* Skip count to find the value of 3 dimes. (10¢, 20¢, 30¢)
- *By what amount do you skip count with nickels? (by 5s)* Skip count to find the value of 4 nickels. (5¢, 10¢, 15¢, 20¢)
- *By what amount do you count on with pennies? (by ones) Count on to find the value of 6 pennies.* (1¢, 2¢, 3¢, 4¢, 5¢, 6¢)
- Draw and label on the chalk board the coins shown in the first example: Ask: *What coin do you see first? (the penny) Then what? (the nickel) Then what? (the dime) What comes next? (the quarter)*
- *When you count coins, group coins with the same value and start with the coins of greatest value.*
- Circle each coin as it is counted. Say: *Let's count these coins. We'll start at 1 quarter, 25¢. What do we do next? (count one dime) Say, 25¢, 35¢. What do we do next? (count the nickels) Say: 35¢, 40¢. What do we count*

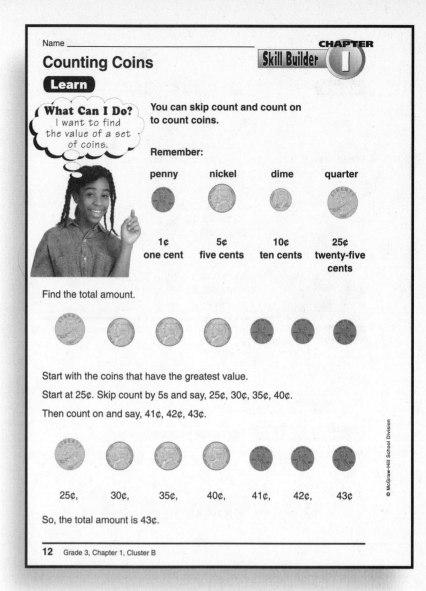

WHAT IF THE STUDENT CAN'T

Identify the Value of a Quarter, Dime, Nickel, and Penny
- Hand out a quarter, dime, nickel, and penny to the student. Have the student read each coin and order the set by value from largest to smallest. Review each coin's name and value daily until the student can recognize it easily.

Skip Count by 5s, 10s, and 25s
- Have the student practice skip counting by 5s, 10s, and 25s a few times a day until the student can do so easily.

Name _____

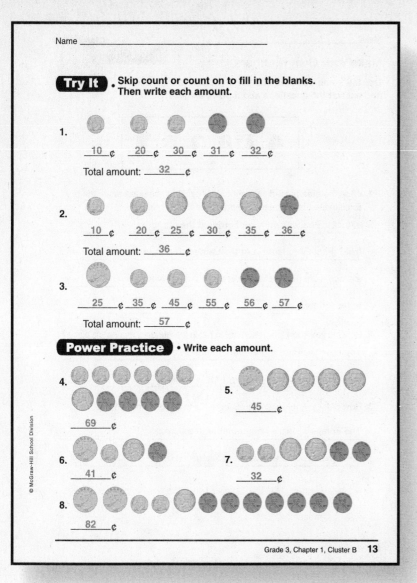

Try It • Skip count or count on to fill in the blanks.
Then write each amount.

1. __10__ ¢ __20__ ¢ __30__ ¢ __31__ ¢ __32__ ¢
Total amount: ___32___ ¢

2. __10__ ¢ __20__ ¢ __25__ ¢ __30__ ¢ __35__ ¢ __36__ ¢
Total amount: ___36___ ¢

3. __25__ ¢ __35__ ¢ __45__ ¢ __55__ ¢ __56__ ¢ __57__ ¢
Total amount: ___57___ ¢

Power Practice • Write each amount.

4. __69__ ¢

5. __45__ ¢

6. __41__ ¢

7. __32__ ¢

8. __82__ ¢

© McGraw-Hill School Division

Grade 3, Chapter 1, Cluster B **13**

WHAT IF THE STUDENT CAN'T

Keep Track of the Coins Counted

• Help the student correct any errors. Have the student draw pictures of the coins they are counting, then circle each coin as they skip count or count on. Make sure the student understands from which amount to start counting.

Complete the Power Practice

• Discuss each incorrect answer. Use play coins to help the student find the correct amount.

---

next? (the penny) *What is the total value?* (41¢)

• Do the same for the coins in the second example.

• *Why is it important to say "cents" when you are finding the value of a set of coins?* (to show that the numbers refer to coins and not some other unit)

• *Why is it easy to skip count with a set of nickels and dimes?* (It is faster to count by 5s or 10s than to count on by ones.)

• *Why should you count the coins in groups, according to their value?* (It is faster and easier to count in groups of quarters, dimes, nickels, and pennies.)

Try It

• Have students name each coin and its value, and count how many there are of each. Ask students to skip count or count on and have them fill in the blanks to show the increasing value. To review, ask:

• *How many dimes are in Exercise 1?* (3) *How do you skip count 3 dimes?* (10¢, 20¢, 30¢)

• *How many pennies are there?* (2) *Count on 2 pennies to find the total amount. Start at 30¢.* (30¢, 31¢, 32¢) *What is the total amount of 3 dimes and 2 pennies?* (32¢)

• Continue the procedure for Exercises 2–3.

Power Practice

• Review students' answers and have them make corrections as needed. Call on volunteers to model their answers with play coins.

• Have students make a chart in their math journal showing a picture of each coin, its name, and its value.

Grade 3, Chapter 1, Cluster B **13**

CHALLENGE

Lesson Goal
- Generate and analyze 3-, 4-, and 6-digit numbers using the digits' place values; round numbers to the nearest thousand, hundred, and ten.

Introducing the Challenge
Find out how comfortable students are in analyzing digits according to place value. Write on the board:

45,629

8,176

Say:

- *Which number is greater?* (45,629) *How does knowing each digit's place value help you compare the numbers?* (The 4 in 45,629 is in the ten thousands place; the 8 in 8,176 is in the one thousands place, and 10,000 is larger than 1,000.)

- *What is 8,176 rounded to the tens place? Explain.* (8,180, because 7 tens and 6 ones are closer to 8 tens than to 7 tens)

Display a place-value chart and have volunteers use it to analyze each number.

Name _____

Make Your Own Numbers
Use the numbers in the box below. Follow the directions and answer the questions about place value.

$$4 \quad 1 \quad 8 \quad 2 \quad 6 \quad 7$$

1. Write the greatest 6-digit number you can with the numbers in the box. Explain the steps you took to make the 6-digit number.

   876,421; Possible answer: I ordered the numbers

   from greatest to least, and then put each number in

   a place from greatest (hundred thousands place)

   to least (ones place).

2. How did you know which number to put in the hundred thousands place?

   The number 8 is the greatest number in the box, so

   I put it in the place with the greatest value.

3. How did you know which number to put in the ones place?

   The number 1 is the least number in the box, so I

   put it in the place with the least value.

Name _____

Use the digits in the box below. Follow the directions about ordering and rounding numbers.

4. Write three 3-digit numbers using the numbers in the box. Then write the 3-digit numbers in order from least to greatest.

   Answers will vary. Possible answer: 159, 519, 953. _____

5. Explain how you ordered the numbers.
   Possible answer: I looked at the digits in each

   hundreds place first, and ordered the numbers

   from least to greatest.

6. Write a 4-digit number using the numbers in the box. Then round the number to the nearest thousand, the nearest hundred, and the nearest ten.

   Possible answer: 3,195. Rounded to the nearest

   thousand: 3,000; nearest hundred: 3,200; ten: 3,200.

7. Explain how you rounded your number to each place.
   Answers will vary. Check students' explanations.

   _____

   _____

Grade 3, Chapter 1, Cluster A **15**

Using the Challenge

Have students read the directions on page 14. Ask:

- *What is the greatest place value of a 6-digit number?* (hundred thousands place)

- *What digit belongs in the hundred thousands place?* (8) *How can you tell?* (8 is the greatest whole number in the box)

- Have students work independently to complete Exercises 1–3. Review any incorrect answers. Provide place-value charts for students to check their work. Ask:

- *Why is it helpful to start with the digit in the hundred thousands place?* (The greatest possible number will have the whole number closest to 9 in the hundred thousands place.)

Have students complete Exercises 4–7. Remind students they can use number lines when rounding to the nearest multiple of ten. Ask:

- *Why is it helpful to think about place value when ordering 3-digit numbers?* (The least number will have the whole number closest to 0 in the hundreds place.)

- *How does a digit's place value help you round the number to the nearest thousand, hundred, and ten?* (Using a digit's place value helps you make sure to round it to the correct amount.)

CHALLENGE

Lesson Goal

- Understand the value of coins and bills to solve riddles.

Introducing the Challenge

Find out how familiar students are with riddles based on the value of coins and bills. Have them solve the following word problems. Encourage them to show their work.

- *Margo has 5 coins with a total value of $0.47 (476 cents). What are her coins?* (1 quarter, 2 dimes, 2 pennies) *How can you check your answer?* (Start with 1 quarter, $0.25. Skip count by two 10s: $0.35, $0.45. Count on by 2 ones: $0.46, $0.47. That equals 5 coins.)

- *Peter paid for a magazine that costs $2.48 with a $5-dollar bill. He received 3 bills and 4 coins in change. What bills and coins did he receive?* (3 one-dollar bills, 2 quarters, and 2 pennies) *How can you check your answer?* (Count on by 3 ones: $1, $2, $3. Skip count by two 25s: $3.25, $3.50. Count on by 2 ones: $3.51, $3.52. That equals 3 bills and 4 coins.)

- *Why is it helpful to group the bills and coins in change by type?* (Possible response: to count the bills and coins more quickly)

Money Riddles

Use what you know about money to solve each riddle.

1. Courtney has 4 coins in her pocket. The value of the coins is $0.45. Two of the coins are nickels. What are the other two coins?

   1 quarter, 1 dime

2. Bill has 7 coins with a total value of $0.83. What are his coins?

   3 quarters, 1 nickel, 3 pennies

3. What is the least number of bills and coins you can use to buy a notebook that costs $1.46? List the bills and coins.

   1 bill and 4 coins: one $1 bill, 1 quarter,

   2 dimes, 1 penny

4. What is the greatest number of coins you can use to buy a bottle of orange juice that costs $1.01? List the coins.

   101; 101 pennies

5. Allison has 2 coins of the same kind in her left hand. In her right hand, she has 4 coins that are alike but are different than the coins in her left hand. She has an equal amount of money in each hand. How much money does she have in all? Explain.

   She has 40¢. She has 2 dimes in her left hand and

   4 nickels in her right hand; 20¢ + 20¢ = 40¢.

Name _____

6. Luther has 3 coins of one kind and 3 of another. James has different coins, but he also has 3 of one kind and 3 of another. Luther has $0.33 more than James. How much does each boy have? What coins do they each have?

   Luther has $0.78. James has $0.45. Luther has 3 quarters and

   3 pennies. James has 3 dimes and 3 nickels.

7. Kelly paid for a magazine that costs $2.79 with a $5 bill. She received 1 bill and 9 coins in change. What bills and coins did she receive?

   She received one $1 bill, 4 quarters,

   4 nickels, and 1 penny.

8. Carlos gave Jane $4.21 using no bills.

   a. What is the greatest number of nickels Jane could get? _____ 84

   b. If Carlos gave Jane 40 dimes, did he give her any quarters? ___ No

9. Felicia has to give $0.25 in change to a customer. If she has pennies, nickels, dimes, and quarters in the cash register, how many different ways could she make change?

   13 ways

10. Make up your own money riddle. Write the riddle and the answer.

   Possible answer: Tony has 5 coins with a total

   value of $1.05. What coins does he have?

   (4 quarters, 1 nickel)

© McGraw-Hill School Division

Grade 3, Chapter 1, Cluster B **17**

CHALLENGE

Using the Challenge

Have students complete Exercises 1–5. Encourage them to draw pictures or use a chart to organize their answers. Review any incorrect answers. Ask:

- *Is it more helpful to start with money of the greatest value or money of the least value when figuring out change?* (It is easier to start with bills or coins of the greatest amounts.)

- *Why is it important in real life to know how many nickels equal 1 quarter, or how many pennies equal 1 dime?* (Possible answers: to see how the coins relate to each other; to receive the correct change)

Have students complete Exercises 6–10. Call on volunteers to read their money riddles for others to solve. Review any incorrect answers. Ask:

- *How can making a chart of coins help you answer money riddles?* (Possible answer: When the coins are arranged by type, they are easier to count.)

- *How can a place-value chart help you organize your answers?* (It can show what digits are in the ones, tens, and hundreds places so the amounts can be added correctly.)

Grade 3, Chapter 1, Cluster B **17**

Name _____

Addition Facts to 20

Add.

1. 2 + 3 = _____

2. 7 + 4 = _____

3. 4
  + 5

4. 8
  + 6

5. 3
  + 9

Add 2-Digit Numbers

Add.

6. 12
  + 23

7. 25
  + 31

8. 57
  + 42

9. 64
  + 14

Regroup Ones

Write the number of tens and ones.

10. 15 = _____ ten _____ ones

11. 68 = _____ tens _____ ones

Hundreds and Tens

Write each number.

12. 8 tens = _____

13. 4 hundreds = _____

14. 5 tens = _____

Name _____

Count Money

Write each money amount.

15. four $1 bills
    2 quarters
    3 nickels
     1 penny

16. one $5 bill
    two $1 bills
    8 dimes
    5 nickels
    2 pennies

_____   _____

Round to Tens, Hundreds, and Thousands

Round to the nearest ten.

17. 68 _____ **18.** 24 _____ **19.** 76 _____

Round to the nearest hundred.

20. 135 _____ **21.** 819 _____ **22.** 462 _____

Round to the nearest thousand.

23. 3,901 _____ **24.** 5,537 _____ **25.** 4,444 _____

CHAPTER 2 PRE-CHAPTER ASSESSMENT

Assessment Goal

This two-page assessment covers skills identified as necessary for success in Chapter 2 Add Whole Numbers. The first page assesses the major prerequisite skills for Cluster A. The second page assesses the major prerequisite skills for Cluster B. When the Cluster A and Cluster B prerequisite skills overlap, the skill(s) will be covered in only one section.

Getting Started

- Allow students time to look over the two pages of the assessment. Point out the labels that identify the skills covered.
- Have students find math vocabulary terms used in the assessment. List vocabulary terms on the board as students identify them. If necessary, review the meanings of all essential math vocabulary.

Introducing the Assessment

- Explain to students that these pages will help you know if they are ready to start a new chapter in their math textbooks.
- Students who have transferred from another school may not have been introduced to some of these skills. Encourage students to do their best and assure them you will help them learn any needed skills.

Cluster A Challenge

Those students who demonstrate mastery of the skills on this page will not need to use the reteaching worksheets. Instead, these students can do the Cluster A Challenge found on pages 28-29.

Name _____

Addition Facts to 20

Add.

1. $2 + 3 =$ ___5___

2. $7 + 4 =$ ___11___

3. $\begin{array}{r} 4 \\ + 5 \\ \hline 9 \end{array}$

4. $\begin{array}{r} 8 \\ + 6 \\ \hline 14 \end{array}$

5. $\begin{array}{r} 3 \\ + 9 \\ \hline 12 \end{array}$

Add 2-Digit Numbers

Add.

6. $\begin{array}{r} 12 \\ + 23 \\ \hline 35 \end{array}$

7. $\begin{array}{r} 25 \\ + 31 \\ \hline 56 \end{array}$

8. $\begin{array}{r} 57 \\ + 42 \\ \hline 99 \end{array}$

9. $\begin{array}{r} 64 \\ + 14 \\ \hline 78 \end{array}$

Regroup Ones

Write the number of tens and ones.

10. $15 =$ ___1___ ten ___5___ ones

11. $68 =$ ___6___ tens ___8___ ones

Hundreds and Tens

Write each number.

12. 8 tens = ___80___

13. 4 hundreds = ___400___

14. 5 tens = ___50___

© McGraw-Hill School Division

17A   Use with Grade 3, Chapter 2, Cluster A

CLUSTER A PREREQUISITE SKILLS

The skills listed in this chart are those identified as major prerequisite skills for students' success in the lessons in Cluster A of the chapter. Each skill is covered by one or more assessment items as shown in the middle column. The right column provides the page number for the lessons in this book that reteach the cluster A prerequisite skills.

Skill Name	Assessment Items	Lesson Pages
Addition Facts to 20	1-5	18-19
Add 2-Digit Numbers	6-9	20-21
Regroup Ones	10-11	22-23
Hundreds and Tens	12-14	24

Name _____

Count Money

Write each money amount.

15. four $1 bills
2 quarters
3 nickels
1 penny

16. one $5 bill
two $1 bills
8 dimes
5 nickels
2 pennies

___$4.66___   ___$8.07___

Round to Tens, Hundreds, and Thousands

Round to the nearest ten.

17. 68 ___70___   **18.** 24 ___20___   **19.** 76 ___80___

Round to the nearest hundred.

20. 135 ___100___   **21.** 819 ___800___   **22.** 462 ___500___

Round to the nearest thousand.

23. 3,901 ___4,000___   **24.** 5,537 ___6,000___   **25.** 4,444 ___4,000___

CLUSTER B PREREQUISITE SKILLS

The skills listed in this chart are those identified as major prerequisite skills for students' success in the lessons in Cluster B of the chapter. Each skill is covered by one or more assessment items as shown in the middle column. The right column provides the page numbers for the lessons in this book that reteach the Cluster B prerequisite skills

Skill Name	Assessment Items	Lesson Pages
Count Money	15-16	25
Round to Tens, Hundreds, and Thousands	17-25	26-27

Alternative Assessment Strategies

- Oral administration of the assessment is appropriate for younger students or those whose native language is not English. Read the skills title and directions one section at a time. Check students' understanding by asking them to tell you how they will do the first exercise in the group.

- For some skill types you may wish to use group administration. In this technique, a small group or pair of students complete the assessment together. Through their discussion, you will be able to decide if supplementary reteaching materials are needed.

Intervention Materials

If students are not successful with the prerequisite skills assessed on these pages, reteaching lessons have been created to help them make the transition into the chapter.

Item correlation charts showing the skills lessons suitable for reteaching the prerequisite skills are found beneath the reproductions of each page of the assessment.

Cluster B Challenge

Those students who demonstrate mastery of the skills on this page will not need to use the reteaching worksheets. Instead, these students can do the Cluster B Challenge found on pages 30–31.

Lesson Goal

- Complete addition facts (sums through 20).

What the Student Needs to Know

- Use a number line to count on.
- Double numbers from 1 through 9.
- Recognize pairs of addends that sum to 10.

Getting Started

Draw on the board a number line from 0 to 20. Ask a student to come to the board and use the line to find the sum of 6 + 4. For example, say:

- *Where should you start on the number line to add 6 + 4?* (at 6)
- *How many numbers should you move to the right, or count on?* (4 numbers to the right)
- *Where did you end up?* (at 10)
- *What is the sum of 6 + 4?* (10)

What Can I Do?

Read the question and the response. Then read and discuss the examples. Ask:

- *How can I use the number line to add 7 + 4?* (Start at 7, and count on 4. You end up at 11, so the sum is 11.)
- *Doubles of numbers such as 8 + 8 = 16 may be easier to remember than some other addition facts, such as 8 + 9 = 17. Even if I don't remember the sum of 6 + 7, I do remember how to double 6. What addition sentence means "double 6"?* (6 + 6 = 12)
- *My second addend is 7. How many more than 6 is 7?* (1 more) *What does 6 + 6 + 1, or 12 + 1 equal?* (13)
- *Name some pairs of numbers that sum to 10.* (Examples: 5 + 5; 2 + 8; 7 + 3; 9 + 1)

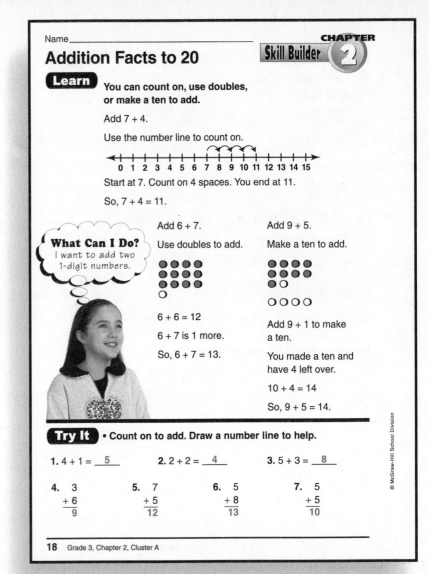

Name_____

Addition Facts to 20

Skill Builder

CHAPTER 2

Learn You can count on, use doubles, or make a ten to add.

Add 7 + 4.

Use the number line to count on.

Start at 7. Count on 4 spaces. You end at 11.

So, 7 + 4 = 11.

What Can I Do? I want to add two 1-digit numbers.

Add 6 + 7.
Use doubles to add.

6 + 6 = 12
6 + 7 is 1 more.
So, 6 + 7 = 13.

Add 9 + 5.
Make a ten to add.

Add 9 + 1 to make a ten.

You made a ten and have 4 left over.

10 + 4 = 14

So, 9 + 5 = 14.

Try It • Count on to add. Draw a number line to help.

1. 4 + 1 = ___5___   2. 2 + 2 = ___4___   3. 5 + 3 = ___8___

4.	5.	6.	7.
3	7	5	5
+6	+5	+8	+5
9	12	13	10

WHAT IF THE STUDENT CAN'T

Use a Number Line to Count On

- Have the student use a number line to practice addition facts to 10. For example, say:
- *To add 2 + 3, place your finger on 2, the first number. How many times will you need to jump to the right to find 2 + 3?* (3 times)
- Count aloud together as the student jumps his or her finger three numbers to the right: *three, four, five.* Then ask: *What is 2 + 3?* (5)
- Repeat with other addition facts to 10 until the student can follow the steps automatically. Next, have him or her use a number line to practice addition facts to 20.

Double Numbers from 1 through 9

- Have the student set out 1 through 9 counters of one color, and then set out the same number of another color, doubling the original number. Invite the student to arrange the counters in memorable symmetrical patterns and count the sum. He or she might copy the patterns on cards using colored markers.
- Practice doubling numbers aloud until the student can do so with ease.

Name _____

Use doubles to add.

8. 2 + 3 = __5__ **9.** 3 + 4 = __7__ **10.** 5 + 6 = __11__

11. 7
      + 8
      ———
       15

12. 8
      + 9
      ———
       17

13. 4
      + 5
      ———
       9

14. 7
      + 6
      ———
       13

Make a ten to add.

15. 9 + 2 = __11__ **16.** 7 + 5 = __12__ **17.** 8 + 4 = __12__

18. 7
      + 4
      ———
       11

19. 3
      + 8
      ———
       11

20. 9
      + 6
      ———
       15

21. 4
      + 9
      ———
       13

Power Practice • Add.

22. 2 + 1 = __3__ **23.** 4 + 3 = __7__ **24.** 3 + 6 = __9__

25. 5 + 4 = __9__ **26.** 3 + 3 = __6__ **27.** 8 + 3 = __11__

28. 6 + 6 = __12__ **29.** 5 + 7 = __12__ **30.** 9 + 6 = __15__

31. 6
      + 4
      ———
       10

32. 3
      + 9
      ———
       12

33. 8
      + 8
      ———
       16

34. 7
      + 4
      ———
       11

35. 9
      + 7
      ———
       16

36. 5
      + 9
      ———
       14

37. 8
      + 9
      ———
       17

38. 7
      + 8
      ———
       15

© McGraw-Hill School Division

Grade 3, Chapter 2, Cluster A **19**

WHAT IF THE STUDENT CAN'T

Recognize Addend Pairs That Sum to 10

- Use connecting cubes or counters of two different colors to model addition facts with sums of 10 (2 + 8 = 10; 6 + 4 = 10; 1 + 9 = 10; and so on). The student might copy the models on cards using colored markers.

Complete the Power Practice

- Discuss each incorrect answer. Have the student model any fact he or she missed using a number line or counters and then write the correct sum.

- *To help me add 9 + 2, I want to make a ten first. What number do I need to add to 9 to make a ten? (1) What number do I have left over after taking 1 from 2? (1) What is 10 + 1? (11) Now I want to make a ten to help me add 9 + 5. After I add 9 + 1 to make a ten, what is left over from 5? (4) What is 10 + 4? (14)*

Try It

- Check students' understanding of how to use a number line, doubles, and making tens to solve addition facts.

- For exercises 15–21, students might begin by modeling the addition sentences using counters. For example, for 7 + 5 they might set out 7 red counters and 5 black ones. Then they might set 3 of the black counters next to the 7 red ones to make 10. This will help them visualize 10 + 2 = 12. Encourage them to rewrite one or more of the facts as follows:

   7   +   5
 + 3   − 3
 ———   ———
  10   +   2 = 12

Power Practice

- Review with students the different methods they have learned to help them add. Tell them they may use mental math for the facts they have memorized. Before students begin, ask how they will decide which methods to use. For example, they will probably use mental math for exercises 26, 28 and 33, since these facts are doubles.

- Select several of the exercises and have volunteers explain which methods they can use to show that the sums they have written are correct. For example, an exercise in which 9 is one of the addends might best be solved by making ten to add.

USING THE LESSON

Lesson Goal

- Complete addition facts with 2-digit addends (sums through 99).

What the Student Needs to Know

- Add two 1-digit numbers with sums through 9.
- Understand place value.
- Use a place-value chart.

Getting Started

Ask what students would do to add the ages of two teenagers: Victoria, 13, and Pablo, 14. Draw a place-value chart on the board. For example, say:

- *Where should I write the 1 in 13?* (in the tens place) *Where should I write the 3 in 13?* (in the ones place)
- Have a volunteer write 14 under 13 in the place-value chart. Ask: *To add these two numbers, what should I do first?* (Add 3 + 4, and write 7 at the bottom of the ones column.)
- *What should I do next?* (Add 1 and 1, and write 2 at the bottom of the tens column.) *So 13 + 14 = ___?___.* (27)

What Can I Do?

Read the question and the response. Then read and discuss the examples. Ask:

- *Why do we put the 1 in 15 in the tens column?* (because 15 has 1 ten) *Why do we put the 5 in the ones column?* (because 15 has 5 ones)
- *How would you write 32 in the place-value chart?* (Put the 3 in the tens place and the 2 in the ones place.)
- *Which column should we add first?* (the ones column) *What does 5 + 2 equal?* (7)
- *Which column should we add next?* (the tens column) *What does 1 + 3 equal?* (4) So 15 + 32 = ___?___ (47)

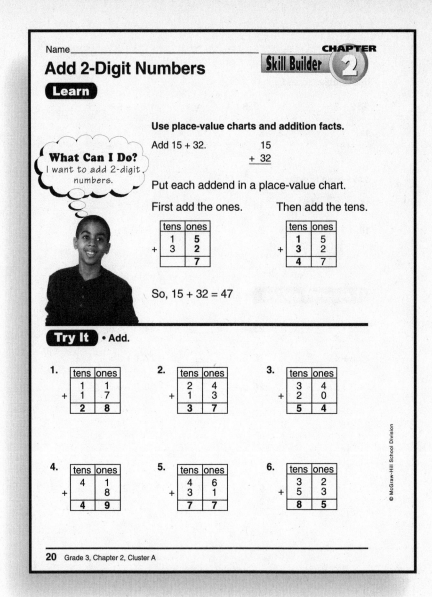

WHAT IF THE STUDENT CAN'T

Add Two 1-Digit Numbers with Sums through 9

- Have the student practice arranging 9 counters to model addition facts with sums through 9. Then they might make models of the facts using sticky dots on cards.
- Practice using mental math to complete addition facts with sums through 9 until the student can do so with ease.

Understand Place Value

- Have the student use connecting cubes to model numbers of tens and ones in 2-digit numbers. For example, give the student 11 unconnected cubes and ask him or her to show how many tens and how many ones there are. He or she can connect ten cubes and show that there is 1 left over.
- Have the student model 2-digit numbers using base-ten rods and ones cubes.

Name_____

7. 18 + 11 29	**8.** 26 + 12 38	**9.** 33 + 13 46	**10.** 15 + 34 49
11. 50 + 17 67	**12.** 24 + 61 85	**13.** 38 + 31 69	
14. 41 + 52 93	**15.** 55 + 22 77	**16.** 11 + 67 78	
17. 34 + 53 87	**18.** 79 + 20 99	**19.** 94 + 4 98	
20. 16 + 82 98	**21.** 44 + 44 88	**22.** 43 + 36 79	

23. 18 + 51 = __69__   **24.** 5 + 52 = __57__

25. 33 + 33 = __66__   **26.** 23 + 21 = __44__

27. 53 + 32 = __85__   **28.** 26 + 43 = __69__

© McGraw-Hill School Division

Learn with Partners & Parents

11, 22, 33 Challenge

- Play with a partner. You will need 2 number cubes. Toss one number cube to see who goes first, then take turns.
- The first player tosses both number cubes and makes a 2-digit number using the digits shown on the number cubes. The digits can be used in any order.
- The second player chooses another number for the first player to add to the number tossed. That number must be 11, 22, or 33.
- The first player adds the two numbers. You must show the addition on paper. A correct sum earns 5 points. No points are earned for an incorrect sum. The first player to earn 75 points is the winner.

WHAT IF THE STUDENT CAN'T

Use a Place-Value Chart

- Have the student use a place-value mat to model 2-digit numbers using connecting cubes and/or base-ten rods and ones cubes. Then have him or her draw place-value charts and show the same numbers with numerals.

- For example, he or she might model 23 on a place-value mat by placing two 10-cube trains in the tens column and 3 cubes in the ones column. Then he or she can write the number as follows:

Tens	Ones
2	3

Complete the Power Practice

- Discuss each incorrect answer. Have the student model any fact he or she missed using place-value charts or base-ten rods and ones cubes.

Try It

- Check students' understanding of how to use a place-value chart to find addition facts with 2-digit addends.

- Students might begin by modeling the addition sentences using base-ten rods and ones cubes. For example, for exercise 1, (11 + 17), they might set out 1 tens rod next to 1 ones cube a few inches away from 1 tens rod next to 7 ones cubes. Then they can combine the rods and cubes to make 2 rods and 8 cubes, or 28.

Power Practice

- Review with students the different methods they have learned to help them add 2-digit numbers. Tell them they do not need to draw a place-value chart unless they want to. Suggest that it may be helpful to draw a vertical line between the ones and tens places.

- Select several of the exercises and have volunteers explain which methods they can use to show that the sums they have written are correct. For example, they might model the addition facts using place-value charts or base-ten rods and ones cubes.

Lesson Goal

* Regroup ones as tens and ones.

What the Student Needs to Know

- Understand that 10 ones equal 1 ten.
- Connect place-value models with numerals.
- Identify ones and tens places in a numeral.

Getting Started

Show students 11 loose connecting cubes. Have a volunteer count the cubes. Ask how many tens and ones students think are in 11 cubes. For example, ask:

- *How can you find out how many tens are in 11 cubes?* (Connect cubes until you have a train of 10.)
- *How many 10-cube trains can you make?* (1) *How many cubes are left over?* (1)
- *How many tens and ones are in 11?* (1 ten and 1 one)

What Can I Do?

Read the question and the response. Then read and discuss the examples. Ask:

- *How many groups of 10 can you make from 25 ones blocks?* (2 groups)
- *Why can't you make 3 groups?* (There are only 5 ones blocks left over after making 2 groups of 10. You can't make another group of 10 from only 5 ones blocks.)
- *What does each tens block equal, or stand for?* (10 ones blocks)
- *So how many tens and ones are there in 25?* (2 tens and 5 ones)
- *How could you figure out the numbers of tens and ones without using blocks?* (The digit in the ones place—the column on the right—shows how many ones. The digit in the tens place—to the left of the ones place—shows how many tens.)

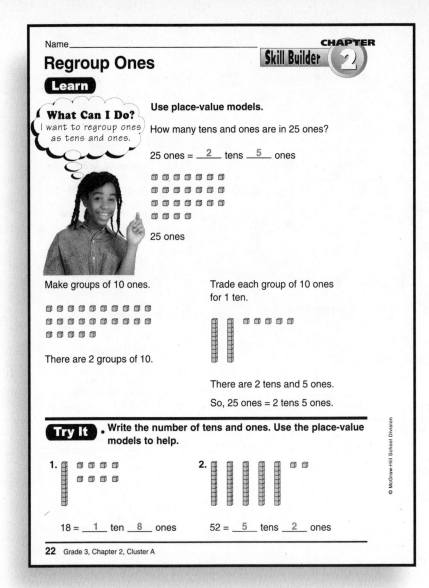

WHAT IF THE STUDENT CAN'T

Understand That 10 Ones Equal 1 Ten

- Provide more practice counting connecting cubes and forming them into 10-cube trains with some cubes left over. For example, give the student 27 cubes and have him or her form two 10-cube trains with 7 cubes left over.
- Then have the student model the same number using tens and ones blocks.

Connect Place-Value Models with Numerals

- After the student uses connecting cubes to model the number of tens and ones in a number, have the student write, for example:

  27 has 2 tens and 7 ones.

- Next, have the student model the same number using tens and ones blocks.

Name_____

Circle groups of 10 ones. Write the number of tens and ones.

3. [blocks shown]

16 ones = __1__ ten __6__ ones

4. [blocks shown]

31 ones = __3__ tens __1__ one

5. [blocks shown]

29 ones = __2__ tens __9__ ones

6. [blocks shown]

43 ones = __4__ tens __3__ ones

Power Practice • Write the number of tens and ones.

7. 11 = __1__ ten __1__ one

8. 17 = __1__ ten __7__ ones

9. 34 = __3__ tens __4__ ones

10. 55 = __5__ tens __5__ ones

11. 67 = __6__ tens __7__ ones

12. 82 = __8__ tens __2__ ones

13. 78 = __7__ tens __8__ ones

14. 96 = __9__ tens __6__ ones

15. 23 = __2__ tens __3__ ones

16. 19 = __1__ ten __9__ ones

13. 41 = __4__ tens __1__ one

18. 92 = __9__ tens __2__ ones

© McGraw-Hill School Division

WHAT IF THE STUDENT CAN'T

Identify Ones and Tens Places in a Numeral

- Have the student look at 2-digit numbers and practice pointing to the digits in the tens and ones places and saying, for example: *There are 2 tens in 27. There are 7 ones in 27.*

- Have the student use a place-value mat to model 2-digit numbers using connecting cubes and/or tens and ones blocks. Then he or she can write each number in a place-value chart as follows:

Tens	Ones
2	7

Complete the Power Practice

- Discuss each incorrect answer. Have the student model any exercise he or she missed using connecting cubes or tens and ones blocks. Help him or her point to the tens place and the ones place in each number.

USING THE LESSON

Try It

- Make sure students recognize tens blocks and ones blocks, and that they understand the value of each tens block (10 ones blocks).

- Students might begin by modeling the exercises using connecting cubes. For example, for exercise 1, they might set out 18 cubes, connect cubes to make a 10-cube train and count the 8 cubes left over.

- For exercises 3–4, students might count by placing a finger on each pictured ones block as they count silently or aloud.

Power Practice

- Review with students the different methods they have learned to help them figure out how many tens and ones in a number. Tell them they may use tens and ones blocks or connecting cubes if they need to. If they complete the exercises by simply copying the digits in the tens and ones places, suggest that they picture tens and ones blocks in their minds.

- Select several of the exercises and have volunteers explain which methods they can use to show that the numbers they have written are correct. For example, they might model the exercises using tens and ones blocks or connecting cubes. Alternatively, they might point to the digits in the tens and ones places and then point to the numbers they wrote.

Lesson Goal
- Write whole numbers for hundreds and tens.

What the Student Needs to Know
- Skip-count by tens and hundreds.
- Use a place-value chart to understand place value.

Getting Started
Find out what students know about tens and hundreds. Say:
- *Let's count to 100 by tens. I'll start: 10, 20, 30... . Now, you continue to count to 100.*
- *Let's count to 900 by hundreds. I'll start: 100, 200, 300... . Now, you continue to count to 900.*

What Can I Do?
Read the question and the response. Then discuss the examples. Draw a place-value chart on the board. Ask:
- *I want to write 70 in my place-value chart. Where should I write the 0?* (the ones column) *Where should I write 7?* (the tens column)
- *What do 3 hundreds equal?* (300) *How can I write 300 in my place-value chart?* (Write 3 in the hundreds column, 0 in the tens column, and 0 in the ones column.)

Try It
Have students write the numbers in the place-value charts. Ask:
- What do 5 hundreds equal? (500) Why did you write 0 in the tens place, and 0 in the ones place? (to show 5 hundreds with no tens and no ones left over)

Power Practice
- Have students complete the practice items. Then review each answer.

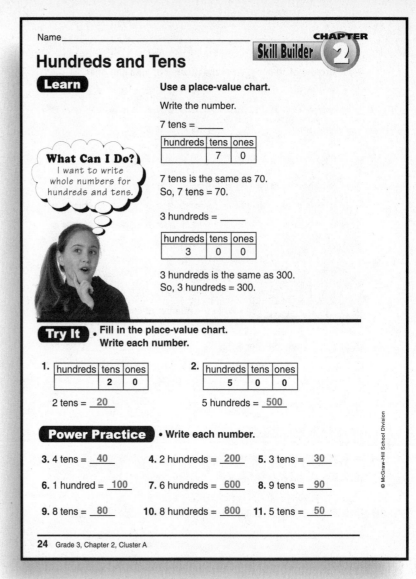

WHAT IF THE STUDENT CAN'T

Skip-Count by Tens and by Hundreds
- Provide more practice skip-counting by tens using tens blocks. The student can set down one tens block at a time, saying "10, 20, 30. . . .," and so on.
- Follow a similar procedure for skip-counting by hundreds using hundreds models.

Use a Place-Value Chart to Understand Place Value
- Have the student use connecting cubes and a place-value mat to model numbers such as 11, 27, and 35. The student can connect cubes to

create 10-cube trains, place these in the tens column, and place the left-over cubes in the ones column.
- Then he or she can write each number in a place-value chart as follows:

Tens	Ones
1	1

Complete the Power Practice
- Discuss each incorrect answer. Have the student model any exercise he or she missed using tens or hundreds models.
- Help the student point to the hundreds place, tens place, and ones place in each number.

Name_____

Count Money

Skill Builder 2 CHAPTER

Learn

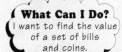
What Can I Do?
I want to find the value of a set of bills and coins.

You can skip count and count on to count bills and coins.

Remember: Put a dollar sign, $, on the left when you write an amount. Put a decimal point between the dollars and the cents.

Find the total amount:
one $5 bill, two $1 bills, 1 quarter, 3 dimes, 1 penny

Start with the bills and coins that have the greatest value.

Start at $5.00.

$5.00, $6.00, $7.00, $7.25, $7.35, $7.45, $7.55, $7.56

So, the total amount is $7.56.

Try It • Skip count and count on to find each amount.

1. $2.36

Power Practice • Write each money amount.

2. $2.81

3.  $7.20

Grade 3, Chapter 2, Cluster B **25**

© McGraw-Hill School Division

WHAT IF THE STUDENT CAN'T

Count on from a Given Number
- Draw a number line on the board. Have the student start at a given number and count on, using a finger to jump to the right.
- Give the student a series of numbers such as 5, 6, 7, _?_. Have the student supply the missing number in each series.

Skip-Count by Fives, Tens, and Twenty-Fives
- Have the student practice skip-counting by fives using play nickels: 5, 10, 15, 20, 25, and so on.
- Provide practice skip-counting by tens using tens blocks

or play dimes: 10, 20, 30, 40, and so on.
- Follow a similar procedure for skip-counting by twenty-fives using play quarters: 25, 50, 75, $1.00, $1.25, and so on.

Complete the Power Practice
- Discuss each incorrect answer. Have the student model any exercise he or she missed using play money.
- Have the student point to the dollar sign and decimal point in each amount. Have him or her also tell what each numeral stands for. For example, in $9.26, the 9 stands for 9 dollars, the 2 stands for 20 cents, and the 6 stands for 6 cents.

USING THE LESSON

Lesson Goal
- Find the value of a set of bills and coins.

What the Student Needs to Know
- Count on from a given number.
- Skip-count by 5s, 10s, and 25s.

Getting Started
Demonstrate with counting play money. Say, for example:
- *Let's start with the bill or coin that is worth the most, the $5 bill, and count on. $5.00, $6.00, $7.00, $7.25, $7.50, $7.60, $7.65, $7.66, $7.67.*
- Then have a volunteer count a different set of bills and coins. Provide prompting as necessary.

What Can I Do?
Read the question and the response. Then read and discuss the examples. Ask:
- *Do the bills and coins go from greater to lesser value or lesser to greater?* (greater to lesser value)
- *What does $5.00 + $1.00 equal?* ($6.00) *What does $6.00 + $1.00 equal?* ($7.00) *$7.00 + $.25?* ($7.25) *Continue counting on.* ($7.35, $7.45, $7.55, $7.56)

Try It
Have students use play money to model the exercises or place their finger on each amount as they count on aloud. For exercise 1, ask:
- *What does $1.00 + $1.00 equal?* ($2.00) *What bill or coin comes next?* (a dime) *What do you say next?* ($2.10) *What coin comes next?* (another dime) *What do you say next?* ($2.20) *How do you continue?* ($2.30, $2.35, $2.36)

Power Practice
- Have students complete the practice items. Then review each answer.

Lesson Goal

- Round numbers to the nearest ten, hundred, or thousand.

What the Student Needs to Know

- Count by tens, hundreds, and thousands.
- Read a number line.
- Identify digits in the ones, tens, hundreds, and thousands places.

Getting Started

Find out what students know about tens, hundreds, and thousands. Say:

- *Let's count to 100 by tens. I'll start: 10, 20, 30... . Now you continue to count to 100.*
- *Now let's count to 1000 by hundreds. I'll start: 100, 200, 300... . Now you continue to count to 1000.*

What Can I Do?

Read the question and the response. Then read and discuss the examples. Ask:

- *What does "round to the nearest ten" mean?* (to go up or down to the nearest ten on the number line) *When do we round a number down?* (when the ones digit is 1, 2, 3, or 4) *When do we round a number up?* (when the ones digit is 5 or greater) *What is 46 rounded to the nearest ten?* (46 rounded to the nearest 10 is 50)
- *How can we round 237 to the nearest hundred?* (Look on the number line and see which hundred it is closest to. It is closest to 200.) *How would we round 250 to the nearest hundred?* (Round up to 300.) *Why doesn't 250 round to 200?* (because there is a 5 in the tens place)
- *Look at the number 3,290. What place is to the right of the thousands place?* (the hundreds place) *What number is in the hundreds place?* (2) *Let's say we want to round 3,590 to the nearest thousand. What should we do?* (Look at the hundreds place, the place to the right of the

---

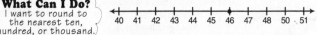
Round to Tens, Hundreds, and Thousands

Learn

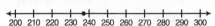

I want to round to the nearest ten, hundred, or thousand.

Use a number line.

Round 46 to the nearest ten.

```
40 41 42 43 44 45 46 47 48 50 51
```

The number 46 is between 40 and 50. It is closer to 50. So, 46 rounded to the nearest ten is 50.

Round 237 to the nearest hundred.

```
200 210 220 230 240 250 260 270 280 290 300
```

The number 237 is between 200 and 300. It is closer to 200. So, 237 rounded to the nearest hundred is 300.

Round 3,290 to the nearest thousand without using a number line.

Look at the place to the right of the thousands place.

3,**2**90

If the digit is less than 5, round down.
If the digit is 5 or greater, round up.

2 < 5; so, round 3,290 down to 3,000.

So, 3,290 rounded to the nearest thousand is 3,000.

Try It • Round to the nearest ten. Use the number line to help.

1.
```
20 21 22 23 24 25 26 27 28 29 30
```

28 __30__

2.
```
80 81 82 83 84 85 86 87 88 89 90
```

83 __80__

WHAT IF THE STUDENT CAN'T

Count by Tens, Hundreds, and Thousands

- Practice counting by tens, hundreds, and thousands a few times each day until the student can do so with ease.
- The student might use tens and hundreds models to count by tens and hundreds.

Read a Number Line

- Sketch on the board three different number lines, one showing tens, one showing hundreds, and one showing thousands. Have the student come to the board and help you insert smaller numbers between the points you have labeled. For example, he or she can add 21, 22, 23, 24, and so on, between 20 and 30; or the student can add 110, 120, 130, and so on, between 100 and 200.

Name_____

Round to the nearest hundred. Use the number line to help.

3.
700 710 720 730 740 750 760 770 780 790 800

721 __700__

4.
400 410 420 430 440 450 460 470 480 490 500

475 __500__

Round to the nearest thousand. Look at the digit to the right of the thousands place to round up or round down.

5. 1,341 __1,000__   6. 6,752 __7,000__   7. 4,901 __5,000__

Power Practice • Round to the nearest ten.

8. 12 __10__   9. 38 __40__   10. 59 __60__

11. 26 __30__   12. 74 __70__   13. 63 __60__

Round to the nearest hundred.

14. 187 __200__   15. 313 __300__   16. 578 __600__

17. 845 __800__   18. 529 __500__   19. 767 __800__

Round to the nearest thousand.

20. 2,399 __2,000__   21. 3,860 __4,000__   22. 7,089 __7,000__

23. 8,615 __9,000__   24. 5,453 __5,000__   25. 6,524 __7,000__

© McGraw-Hill School Division

WHAT IF THE STUDENT CAN'T

Identify Digits in the Ones, Tens, Hundreds, and Thousands Places

- Emphasize that in a whole number the last digit is in the ones place. Make sure the student knows that the digit to the left of the ones place is in the tens place. Have the student also point to the hundreds and thousands places.

- Have the student point to each number in the Power Practice and identify the digit in the ones, tens, hundreds, and thousands places as appropriate.

Complete the Power Practice

- Discuss each incorrect answer. Have the student model any exercise he or she missed using a sketched number line.

- Have the student identify the digit to the right of the place he or she is rounding to. Then have him or her round up or down according to the rule.

USING THE LESSON

thousands place. There is a 5 there, so we round up to 4,000.)

Try It

Have students say the number to be rounded and then find it on the number line. Have them identify the lesser ten and the greater ten on the number line. Ask:

- *Is the number closer to the lesser ten or the greater ten?* (Answers will vary.)

- *In 28, what number is in the ones place?* (8) *How does this number help you figure out whether to round up or down?* (I know that if the ones digit is 5 or greater, I should round up. 8 is greater than 5, so I round up to 30.)

- *In 83, what is the ones digit?* (3) *Should you round up or down, and why?* (I should round down, because 3 is less than 5. I'll round down to 80.)

Power Practice

- Select several of the exercises and have volunteers describe some different methods they can use to show that the answer they have written is correct.

- Review some ways that students can help themselves decide whether to round up or down. For example, they can sketch a number line and use it to estimate whether the number they are rounding is closest to the greater or lesser ten, hundred, or thousand. Or they can look at the digit to the right of the place they are rounding to. If that digit is 5 or greater, they should round up. If it is 4 or less, they should round down.

CHALLENGE

Lesson Goal

- Use properties of addition and subtraction to solve missing-number puzzles.

Introducing the Challenge

- Review the vocabulary needed for the lesson by having students use each term in a sentence. Vocabulary used in this lesson includes: *sum*, *straight line*, and *triangle*.

- Write the following addition sentences on the board:

  $1 + 6 + 2 = 9$
  $2 + 4 + 3 = 9$
  $3 + 5 + 1 = 9$

  Ask: *What is the same about these three addition sentences?* (They all sum to 9. They all have three addends. They have some of the same addends.)

- Ask a volunteer to draw on the board the triangle shown in the example and point out on the triangle the addition sentences you wrote.

Equal Lines

The sum of the numbers in each straight line should be the same.

Example:

$1 + 6 + 2 = 9$

$2 + 4 + 3 = 9$

$3 + 5 + 1 = 9$

Write the missing numbers for each triangle.

1.
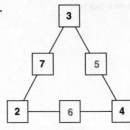

2.
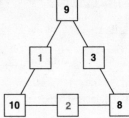

3.
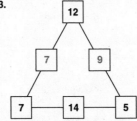

4.
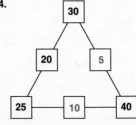

Name _____

The sum of the numbers in each straight line should be the same. Write the missing numbers for each triangle.

5.
```
            1
        1       2
      3     0     2
```

6.
```
            6
        3       5
      4     7     2
```

7.
```
           50
       40      20
      60    10    80
```

8.
```
          150
      250      400
     350   200   200
```

9.
```
           71
       18      31
      42    60    29
```

10.
```
          267
      216      173
     105   335   148
```

CHALLENGE

Using the Challenge

- Have a volunteer read the directions aloud. Copy the first puzzle on the board for discussion. Students need to understand the following:

- The object of the puzzle is to find the numbers that belong in the blanks.

- When finished, the sum of the three numbers in each straight line should be the same.

- Students may need help getting started. If so, tell them to find a line that has no blanks in it. For example, in exercise 1, there is no blank on the left side of the triangle. The three numbers in this line sum to 12.

- Therefore, the other two lines need to have numbers that also sum to 12. The line on the right side of the triangle has a 3, a blank, and a 4. 3 + 4 = 7 and 12 – 7 = 5, so a 5 should go in the blank.

- The line on the bottom of the triangle has a 2, a blank, and a 4. 2 + 4 = 6, and 12 – 6 = 6, so a 6 should go in the blank.

- Encourage students to use mental math to solve exercises 1–8; however, you may wish to allow them to use a calculator to solve exercises 9–10. Otherwise, they will probably need to calculate the sums and differences using pencil and paper.

CHALLENGE

Lesson Goal
- Use reversing digits and addition to find palindrome numbers.

Introducing the Challenge
- Review the vocabulary needed for the lesson by having a volunteer use each term in a sentence. Vocabulary used in this lesson includes: *reverse* and *digit*. The word *palindrome* is defined in the lesson.

- Have a volunteer read aloud the first paragraph on the page. Next, write the words *mom*, *yummy*, and *tot* on the board. Ask which two words read the same forward or backward. (*mom* and *tot*) Ask why *yummy* is not a palindrome. (There is no *u* following the second *m*.)

- Go over the examples with students. You may wish to point out that unlike 13 + 31, 75 + 57 does not produce a palindrome in one step because while 1 + 3 or 3 + 1 = 4, a 1-digit number, 5 + 7 or 7 + 5 = 12, a 2-digit number. However, if you reverse 132 (231) and add 132 + 231, the sum is a palindrome, 363. This happens because the digits in the ones, tens, and hundreds places all sum to 1-digit numbers.

CHALLENGE — CHAPTER 2

Palindrome Numbers

A *palindrome* is a word, phrase, or sentence that reads the same forward or backward. For example, the names *Anna* and *Bob* are palindromes. So are the words *kayak*, *level*, and *madam*. This sentence is a palindrome: *Enid and Edna dine.*

Numbers can also be palindromes. For example, 55, 171, and 34,943 are all palindrome numbers.

You can use addition to make your own palindrome numbers.

Choose any 2- or 3-digit number.

Reverse the digits and add.

```
  13
+ 31
  44
```

The sum, 44, is a palindrome. It reads the same forward and backward.

Choose any 2- or 3-digit number.

Reverse the digits and add.

```
  75
+ 57
 132
```

Now reverse the digits of the sum and add again.

```
  132
+ 231
  363
```

The number 363 is a palindrome.

Reverse the digits and add until you get a palindrome number.

1.
```
   45
 + 54
   99
```

2.
```
     318
 +   813
   1,131
 + 1,311
   2,442
```

3.
```
    94
 + 49
  143
+ 341
  484
```

© McGraw-Hill School Division

Name _____

Reverse the digits and add until you get a palindrome number.

4.   68
     + 86

     154
    + 451

     605
    + 506

    1,111

5.   152
    + 251

     403
    + 304

     707

6.   895
     + 598

    1,493
    + 3,941

    5,434
    + 4,345

    9,779

Make your own palindrome numbers. For 7–9, choose a 2- or 3-digit number, reverse the digits, and add. Continue until you get a palindrome number.

7. Answers will vary.   8. Answers will vary.   9. Answers will vary.

Using the Challenge

- Have a volunteer read the directions aloud. Copy the first two exercises on the board for discussion. Students need to understand the following:

- The object is to reverse digits and use addition to produce a palindrome.

- When finished, each sum should read the same both forward and backwards.

- Students may need help getting started. If so, help them practice reversing digits in various 2- and 3-digit numbers. For example 126 becomes 621, 14 becomes 41 and 986 becomes 689.

- Point out that while 45 + 54 produces a palindrome in one step, it takes two steps to produce a palindrome from 318.

- First, students should reverse 318 (813) and add 318 + 813 for a sum of 1131. Then they need to reverse 1131 (1311) and add 1131 + 1311 for a sum of 2442, which is a palindrome.

- Remind students to be patient. Producing a palindrome sometimes takes several steps. (Exercise 4 and 6 each require three addition steps.)

- For exercises 7–9, depending on the numbers students begin with, they may wish to use a calculator to help them add large numbers.

Count Back

Complete each subtraction pattern.

1. 10, 9, 8, 7, _____, _____

2. 35, 34, 33, 32, _____, _____

3. 403, 402, 401, 400, _____, _____

Basic Addition Facts

Find each sum.

4. $5 + 0 =$ _____   **5.** $4 + 7 =$ _____   **6.** $9 + 8 =$ _____

Subtraction Facts to 20

Subtract.

7. $10 - 4 =$ _____   **8.** $16 - 8 =$ _____

9. 15
   $-\ 7$

10. 14
   $-\ 9$

Addition Patterns

Add. Use mental math.

11. $40 + 30 =$ _____

12. $600 + 500 =$ _____

13. $50 + 90 =$ _____

Name_____

Subtract 2-Digit Numbers

Subtract.

14. 26
       − 13
       ——

15. 45
       − 11
       ——

16. 98
       − 54
       ——

17. 79
       − 22
       ——

Rename Tens and Ones

Write each missing number.

18. 1 ten 9 ones = _____ ones

19. 8 tens 4 ones = _____ ones

Round to the Nearest Ten, Hundred, or Thousand

**Write which two tens the number is between.
Round to the nearest ten.**

20. 72 is between _____ and _____.   72 rounds to _____.

21. 16 is between _____ and _____.   16 rounds to _____.

**Write which two hundreds the number is between.
Round to the nearest hundred.**

22. 159 is between _____ and _____.   159 rounds to _____.

23. 546 is between _____ and _____.   546 rounds to _____.

**Write which two thousands the number is between.
Round to the nearest thousand.**

24. 5,399 is between _____ and _____.   5,399 rounds to _____.

25. 8,601 is between _____ and _____.   8,601 rounds to _____.

Assessment Goal

This two-page assessment covers skills identified as necessary for success in Chapter 3 Subtract Whole Numbers. The first page assesses the major prerequisite skills for Cluster A. The second page assesses the major prerequisite skills for Cluster B. When the Cluster A and Cluster B prerequisite skills overlap, the skill(s) will be covered in only one section.

Getting Started

- Allow students time to look over the two pages of the assessment. Point out the labels that identify the skills covered.
- Have students find math vocabulary terms used in the assessment. List vocabulary terms on the board as students identify them. If necessary, review the meanings of all essential math vocabulary.

Introducing the Assessment

- Explain to students that these pages will help you know if they are ready to start a new chapter in their math textbooks.
- Students who have transferred from another school may not have been introduced to some of these skills. Encourage students to do their best and assure them you will help them learn any needed skills.

Cluster A Challenge

Those students who demonstrate mastery of the skills on this page will not need to use the reteaching worksheets. Instead, these students can do the Cluster A Challenge found on pages 40-41.

Name_____

Count Back

Complete each subtraction pattern.

1. 10, 9, 8, 7, __6__, __5__

2. 35, 34, 33, 32, __31__, __30__

3. 403, 402, 401, 400, __399__, __398__

Basic Addition Facts

Find each sum.

4. $5 + 0 =$ __5__   5. $4 + 7 =$ __11__   6. $9 + 8 =$ __17__

Subtraction Facts to 20

Subtract.

7. $10 - 4 =$ __6__   8. $16 - 8 =$ __8__

9. 15
   $-\ 7$
   ‾‾‾‾
     8

10. 14
    $-\ 9$
    ‾‾‾‾
      5

Addition Patterns

Add. Use mental math.

11. $40 + 30 =$ __70__

12. $600 + 500 =$ __1,100__

13. $50 + 90 =$ __140__

© McGraw-Hill School Division

31A   Use with Grade 3, Chapter 3, Cluster A

CLUSTER A PREREQUISITE SKILLS

The skills listed in this chart are those identified as major prerequisite skills for students' success in the lessons in Cluster A of the chapter. Each skill is covered by one or more assessment items as shown in the middle column. The right column provides the page number for the lessons in this book that reteach the cluster A prerequisite skills.

Skill Name	Assessment Items	Lesson Pages
Count Back	1-3	32
Basic Addition Facts	4-6	33
Subtraction Facts to 20	7-10	34
Addition Patterns	11-13	35

Name_____

Subtract 2-Digit Numbers

Subtract.

14.	26	15.	45	16.	98	17.	79
	− 13		− 11		− 54		− 22
	13		34		44		57

Rename Tens and Ones

Write each missing number.

18. 1 ten 9 ones = __19__ ones   19. 8 tens 4 ones = __84__ ones

Round to the Nearest Ten, Hundred, or Thousand

**Write which two tens the number is between.
Round to the nearest ten.**

20. 72 is between __70__ and __80__ .   72 rounds to __70__ .

21. 16 is between __10__ and __20__ .   16 rounds to __20__ .

**Write which two hundreds the number is between.
Round to the nearest hundred.**

22. 159 is between __100__ and __200__ .   159 rounds to __200__ .

23. 546 is between __500__ and __600__ .   546 rounds to __500__ .

**Write which two thousands the number is between.
Round to the nearest thousand.**

24. 5,399 is between __5,000__ and __6,000__   5,399 rounds to __5,000__ .

25. 8,601 is between __8,000__ and __9,000__   8,601 rounds to __9,000__ .

© McGraw-Hill School Division

Use with Grade 3, Chapter 3, Cluster B **31B**

CLUSTER B PREREQUISITE SKILLS

The skills listed in this chart are those identified as major prerequisite skills for students' success in the lessons in Cluster B of the chapter. Each skill is covered by one or more assessment items as shown in the middle column. The right column provides the page numbers for the lessons in this book that reteach the Cluster B prerequisite skills

Skill Name	Assessment Items	Lesson Pages
Subtract 2-Digit Numbers	14-17	36-37
Rename Tens and Ones	18-19	38
Round to the Nearest Ten, Hundred, or Thousand	20-25	39

CHAPTER 3 PRE-CHAPTER ASSESSMENT

Alternative Assessment Strategies

- Oral administration of the assessment is appropriate for younger students or those whose native language is not English. Read the skills title and directions one section at a time. Check students' understanding by asking them to tell you how they will do the first exercise in the group.

- For some skill types you may wish to use group administration. In this technique, a small group or pair of students complete the assessment together. Through their discussion, you will be able to decide if supplementary reteaching materials are needed.

Intervention Materials

If students are not successful with the prerequisite skills assessed on these pages, reteaching lessons have been created to help them make the transition into the chapter.

Item correlation charts showing the skills lessons suitable for reteaching the prerequisite skills are found beneath the reproductions of each page of the assessment.

Cluster B Challenge

Those students who demonstrate mastery of the skills on this page will not need to use the reteaching worksheets. Instead, these students can do the Cluster B Challenge found on pages 42-43.

Grade 3, Chapter 3, Cluster B **31D**

Lesson Goal
- Complete a subtraction pattern.

What the Student Needs to Know
- Use a number line.
- Count back by ones.

Getting Started
Draw on the board a number line from 0 to 10. Place your finger on 10 and begin counting backward. Say 9, 8, 7, 6 and so on. Ask:
- *What am I doing?* (counting back by ones)
- *How can I count back by ones from 5?* (5, 4, 3, 2, 1, 0)

What Can I Do?
Read the question and the response. Then read and discuss the examples. Ask:
- *If I start at 9 on the number line and count back by ones, what should I say?* (9, 8, 7, 6, 5, 4)
- *If I start at 264 and count back by ones, what should I say?* (264, 263, 262, 261, 260, 259)

Try It
Have students say the series of numbers after they complete them. Ask:
- *What follows 13 in the pattern in exercise 1?* (12) *What follows 12?* (11)
- *What follows 79 in the pattern in exercise 2?* (78) *What follows 78?* (77)

Power Practice
- Have students complete the practice items. Then review each answer.

Name_____

Count Back

Learn

What Can I Do?
I want to complete a subtraction pattern.

Use a number line to count back.

Complete each subtraction pattern.

9, 8, 7, 6, ____, ____

0 1 2 3 4 5 6 7 8 9 10

Count back by ones. Start at 9.
9, 8, 7, 6, 5, 4

264, 263, 262, 261, ____, ____

255 256 257 258 259 260 261 262 263 264 265

Count back by ones. Start at 264.
264, 263, 262, 261, 260, 259

Try It • Complete each subtraction pattern. Use the number line to help.

1.
10 11 12 13 14 15 16 17 18 19 20

16, 15, 14, 13, __12__, __11__

2.
72 73 74 75 76 77 78 79 80 81 82

82, 81, 80, 79, __78__, __77__

Power Practice • Complete each subtraction pattern.

3. 25, 24, 23, 22, __21__, __20__

4. 44, 43, 42, 41, __40__, __39__

5. 587, 586, 585, __584__, __583__

6. 152, 151, 150, __149__, __148__

7. 770, 769, 768, __767__, __766__

8. 803, 802, 801, __800__, __799__

32   Grade 3, Chapter 3, Cluster A

WHAT IF THE STUDENT CAN'T

Use a Number Line
- Have the student use a number line to practice counting forward by ones. For example, say:
- *Start at 5 and count forward by ones.* (5, 6, 7, 8, 9, 10)
- *Let's draw a number line from 250 to 260. Start at 252 and count forward by ones.* (252, 253, 254, 255, 256....)

Count Back by Ones
- Have the student use number lines to practice counting back by ones. For example, say:

- *Now start at 5 and count back by ones.* (5, 4, 3, 2, 1, 0)
- *Let's draw a number line from 50 to 60. Start at 55 and count back by ones.* (55, 54, 53, 52, 51, 50)
- Repeat with other subtraction patterns until the student can follow the steps with ease.

Complete the Power Practice
- Discuss each incorrect answer. Have the student model any exercise he or she missed using a sketched number line.

Basic Addition Facts

Name_____

Skill Builder CHAPTER **3**

Learn

What Can I Do?
I want to find the sum of two 1-digit numbers.

Use Doubles

Find the sum of 7 + 8.

7 + 7 = 14
7 + 8 is 1 more.
So, 7 + 8 = 15.

Count On

Find the sum of 4 + 3.

Start at 4. Say 5, 6, 7.
So, 4 + 3 = 7.

Make a Ten

Find the sum of 8 + 6.

Add 8 + 2 to make a ten with 4 left over.

10 + 4 = 14
So, 8 + 6 = 14.

Try It • Count on, use doubles, or make a ten to find each sum.

1. 3 + 2 = __5__   2. 4 + 5 = __9__   3. 9 + 4 = __13__

4. 8   5. 4   6. 9   7. 6
  + 5   + 7   + 8   + 6
  ‾‾13   ‾‾11   ‾‾17   ‾‾12

Power Practice • Find each sum.

8. 3 + 7 = __10__   9. 2 + 0 = __2__   10. 4 + 8 = __12__

11. 8 + 3 = __11__   12. 7 + 7 = __14__   13. 1 + 9 = __10__

14. 7   15. 0   16. 8   17. 9
   + 5   + 9   + 6   + 7
   ‾‾12   ‾‾9   ‾‾14   ‾‾16

© McGraw-Hill School Division

Grade 3, Chapter 3, Cluster A **33**

WHAT IF THE STUDENT CAN'T

Count on Mentally

- Have the student use a number line to practice adding 1-digit numbers by counting on. Repeat until the student can follow the steps automatically.
- Next, have him or her add 1-digit numbers by counting on mentally.

Double Numbers from 1 through 9

- Have the student set out 1 through 9 counters of one color, and then set out the same number of another color, doubling the original number. Invite him or her to arrange the doubles in memorable patterns and copy the patterns on cards using stick-on dots.

Recognize Addend Pairs That Sum to 10

- Use connecting cubes or counters of two different colors to model addition facts with sums of 10 (2 + 8 = 10; 6 + 4 = 10; 1 + 9 = 10; and so on).

Complete the Power Practice

- Discuss each incorrect answer. Have the student model any fact he or she missed by counting on, making doubles, or making tens to add.

USING THE LESSON

Lesson Goal

- Add two 1-digit numbers (sums through 18).

What the Student Needs to Know

- Count on mentally.
- Double numbers from 1 through 9.
- Recognize pairs of addends that sum to 10.

Getting Started

Find out what students know about adding two 1-digit numbers. Ask, for example:

- *How could you use doubles to add 4 + 5?* (First, double 4 for a sum of 8. 5 is 1 more than 4, so add 1 to 8 for a sum of 9.)

What Can I Do?

Read the question and the response. Then read and discuss the examples. Ask:

- *What addition sentence means "double 7"?* (7 + 7 = 14) *How many more than 7 is 8?* (1 more) *What does 7 + 7 + 1 equal?* (15)
- *How can I count on mentally to add 4 + 3?* (Start at 4, and count on 3 times: 5, 6, 7. The sum is 7.)
- *To help me add 8 + 6, I want to make a ten first. What number do I need to add to 8 to make a ten?* (2) *What number do I have left over after taking 2 from 6?* (4) *What is 10 + 4?* (14)

Try It

- Help students decide which method to use to help them add. For example, they might use counting on mentally for exercise 1; doubles for exercises 2 and 7; and making tens for exercises 3–6.

Power Practice

- Have students complete the practice items. Then review each answer.

Grade 3, Chapter 3, Cluster A **33**

USING THE LESSON

Lesson Goal
- Complete subtraction facts to 20.

What the Student Needs to Know
- Count back by ones.
- Double numbers from 1 through 9.

Getting Started
Draw on the board a number line from 0 to 10. Place your finger on 8. Ask:

- *How can I use the number line to subtract 8 – 3?* (Count back 3 numbers, 7, 6, 5.) *What is 8 – 3?* (5)

What Can I Do?
Read the question and the response. Then read and discuss the examples. Ask:

- *If I start at 11 and count back to subtract 11 – 3, what should I say?* (10, 9, 8) *What does 11 – 3 equal?* (8)
- *What do you get if you double 3?* (6) *So what does 6 – 3 equal?* (3)
- *What do you get if you double 6?* (12) *So what does 12 – 6 equal?* (6)

Try It
- Have students identify the exercises for which they will use doubles to subtract (exercises 3–7). Ask:
- *In exercise 1, at what number will you start?* (6) *How many times should you count back?* (2 times) *Let's try it: 5, 4. So what does 6 – 2 equal?* (4)
- *In exercise 4, how will you use doubles to subtract?* (9 + 9 = 18, so 18 – 9 = 9)

Power Practice
- Have students complete the practice items. Then review each answer.

Subtraction Facts to 20

Learn

What Can I Do?
I want to find the difference between two numbers.

Count Back
Subtract 11 – 3.
Start at 11.
Say 10, 9, 8.
So, 11 – 3 = 8.

Use Doubles
Subtract 12 – 6.
You know that 6 + 6 = 12.
So, 12 – 6 = 6.

Try It • Count back or use doubles to subtract.

1. 6 – 2 = __4__   2. 4 – 3 = __1__   3. 8 – 4 = __4__

4. 18	5. 10	6. 14	7. 16
− 9	− 5	− 7	− 8
9	5	7	8

Power Practice • Subtract.

8. 3 – 1 = __2__   9. 9 – 4 = __5__   10. 12 – 5 = __7__

11. 12 – 7 = __5__   12. 16 – 9 = __7__   13. 13 – 4 = __9__

14. 11 – 6 = __5__   15. 14 – 8 = __6__   16. 16 – 7 = __9__

17. 6	18. 10	19. 8	20. 17
− 3	− 8	− 0	− 9
3	2	8	8

WHAT IF THE STUDENT CAN'T

Count Back by Ones
- Have the student use a number line to practice counting back by ones. For example, say:
- *Start at 9 and count back by ones.* (9, 8, 7, 6, 5, 4, 3, 2, 1, 0)
- *Let's use the number line to subtract 9 – 4. Where should we start?* (at 9) *Now what should we do?* (Count back 4 numbers.) *Let's say this together: 8, 7, 6, 5. What does 9 – 4 equal?* (5)
- Next, follow a similar process using mental math instead of a number line.

Double Numbers from 1 through 9
- Have the student set out counters of one color, and then set out the same number of another color, doubling the original number. On a separate sheet of paper the student should write an addition sentence for the double shown.

Complete the Power Practice
- Discuss each incorrect answer. Have the student model any exercise missed using connecting cubes.

Name_____

Addition Patterns

Learn

What Can I Do?
I want to add greater numbers mentally.

Use basic facts and patterns to find sums mentally.

Find 700 + 500.

You know the basic fact 7 + 5 = 12.

7 + 5 = 12
Think: 7 ones + 5 ones = 12 ones

70 + 50 = 120
Think: 7 tens + 5 tens = 12 tens

700 + 500 = 1,200
Think: 7 hundreds + 5 hundreds = 12 hundreds

So, 700 + 500 = 1,200.

Try It • Write each sum.

1. 4 + 1 = __5__

    40 + 10 = __50__

    400 + 100 = __500__

2. 5 + 6 = __11__

    50 + 60 = __110__

    500 + 600 = __1,100__

Power Practice • Add. Use mental math.

3. 200 + 600 = __800__

5. 80 + 10 = __90__

7. 800 + 500 = __1,300__

9. 900 + 600 = __1,500__

11. 90 + 90 = __180__

4. 30 + 40 = __70__

6. 600 + 600 = __1,200__

8. 70 + 30 = __100__

10. 500 + 500 = __1,000__

12. 70 + 80 = __150__

© McGraw-Hill School Division

Grade 3, Chapter 3, Cluster A **35**

WHAT IF THE STUDENT CAN'T

Complete Basic Addition Facts with Sums to 20

- Have the student use counters or connecting cubes to practice addition facts with sums to 20. The student might copy the models he or she creates on cards using colored markers. Have the student write the addition sentence below each drawing.

Count by Tens and Hundreds

- Practice counting by tens and hundreds a few times each day until the student can do so with ease.
- The student might use tens and hundreds models to count by tens and hundreds.

Understand Place Value

- Have the student use hundreds, tens, and ones blocks and a place-value mat to model a series of numbers such as 7, 70, and 700.
- Then he or she can write each number in a place-value chart as follows:

Hundreds	Tens	Ones
7	0	0

Complete the Power Practice

- Discuss each incorrect answer. Have the student model any exercise he or she missed using tens and hundreds blocks.

USING THE LESSON

Lesson Goal
- Add greater numbers mentally.

What the Student Needs to Know
- Basic addition facts (sums to 20).
- Count by tens and hundreds.
- Understand place value.

Getting Started
Find out what students know about patterns among ones, tens, and hundreds. Ask:
- *What does 1 + 5 equal?* (6) *What does 10 + 50 equal?* (60) *What does 100 + 500 equal?* (600)
- *How could you use the addition sentence 8 + 5 = 13 to figure out what 80 + 50 equals?* (I could add a 0 after 13 to make 130. Then I would know that 80 + 50 = 130.)

What Can I Do?
Read the question and the response. Then read and discuss the example. Ask:
- *How can you use 7 + 5 = 12 to figure out what 70 + 50 equals?* (I can add a 0 after 12 to make 120.)
- *How can you use 7 + 5 = 12 to figure out what 700 + 500 equals?* (I can add two zeros after 12 to make 1,200.)

Try It
For exercise 1, have students describe their thinking. To prompt them, ask:
- *How did you use 4 + 1 = 5 to figure out the next sum?* (I added a 0 after 5 to make 50.)
- *How did you use 4 + 1 = 5 to figure out what 400 + 100 equals?* (I added two zeros after 5 to make 500.)

Power Practice
- Have the student complete the practice items. Then review each answer.

Lesson Goal

- Complete subtraction facts with 2-digit numbers.

What the Student Needs to Know

- Subtract 1-digit numbers.
- Understand place value.
- Use a place-value chart.

Getting Started

Write the numbers 39 and 21 on the board. Ask what students would do to find out how many years older a 39-year-old is than a 21-year-old. Draw a place-value chart on the board. For example, say:

- *Where should I write the 3 in 39?* (in the tens place) *Where should I write the 9 in 39?* (in the ones place)

- Have a volunteer write 21 under 39 in the place-value chart. Ask: *To subtract 21 from 39, what should I do first?* (Subtract 1 from 9, and write 8 at the bottom of the ones column.)

- *What should I do next?* (Subtract 2 from 3, and write 1 at the bottom of the tens column.) *So 39 – 21 = ?* . (18)

What Can I Do?

Read the question and the response. Then read and discuss the example. Ask:

- *Why do we put the 5 in 59 in the tens column?* (because 59 has 5 tens) *Why do we put the 9 in the ones column?* (because 59 has 9 ones)

- *How would you write 24 in the place-value chart?* (Put the 2 in the tens place and the 4 in the ones place.)

- *Which column should we subtract first?* (the ones column) *What does 9 – 4 equal?* (5)

- *What should we do next?* (Subtract the numbers in the tens column.) *What does 5 – 2 equal?* (3) *So 59 – 24 = ?* . (35)

WHAT IF THE STUDENT CAN'T

Subtract 1-Digit Numbers

- Have the student use 9 connecting cubes to model subtraction sentences with 1-digit numbers. For example, he or she might begin with an 8-cube train and take away 2 cubes to create a 6-cube train. Then have the student draw each model on a card. He or she should write the subtraction sentence below the picture.

- The student should practice using mental math to complete subtraction facts with 1-digit numbers until he or she can do so with ease.

Understand Place Value

- Have the student use tens and ones blocks to model 2-digit numbers. For example, the student can model 11 by setting out 1 tens block and 1 ones block. He or she can model 95 by setting out 9 tens blocks and 5 ones blocks.

- Have the student practice identifying the numbers of tens and ones in two-digit numbers.

Name_____

Power Practice • Subtract.

7. 19 − 11 8	8. 27 − 12 15	9. 46 − 15 31	10. 48 − 34 14
11. 54 − 24 30	12. 65 − 21 44	13. 34 − 11 23	14. 49 − 24 25
15. 74 − 33 41	16. 66 − 22 44	17. 58 − 46 12	18. 79 − 41 38
19. 94 − 13 81	20. 88 − 17 71	21. 75 − 44 31	22. 99 − 75 24

23. 38 − 13 = __25__

24. 29 − 6 = __23__

25. 45 − 21 = __24__

26. 66 − 35 = __31__

27. 87 − 34 = __53__

28. 76 − 53 = __23__

Learn with Partners & Parents

99 Subtraction

Play with a partner. You need four sets of digit cards 0–9, paper, and a pencil.

• Mix the cards well. Place them facedown in the middle of the table. Take turns drawing 2 cards each, but do not show them to the other player.

• Each player makes a number with the two digits on the cards and subtracts that number from 99. The player with the greatest remainder gets 2 points. The player with the most points after all the cards are used wins the game.

WHAT IF THE STUDENT CAN'T

Use a Place-Value Chart

• Have the student use a place-value mat to model 2-digit numbers using tens and ones blocks. Then have him or her draw place-value charts and show the same numbers with numerals.

• For example, he or she might model 35 on a place-value mat by placing 3 tens blocks in the tens column and 5 ones blocks in the ones column. Then he or she can write the number as follows:

Tens	Ones
3	5

Complete the Power Practice

• Discuss each incorrect answer. Have the student model any fact he or she missed using place-value charts or tens and ones blocks.

USING THE LESSON

Try It

Check students' understanding of how to use a place-value chart to find subtraction facts.

• Students might begin by modeling the subtraction sentences using tens and ones blocks.

• For example, for exercise 1 (25 – 11), they can set out 2 tens blocks and 5 ones blocks and then take away 1 tens block and 1 ones block, leaving 1 tens block and 4 ones blocks, or 14.

Power Practice

• Review with students the steps they can follow to help them subtract 2-digit numbers. Tell them they do not need to draw place-value charts unless they want to. Suggest that it may be helpful to draw a vertical line between the ones and tens columns.

• Select several of the exercises and have volunteers describe the steps they followed to find the differences.

Learn with Partners & Parents

• As an alternative, have students make cards for several 2-digit numbers. Students can take turns drawing cards and subtracting the number on the card from 99.

USING THE LESSON

Lesson Goal
- Rename tens and ones as ones.

What the Student Needs to Know
- Understand that 1 ten equals 10 ones.
- Count by tens.
- Add 1-digit numbers to multiples of 10 through 90.

Getting Started
Show students one 10-cube train of connecting cubes and 2 loose cubes. Ask:
- *How many tens and ones do I have?* (1 ten and 2 ones) *If I take apart the 10-cube train and add the cubes to the 2 ones, how many ones will I have?* (12)
- *How can you find out how many ones are in 1 ten and 2 ones?* (Add 10 + 2 for a sum of 12.)

What Can I Do?
Read the question and the response. Then read and discuss the example. Ask:
- *How many ones are in each tens block?* (10) *How can you find out how many ones are in 3 tens blocks?* (Count by tens: 10, 20, 30. There are 30 ones in 3 tens.)
- *What does 30 ones + 4 ones equal?* (34 ones)

Try It
Students might begin by modeling the exercises using connecting cubes. For example, for exercise 1 they might set out a 10-cube train and 6 loose cubes. Then they can take apart the train and count all of the cubes for a total of 16.

Power Practice
- Review with students the steps they have learned to help them rename tens and ones as ones. Allow them to use tens and ones blocks or connecting cubes if they need to.

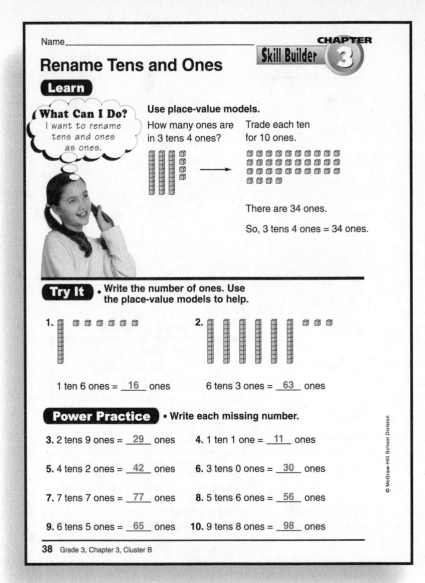

WHAT IF THE STUDENT CAN'T

Understand That 1 Ten Equals 10 Ones
- Make sure the student recognizes tens blocks and ones blocks, and that he or she understands the value of each tens block (10 ones blocks).
- Provide more practice connecting cubes into 10-cube trains and using the trains along with loose cubes to model various 2-digit numbers.

Count by Tens
- Provide daily practice counting by tens from 10 through 100 until the student can do so with ease.

Add 1-Digit Numbers to Multiples of 10 through 90
- Write multiples of 10 on the board and have the student mentally add 1-digit numbers to each. For example, ask:
- What does 10 + 1 equal? (11) What does 50 + 6 equal? (56)
- Continue such practice until the student can complete the addition sentences with ease.

Complete the Power Practice
- Discuss each incorrect answer. Have the student model any exercise he or she missed using connecting cubes or tens and ones blocks.

Name_____

Round to the Nearest Ten, Hundred, or Thousand

Learn

What Can I Do?
I want to round to the nearest ten, hundred, or thousand.

Round 6,803 to the nearest thousand.

Step 1
Look at the place to the right of the thousands place.

6,803

Step 2
If the digit is less than 5, round down to 6,000.

If the digit is 5 or greater, round up to 7,000.

So, 6,803 rounded to the nearest thousand is 7,000.

Try It • Round to the nearest ten, hundred, or thousand. Fill in the blanks.

1. Round 29 to the nearest ten.

   29 is between __20__ and __30__.

   29 rounds to __30__.

2. Round 538 to the nearest hundred.

   538 is between __500__ and __600__.

   538 rounds to __500__.

Power Practice • Round to the nearest ten.

3. 22 __20__   4. 86 __90__   5. 45 __50__

Round to the nearest hundred.

6. 271 __300__   7. 749 __700__   8. 615 __600__

Round to the nearest thousands.

9. 4,672 __5,000__   10. 3,333 __3,000__   11. 8,501 __9,000__

Grade 3, Chapter 3, Cluster B **39**

WHAT IF THE STUDENT CAN'T

Count by Tens, Hundreds, and Thousands

• Practice counting by tens, hundreds, and thousands a few times each day until the student can do so with ease.

• The student might use tens and hundreds blocks to count by tens and hundreds.

Identify Digits in the Ones, Tens, Hundreds, and Thousands Places

• Emphasize that in a whole number the last digit is in the ones place. Make sure the student knows that the digit to the left of the ones place is in the tens place. Have the student also point to the hundreds and thousands places.

• Have the student point to each number in the Power Practice and identify the digit in the ones, tens, hundreds, and thousands places as appropriate.

Complete the Power Practice

• Discuss each incorrect answer. Have the student model any exercise he or she missed using a sketched number line.

• Have the student identify the digit to the right of the place he or she is rounding to. Then have him or her round up or down according to the rule.

USING THE LESSON

Lesson Goal

• Round numbers to the nearest ten, hundred, or thousand.

What the Student Needs to Know

• Count by tens, hundreds, and thousands.

• Identify digits in the ones, tens, hundreds, and thousands places.

Getting Started

Write the number 4,321 on the board. Ask:

• *What number is in the hundreds place?* (3) *What number is in the ones place?* (1) *What number is in the thousands place?* (4) *What number is in the tens place?* (2)

What Can I Do?

Read the question and the response. Then read and discuss the examples. Ask:

• *What does "round to the nearest thousand" mean?* (to go up or down to the nearest thousand)

• *Should we round 6,803 up or down?* (up) *Why should we round this number up?* (The digit to the right of the thousands place is 8. 8 is greater than 5, so we round up.)

• *What is 6,803 rounded to the nearest thousand?* (7,000)

Try It

For each of the exercises, have the students say the number to be rounded and then tell which multiples of 10 or 100 it falls between. Ask:

• *Should you round 29 up or down?* (up) *Why?* (because 9 is greater than 5)

• *In exercise 2, is 538 closer to 500 or 600?* (500) *Should you round up or down?* (down) *Why?* (because 3 is less than 5)

Power Practice

• Have the student complete the practice items. Then review each answer.

CHALLENGE

Lesson Goal
- Use addition, subtraction, guessing and checking to solve number puzzles involving two variables.

Introducing the Challenge
- Review the meaning of the word *represents* by having a volunteer use it in a sentence.(stands for)
- Write the addition sentence 4 + 1 = 5 on the board. Next, draw a box around the 4 and a circle around the 1. Explain that in this lesson, shapes such as squares, circles, and triangles stand for numbers.
- Work through the example exercise with students. Emphasize that they may need to try several different pairs of numbers that the shapes might represent before they find the correct numbers.

Guess and Check Shapes

For each pair of number sentences, each shape represents one number. Guess the numbers for each shape. Then put the numbers in each number sentence to check your guesses. Keep guessing and checking until you figure out the number that each shape represents.

Example:

☐ + △ = 5   Think: What are some basic addition facts for 5?

☐ − △ = 1   4 + 1 = 5, 3 + 2 = 5, 5 + 0 = 5

                   Try 4 and 1.

                   4 + 1 = 5

                   4 − 1 = 3, not 1. Try another fact.

                   Try 3 and 2.

3 + 2 = 5   3 + 2 = 5

3 − 2 = 1   3 − 2 = 1

                   So, ☐ = 3 and △ = 2.

1. Write the number inside each shape to make each number sentence true.

☐ + △ = 10

☐ − △ = 6   ☐ = _8_ , △ = _2_

Name _____

2. Explain how you found the answer to Exercise 1.

Answers will vary. Possible answer: I tried different addition facts

for 10. I tried 9 + 1 = 10, but 9 − 1 = 8, not 6. I tried 8 + 2 = 10.

Since 8 − 2 = 6, 8 is the square and 2 is the triangle.

Now try these problems. Write the number inside each shape.

3. $\boxed{11} + \triangle_4 = 15$

$\boxed{11} - \triangle_4 = 7$

4. $\bigcirc_4 + \boxed{0} = 4$

$\bigcirc_4 - \boxed{0} = 4$

5. $\boxed{14} + \bigcirc_{12} = 26$

$\boxed{14} - \bigcirc_{12} = 2$

6. $\bigcirc_{75} + \triangle_{25} = 100$

$\bigcirc_{75} - \triangle_{25} = 50$

7. $\triangle_{70} + \boxed{24} = 94$

$\triangle_{70} - \boxed{24} = 46$

8. $\boxed{211} + \triangle_{98} = 309$

$\boxed{211} - \triangle_{98} = 113$

© McGraw-Hill School Division

Using the Challenge

- Have a volunteer read the directions aloud. Copy the first exercise on the board for discussion. Students need to understand the following:

- The object of each exercise is to find the numbers that the shapes represent.

- When finished, both the addition sentence and the subtraction sentence need to be correct once the numbers students find are substituted for the shapes.

- Students may need help getting started on exercise 1. If so, tell them to think of several different pairs of addends that sum to 10. (5 + 5; 9 + 1; 6 + 4; 7 + 3; 10 + 0; 8 + 2)

- Point out that any of these pairs will work for the addition sentence, but only one of them will work for the subtraction sentence. Students will need to try each one until they find the one that works. (5 − 5 does not equal 6; neither does 9 − 1; 6 − 4; 7 − 3; nor 10 − 0; but 8 − 2 does equal 6.)

- If students need help with exercises 5–8, explain that the sums and differences given will help them figure out which pairs of numbers to try. For example, in exercise 5, one of the two numbers is only 2 more than the other. Since the sum of the two numbers is 26, and 13 + 13 = 26, the two numbers must be close to 13. (They are 14 and 12, because 14 − 12 = 2.)

CHALLENGE

Lesson Goal

- Use properties of subtraction to supply missing digits in subtraction problems involving 3-digit numbers.

Introducing the Challenge

- Write the following subtraction problem vertically on the board: 50 – 20 = 30. Erase the 5 and draw a box in its place. Do the same with the zero in 20. Discuss with students how they might figure out what the missing digits are. Say:

- *Look at the ones column. There is a 0 in the first line, an empty box beneath it, and another 0 in the answer line. What digit belongs in the box, and why?* (0, because 0 – 0 = 0)

- *Look at the tens column. There is an empty box in the first line, a 2 beneath it, and a 3 in the answer line. What digit belongs in the box, and why?* (5, because 5 – 2 = 3) *How could you use addition to figure this out?* (by adding 3 + 2)

Using the Challenge

- Have a volunteer read the directions aloud. Copy the first exercise on the board for discussion. Students need to understand the following:

- The object of each exercise is to find the missing digits that belong in the empty boxes.

- When finished, the answer to each subtraction problem should be correct. If students are not sure that they wrote the correct digits in the boxes, they should compute the problem to see whether they get the same answer.

- Students may need help getting started with exercise 1. Say:

- *Look first at the ones column. It shows an empty box in the first row, a 2 beneath that, and a 6 in the answer row. What mystery number minus 2 equals 6?* (8)

- Point out that another way to find the missing number in the

---

Missing Digits

Some digits are missing from these problems. Use what you know about subtraction to find the missing digits.

Write each missing digit.

1.
```
    2   5  [8]
  -  1   3   2
  ─────────────
   [1]  2   6
```

2.
```
    3   6   9
  -  1   1  [4]
  ─────────────
    2  [5]  5
```

3.
```
    4   9  [1]
  -  1   7   4
  ─────────────
    3  [1]  7
```

4.
```
    5   5   3
  -  2  [2]  5
  ─────────────
   [3]  2   8
```

5.
```
    7  [1]  5
  -  3   3   2
  ─────────────
   [3]  8   3
```

6.
```
   [7]  4   0
  -  1   2  [9]
  ─────────────
    6   1   1
```

Write each missing digit.

7.
```
    3   7  [9]
-   1  [3]  1
_____
    2   4   8
```

8.
```
    5  [1]  5
-   1   3  [9]
_____
    3   7   6
```

9.
```
    7   2  [3]
-   4   7   7
_____
    2  [4]  6
```

10.
```
  [8]  0   4
-   1   1   9
_____
    6   8  [5]
```

11.
```
    9  [0]  1
-   3   0   2
_____
    5   9  [9]
```

12.
```
    8   4  [2]
-      [6]  5
_____
    7   7   7
```

13. Make up a subtraction problem that has some missing digits. Explain how your problem can be solved.

Answers will vary.

_____

_____

CHALLENGE

ones column would be to add 6 + 2.

- Next, have students supply the missing digit in the hundreds column of the answer line. (1)

- Some students may need help with exercises that involve regrouping hundreds, tens, and ones. You may wish to work through one such problem with students.

- For example, write exercise 4 on the board. Say:

  Look first at the ones column. Since we can't subtract 5 from 3, we must regroup 53 as 4 tens and 13 ones; then we can subtract 5 from 13 for a difference of 8.

- *Next, look at the tens column. What mystery number can be subtracted from 4 (not 5, since we had to regroup 53 as 4 tens and 13 ones) for a difference of 2? (2) How do you know? (because 2 + 2 = 4)*

- *Last, look at the hundreds column. What does 5 – 2 equal? (3)*

- For exercise 13, suggest that students first write their problem without missing digits, find the correct answer, and then decide which digits to represent with empty boxes.

Name_____

Time to the Hour, Half Hour, and Quarter Hour

Write each time.

1.

2.

3.

_____   _____   _____

Skip Counting by 5s

Skip count by 5s. Write the next two numbers in each pattern.

4. 5, 10, 15, 20, _____, _____

5. 15, 20, 25, 30, _____, _____

6. 30, 35, 40, 45, _____, _____

7. 25, 30, 35, 40, _____, _____

8. 20, 25, 30, 35, _____, _____

9. 10, 15, 20, 25, _____, _____

Ordinal Numbers

Name the correct place of the shaded object. Circle a, b, c, or d.

10.

a. first

b. second

c. third

d. fourth

11.

a. fifth

b. sixth

c. seventh

d. eighth

Name_____

Tally Marks and Charts

Use the tally chart.

12. How many girls are in the class? _____

13. How many boys are in the class? _____

Mrs. Jackson's Class	
girls	ⵑⵑⵑⵑ ⵑⵑⵑⵑ
boys	ⵑⵑⵑⵑ ⵑⵑⵑⵑ ⵑⵑ

Addition Patterns

Complete.

14. If ◯ = 2 then ◯◯◯ = _____

15. If △ = 10 then △△△△ = _____

Read Pictographs

Use the pictograph.

16. How many red apples are there? _____

17. How many more green apples are there

than red apples? _____

Apples in a Bowl	
green apples	🍎🍎🍎🍎 🍎🍎🍎🍎
red apples	🍎🍎🍎🍎 🍎

Key: 🍎 = 1 apple

Read Bar Graphs

Use the bar graph.

18. Which sport does the

class like best? _____

19. Which sport do they like the least?_____

20. How many students like softball? _____

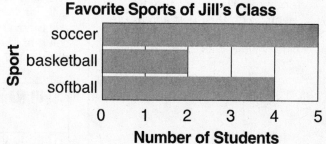

Favorite Sports of Jill's Class

Assessment Goal

This two-page assessment covers skills identified as necessary for success in Chapter 4 Time, Data, and Graphs. The first page assesses the major prerequisite skills for Cluster A. The second page assesses the major prerequisite skills for Cluster B. When the Cluster A and Cluster B prerequisite skills overlap, the skill(s) will be covered in only one section.

Getting Started

- Allow students time to look over the two pages of the assessment. Point out the labels that identify the skills covered.

- Have students find math vocabulary terms used in the assessment. List vocabulary terms on the board as students identify them. If necessary, review the meanings of all essential math vocabulary.

Introducing the Assessment

- Explain to students that these pages will help you know if they are ready to start a new chapter in their math textbooks.

- Students who have transferred from another school may not have been introduced to some of these skills. Encourage students to do their best and assure them you will help them learn any needed skills.

Cluster A Challenge

Those students who demonstrate mastery of the skills on this page will not need to use the reteaching worksheets. Instead, these students can do the Cluster A Challenge found on pages 54-55.

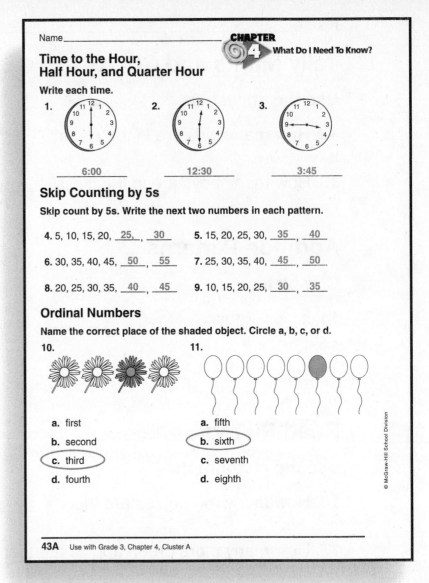

Name_____

CHAPTER 4 — What Do I Need To Know?

**Time to the Hour,
Half Hour, and Quarter Hour**

Write each time.

1. ___6:00___   2. ___12:30___   3. ___3:45___

Skip Counting by 5s

Skip count by 5s. Write the next two numbers in each pattern.

4. 5, 10, 15, 20, __25,__ , __30__   5. 15, 20, 25, 30, __35__ , __40__

6. 30, 35, 40, 45, __50__ , __55__   7. 25, 30, 35, 40, __45__ , __50__

8. 20, 25, 30, 35, __40__ , __45__   9. 10, 15, 20, 25, __30__ , __35__

Ordinal Numbers

Name the correct place of the shaded object. Circle a, b, c, or d.

10.
a. first
b. second
c. third
d. fourth

11.
a. fifth
b. sixth
c. seventh
d. eighth

© McGraw-Hill School Division

43A   Use with Grade 3, Chapter 4, Cluster A

CLUSTER A PREREQUISITE SKILLS

The skills listed in this chart are those identified as major prerequisite skills for students' success in the lessons in Cluster A of the chapter. Each skill is covered by one or more assessment items as shown in the middle column. The right column provides the page number for the lessons in this book that reteach the cluster A prerequisite skills.

Skill Name	Assessment Items	Lesson Pages
Time to the Hour, Half Hour, and Quarter Hour	1-3	44-45
Skip Count by 5s	4-9	46
Ordinal Numbers	10-11	47

Name_____

Tally Marks and Charts

Use the tally chart.

12. How many girls are in the class? __9__

13. How many boys are in the class? __12__

Mrs. Jackson's Class	
girls	‖‖‖ ‖‖‖
boys	‖‖‖ ‖‖‖ ‖‖

Addition Patterns

Complete.

14. If ◯ = 2 then ◯◯◯ = __6__

15. If △ = 10 then △△△△ = __40__

Read Pictographs

Use the pictograph.

16. How many red apples are there? __5__

17. How many more green apples are there

than red apples? __3__

Apples in a Bowl	
green apples	🍎🍎🍎🍎 🍎🍎🍎🍎
red apples	🍎🍎🍎🍎 🍎

Key: 🍎 = 1 apple

Read Bar Graphs

Use the bar graph.

18. Which sport does the

class like best? __soccer__

19. Which sport do they like the least? __basketball__

20. How many students like softball? __4__

Favorite Sports of Jill's Class

Sport: soccer, basketball, softball

Number of Students: 0 1 2 3 4 5

© McGraw-Hill School Division

CLUSTER B PREREQUISITE SKILLS

The skills listed in this chart are those identified as major prerequisite skills for students' success in the lessons in Cluster B of the chapter. Each skill is covered by one or more assessment items as shown in the middle column. The right column provides the page numbers for the lessons in this book that reteach the Cluster B prerequisite skills

Skill Name	Assessment Items	Lesson Pages
Tally Marks and Charts	12-13	48
Addition Patterns	14-15	49
Read Pictographs	16-17	50-51
Read Bar Graphs	18-20	52-53

CHAPTER 4 PRE-CHAPTER ASSESSMENT

Alternative Assessment Strategies

- Oral administration of the assessment is appropriate for younger students or those whose native language is not English. Read the skills title and directions one section at a time. Check students' understanding by asking them to tell you how they will do the first exercise in the group.

- For some skill types you may wish to use group administration. In this technique, a small group or pair of students complete the assessment together. Through their discussion, you will be able to decide if supplementary reteaching materials are needed.

Intervention Materials

If students are not successful with the prerequisite skills assessed on these pages, reteaching lessons have been created to help them make the transition into the chapter.

Item correlation charts showing the skills lessons suitable for reteaching the prerequisite skills are found beneath the reproductions of each page of the assessment.

Cluster B Challenge

Those students who demonstrate mastery of the skills on this page will not need to use the reteaching worksheets. Instead, these students can do the Cluster B Challenge found on pages 56–57.

Lesson Goal
- Tell time on an analog clock.

What the Student Needs to Know
- Identify the hour hand and minute hand on an analog clock.
- Count by fives.
- Understand how to write times.

Getting Started
Use an analog clock. Ask:
- *Which is the hour hand?* (the shorter one) *What is the longer hand called?* (the minute hand)
- *In one hour, how far does the minute hand move?* (all the way around the clock) *How far does the hour hand move in one hour?* (from one numeral to the next)
- *If the minute hand is on the 3, how many minutes after the hour does it show?* (15 minutes) *What part of an hour is 15 minutes?* (a quarter of an hour)
- *If it is 30 minutes, or half an hour after the hour, where will the minute hand be?* (on the 6)

What Can I Do?
- Read the question and the response. Then read and discuss the examples. Ask:
- *Where is the hour hand on the first clock?* (on 5) *Where is the minute hand?* (on 12) *How would you read this time?* (five o'clock) *How would you write it?* (5:00)
- *Where is the minute hand on the second clock?* (on the 6) *How many minutes after the hour does it show?* (30 minutes)
- *On the third clock, where are the hour and minute hands?* (The hour hand is a little past the 7, and the minute hand is on the 3.) *How many minutes after seven o'clock does it show?* (15 minutes) *Why do we put a colon between the 7 and the 15?* (to separate the hour from the minutes after the hour)

Name _____

Time to the Hour, Half Hour, and Quarter Hour

Learn

What Can I Do? I want to tell time on a clock.

Look at the hour hand and the minute hand.

The hour hand is the short hand. The minute hand is the long hand.

Read: five o'clock   Read: ten-thirty   Read: seven-fifteen

Write: 5:00   Write: 10:30   Write: 7:15

Try It • Complete. Write each time.

1.
The hour hand is on the __3__.

The minute hand is on the __12__.

The time is __3:00__.

2.
The hour hand is on the __11__.

The minute hand is on the __12__.

The time is __11:00__.

WHAT IF THE STUDENT CAN'T

Identify the Hour Hand and Minute Hand on an Analog Clock
- Use an analog clock. Have the student observe how its hands move during the course of the school day. Ask, for example:
- *It's 9 o'clock—where is the hour hand?* (on the 9) *Where is the minute hand?* (on the 12)
- *It's 10:30—time when some students go to speech class. Where is the minute hand?* (on the 6) *What does the minute hand on the 6 show?* (that it is 30 minutes after the hour)

Count by Fives
- Use a number line from 0 to 60. Have the student practice jumping his or her finger from 0 to 5 to 10 to 15, and so on, counting aloud by fives: "five, ten, fifteen, twenty," and so on. Repeat a few times a day until the student can count by fives with ease.
- Next, have the student count by fives on an analog clock, starting at 12 and counting by fives while jumping his or her finger clockwise from numeral to numeral: "five, ten, fifteen, ... sixty."

Name_____

Complete. Write each time.

3.

4.

The hour hand is past the ___1___ .   The hour hand is past the ___9___ .

The minute hand is on the ___6___ .   The minute hand is on the ___3___ .

The time is ___1:30___ .   The time is ___9:15___ .

Power Practice

Write each time.

5.

6.

6:00   12:15

7.

8.

4:30   2:00

© McGraw-Hill School Division

Learn with Partners & Parents

How Long?

You need one set of alphabet cards, paper, and pencil.

- Each player marks a paper with 3 columns titled *15 Minutes, Half Hour,* and *Hour.*
- Shuffle the cards and place them facedown. One player turns over the top card and lets every player see the letter.
- All players have 5 minutes to think of as many activities as they can for each column. Each activity must start with the letter that was drawn. For example, for the letter G, the player might write "Go to the store" in the hour column.
- The player with the most activities wins 5 points.

Grade 3, Chapter 4, Cluster A **45**

Try It

Check students' understanding of how to write times.

- Make sure students know that the hour goes before the colon, and the number of minutes after the hour follow the colon.
- If students need help counting minutes after the hour, show them how to place their finger on the 12 and jump it from numeral to numeral, clockwise, while counting by fives.
- For example, for exercise 4, they should count "five, ten, fifteen" as they jump their finger from the 12 to the 1, 2, and 3. Since the minute hand is on the 3, students can conclude that it is 15 minutes after the hour.

Power Practice

- Review with students the steps they can follow to help them write times.
- Select several of the exercises and have volunteers describe the steps they followed to find the times and write them.

WHAT IF THE STUDENT CAN'T

Understand How to Write Times

- Draw on the board several clock faces showing different times. Write the times beneath the clocks. Show the student that the number before the colon corresponds to the number the hour hand is on or closest to.
- Next, show the student that the number following the colon corresponds to the number of minutes after the hour.
- Erase the times under the clocks you drew, and have the student rewrite them.

Complete the Power Practice

- Discuss each incorrect answer. Have the student tell what hour each clock face shows, and how many minutes after the hour it shows. Then have him or her rewrite the answer with your prompting.

Lesson Goal

- Skip count by 5s to complete a pattern.

What the Student Needs to Know

- Recognize and continue an addition pattern.
- Understand skip counting.
- Add 5 to different multiples of 5.

Getting Started

Find out what students know about patterns. Ask:

- *What comes next in this pattern: ababa?* (b) *What comes next in this pattern: 1, 2, 3, 4?* (5)
- *How would you describe this pattern: 2, 4, 6, 8?* (skip counting by 2s beginning with 2) *How would you describe this pattern: 0, 5, 10, 15?* (skip counting by 5s, beginning with 0)

What Can I Do?

Read the question and the response. Then read and discuss the example. Ask:

- *How would you describe this pattern?* (skip counting by 5s beginning with 10)
- *How can you find the next number in the pattern?* (Add 25 + 5, which equals 30.) *What comes after 30 in the pattern?* (35)

Try It

For exercise 4, have students describe their thinking. To prompt them, ask:

- *How would you describe this pattern?* (skip counting by 5s beginning with 35)
- *What number comes before the blank?* (50) *What number comes next in the pattern?* (55)

Power Practice

- Have the student complete the practice items. Then review each answer.

Name_____

Skip Counting by 5s

Learn

What Can I Do?
I want to complete a pattern.

Skip count to complete the pattern.

10, 15, 20, 25, _____, _____

Each number in the pattern goes up by 5.

Skip count by 5s. Start at 10.

Count 10, 15, 20, 25, 30, 35.

The last two numbers in the pattern are 30 and 35.

Try It • Skip count by 5s. Write the next number in each pattern.

1. 5, 10, 15, 20, __25__   2. 20, 25, 30, 35, __40__

3. 15, 20, 25, 30, __35__   4. 35, 40, 45, 50, __55__

Power Practice • Write the next two numbers in each pattern.

5. 25, 30, 35, 40, __45__, __50__   6. 0, 5, 10, 15, __20__, __25__

7. 35, 40, 45, 50, __55__, __60__   8. 30, 35, 40, 45, __50__, __55__

9. 45, 50, 55, 60, 65, __70__, __75__

10. 60, 65, 70, 75, 80, __85__, __90__

WHAT IF THE STUDENT CAN'T

Recognize and Continue an Addition Pattern

- Tell the student that in an addition pattern such as 2, 4, 6, 8, the same number (in this case, 2) is added over and over again.
- Write several simple addition patterns on the board and have the student continue them. Repeat a few times a day until the student can continue such patterns with ease.

Understand Skip Counting

- Have the student practice skip counting by 2s, 5s, and 10s on the number line, saying the numbers aloud. Next, have him or her skip count without using a number line.

Add 5 to Different Multiples of 5

- Have the student create several 5-cube trains of connecting cubes and then count the cubes in 1 train, 2 trains, 3 trains, and so on.

Complete the Power Practice

- Discuss each incorrect answer. Have the student model any exercise he or she missed using connecting cubes or a sketched number line.

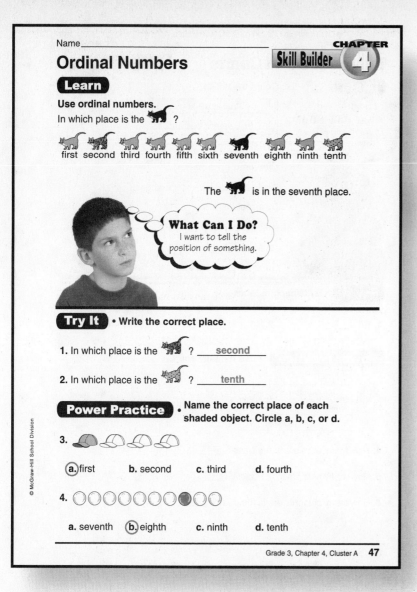

Name_____

Ordinal Numbers

Learn

Use ordinal numbers.
In which place is the 🐱 ?

first second third fourth fifth sixth seventh eighth ninth tenth

The 🐱 is in the seventh place.

What Can I Do?
I want to tell the position of something.

Try It • Write the correct place.

1. In which place is the 🐱 ? ____second____

2. In which place is the 🐱 ? ____tenth____

Power Practice • Name the correct place of each shaded object. Circle a, b, c, or d.

3. (a.)first   b. second   c. third   d. fourth

4. ○○○○○○●○○

   a. seventh   (b.)eighth   c. ninth   d. tenth

Grade 3, Chapter 4, Cluster A **47**

© McGraw-Hill School Division

WHAT IF THE STUDENT CAN'T

Understand That Ordinal Numbers Correspond to Cardinal Numbers

- Have the student write the numbers 1 through 10 on a sheet of paper. Below these cardinal numbers, he or she can write the corresponding ordinal number words. For example, under numeral 5, he or she should write "fifth."

- Ask, for example: *If there are 3 people in a line, what place in line does the last one have?* (the third) *If there are 7 people in a line, what position does the last person have?* (the seventh)

Complete the Power Practice

- Discuss each incorrect answer. Have the student model any exercise he or she missed by counting from left to right.

Lesson Goal

- Use ordinal numbers.

What the Student Needs to Know

- Ordinal numbers that correspond to cardinal numbers.

Getting Started

Find out what students know about ordinal numbers. Ask:

- *If you are the third person in line, how many people are in front of you?* (2)

- *What is the next word in this pattern: first, second, third....?* (fourth)

What Can I Do?

Read the question and the response. Then read and discuss the example. Ask:

- *How many cats are in front of the black cat?* (6)

- *Which place in line does the cat in front of the black cat have?* (the sixth place) *Which place in line does the cat behind the black cat have?* (the eighth place)

Try It

Ask:

- *How many cats are in front of the striped cat?* (1) *Which place in line does the striped cat have?* (the second place)

- *How many cats are in the line?* (10) *Which cat is last in line?* (the spotted cat) *Which place in line does the last cat have?* (the tenth place)

Power Practice

- Have the student complete the practice items. Then review each answer.

USING THE LESSON

Lesson Goal
- Read a tally chart.

What the Student Needs to Know
- Count on from a given number.
- Count by 5s.

Getting Started
Write on the board tally marks showing the number of students in the group. Ask:

- *How many marks did I make for each student?* (1) *What did I draw to show 5 students?* (4 tally marks with 1 tally mark across them)
- *How many students are in our group?* (Answers will vary.)

What Can I Do?
Read the question and the response. Then read and discuss the example. Ask:

- *What does the chart show?* (numbers of oranges and pears in a box) *How many tally marks are next to the word oranges?* (8)
- *How can you tell there are 8 tally marks?* (There are 5 marks in one group and 3 marks in another group.)
- *Why should we start with 5 when we count the marks?* (to add the group of 3 to the group of 5)

Try It
Have students describe their thinking. To prompt them, ask:

- *For exercise 2, how can you count on to find the answer?* (Begin at 5, and count 2 more: 6, 7 — there are 7 tally marks.)
- *For exercise 3, what is the quickest way to count the tally marks?* (Count by 5s: 5, 10, 15.)

Power Practice
- Have the student complete the practice items. Then review each answer.

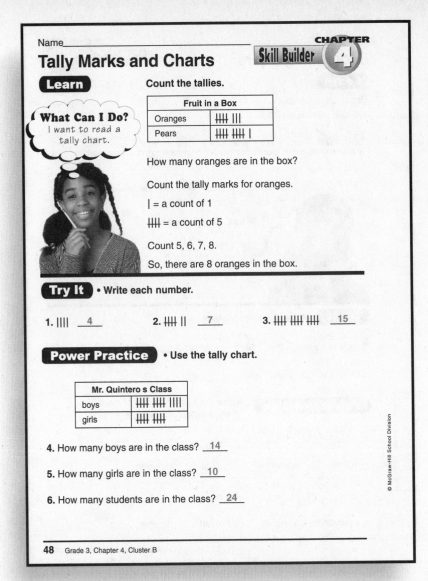

Name_____

Tally Marks and Charts

Learn   Count the tallies.

What Can I Do? I want to read a tally chart.

Fruit in a Box	
Oranges	ＨＨ |||
Pears	ＨＨ ＨＨ	

How many oranges are in the box?

Count the tally marks for oranges.

| = a count of 1

ＨＨ = a count of 5

Count 5, 6, 7, 8.

So, there are 8 oranges in the box.

Try It • Write each number.

1. |||| ___4___   2. ＨＨ || ___7___   3. ＨＨ ＨＨ ＨＨ ___15___

Power Practice • Use the tally chart.

Mr. Quintero s Class	
boys	ＨＨ ＨＨ ||||
girls	ＨＨ ＨＨ

4. How many boys are in the class? ___14___

5. How many girls are in the class? ___10___

6. How many students are in the class? ___24___

WHAT IF THE STUDENT CAN'T

Count on from a Given Number
- Have the student use a number line to practice counting on from 5 or 10. For example, draw on the board tally marks showing 8. Say:
- *Place your finger on 5. How many times will you need to jump to the right to find the number of tally marks?* (3 times)
- Have the student count aloud as he or she jumps a finger 3 numbers to the right: *6, 7, 8.* Then ask: *what number do the tally marks show?* (8)
- Repeat with numbers shown with tally marks such as 9, 12

(count on from 10), and 17 (count on from 15).

Count by 5s
- Use a number line from 0 to 60. Have the student practice jumping his or her finger from 0 to 5 to 10 to 15, and so on, counting aloud by fives: "five, ten, fifteen, twenty," and so on. Repeat a few times a day until the student can count by fives with ease.

Complete the Power Practice
- Discuss each incorrect answer. Have the student model any exercise he or she missed using loose connecting cubes and 5-cube trains.

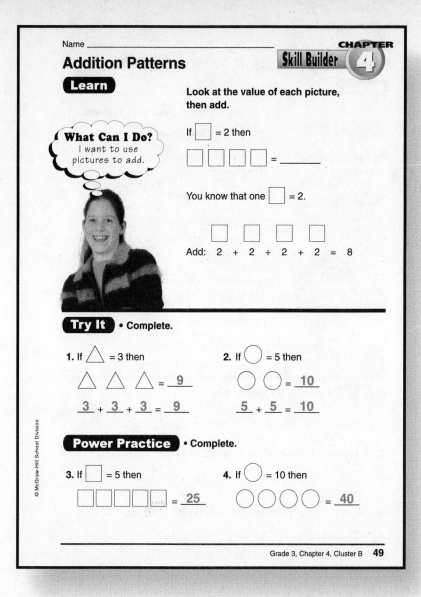

Addition Patterns

Learn

What Can I Do?
I want to use pictures to add.

Look at the value of each picture, then add.

If ☐ = 2 then

☐ ☐ ☐ ☐ = _____

You know that one ☐ = 2.

☐ ☐ ☐ ☐

Add: 2 + 2 + 2 + 2 = 8

Try It • Complete.

1. If △ = 3 then

△ △ △ = __9__

__3__ + __3__ + __3__ = __9__

2. If ◯ = 5 then

◯ ◯ = __10__

__5__ + __5__ = __10__

Power Practice • Complete.

3. If ☐ = 5 then

☐ ☐ ☐ ☐ ☐ = __25__

4. If ◯ = 10 then

◯ ◯ ◯ ◯ = __40__

WHAT IF THE STUDENT CAN'T

Connect Symbols with Numerical Values

- Talk with the student about the words "stands for." For example, a nickel stands for, or is worth, 5 pennies.
- Use attribute blocks and counters. Tell the student that, for example, a triangle is worth 3 counters. Make exchanges with the student. For example, exchange 2 triangles for 6 counters.

Add Several 1-Digit Numbers

- Have the student use a number line to practice adding several 1-digit numbers. Say:
- *To add 3 + 3 + 3, place your finger on 3, the first number.*

How many times will you need to jump to the right to find 3 + 3? (3 times) *What is 3 + 3?* (6)

- *What should you do to add the last 3?* (Jump 3 more numbers to the right.) *What does 3 + 3 + 3 equal?* (9)

Complete the Power Practice

- Discuss each incorrect answer. Have the student model any exercise he or she missed by exchanging attribute blocks for counters.

Lesson Goal
- Use picture symbols to add.

What the Student Needs to Know
- Connect symbols with numerical values.
- Add several 1-digit numbers.

Getting Started
Draw a star on the board. Tell students that the star stands for 2. Then ask:

- *If each star stands for 2, what would 2 stars equal? (4) What would 3 stars equal? (6, or 2 + 2 + 2)*

What Can I Do?
Read the question and the response. Then read and discuss the example. Ask:

- *What does 1 square equal? (2) What would 2 squares equal? (2 + 2, or 4)*
- *What would 3 squares equal? (2 + 2 + 2, or 6)*
- *How can you write an addition sentence to show the value of 4 squares? (2 + 2 + 2 + 2 = 8)*

Try It
Have students describe their thinking. To prompt them, ask:

- *What does 1 triangle equal? (3) If you add 3 triangles, and each equals 3, what do you get? (9)*
- *What does 1 circle equal? (5) What is the quickest way to add 2 circles (2 fives)? (count by 5s — 5, 10)*

Power Practice
- Have students complete the practice items. Make sure they understand that in exercise 3, a square is worth 5, rather than 2 (as in the example at the top of the page).

Lesson Goal

- Compare information in a pictograph.

What the Student Needs to Know

- Connect symbols with numerical values.
- Understand information presented in chart form.
- Compare, add, and subtract numbers from 2 to 11.

Getting Started

Create on the board a simple pictograph showing favorite ice-cream flavors of students in the group. Your chart should resemble the ones in the lesson. Include one row for each ice-cream flavor; draw 1 small ice-cream cone for each student who prefers that flavor. Ask:

- *What does this chart show?* (our favorite ice-cream flavors) *What does each ice-cream cone stand for?* (1 student) *How many students like chocolate ice cream best?* (Answers will vary.)

What Can I Do?

Read the question and the response. Then read and discuss the examples. Ask:

- *What does this chart show?* (how many books Jessie, Eric, and Anna read) *What does the Key show?* (that each 📕 stands for 1 book)
- *How many books did Eric read?* (2) *How many did Jessie read?* (3) *How about Anna?* (She read 5.) *So who read the greatest number?* (Anna)

Name_____

Read Pictographs

Learn

What Can I Do?
I want to compare information in a pictograph.

Use the key and count the symbols.

Books Read	
Jessie	📕📕📕
Eric	📕📕
Anna	📕📕📕📕📕

Key: 📕 = 1 book

Who read the most books?

Use the key to find how many books each student read.

Jessie: 1 + 1 + 1 = 3 books

Eric: 1 + 1 = 2 books

Anna: 1 + 1 + 1 + 1 + 1 = 5 books

5 books > 3 books > 2 books

So, Anna read the most books.

Try It • Use the pictograph above.

1. Who read the least number of books? ___Eric___

2. How many more books did Anna read than Jessie? ___2 books___

3. How many books did Eric and Anna read? ___7 books___

4. How many books did the students read in all? ___10 books___

50 Grade 3, Chapter 4, Cluster B

© McGraw-Hill School Division

WHAT IF THE STUDENT CAN'T

Connect Symbols with Numerical Values

- Talk with the student about the words "stands for." For example, if you were making a pictograph showing favorite kinds of fruit, you could use red sticky dots to stand for apples, orange sticky dots to stand for oranges, and yellow sticky dots to stand for bananas.
- Have the student use attribute blocks to invent symbols for various objects. For example, a group of red squares might stand for the number of red cars in a parking lot.

Understand Information Presented in Chart Form

- Talk with the student about the charts shown in the lesson. Ask what each shows, and point out its title.
- Make sure the student understands that a Key shows what symbols stand for.
- Have the student point to the symbols that stand for the number of books Jessie read and the number of pink roses in Mr. Finch's flower shop. Make sure he or she knows that the symbols appear in the same row as the words that tell what they stand for.

Name_____

Roses at Mr. Finch's Flower Shop	
Yellow roses	🌼🌼🌼🌼🌼🌼🌼
Red roses	🌼🌼🌼🌼🌼🌼🌼🌼🌼🌼
Pink roses	🌼🌼🌼🌼🌼
White roses	🌼🌼🌼

Key: 🌼 = 1 rose

3. How many different color roses does the pictograph show?

List the colors. _____4; yellow, red, pink, and white_____

4. Which color of roses are there the greatest number of? The least?

Greatest: _____red_____ Least: _____white_____

5. How many pink roses are there? _____5_____

6. How many more red roses are there than white roses? _____8_____

7. How many yellow and pink roses are there altogether? _____13_____

8. How many roses are there in all? _____27_____

Grade 3, Chapter 4, Cluster B   51

© McGraw-Hill School Division

Try It

Have students explain their thinking. To prompt them, ask:

- *What is the quickest way to answer question 1?* (Look quickly at the chart. The line of books next to Eric's name is shortest.)
- *What do you need to do to answer question 2?* (Count the number of books next to Anna's and Jessie's names. Subtract 5 – 3.) *How could you answer the question without subtracting?* (Compare the rows of books. There are 2 more books in Anna's row than in Jessie's.)

Power Practice

- Select several of the exercises and have volunteers describe what they did to answer the questions.

WHAT IF THE STUDENT CAN'T

Compare, Add, and Subtract Numbers from 2 to 11

- Have the student compare on a number line pairs of numbers from 2 to 11. Ask him or her to tell which number is greater and which is smaller.
- Students might practice simple addition and subtraction sentences using a number line, counters, and/or mental math. Practice completing sentences such as 2 + 3; 11 – 7; 2 + 3 + 5; and so on until students can do so with ease.

Complete the Power Practice

- Discuss each incorrect answer. Have the student model any exercise he or she answered incorrectly using connecting cubes to stand for the amounts shown in the charts.

Lesson Goal

- Compare information in a bar graph.

What the Student Needs to Know

- Understand information presented on a bar graph.
- Compare numbers shown on a bar graph.
- Compare, add, and subtract numbers from 1 to 7.

Getting Started

Create on the board a simple bar graph showing kinds of pets owned by students' families. Your bar graph should resemble the ones in the lesson. Include one bar for each type of pet. Ask:

- *What does this bar graph show?* (kinds of pets we own; how many of each kind we own) *What do the words on the side tell?* (kinds of pets) *What do the numbers on the bottom tell?* (numbers of each type) *How many dogs do we own?* (Answers will vary.)
- Ask other questions as appropriate.

What Can I Do?

Read the question and the response. Then read and discuss the example. Ask:

- *What does this bar graph show?* (favorite colors of Kate's friends) *What colors are shown in the graph?* (red, blue, and yellow)
- *What is the greatest number of friends who have the same favorite color?* (5) *What is the smallest number who like a certain color best?* (1)
- *How many friends like yellow best?* (2) *How can you tell?* (The bar for yellow reaches to the 2.)

Name_____

Read Bar Graphs

Learn

What Can I Do?
I want to compare information.

Read a bar graph.

How many of the friends chose yellow as their favorite color?

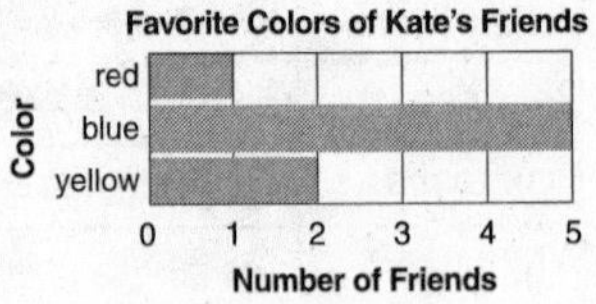

Favorite Colors of Kate's Friends

Color: red, blue, yellow

Number of Friends: 0 1 2 3 4 5

Look at the bar for yellow.
The bar ends at 2.
So, 2 friends chose yellow.

Try It • Use the bar graph above.

1. How many friends chose red? _____1_____

2. How many friends chose blue? _____5_____

3. Does the graph show that the friends liked

   blue or yellow better? _____blue_____

4. How many more friends chose blue than

   chose yellow? _____3_____

5. Which color do the friends like least? _____red_____

© McGraw-Hill School Division

WHAT IF THE STUDENT CAN'T

Understand Information Presented on a Bar Graph

- Talk with the student about the bar graphs shown in the lesson. Ask what each shows, and point out its title.
- Have the student point to the bars that stand for the number of friends who like red best and the number of students who like crackers best.

Compare Numbers Shown on a Bar Graph

- Make sure the student knows that a bar graph is a good way to compare amounts. Point out that you can see which is the longest and shortest bar without even looking at the numbers on the bottom of the graph.
- Work with the student to create his or her own bar graph comparing hair colors of students in the group or class. Show the student how to use the numbers at the bottom of the graph to create each bar.

Name_____

Favorite Snacks of Justin's Class

Snack:
- fruit
- crackers
- popcorn

0 1 2 3 4 5 6 7 8
Number of Students

6. What is the title of the bar graph? <u>Favorite Snacks of Justin's Class</u>

7. Which snack is the class favorite? _____ popcorn _____

8. How many students chose fruit as their

favorite snack? <u>6 students</u>

9. How many more students like popcorn best than

like crackers best? _____ <u>4 more students</u>

10. How many students voted in all? <u>16 students</u>

© McGraw-Hill School Division

WHAT IF THE STUDENT CAN'T

Compare, Add, and Subtract Numbers from 1 to 7

- Have the student compare on a number line pairs of numbers from 1 to 7. Ask him or her to tell which number is greater and which is smaller.

- Students might practice simple addition and subtraction sentences using a number line, counters, and/or mental math. Practice completing sentences such as 2 + 3; 7 – 5; 2 + 3 + 1; and so on until students can do so with ease.

Complete the Power Practice

- Discuss each incorrect answer. Have the student model any exercise he or she answered incorrectly using connecting cubes to stand for the bars shown in the graphs.

USING THE LESSON

Try It

Have students explain their thinking. To prompt them, ask:

- *What is the quickest way to answer question 3?* (Look quickly at the graph. The bar for blue is much longer than the one for yellow.)

- *What is another way to answer question 3?* (The blue bar reaches to 5; the yellow one reaches to 2; 5 is greater than 2.)

- *What is the quickest way to answer question 5?* (Look quickly at the bar graph. The shortest bar is the one for red.)

Power Practice

- Select several of the exercises and have volunteers describe what they did to answer the questions. To prompt them, ask:

- *Which is the longest bar?* (the one for popcorn) *Which is the shortest bar?* (the one for crackers)

- *How can you find the answer to question 9 without subtracting?* (count on from 3 to 7)

- *For exercise 10, what addition sentence do you need to complete?*
(6 + 3 + 7 = 16)

CHALLENGE

Lesson Goal

- Use facts about analog clocks and telling time to figure out times shown on clock faces without numbers.

Introducing the Challenge

- Draw on the board an analog clock with numbers but no hands. Next, erase the numbers and replace them with ticks or dots around perimeter of the clock face. Ask a volunteer to come to the board and tell which number each tick or dot represents.

- Finally, draw 8 different clock faces without numbers. Draw hands to show the following times in scrambled order: 3:00; 6:00; 9:00; 12:00; 3:30; 6:30; 9:30; 12:30. Ask volunteers to come to the board and write the correct time under each clock face. Have students explain how they can tell times on clock faces that do not have numbers.

Using the Challenge

- Ask a volunteer to read the directions aloud. Copy the first clock face on the board for discussion. Students need to understand the following:

- The object of each exercise is to find the time that each clock face shows and write it in the blank.

- Students should write the hour before the colon, and the minutes after the colon.

- Students may need help getting started. If so, suggest that they draw dots or ticks to represent 12, 3, 6, and 9 on the clock faces. Then they will be able to tell which numbers the hands are closest to.

- For example, in exercise 1, the minute hand is pointing straight up (where the 12 would be). The hour hand is closer to the point where the 3 would be than it is to where the 12 would be. This suggests that it is pointing to 2 rather than 1.

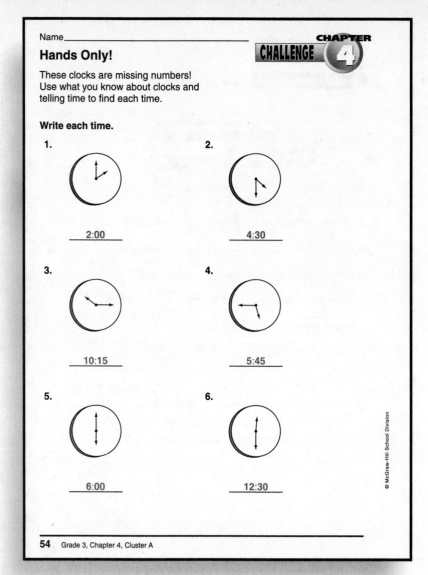

Hands Only!

These clocks are missing numbers! Use what you know about clocks and telling time to find each time.

Write each time.

1.
2:00

2.
4:30

3.
10:15

4.
5:45

5.
6:00

6.
12:30

Name_____

Write each time.

7.

_____5:25_____

8.

_____1:40_____

9.

_____7:55_____

10.

_____11:10_____

11. How much time has passed between the time shown in Problem 9 and the time shown in Problem 10? _____3 hours 15 minutes_____

12. Describe how you found the times on the clocks without any numbers.

_____Possible answer: I looked at the hour hand and wrote the number_____

_____that it would be pointing at. I looked at the minute hand and wrote_____

_____the number that it would be pointing at. Then I figured out the time._____

CHALLENGE

- If students need help, you might suggest that they look at a classroom clock that does have numbers on it.
- You may wish to use exercise 9 to show that when an analog clock is showing a time such as 7:55—when the hour is just about to change—the hour hand will be pointing somewhere between the earlier and the later hour. That is why the hour hand in exercise 9 is closer to 8 than to 7.
- Before students write their responses to exercise 12, you may wish to have them discuss this question aloud. This may help them figure out what to write.

CHALLENGE

Lesson Goal

- Take a survey and use the results to create a pictograph and a bar graph.

Introducing the Challenge

- Take a quick survey to find out how many students are wearing shoes with shoelaces, how many have shoes with zippers, how many have slip-on shoes, and how many have shoes that fasten in other ways. Show the results of your survey with tally marks.

- Create on the board a pictograph showing the results of your survey. Have students suggest a symbol or symbols you might use in your pictograph. With students' help, draw a key for your pictograph. Ask volunteers to suggest titles for your graph; choose the most appropriate title and write it above the pictograph.

- Next, use your survey results to create a bar graph. Draw a grid on the board and use it to draw bars for your graph. Have students suggest a title for the bar graph and headings to write along the left side and the bottom.

Using the Challenge

- The object of the lesson is to conduct a survey, use the results to create a pictograph (including a key), and then use the same survey results to create a bar graph.

- To complete the lesson, students should use what they have learned about tally marks, surveys, pictographs, symbols, keys, and bar graphs.

- Students may need help getting started. If so, help them brainstorm lists of subjects they might use in their surveys. (Examples: favorite pizza toppings, favorite muffin flavors, favorite yogurt flavors, favorite colors, favorite movies, favorite sports, favorite school subjects, favorite books)

Name_____

Make Your Own Chart and Graph

Think of an idea for making a pictograph.
You may want to take a survey of your
classmates or friends, or collect data about a subject.

1. Make a tally chart of your data in the space below.

Answers will vary. Check students' tally charts.

2. How did you decide on the subject for your pictograph?_____

Answers will vary.

_____

3. Choose a symbol and key for the pictograph. Draw it in the space below.

Answers will vary. Check that students use a key
and symbol that works with their data.

Key: _____ = _____

4. Write a title for your pictograph. Answers will vary.

_____

Name_____

Make Your Own Chart and Graph

CHALLENGE **CHAPTER 4**

Think of an idea for making a pictograph.
You may want to take a survey of your
classmates or friends, or collect data about a subject.

1. Make a tally chart of your data in the space below.

Answers will vary. Check students' tally charts.

2. How did you decide on the subject for your pictograph?_____

Answers will vary.

_____

3. Choose a symbol and key for the pictograph. Draw it in the space below.

Answers will vary. Check that students use a key
and symbol that works with their data.

Key: _____ = _____

4. Write a title for your pictograph. Answers will vary.

_____

_____

CHALLENGE

- Students may wish to work in pairs or groups of three to complete their surveys and create their graphs.

- Make sure students understand that their symbols should reflect their survey subjects. For example, if they conducted a survey on favorite muffin flavors, they might use a simple drawing of a muffin to stand for each person who preferred a certain flavor.

- You may wish to provide grid paper that students can use to help them create their bar graphs. Remind them to write headings and titles on their graphs. For example, one bar graph might be titled Our Favorite Muffins. A student might write Numbers of People along the left side of the graph, and Muffin Flavors along the bottom. Then he or she might label each bar with the appropriate muffin flavor.

- If students have difficulty writing word problems to go with their graphs, suggest that they look back at pages 52–53 of Chapter 4 to help them think of ideas.

Name_____

Equal Groups

Complete.

1.

_____ groups of 2

2.
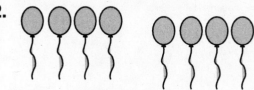
_____ groups of 4

3.

4 groups of _____

4.

6 groups of _____

5.
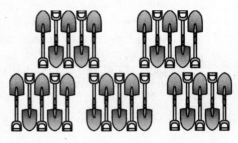
_____ groups of _____

6.
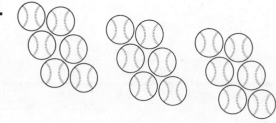
_____ groups of _____

Add 3 or More Numbers

Add.

7. $2 + 5 + 3 =$ _____

8. $4 + 3 + 0 + 4 =$ _____

9.
```
   6
   3
 + 5
```

10.
```
   9
   1
   1
 + 4
```

11.
```
   7
   4
   2
 + 5
```

Name_____

Skip Counting

Each pattern is a skip counting pattern.
Write the missing number in each pattern.

12. 2, 4, _____, 8, 10   **13.** 3, _____, 9, 12, 15

14. 5, 10, 15, _____, 25   **15.** _____, 8, 12, 16, 20

Commutative Property of Addition

Complete.

16. 2 + 3 = 3 + _____   **17.** 5 + 4 = _____ + 5

18. 7 + _____ = 6 + 7   **19.** _____ + 2 = 2 + 9

Doubles to Add

Find each sum.

20. 2 + 2 = _____   **21.** 5 + 5 = _____   **22.** 8 + 8 = _____

23.   4   **24.**   9   **25.**   6
         + 4   + 9   + 6
         ___   ___   ___

© McGraw-Hill School Division

CHAPTER 5 PRE-CHAPTER ASSESSMENT

Assessment Goal

This two-page assessment covers skills identified as necessary for success in Chapter 5 Mutiplication Concepts. The first page assesses the major prerequisite skills for Cluster A. The second page assesses the major prerequisite skills for Cluster B. When the Cluster A and Cluster B prerequisite skills overlap, the skill(s) will be covered in only one section.

Getting Started

- Allow students time to look over the two pages of the assessment. Point out the labels that identify the skills covered.

- Have students find math vocabulary terms used in the assessment. List vocabulary terms on the board as students identify them. If necessary, review the meanings of all essential math vocabulary.

Introducing the Assessment

- Explain to students that these pages will help you know if they are ready to start a new chapter in their math textbooks.

- Students who have transferred from another school may not have been introduced to some of these skills. Encourage students to do their best and assure them you will help them learn any needed skills.

Cluster A Challenge

Those students who demonstrate mastery of the skills on this page will not need to use the reteaching worksheets. Instead, these students can do the Cluster A Challenge found on pages 64–65.

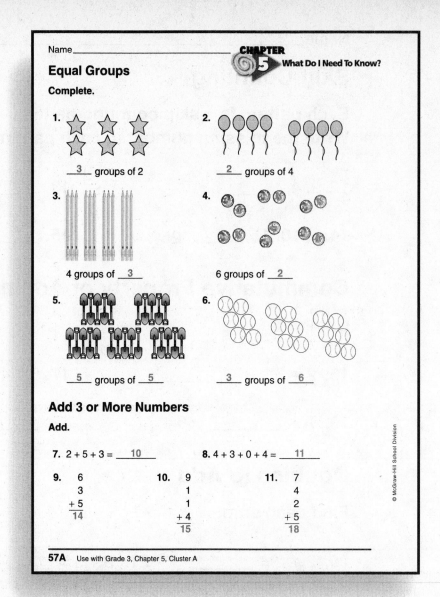

Name_____

Equal Groups

Complete.

1. ___3___ groups of 2

2. ___2___ groups of 4

3. 4 groups of ___3___

4. 6 groups of ___2___

5. ___5___ groups of ___5___

6. ___3___ groups of ___6___

Add 3 or More Numbers

Add.

7. $2 + 5 + 3 =$ ___10___

8. $4 + 3 + 0 + 4 =$ ___11___

9.
$$\begin{array}{r} 6 \\ 3 \\ +\,5 \\ \hline 14 \end{array}$$

10.
$$\begin{array}{r} 9 \\ 1 \\ 1 \\ +\,4 \\ \hline 15 \end{array}$$

11.
$$\begin{array}{r} 7 \\ 4 \\ 2 \\ +\,5 \\ \hline 18 \end{array}$$

57A Use with Grade 3, Chapter 5, Cluster A

© McGraw-Hill School Division

CLUSTER A PREREQUISITE SKILLS

The skills listed in this chart are those identified as major prerequisite skills for students' success in the lessons in Cluster A of the chapter. Each skill is covered by one or more assessment items as shown in the middle column. The right column provides the page number for the lessons in this book that reteach the cluster A prerequisite skills.

Skill Name	Assessment Items	Lesson Pages
Equal Groups	1-6	58-59
Add 3 or More Numbers	7-11	60

Name_____

Skip Counting

Each pattern is a skip counting pattern.
Write the missing number in each pattern.

12. 2, 4, <u>6</u>, 8, 10   **13.** 3, <u>6</u>, 9, 12, 15

14. 5, 10, 15, <u>20</u>, 25   **15.** <u>4</u>, 8, 12, 16, 20

Commutative Property of Addition

Complete.

16. $2 + 3 = 3 + $ <u>2</u>   **17.** $5 + 4 = $ <u>4</u> $+ 5$

18. $7 + $ <u>6</u> $= 6 + 7$ **19.** <u>9</u> $+ 2 = 2 + 9$

Doubles to Add

Find each sum.

20. $2 + 2 = $ <u>4</u>   **21.** $5 + 5 = $ <u>10</u>   **22.** $8 + 8 = $ <u>16</u>

23.   4   **24.**   9   **25.**   6
      $\underline{+\ 4}$ $\underline{+\ 9}$ $\underline{+\ 6}$
         8   18   12

CLUSTER B PREREQUISITE SKILLS

The skills listed in this chart are those identified as major prerequisite skills for students' success in the lessons in Cluster B of the chapter. Each skill is covered by one or more assessment items as shown in the middle column. The right column provides the page numbers for the lessons in this book that reteach the Cluster B prerequisite skills

Skill Name	Assessment Items	Lesson Pages
Skip Counting	12-15	61
Commutative Property of Addition	16-19	62
Doubles to Add	20-25	63

Alternative Assessment Strategies

- Oral administration of the assessment is appropriate for younger students or those whose native language is not English. Read the skills title and directions one section at a time. Check students' understanding by asking them to tell you how they will do the first exercise in the group.

- For some skill types you may wish to use group administration. In this technique, a small group or pair of students complete the assessment together. Through their discussion, you will be able to decide if supplementary reteaching materials are needed.

Intervention Materials

If students are not successful with the prerequisite skills assessed on these pages, reteaching lessons have been created to help them make the transition into the chapter.

Item correlation charts showing the skills lessons suitable for reteaching the prerequisite skills are found beneath the reproductions of each page of the assessment.

Cluster B Challenge

Those students who demonstrate mastery of the skills on this page will not need to use the reteaching worksheets. Instead, these students can do the Cluster B Challenge found on pages 66–67.

Lesson Goal
- Describe equal groups.

What the Student Needs to Know
- Recognize equal groups.
- Count the number of equal groups and the number in each group.

Getting Started
Determine what students know about equal groups. Display 6 groups of 2 connecting cubes each. Write on the board "Number of groups" and "Number in each group." Ask the following questions and record the answers under the correct heading:

- *How many groups are there?* (6) *How many cubes are in each group?* (2) *Are the groups equal?* (Yes.) *So, there are 6 groups of 2.*

- If necessary, repeat the steps with 3 groups of 3 pencils each.

What Can I Do?
- Read the question and the response. Then discuss the example. Ask:

- *What is the first step?* (Count the number of groups.) *What is the second step?* (Count the number in each group.) *Why is it helpful to do these steps in order?* (To help you keep track of the number of groups, then the number in each group.)

- *How do the pictures help you count the groups or items in each group?* (You can point to each item or group as you count.)

- *Why is it important to count then recount the number of groups?* (to make sure you counted correctly)

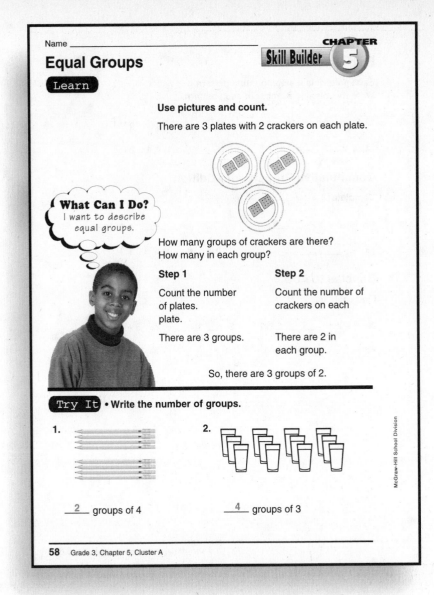

WHAT IF THE STUDENT CAN'T

Recognize Equal Groups
- Display 2 equal groups of 4 connecting cubes each and 2 unequal groups, one with 3 connecting cubes and one with 5. Have the student count the number in each group to find the pair of equal groups. (the pair with 4 cubes each) Have the student draw and label pictures of equal groups in his or her math journal.

Count the Number of Equal Groups and the Number in Each Group
- Draw four circles on the board with two stars in each.

Tell the student that each circle is a group of stars. Have him or her count the groups. (4) Have him or her count the stars in each group. (2) Then have the student repeat after you, "4 groups of 2." Practice daily until the student can follow the steps without hesitation.

- Help the student correct any errors. Remind the student that he or she can tally the items in one group while counting on by ones, or circle the items while counting. Make sure the student remembers to recount before completing the work.

Name _____

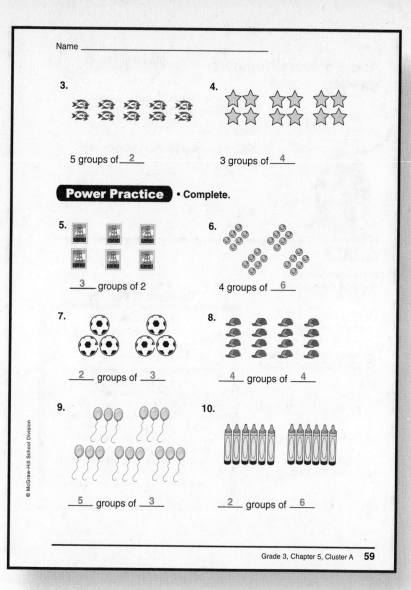

3.

5 groups of __2__

4.

3 groups of __4__

Power Practice • Complete.

5.

__3__ groups of 2

6.

4 groups of __6__

7.

__2__ groups of __3__

8.

__4__ groups of __4__

9.

__5__ groups of __3__

10.

__2__ groups of __6__

© McGraw-Hill School Division

WHAT IF THE STUDENT CAN'T

Complete the Power Practice
- Discuss each incorrect answer. Have the student model any missed exercise using connecting cubes or pictured sets.

- The most common error that will occur in exercises 5–10 is that students will miscount the number of groups. Determine if students understand "3 groups of 2," for instance, by having them draw pictures.

USING THE LESSON

Try It
Check students' understanding of counting equal groups. Look at exercise 1 and ask:

- *What do you count first?* (the number of groups) *How many groups are there?* (2) *How many pencils are in each group?* (4) *Are the groups equal?* (Yes.) Repeat the procedure for exercise 2.

For exercises 3–4, make sure students are counting the number in each group. Review students' answers. Ask:

- *What number are you asked to find in exercises 3 and 4?* (the number in each group) *Is that the first step or second step in describing equal groups?* (the second step)

Power Practice
Have students complete the practice exercises. Review students' answers and have them make corrections as needed. Call on volunteers to model several of their answers with connecting cubes.

USING THE LESSON

Lesson Goal
- Add 3 or more numbers.

What the Student Needs to Know
- Add pairs of whole numbers mentally.
- Understand the Associative Property of Addition.

Getting Started
Find out what students know about grouping numbers to make addition easier. Write on the board:

2 + 8 + 7 = _____. Say:
- *Add 2 + 8. (10) Add 10 + 7. (17)*
- *How does adding 2 + 8 first make the addition easier? (You can use mental math to add 2 + 8 quickly to get 10, then add 10 to 7.)*
- *Which is easier, adding the group 2 + 8 first or the group 8 + 7? (Answers will vary.)*

What Can I Do?
- Read the question and the response. Remind students that the parentheses mean "do this first." Then read and discuss the example. Ask:
- *What is the first step in adding 3 or more numbers? (Group the numbers in pairs.)*
- *How does grouping pairs of numbers make adding easier? (You can use mental math to add 2 numbers quickly.)*

Try It
Have students use parentheses to show how they grouped the numbers. Remind students that there is no right or wrong way to group them.

Power Practice
- Have students complete the practice items. Then review each answer.

Add 3 or More Numbers

Learn

What Can I Do?
I want to add 3 or more numbers.

Use the Associative Property to add two numbers at a time.

Find 4 + 2 + 8.

Group the numbers to make addition easier.

4 + (2 + 8) =
↓
4 + 10 = 14   Make a ten. Add mentally.

So, 4 + 2 + 8 = 14.

Try It

Add. Show how you grouped the numbers.

1. 3 + 2 + 9 = __14__
   Possible answer:
   (3 + 2) + 9 = 5 + 9 = 14

Power Practice

Add.

2. 7 + 1 + 2 = __10__

3. 5 + 3 + 4 = __12__

4. 2 + 2 + 5 + 3 = __12__

5. 4 + 6 + 6 = __16__

Learn with Partners & Parents

Number Cube Roll
You need four 1–6 number cubes.
- The first player rolls the four cubes.
- The second player writes a number sentence to add the four numbers rolled.
- The first player then writes a number sentence in which the numbers are grouped differently.
- Each player checks the other's number sentence. If both players agree, both get a point for the round, and the second player rolls. If a player misses a sentence, that player loses a point, and the other player rolls.
- Play until one or both players have earned 10 points.

WHAT IF THE STUDENT CAN'T

Use Mental Math to Add Whole Numbers
- Have the student practice adding pairs of whole numbers using flash cards until he or she can do so with ease.

Understand the Associative Property of Addition
- Discuss the meaning of "Associative Property" (when adding or multiplying, the grouping of the numbers does not affect the result). Then have the student write the term, its meaning, and an example in the math journal.

Complete the Power Practice
- Discuss each incorrect answer. Have the student use connecting cubes to check his or her work, or group different pairs to see if the addition is easier.
- For exercises 7 and 8, have volunteers use a place-value chart.

Name _____

Skip Counting

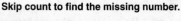

Learn

What Can I Do?
I want to find a missing number in a skip-counting pattern.

Skip count to find the missing number.

2, 4, 6, _____, 10

Each number in the pattern goes up by 2.

Skip count by 2s.

Start at 2 and end at 10.

Count 2, 4, 6, 8, 10.

The number that comes between 6 and 10 is 8.

Try It • Write the missing number in each skip-counting pattern.

1. Skip count by 3s.

   9, 12, _15_, 18, 21

2. Skip count by 5s.

   5, _10_, 15, 20, 25

Power Practice • Write the missing number in each pattern.

3. 4, 8, _12_, 16, 20

4. 6, 8, 10, _12_, 14

5. 6, _9_, 12, 15, 18

6. _5_, 10, 15, 20, 25

7. 12, 16, 20, _24_, 28

8. 25, 30, _35_, 40, 45

Grade 3, Chapter 5, Cluster B **61**

© McGraw-Hill School Division

WHAT IF THE STUDENT CAN'T

Skip Count in 2s, 3s, 4s, and 5s

- Have the students practice skip-counting in 2s, 3s, 4s, and 5s, beginning with the first number, until he or she can do so easily.

Recognize a Skip Counting Pattern

- Have the student make a number line for the exercises they missed, and draw arrows to show the skips from one number to the next. Encourage the student to explain how the number line helps him or her recognize the pattern.

Understand Place Value in Skip Counting Patterns

- Have the student use place-value charts with the patterns they missed to show what happens to the digits in the ones and tens places as the numbers in a pattern increase.

Complete the Power Practice

- Discuss each incorrect answer. Have the student skip count to complete the pattern correctly.

- Provide the student with a hundred chart to circle the numbers in a pattern he or she missed.

Lesson Goal

- Find a missing number in a skip counting pattern.

What the Student Needs to Know

- Skip count by 2s, 3s, 4s, and 5s.
- Recognize a skip counting pattern.
- Understand place value in skip counting patterns.

Getting Started

Find out what students know about skip counting. Write on the board a number line from 0 to 12. Start counting at 2.

0 1 2 3 4 5 6 7 8 9 10 11 12

2, 4, 6, 8, _____, 12

- Ask: *By how many does each number in the pattern go up?* (2)
- *Skip count by 2s, starting at 2.* (2, 4, 6, 8, 10, 12) *What is the missing number?* (10)

What Can I Do?

- Read the question and the response. Then read and discuss the example. Ask:
- *What is the first step in finding the missing number in a skip counting pattern?* (Find the amount each number goes up by.)

Try It

Have students practice skip-counting by 3s and 5s. Review their answers. Ask:

- *What number comes just after 21 in the pattern in exercise 1?* (24) *How can you tell?* (By skip counting in 3s, you know the number after 21 is 24. Point out that in exercise 1, the student skip counts by 3s, but the first number is not 3 but 9.)

Power Practice

- Have students complete the practice items. Then review each answer.

Lesson Goal
- Write a different addition sentence using the same addends and sum.

What the Student Needs to Know
- Identify the missing number as an addend.
- Use the Commutative Property of Addition.

Getting Started
Find out what students know about writing different addition sentences using the same addends and sum. Display 4 red cubes and 2 blue cubes. Say:

- *Write a number sentence for the cubes. (4 + 2) What is the sum? (6)*
- *Change the order of the cubes. Write another addition sentence. (2 + 4) What is the sum? (6)*
- *Does the order in which you add the red cubes and blue cubes matter? (no) Why? (The sum is the same.)*

What Can I Do?
- Read the question and the response. Then read and discuss the example. Ask volunteers to model the example with colored connecting cubes. Ask:
- *What numbers can you reorder in an addition sentence? (the addends)*
- *Can you reorder the sum and an addend to make two addition sentences that are equal? (No.)*

Try It
Have students complete Exercises 1–2. Review their answers.

Power Practice
- Have students complete the practice exercises. Then review each answer.

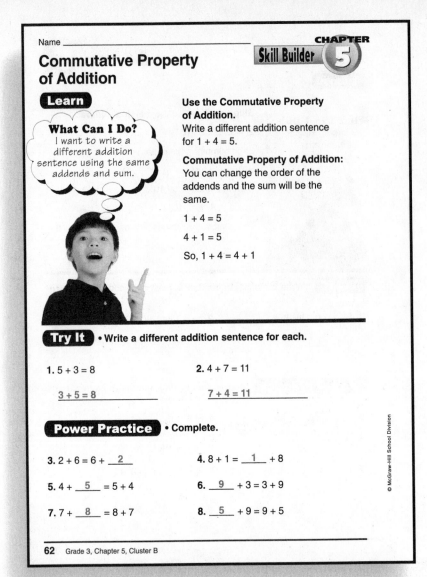

Name _____

Commutative Property of Addition

Learn

What Can I Do?
I want to write a different addition sentence using the same addends and sum.

Use the Commutative Property of Addition.
Write a different addition sentence for $1 + 4 = 5$.

Commutative Property of Addition: You can change the order of the addends and the sum will be the same.

$1 + 4 = 5$

$4 + 1 = 5$

So, $1 + 4 = 4 + 1$

Try It • Write a different addition sentence for each.

1. $5 + 3 = 8$

   $3 + 5 = 8$

2. $4 + 7 = 11$

   $7 + 4 = 11$

Power Practice • Complete.

3. $2 + 6 = 6 + \underline{\ 2\ }$

4. $8 + 1 = \underline{\ 1\ } + 8$

5. $4 + \underline{\ 5\ } = 5 + 4$

6. $\underline{\ 9\ } + 3 = 3 + 9$

7. $7 + \underline{\ 8\ } = 8 + 7$

8. $\underline{\ 5\ } + 9 = 9 + 5$

WHAT IF THE STUDENT CAN'T

Identify the Missing Number as an Addend
- For exercises 3–8, the student may incorrectly write the sum in the blank instead of the missing addend. Emphasize that the student is combining the same addends, just in a different way. Have the student use counters to demonstrate each addition sentence missed.

Use the Commutative Property
- Direct the student's attention to exercise 3. Explain that the Commutative Property of Addition can help him or her find $6 + 2$ if he or she knows that $2 + 6 = 8$. Have the student use flashcards to change the order of addends in basic sums until this can done with ease.

Complete the Power Practice
- Discuss each incorrect answer. Have the student use colored squares to help show the correct answers.

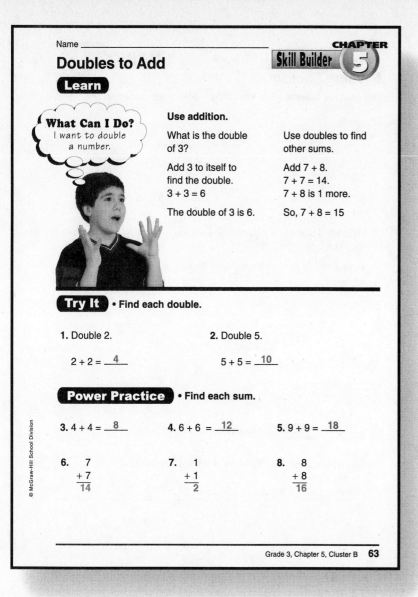

Name _____

Doubles to Add

Skill Builder CHAPTER **5**

Learn

What Can I Do?
I want to double a number.

Use addition.

What is the double of 3?

Add 3 to itself to find the double.
3 + 3 = 6

The double of 3 is 6.

Use doubles to find other sums.

Add 7 + 8.
7 + 7 = 14.
7 + 8 is 1 more.

So, 7 + 8 = 15

Try It • Find each double.

1. Double 2.

2 + 2 = _4_

2. Double 5.

5 + 5 = _10_

Power Practice • Find each sum.

3. 4 + 4 = _8_   4. 6 + 6 = _12_   5. 9 + 9 = _18_

6.   7
  + 7
  ‾14‾

7.   1
  + 1
  ‾2‾

8.   8
  + 8
  ‾16‾

Grade 3, Chapter 5, Cluster B   **63**

WHAT IF THE STUDENT CAN'T

Identify the Ones and Tens Places in 2-Digit Numbers

• Direct the student's attention to exercise 4. Ask what the double of 6 is. (12) Have the student identify the number of tens and ones. (1 ten, 2 ones) Do the same with the sums of exercises 2, 5, 6, and 8. Stress that doubling whole numbers from 5 to 9 will produce 2-digit numbers.

Choose Addition Strategies

• Have the student use flash cards to find basic sums until he or she can do so easily. Stress that the student can use these addition strategies:

counting on, using doubles, using doubles plus 1, or using doubles minus 1.

Recognize Doubled Numbers

• Remind the student that an addition sentence that adds a number to itself means doubling that number. Ask the student to create an illustrated chart showing the doubles of numbers from 1 to 10.

Complete the Power Practice

• Discuss each incorrect answer. Have the student draw pictures to show the correct answers.

USING THE LESSON

Lesson Goal

• Double a number.

What the Student Needs to Know

• Identify the ones and tens places in 2-digit numbers.

• Choose addition strategies.

• Recognize doubled numbers.

Getting Started

Find out what students know about doubling numbers. Display 2 blue cubes. Say:

• *What is the double of 2?* (4) Display 2 red cubes. Say: *Let's check. Count the 2 blue cubes and 2 red cubes.* (4) *So, 2 + 2 = 4.*

• *How can doubling 2 help you if you need to add 2 + 3?* (Double 2 and count on by 1.)

What Can I Do?

Read the question and the response. Then read and discuss the examples. Ask volunteers to model the examples with colored connecting cubes. Ask:

• *What addition sentence means the same as "double 3"?* (3 + 3)

• *Why is it easier to find the sum of 7 + 8 if you double 7 first?* (It is faster to double 7 and add 1 than to use the counting-on method.)

Try It

Have students complete exercises 1–2. Review their answers. Call on volunteers to show their work on number lines. Ask:

• *Did you use mental math to find the sum? Why or why not?* (Possible answer: Yes, because I know that 2 + 2 = 4, and 5 + 5 = 10.)

• *How can you practice your mental math?* (Possible answer: You can use flash cards.)

Power Practice

• Have students complete the practice exercises. Then review each answer.

CHALLENGE

Lesson Goal

- Use multiplication and division to solve problems.

Introducing the Challenge

Find out how familiar students are with multiplication and division word problems. Have them solve the following word problems:

- *Marisa has 2 bookshelves with 2 soccer trophies on each. How many trophies does she have in all? (4)*

- *Hank sold 10 muffins at the bake sale. He sold the same number to 5 people. How many muffins did each person buy? (2)*

Using the Challenge

Have students read the directions to the challenge. Complete problems 1–2 as a group. Use connecting cubes to model each problem. Ask:

- *How can division help you find the first missing factor in problem 1?* (8 divided by 2 = 4, so 4 is the missing factor)

Have students complete problems 3–4 individually. Review students' answers. Ask:

- *How does drawing an array in problem 3 help you find the product?* (Possible answer: It makes it easier to count the groups, then the items in each group.)

- *Why is it easier to write and solve a multiplication sentence than an addition sentence for the word problem in problem 3?* (It is faster to multiply 3 × 4 than to add 4 + 4 + 4.)

Have students work independently to complete problems 5–14. Review any incorrect answers. Have students draw pictures to show their work for several problems.. Ask:

- *How does using division help you find the missing factors?* (You can divide the product by one of the factors to find the missing factor.)

Name _____

Logical Thinking: Missing Factors

Use what you know about multiplication to solve these problems.

Complete.

1. $2 \times 4 = \underline{\quad 8 \quad}$

$2 \times \underline{\quad 4 \quad} = 8$

$\underline{\quad 2 \quad} \times 4 = 8$

2. $5 \times 3 = \underline{\quad 15 \quad}$

$5 \times \underline{\quad 3 \quad} = 15$

$\underline{\quad 5 \quad} \times 3 = 15$

3. Ming has 3 boxes with 4 crayons in each box. How many crayons does she have in all?

Draw a picture to solve the problem. Then complete the addition sentence.

Students should draw 3 groups of 4, or 3 rows with 4 in each row.

$\underline{\quad 4 \quad} + \underline{\quad 4 \quad} + \underline{\quad 4 \quad} = \underline{\quad 12 \quad}$

4. Explain how to write a multiplication sentence for Exercise 3.

Possible answer: There are 3 groups of 4, so $3 \times 4 = 12$.

Name _____

Write each missing factor.

5. __2__ × 3 = 6   6. 5 × __4__ = 20

7. 3 × __5__ = 15   8. __2__ × 6 = 12

9. 5 × __8__ = 40   10. __9__ × 2 = 18

11. How did you find the missing factor for Exercise 5? Explain.

Answers will vary. Possible answer: I drew groups of 3 Xs until

there were a total of 6 Xs. I counted the number of groups. There

were 2 groups of 3, so 2 is the missing factor.

12. Write an addition sentence for 4 × 7.   **7 + 7 + 7 + 7 = 28**

13. The product of two numbers is 45. What are the two numbers?

Possible answer: 5 and 9

14. Jake gave away 14 baseball cards. He gave the same number of cards to each of 7 friends. How many cards did each friend get?

2 cards

CHALLENGE

- Point out to students that for problem 11, there are several ways to find the missing factor. Encourage students to share their answers and explain why their method helped them solve the problem.

- Point out that for problem 13, the correct answer could be 9 × 5 or 5 × 9.

- Ask: *Why are both answers correct, according to the Commutative Property?* (When multiplying or adding, the order of the numbers does not affect the result.)

- Ask: *What other numbers could have a product of 45?* (15 and 3)

- Ask students to write a division sentence for problem 14. (14 ÷ 7 = 2) Ask how they could check the answer. (Show that 7 × 2 = 14)

CHALLENGE

Lesson Goal
- Find the sums of products in two sets and compare the sums.

Introducing the Challenge
Find out how familiar students are with solving 1 and zero multiplication facts and comparing products. Have them solve the following:

- *What is 121 × 0?* (0)
- *Which is greater, the product of 23 × 1 or the product of 88 × 0? Why?* (the product of 23 × 1, because 23 is greater than 0)
- Write on the board:

  23 > 0

  Remind students that > means "greater than."

Using the Challenge
- Have students read the directions to the challenge. Find the products in Set A and Set B of problem 1 as a group. Ask:
- *What is the first step in finding the set with the greater number?* (Find the product in each multiplication sentence.)
- *What is the second step?* (Add the products in each step.)
- *What is the third step?* (Compare the sum of the products in Set A to the sum of the products in Set B.)

Number Sense: Choose the Greater Set

Look at the two sets in each problem. If you add all the products in each set, which set shows the greater number? Use number sense to solve.

1. | Set A | Set B |
    |-------|-------|
    | 3 × 1 | 4 × 1 |
    | 3 × 2 | 4 × 2 |

    a. Which set shows the greater number? __Set B__

    b. Explain how you know.
    Possible answer: Because 4 > 3, and the

    second factors are the same in each set.

2. | Set A | Set B |
    |--------|---------|
    | 0 × 1 | 160 × 0 |
    | 1 × 16 | 1 × 1 |

    a. Which set shows the greater number? __Set A__

    b. Explain how you know.
    Possible answer: For Set A, 0 + 16 = 16.

    For Set B, 0 + 1 = 1; 16 > 1.

Name _____

3.

Set A	Set B
0×72	1×27
27×1	72×0
725×0	275×1

a. Which set shows the greater number? <u>Set B</u>

b. Explain how you know. <u>Possible answer: Because the first two</u>

<u>products in each set are the same, and 275 > 0.</u>

4.

Set A	Set B
$1 \times 1,654,987$	$1,654,987 \times 0$

a. Which set shows the greater number? <u>Set A</u>

b. Explain how you know. <u>Possible answer:</u>

<u>Because 1,654,987 > 0.</u>

5. Write your own set problem. Use 3 and 4 or 0 and 1 as factors.

<u>Problems will vary. Check students' problems.</u>

_____

CHALLENGE

Have students complete problems 2–5 individually. Review students' answers. Ask:

- *How does knowing multiplication facts for 1 and zero help you solve these problems quickly?* (You can do mental math when a factor is 1 or zero, because a number multiplied by 1 equals that number, and a number multiplied by zero equals zero.)

- *Why is it helpful to check your work?* (Possible answer: There are several steps to find the set with the greater number, so you need to check that you did each step correctly.)

- Call on volunteers to share their set problems for problem 5, omitting the answers. Have other students solve the problems and explain how they know which sets have the greater numbers.

Use Arrays to Multiply

Write the multiplication sentence that each array shows.

1.

$\underline{\ 2\ } \times \underline{\ 4\ } = \underline{\ 8\ }$

2.

$\underline{\ 3\ } \times \underline{\ 5\ } = \underline{\ \ \ \ }$

Equal Groups

Write the multiplication sentence that each picture shows.

3.

$\underline{\ \ \ \ } \times \underline{\ \ \ \ } = \underline{\ \ \ \ }$

4.

$\underline{\ \ \ \ } \times \underline{\ \ \ \ } = \underline{\ \ \ \ }$

Repeated Addition

Find each sum.

5. $3 + 3 + 3 + 3 = \underline{\ \ \ \ }$

6. $2 + 2 + 2 + 2 + 2 + 2 = \underline{\ \ \ \ }$

7. $5 + 5 + 5 + 5 + 5 = \underline{\ \ \ \ }$

8. $4 + 4 + 4 + 4 + 4 = \underline{\ \ \ \ }$

Multiplication Facts Through 5s

Multiply.

9. $2 \times 3 = \underline{\ \ \ \ \ \ \ }$

10. $6 \times 5 = \underline{\ \ \ \ \ \ \ }$

11. $\begin{array}{r} 4 \\ \times\, 4 \\ \hline \end{array}$

12. $\begin{array}{r} 8 \\ \times\, 2 \\ \hline \end{array}$

13. $\begin{array}{r} 3 \\ \times\, 7 \\ \hline \end{array}$

Name _____

Place Value

Complete.

14. 40 = _____ tens   **15.** 90 = _____ tens   **16.** 70 = _____ tens

Use a Multiplication Table

Use the multiplication table.

0	1	2	3	4	5	6	7	8	9	10
0	0	0	0	0	0	0	0	0	0	0
0	1	2	3	4	5	6	7	8	9	10
0	2	4	6	8	10	12	14	16	18	20
0	3	6	9	12	15	18	21	24	27	30
0	4	8	12	16	20	24	28	32	36	40
0	5	10	15	20	25	30	35	40	45	50
0	6	12	18	24	30	36	42	48	54	60
0	7	14	21	28	35	42	49	56	63	70
0	8	16	24	32	40	48	56	64	72	80
0	9	18	27	36	45	54	63	72	81	90
0	10	20	30	40	50	60	70	80	90	100

17. Draw a line through the **rows** that have both odd and even numbers.

18. Circle the **columns** that have only even numbers.

Associative Property of Addition

Find each sum. Add the grouped addends first.

19. (3 + 7) + 4   **20.** 6 + (2 + 9)

_____ + 4 = _____   6 + _____ = _____

CHAPTER 6 PRE-CHAPTER ASSESSMENT

Assessment Goal

This two-page assessment covers skills identified as necessary for success in Chapter 6 Multiplication Facts. The first page assesses the major prerequisite skills for Cluster A. The second page assesses the major prerequisite skills for Cluster B. When the Cluster A and Cluster B prerequisite skills overlap, the skill(s) will be covered in only one section.

Getting Started

- Allow students time to look over the two pages of the assessment. Point out the labels that identify the skills covered.
- Have students find math vocabulary terms used in the assessment. List vocabulary terms on the board as students identify them. If necessary, review the meanings of all essential math vocabulary.

Introducing the Assessment

- Explain to students that these pages will help you know if they are ready to start a new chapter in their math textbooks.
- Students who have transferred from another school may not have been introduced to some of these skills. Encourage students to do their best and assure them you will help them learn any needed skills.

Cluster A Challenge

Those students who demonstrate mastery of the skills on this page will not need to use the reteaching worksheets. Instead, these students can do the Cluster A Challenge found on pages 78-79.

Name _____

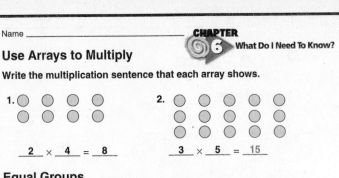

CHAPTER 6 What Do I Need To Know?

Use Arrays to Multiply

Write the multiplication sentence that each array shows.

1. __2__ × __4__ = __8__

2. __3__ × __5__ = __15__

Equal Groups

Write the multiplication sentence that each picture shows.

3. __3__ × __4__ = __12__

4. __2__ × __5__ = __10__

Repeated Addition

Find each sum.

5. $3+3+3+3 =$ __12__

6. $2+2+2+2+2+2 =$ __12__

7. $5+5+5+5+5 =$ __25__

8. $4+4+4+4+4 =$ __20__

Multiplication Facts Through 5s

Multiply.

9. $2 \times 3 =$ __6__

10. $6 \times 5 =$ __30__

11. $\begin{array}{r} 4 \\ \times 4 \\ \hline 16 \end{array}$

12. $\begin{array}{r} 8 \\ \times 2 \\ \hline 16 \end{array}$

13. $\begin{array}{r} 3 \\ \times 7 \\ \hline 21 \end{array}$

67A Use with Grade 3, Chapter 6, Cluster A

CLUSTER A PREREQUISITE SKILLS

The skills listed in this chart are those identified as major prerequisite skills for students' success in the lessons in Cluster A of the chapter. Each skill is covered by one or more assessment items as shown in the middle column. The right column provides the page number for the lessons in this book that reteach the cluster A prerequisite skills.

Skill Name	Assessment Items	Lesson Pages
Use Arrays to Multiply	1-2	68-69
Equal Groups	3-4	70-71
Repeated Addition	5-8	72
Multiplication Facts Through 5s	9-13	73-74

Name _____

Place Value

Complete.

14. 40 = __4__ tens   **15.** 90 = __9__ tens   **16.** 70 = __7__ tens

Use a Multiplication Table

Use the multiplication table.

0	1	2	3	4	5	6	7	8	9	10
0	0	0	0	0	0	0	0	0	0	0
0	1	2	3	4	5	6	7	8	9	10
0	2	4	6	8	10	12	14	16	18	20
0	3	6	9	12	15	18	21	24	27	30
0	4	8	12	16	20	24	28	32	36	40
0	5	10	15	20	25	30	35	40	45	50
0	6	12	18	24	30	36	42	48	54	60
0	7	14	21	28	35	42	49	56	63	70
0	8	16	24	32	40	48	56	64	72	80
0	9	18	27	36	45	54	63	72	81	90
0	10	20	30	40	50	60	70	80	90	100

17. Draw a line through the **rows** that have both odd and even numbers.

18. Circle the **columns** that have only even numbers.

Associative Property of Addition

Find each sum. Add the grouped addends first.

19. (3 + 7) + 4   **20.** 6 + (2 + 9)

__10__ + 4 = __14__   6 + __11__ = __17__

Alternative Assessment Strategies

- Oral administration of the assessment is appropriate for younger students or those whose native language is not English. Read the skills title and directions one section at a time. Check students' understanding by asking them to tell you how they will do the first exercise in the group.

- For some skill types you may wish to use group administration. In this technique, a small group or pair of students complete the assessment together. Through their discussion, you will be able to decide if supplementary reteaching materials are needed.

Intervention Materials

If students are not successful with the prerequisite skills assessed on these pages, reteaching lessons have been created to help them make the transition into the chapter.

Item correlation charts showing the skills lessons suitable for reteaching the prerequisite skills are found beneath the reproductions of each page of the assessment.

CLUSTER B PREREQUISITE SKILLS

The skills listed in this chart are those identified as major prerequisite skills for students' success in the lessons in Cluster B of the chapter. Each skill is covered by one or more assessment items as shown in the middle column. The right column provides the page numbers for the lessons in this book that reteach the Cluster B prerequisite skills

Skill Name	Assessment Items	Lesson Pages
Place Value	14-16	75
Use a Multiplication Table	17-18	76
Associative Property of Addition	19-20	77

Cluster B Challenge

Those students who demonstrate mastery of the skills on this page will not need to use the reteaching worksheets. Instead, these students can do the Cluster B Challenge found on pages 80-81.

USING THE LESSON

Lesson Goal
- Write a multiplication sentence for an array.

What the Student Needs to Know
- Recall basic addition facts.
- Recognize an array as a model for multiplication.

Getting Started
- Ask students to think of an addition fact for a double, such as 4 + 4. Then say:
- *Think of 4 + 4 as 2 fours or 2 × 4. Since 4 + 4 = 8, then 2 × 4 also = __?__. (8)*
- *I'm going to place those 2 fours into 2 rows of counters, each with 4 in a row. That is how we can picture 2 × 4.*

What Can I Do?
- Read the question and the response. Then read and discuss the example. Ask:
- *If I count across 4 counters on each of 3 rows, how do I show how many counters I have? (4 + 4 + 4 = 12)*
- *I have 3 rows of 4 counters. That is the same as adding 3 fours. So 4 + 4 + 4 = 3 × 4 = 12.*
- *What if I have 4 rows of fours? I add another 4: 4 + 4 + 4 + 4. If 3 × 4 was 12, then what do I get if I add 4 more? (16) So 4 × 4 = 16.*
- *What multiplication sentence can you write for 6 rows of 4? (6 × 4 = 24) For 7? (7 × 4 = 28)*

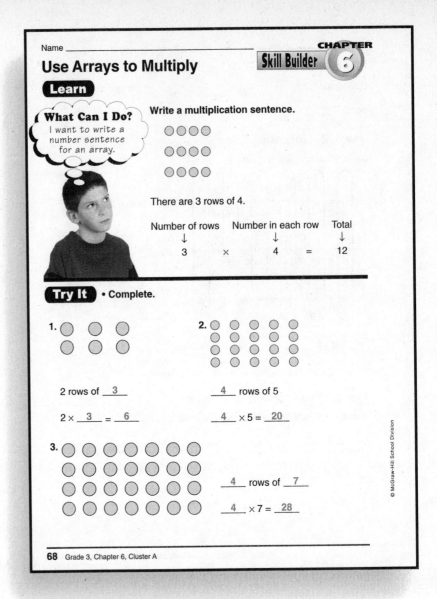

Name _____

Use Arrays to Multiply

Learn

What Can I Do?
I want to write a number sentence for an array.

Write a multiplication sentence.

○ ○ ○ ○
○ ○ ○ ○
○ ○ ○ ○

There are 3 rows of 4.

Number of rows		Number in each row		Total
↓		↓		↓
3	×	4	=	12

Try It • Complete.

1. ○ ○ ○
   ○ ○ ○

   2 rows of __3__

   2 × __3__ = __6__

2. ○ ○ ○ ○ ○
   ○ ○ ○ ○ ○
   ○ ○ ○ ○ ○
   ○ ○ ○ ○ ○

   __4__ rows of 5

   __4__ × 5 = __20__

3. ○ ○ ○ ○ ○ ○ ○
   ○ ○ ○ ○ ○ ○ ○
   ○ ○ ○ ○ ○ ○ ○
   ○ ○ ○ ○ ○ ○ ○

   __4__ rows of __7__

   __4__ × 7 = __28__

© McGraw-Hill School Division

WHAT IF THE STUDENT CAN'T

Recall Basic Addition Facts
- Practice basic addition facts for 10 to 15 minutes daily until students can recall the sums for addition facts automatically.

Recognize an Array as a Model for Multiplication
- Have the student repeatedly use counters or draw arrays. Have the student start with simple numbers—say, up to 5 rows of 5 counters each. Have him or her count by 1s if necessary. Ask the student to write a multiplication sentence for each array.

Name _____

Complete.

4.

____6____ rows of ____2____

____6____ × ____2____ = ____12____

5.

____3____ rows of ____3____

____3____ × ____3____ = ____9____

Power Practice • Write the multiplication sentence that each array shows.

6.

____2____ × ____5____ = ____10____

7.

____5____ × ____3____ = ____15____

8.

____4____ × ____3____ = ____12____

9.

____5____ × ____6____ = ____30____

© McGraw-Hill School Division

Try It

- For exercises 1–4, students might think of the multiplication sentence they would write if they had just 1 row of counters. For example in exercise 1, there are 3 counters: $1 \times 3 = 3$. From that, they can add another 3 to give them 6, which is the same as 2×3. They need not start with 1 row each time. For example, in exercise 2, if they already know 2×5, they could add another 5 to get 3×5, then another to get 4×5.

Power Practice

- For each exercise, have volunteers describe some different methods they can use to show that the product they have written is correct. (count the number of counters, use a drawing, use a number line)
- Remind students they can use addition to check their work.

WHAT IF THE STUDENT CAN'T

Complete the Power Practice

- Discuss each incorrect answer. Have the student model any fact he or she missed, using physical counters rather than drawn ones.

Lesson Goal
- Write a multiplication sentence to describe a number picture.

What the Student Needs to Know
- Recall basic addition and multiplication facts.
- Recognize multiplication as repeated addition.

Getting Started
- Ask students to think of an addition fact for a double, such as 3 + 3. For example, say:
- *Think of 3 + 3 as 2 threes or 2 × 3. Since 3 + 3 = 6, then 2 × 3 = __?__. (6)*
- *Think of 3 × 3 as 2 × 3 + __?__. (3)*
- *I'm going to skip-count by 3s. When I stop, say the next number. 3, 6, __?__. (9)*
- *You know that 2 × 3 = 6, that 3 × 3 = 2 × 3 + 3, and that 6 + 3 = 9. So 3 × 3 = __?__. (9)*
- *What if I have 4 rows of fours? I add another 4: 4 + 4 + 4 + 4. If 3 × 4 was 12, then what do I get if I add 4 more? (16) So 4 × 4 = 16.*
- *What do I get if I have 5 rows of 4? (20) How do I get that? (by adding 4 to 16; 4 + 4 + 4 + 4 + 4 = 20; 5 × 4 = 20)*

What Can I Do?
- Read the question and the response. Then read and discuss the example. Ask:
- *If I count 5 marbles in each of 4 groups, how do I show how many counters I have? (5 + 5 + 5 + 5 = 20)*
- *I have 4 groups of 5 marbles. That is the same as adding 4 fives. So 5 + 5 + 5 + 5 = 4 × 5 = 20.*
- *What if I have 5 groups of 5? I would add another 5. If 4 × 5 is 20, then what do I get if I add 5 more? (25) So 5 × 5 = 25.*
- *What do I get if I have 6 rows of 5? (30) How do I get that? (by adding 5 to 25)*

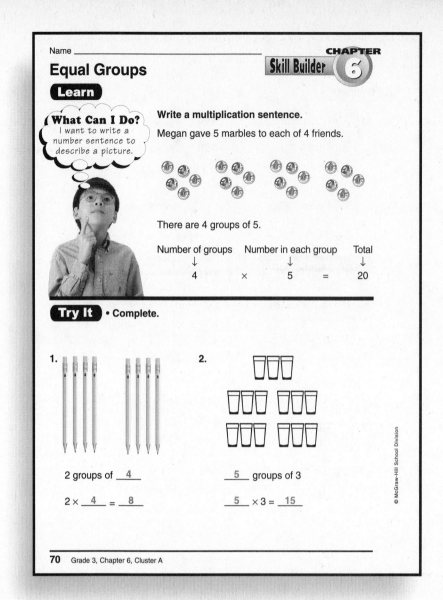

Name _____

Equal Groups

Learn

What Can I Do? I want to write a number sentence to describe a picture.

Write a multiplication sentence.

Megan gave 5 marbles to each of 4 friends.

There are 4 groups of 5.

Number of groups	Number in each group	Total
↓	↓	↓
4	× 5	= 20

Try It • Complete.

1.

2 groups of __4__

2 × __4__ = __8__

2.

__5__ groups of 3

__5__ × 3 = __15__

70   Grade 3, Chapter 6, Cluster A

© McGraw-Hill School Division

WHAT IF THE STUDENT CAN'T

Recall Basic Addition and Multiplication Facts
- Practice addition and multiplication facts for 10 to 15 minutes daily until the student can recall the sums for addition facts automatically.

Recognize Multiplication as Repeated Addition
- Have the student repeatedly use counters or other objects in equal groups or draw their own equal groups. Have them start with simple numbers—say, up to 5 rows of 5 counters each. Have them count by 1s if necessary. Ask them to write a multiplication sentence for each array of group.

Name _____

Complete.

3.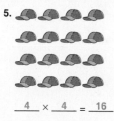

___3___ groups of ___4___

___3___ × ___4___ = ___12___

4. ★★ ★★ ★★
★ ★ ★
★★ ★★ ★★
★ ★ ★

___6___ groups of ___3___

___6___ × ___3___ = ___18___

Power Practice

Write the multiplication sentence that each picture shows.

5. (caps)

___4___ × ___4___ = ___16___

6. (apples)

___5___ × ___4___ = ___20___

Learn with Partners & Parents

Spinning Groups

- You will need a spinner numbered 1 to 8, and many counters, pennies, or beans in a paper bag.

- Take turns. The first player spins the spinner, and takes a handful of counters from the bag without looking.

- Make equal groups using the counters. Each group should have the number of counters shown on the spinner. (If there are any left over counters, put them back in the bag.)

- Players get 2 points for each equal group. For instance, if you make 5 equal groups of 3 counters each, you get 10 points.

- Each player gets 10 turns. The player with the most points after 10 turns wins the game.

© McGraw-Hill School Division

WHAT IF THE STUDENT CAN'T

Complete the Power Practice

- Discuss each incorrect answer. Have the student model any fact he or she missed, using physical counters rather than drawn ones.

USING THE LESSON

Try It

- Check students' understanding of how to use a multiplication fact they already know to find another multiplication fact.

- For exercises 1–4, students might think of the multiplication sentence they would write if they had just 1 group of objects. For example in exercise 1 they could start with 4 pencils: $1 \times 4 = 4$. From that, they could add another 4 pencils to give them 8 in all, which is the same as 2×4. In exercise 2, if they already know 3×3, they could add another 3 to get 4×3, then another to get 5×3.

Power Practice

- For each of the exercises, have volunteers describe some different methods they can use to show that the product they have written is correct. (count the number of objects, use counters, use a number line)

- Review that if a product does not immediately come to mind, students can add to a product they know.

- Remind students they can use addition to check their work.

Learn with Partners & Parents

- Players should realize that the least number of counters in any group will be 1, and the greatest number of counters in any group will be 8.

- Tell players that they could decide to give a player 2 points for writing a correct multiplication statement for the array of groups he or she has created; for example, for 5 groups of 3 the statement would be $5 \times 3 = 15$.

Lesson Goal
- Use skip counting to add the same number three or more times.

What the Student Needs to Know
- Use skip counting

Getting Started
Ask students to look at this example: 2 + 2 + 2. Say:
- When you add these numbers, you skip the numbers between them.
- *The numbers you count are ? .* (2, 4, 6)
- *The numbers you skip are ? .* (3, 5)
- *How many times have you skip-counted?* (2)

What Can I Do?
- Read the question and the response. Then look at the example. Ask:
- *How many 4s are being added?* (5)
- *How many times do you skip count 4?* (5)

Skip count with students: 4, 8, 12, 16, 20. You may want to have students count the in-between numbers with fingers: Say: *4; use fingers when counting 5, 6, and 7.*

Try It
- Have students read exercise 1 and count the number of 2s. Have students write the correct numbers on the lines at the bottom of the example and place the answer on the top write-on line.
- Have students follow the same procedure for exercise 2.

Power Practice
- Have students complete the practice items. Then review each answer.

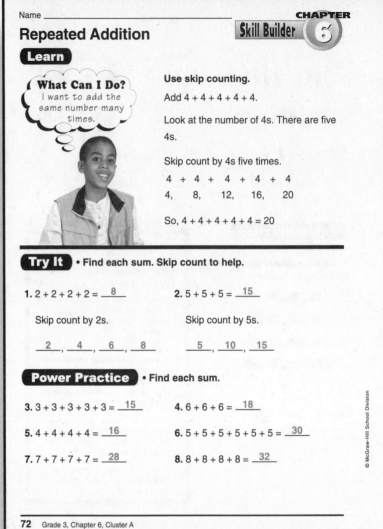

Name _____

Repeated Addition

Learn

What Can I Do?
I want to add the same number many times.

Use skip counting.

Add 4 + 4 + 4 + 4 + 4.

Look at the number of 4s. There are five 4s.

Skip count by 4s five times.

$$4 + 4 + 4 + 4 + 4$$
$$4, \quad 8, \quad 12, \quad 16, \quad 20$$

So, 4 + 4 + 4 + 4 + 4 = 20

Try It • Find each sum. Skip count to help.

1. 2 + 2 + 2 + 2 = __8__   2. 5 + 5 + 5 = __15__

Skip count by 2s.   Skip count by 5s.

__2__, __4__, __6__, __8__   __5__, __10__, __15__

Power Practice • Find each sum.

3. 3 + 3 + 3 + 3 + 3 = __15__   4. 6 + 6 + 6 = __18__

5. 4 + 4 + 4 + 4 = __16__   6. 5 + 5 + 5 + 5 + 5 + 5 = __30__

7. 7 + 7 + 7 + 7 = __28__   8. 8 + 8 + 8 + 8 = __32__

72 Grade 3, Chapter 6, Cluster A

WHAT IF THE STUDENT CAN'T

Use Skip Counting
- Use counters to form groups for skip counting. Show the student that by gathering the counters into groups of, say, 4, they can count 1-2-3-4, then 5-6-7-8, and so on. The last number in each group of 4 becomes the next number in the skip counting pattern.
- Practice selected addition facts daily for 5 or 10 minutes: adding equal numbers, such as 4 + 4, then 4 to the sum of that (8 + 4), and so on. Repeat until the student can recall the sums for these addition facts automatically.

Complete the Power Practice
- Discuss each incorrect answer.
- Perhaps the student will understand the concept of skip counting if presented in a different modality; for example, doing artwork (color every fourth frog he or she draws) or playing a game (every fourth student stands up).

Multiply by 3 and 4

Skill Builder

CHAPTER 6

Learn

Use equal groups.

Multiply 3×5.

Draw 3 groups of 5 circles.

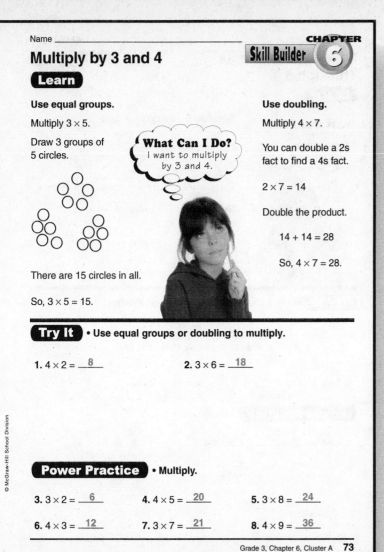

What Can I Do?
I want to multiply by 3 and 4.

There are 15 circles in all.

So, $3 \times 5 = 15$.

Use doubling.

Multiply 4×7.

You can double a 2s fact to find a 4s fact.

$2 \times 7 = 14$

Double the product.

$14 + 14 = 28$

So, $4 \times 7 = 28$.

Try It · Use equal groups or doubling to multiply.

1. $4 \times 2 = \underline{8}$ 　　　　2. $3 \times 6 = \underline{18}$

© McGraw-Hill School Division

Power Practice · Multiply.

3. $3 \times 2 = \underline{6}$ 　　4. $4 \times 5 = \underline{20}$ 　　5. $3 \times 8 = \underline{24}$

6. $4 \times 3 = \underline{12}$ 　　7. $3 \times 7 = \underline{21}$ 　　8. $4 \times 9 = \underline{36}$

Grade 3, Chapter 6, Cluster A   **73**

WHAT IF THE STUDENT CAN'T

Recall Basic Addition and Multiplication Facts

- Practice addition and multiplication facts 10 to 15 minutes daily until the student can recall the sums for the addition facts and the products for the multiplication facts with ease.

Complete the Power Practice

- Discuss each incorrect answer.
- Have the student model any fact he or she missed.

USING THE LESSON

Lesson Goal

- Use equal groups or doubling to multiply by 3 and 4.

What the Student Needs to Know

- Recall basic addition and multiplication facts.

Getting Started

- Ask students to draw and count a group of 3 objects. Then ask:
- *How can you find out how many are in 3 groups?* (Draw the other 2 groups, then count the total number.)

What Can I Do?

- Read the question and the response. Then discuss the first example. Ask:
- *In the first example, what would you draw to show equal groups?* (3 groups of 5 circles)
- *How many circles are there in all?* (15)
- *What multiplication sentence shows this?* ($3 \times 5 = 15$)

Read and discuss the second example. Ask:

- *What method are you going to use to solve this?* (doubling a 2s multiplication fact)
- *What multiplication sentence will you use first?* ($2 \times 7 = 14$)
- *How do you double the product?* (by adding $14 + 14$)

Try It

- Have students read exercise 1: $4 \times 2 = \underline{\quad}$. Ask whether to use equal groups or doubling a 2s fact to multiply. (doubling)
- Now, have students read and go through the steps on the second exercise.

Power Practice

- Have students complete the practice items. Then review each answer and method.

USING THE LESSON

Lesson Goal
- Practice multiplication facts through 5s by skip-counting on a number line.

What the Student Needs to Know
- Skip-count by numbers from 2 through 5.
- Recognize which number to use to skip count.

Getting Started
- Write on the chalkboard the multiplication fact 5×2.
- Ask students to tell how to find the answer by skip counting. (2, 4, 6, 8, 10.) Then say:
- *Now we are going to show this on a number line.*

  Use an existing number line or draw one. Then say:
- *I am marking the number line at each 2 through 10: 2, 4, 6, 8, 10.*
- Count the number of 2s: 1, 2, 3, 4, 5.

What Can I Do?
- Read the question and the response. Use an existing number line or draw a new one and mark it as on the PE. Demonstrate skip counting by 5s, as is shown on the number line.

Try It
- Have students do exercise 1. Be sure students understand the number by which they are going to skip count (5) and the number of times that they are going to count it (3).
- Check students' marked number lines. (arrows from 0 to 5; 5 to 10; 10 to 15)

Power Practice
- Have students complete the practice items. Then review each answer.

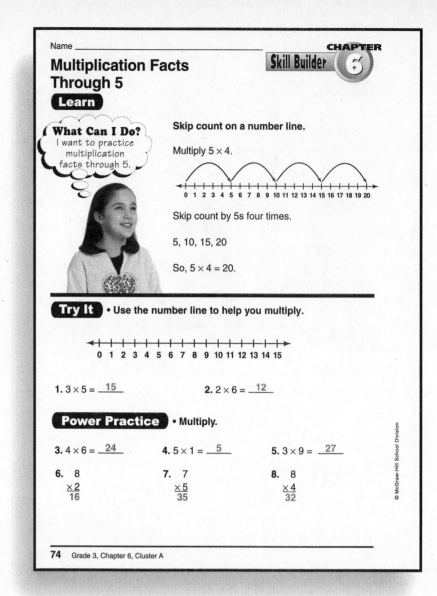

Name _____

Multiplication Facts Through 5

Learn

What Can I Do?
I want to practice multiplication facts through 5.

Skip count on a number line.

Multiply 5×4.

0 1 2 3 4 5 6 7 8 9 10 11 12 13 14 15 16 17 18 19 20

Skip count by 5s four times.

5, 10, 15, 20

So, $5 \times 4 = 20$.

Try It • Use the number line to help you multiply.

0 1 2 3 4 5 6 7 8 9 10 11 12 13 14 15

1. $3 \times 5 =$ __15__   2. $2 \times 6 =$ __12__

Power Practice • Multiply.

3. $4 \times 6 =$ __24__   4. $5 \times 1 =$ __5__   5. $3 \times 9 =$ __27__

6. 8
   $\times 2$

   16

7. 7
   $\times 5$

   35

8. 8
   $\times 4$

   32

© McGraw-Hill School Division

74   Grade 3, Chapter 6, Cluster A

WHAT IF THE STUDENT CAN'T

Understand Skip Counting
- Use counters to form groups for skip counting. Show students that by gathering the counters into groups of, say, 4, they can count 1-2-3-4, then 5-6-7-8, and so on. The last number in each group of 4 becomes the next number in skip counting.
- Practice selected addition facts daily for 5 or 10 minutes: adding equal numbers, such as $4 + 4$, then 4 to the sum of that ($8 + 4$), and so on. Repeat until the student can recall the sums for these addition facts automatically.

Recognize Which Number to use to Skip Count
- Point out and practice that in a horizontal fact, $a \times b$, b is the number in a group or the number to be skip counted and a is the number of groups or the number of times to skip count. When the multiplication fact is vertical, the top number is the number in a group or the number to be skip counted, and the bottom number is the number of groups or the number of times to skip-count.

Complete the Power Practice
- Discuss each incorrect answer and review the previous points if necessary.

Place Value

Skill Builder

CHAPTER 6

Learn

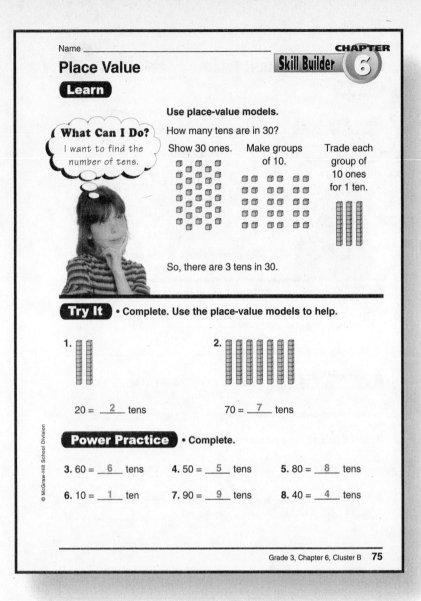

What Can I Do?
I want to find the number of tens.

Use place-value models.

How many tens are in 30?

| Show 30 ones. | Make groups of 10. | Trade each group of 10 ones for 1 ten. |

So, there are 3 tens in 30.

Try It • Complete. Use the place-value models to help.

1. 20 = __2__ tens

2. 70 = __7__ tens

Power Practice • Complete.

3. 60 = __6__ tens

4. 50 = __5__ tens

5. 80 = __8__ tens

6. 10 = __1__ ten

7. 90 = __9__ tens

8. 40 = __4__ tens

© McGraw-Hill School Division

WHAT IF THE STUDENT CAN'T

Recognize the Ones and the Tens Digits in a Number

- Stress that in a whole number the last digit is in the 1s column.
- The 10s column is the digit before the 1s.
- Have students practice reading 2-digit numbers and identifying the 1s and the 10s.

Complete the Power Practice

- Discuss each incorrect answer. Make sure the student knows that the non-zero digit names the number of tens.

USING THE LESSON

Lesson Goal

- Use place-value models to find the number of tens in 2-digit numbers ending in 0.

What the Student Needs to Know

- Recognize the ones and tens digits in a number.

Getting Started

Ask students to count by 1s from 10 to 20. Say:

- *When you get to 20, how many 1s have you counted?* (10)
- *Ten 1s is the same as how many 10s?* (1)
- *So if you started with one 10 and now you have another 10, how many 10s do you have?* (2)
- *20 is the same as how many 10s?* (2)
- *What does the 2 in the number 20 show?* (that there are two 10s)

What Can I Do?

Read the question and the response. Then follow the steps of the example by using the place-value models. Ask:

- *What does it mean to "trade" each group of ten 1s for one 10?* (to exchange equal amounts)

Try It

- Have students use place-value models to help do exercises 1 and 2. Note that example 1 uses 20 = 2 10s, the same as you used in the "Getting Started" section.

Power Practice

- Have students complete practice items. Then review each answer.

Lesson Goal
- Use the rows and columns in a multiplication table to find patterns in multiplication.

What the Student Needs to Know
- Track accurately across a row or down a column in a multiplication table.
- Identify odd and even numbers.

Getting Started
Have students look at the table. Ask:
- *What does the table show about any number multiplied by 0?* (the product is 0)
- *Reading across a row or down a column is like what process?* (skip counting)

What Can I Do?
Read the question and the response. Then examine the exercise. Ask:
- *How can you compare the 2s row and the 4s row?* (Look at the pairs of numbers in the same column to look for relationships)
- *How do the numbers in the 4s row compare to the numbers in the 2s row?* (The 4s row is 2 times the 2s row.)

Try It
Have students read exercise 1 and then read the choices—*odd, even,* or *odd and even.* Have students look along the row until one of the choices is clear. Ask:
- *How far do you have to look?* (until the 4s column)

Do the same for exercise 2. Students should see by the 3s row that the numbers are even.

Power Practice
- Have students complete the practice items. Then review each answer.

Name _____

Use a Multiplication Table

Learn

What Can I Do?
I want to find patterns in a multiplication table.

Look at the rows and the columns.

What pattern do you see in the 2s row and the 4s row?

Columns

x	0	1	2	3	4	5	6	7	8	9	
0	0	0	0	0	0	0	0	0	0	0	
1	0	1	2	3	4	5	6	7	8	9	
2	0	2	4	6	8	10	12	14	16	18	←2s Row
3	0	3	6	9	12	15	18	21	24	27	
4	0	4	8	12	16	20	24	28	32	36	←4s Row
5	0	5	10	15	20	25	30	35	40	45	

Rows

The numbers in the 4s row are double the numbers in the 2s row.

Try It • Complete. Write *odd, even,* or *odd and even.*

1. The numbers in the 3s row are _____ odd and even _____.

2. The numbers in the 6s column are _____ even _____.

Power Practice • Use the multiplication table.

3. Which rows have only even numbers? _rows 0, 2, and 4_

4. Which columns have both odd and even numbers? _____

   columns 1, 3, 5, 7, and 9

5. What do you notice about the first 6 numbers in the 5s row and the 5s column? _The numbers are the same._

   _____

WHAT IF THE STUDENT CAN'T

Track Accurately Across or Down a Column in a Multiplication Table
- Suggest using a 6-inch ruler or a 3 × 5 card to help tracking.

Identify Odd and Even Numbers
- Point out that all even numbers can be divided by 2; odd numbers cannot. In the multiplication table even and odd numbers alternate in odd-numbered rows and columns.

Complete the Power Practice
- Discuss any incorrect answers.
- Have the student model exercises that were answered incorrectly.

Associative Property of Addition

Skill Builder

Learn

What Can I Do?
I want to add 3 numbers.

Use the Associative Property of Addition.

Add $5 + 1 + 9$.

Associative Property of Addition: The grouping of the addends does not change the sum.

Group the numbers to make addition easier. Use parentheses.

$5 + (1 + 9) = \underline{\quad?\quad}$

$5 + 10 = 15$

So, $5 + 1 + 9 = 15$.

Try It • Find each sum. Add the grouped addends first.

1. $(8 + 2) + 3$

$\underline{10} + 3 = \underline{13}$

2. $7 + (2 + 2)$

$7 + \underline{4} = \underline{11}$

Power Practice • Find each sum.

3. $6 + 9 + 1 = \underline{16}$

4. $3 + 7 + 3 = \underline{13}$

5. $9 + 5 + 4 = \underline{18}$

6. $3 + 2 + 7 = \underline{12}$

7. $5 + 8 + 2 = \underline{15}$

8. $4 + 6 + 5 = \underline{15}$

9. $8 + 4 + 6 = \underline{18}$

10. $9 + 3 + 7 = \underline{19}$

© McGraw-Hill School Division

Grade 3, Chapter 6, Cluster B **77**

WHAT IF THE STUDENT CAN'T

Recall Basic Addition Facts through 18

- Practice addition facts through 18 for about 10 minutes daily, until the student can recall the sums for the addition facts automatically.

Complete the Power Practice

- Discuss each incorrect answer. Use counters, other physical objects, or pictured objects in groups to reinforce the concept of grouping.

USING THE LESSON

Lesson Goal

- Use the Associative Property of Addition to add 3 numbers.

What the Student Needs to Know

- Recall basic addition facts through 180.

Getting Started

Ask students to think of using the Associative Property as a way to make addition easier. Say:

- *When adding, look for number combinations that you know well.*
- *Think of this pair of sums. Which one is easier to add, $4 + 2$ or $4 + 8$? Why?* ($4 + 2$; you don't have to regroup.)
- *In adding $4 + 2 + 8$, which two addends would you group? Why?* ($2 + 8$, because they make 10; and $4 + 10$ is easier to add than $6 + 8$)

What Can I Do?

Read the question and the response. Then review the exercise: $5 + 1 + 9$. Tell students that parentheses are used around the two numbers that are grouped. Ask:

- *Which two numbers will you group? Why?* ($1 + 9$, because they add up to 10, and $5 + 10$ is easier to add than $6 + 9$)
- *The Associative Property will not always provide an easier group to add. How would you group $5 + 4 + 7$?* (Answers will vary.)

Try It

- Have students do exercises 1 and 2 by using the groupings suggested. Ask:
- *Would you choose different groupings for either exercise?* (in exercise 2, some students may think $9 + 2$ easier than $7 + 4$)

Power Practice

- Have students complete the practice items. Then review each answer. Each student should tell what grouping they used.

CHALLENGE

Lesson Goal
- Understand a reading timetable.

Introducing the Challenge
- Explore the uses of a timetable. Say:
- *A timetable is useful when you want to show amounts at different times or track events over a period of time.*
- *Think of some uses of a timetable.* (Possible answers: Show how many exercises you do each day, show what time you have different classes; show the departure times of buses, trains, or planes, and so on)
- A timetable can take the form of a list or a table or chart.

Name _____

Reading Timetable

Tonya is reading a book about Native Americans for a Social Studies project. She has made a reading plan. She will read 6 pages the first day, 7 pages the next day, and 8 pages the day after that. Then she will repeat the plan until she finishes the book.

Here is the table of contents for Tonya's book.

Table of Contents

Chapter	Page Number
Chapter 1 1	
Chapter 2.................................. 20	
Chapter 3.................................. 28	
Chapter 4.................................. 42	
Chapter 5.................................. 56	
Chapter 6.................................. 66	
Chapter 7.................................. 74	
Chapter 8.................................. 88	

1. How many chapters are in the book? 8 chapters

2. On what day of reading will Tonya begin Chapter 2? Day 3

3. How many pages will Tonya have read after 3 days? 21 pages

4. How many pages will Tonya read on her twelfth day of reading:

6 pages, 7 pages, or 8 pages? 8 pages

© McGraw-Hill School Division

Name _____

5. How many pages will Tonya have read after 6 days?
Explain how you know.

42 pages; Possible answer: In 6 days, Tonya will complete her

reading plan twice. $2 \times 6 = 12, 2 \times 7 = 14, 2 \times 8 = 16$;

$12 + 14 + 16 = 42$

6. What chapter will Tonya be on after reading for 9 days?
How do you know?

Chapter 5; Possible answer: In 9 days, Tonya

will complete her reading plan 3 times. $3 \times 6 = 18, 3 \times 7 = 21$,

$3 \times 8 = 24; 18 + 21 + 24 = 63$; Since Chapter 5 is between pages

56 and 65, she will be on Chapter 5.

7. On what day of reading will Tonya begin Chapter 7? Explain.

Day 11; Possible answer: Tonya is on p. 63 after 9 days.

Chapter 7 starts on p. 74. Tonya will read 6 pages on Day 10,

$63 + 6 = 69$. She will read 7 pages on Day 11, $69 + 7 = 76$. So

she will start reading Chapter 7 on Day 11.

8. The book has 102 pages. If Tonya uses her reading plan, how
many days will it take her to finish the book? Explain how you found
your answer.

15 days; Possible answer: Every 3 days, Tonya reads 21 pages.

If I add 21 to itself 4 times, she reads 84 pages in 12 days.

If I add 21 pages 5 times, she reads 105 pages in 15 days.

CHALLENGE

Using the Challenge

Read the introduction. Look at the table of contents. Ask:

- *What do the page numbers mean?* (the page on which each chapter begins)
- *Without looking ahead, do we know yet how many pages the book has altogether?* (No.)
- *How often does Tonya's reading plan repeat?* (every 3 days)
- *How many pages does she read in 3 days?* ($6 + 7 + 8 = 21$ pages)

Read each problem with students. Ask:

- *What operation do you think you will use to answer Problem 3?* (addition)
- *What facts help you to answer Problem 4?* (the fact that the page pattern repeats every three days and $4 \times 3 = 12$) You may want to help students use multiples of 3 as a way to answer Problem 6.
- Have students complete the questions. Then review each answer.

CHALLENGE

Lesson Goal

- Use multiplication facts and strategies to help find factors.

Introducing the Challenge

Say:

- *You will be using your knowledge of multiplication facts together with your knowledge of addition and subtraction to solve some math riddles.*

Remind students that factors are the two numbers that are multiplied to give a product.

Begin with a single example. Give students this riddle:

- *Name two numbers that have a product equal to 6 + 6 ?*
- *How many pairs can you think of that have that sum?* (Possible answers: $1 \times 2, 2 \times 6, 3 \times 4$)

Using the Challenge

Read the first question. Ask:

- *What is the first thing you have to do to solve this riddle?* (Add the two numbers to find out what product the factors will have to make.)
- *What visual aids could you use to help you?* (multiplication table, number line)
- *If you cannot see the answer right away, what problem-solving strategy might you use?* (guess and check)

Say:

- *For problems 3 through 8, you have to match existing answers. You need to look down the row of possible answers and eliminate them one by one, until you come to a correct answer.*
- *Problems 9 through 12 are trickier still. To find the answer to number 9, what steps would you take?* (Possible answer: write all the pairs of numbers that add up to 13; then see which ones used as factors give a product of 36.)

Name _____

Find Factors: Multiplication Riddles

Use multiplication facts and strategies to help you find factors.

1. Name a pair of factors that have a product equal to 10 + 10.

   Possible answers: 4 and 5, 2 and 10, 1 and 20

2. Name a pair of factors that have a product equal to 40 − 8.

   Possible answers: 4 and 8, 1 and 32, 2 and 16

Write the letter of the factor pair that matches each description.

	Factor Pair
3. Their product is equal to 36 − 11. ___B___	**A.** 9, 7
4. Their product is even. Their difference is 2. ___F___	**B.** 5, 5
5. Their product is greater than 60. ___A___	**C.** 7, 3
6. Their product is equal to 25 + 25. ___E___	**D.** 6, 7
7. Their product is between 40 and 45. ___D___	**E.** 5, 10
8. Their product is odd. Their difference is 4. ___C___	**F.** 4, 6

Name _____

Use multiplication facts and strategies to help you solve these riddles.

9. Which two numbers have a sum of 13 and a product of 36?

   4 and 9

10. I am a 2-digit number. If you subtract my first digit from my second digit, the difference is 7. The product of my digits is 18. What number am I?

    29

11. Which three numbers have a sum of 10 and a product of 14?

    1, 2, and 7

12. I am a 3-digit number. The sum of my digits is 6. The product of my digits is 0. My first digit is the same as my last digit. What number am I?

    303

13. Write your own multiplication riddle.

    Answers will vary. Check students' riddles.

    _____

    _____

CHALLENGE

- Look over all the riddles before you come up with your own. Decide what steps you need to take to solve it.

Riddle

Before students write their own riddles for Problem 1, you might want to review the steps students have taken to solve existing riddles.

If necessary, provide numbers or pairs of numbers that students can use to develop their own riddles.

Equal Groups

Draw each picture. Then write the total amount.

1. 3 groups of 6 squares

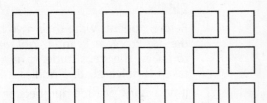

Total = __ squares

2. 7 groups of 5 circles

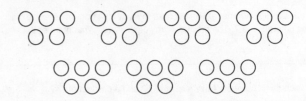

Total = __ circles

Subtraction

Subtract.

3. 10
  − 2

4. 24
  − 6

5. 21
  − 7

6. 36 − 9 = _____

7. 40 − 5 = _____

Skip Count Backwards

Each pattern is a skip counting pattern. Write the next number in each pattern.

8. 15, 12, 9, 6, _____

9. 18, 16, 14, 12, _____

10. 36, 30, 24, 18, _____

11. 40, 36, 32, 28, _____

Missing Factors

Write each missing factor.

12. $2 \times$ _____ $= 8$ **13.** $3 \times$ _____ $= 18$

14. $5 \times$ _____ $= 45$ **15.** $4 \times$ _____ $= 32$

Multiplication Facts Through 9

Find each product.

16. $4 \times 7 =$ _____   **17.** $6 \times 6 =$ _____

18. $\begin{array}{r} 5 \\ \times 8 \\ \hline \end{array}$ **19.** $\begin{array}{r} 7 \\ \times 3 \\ \hline \end{array}$ **20.** $\begin{array}{r} 8 \\ \times 9 \\ \hline \end{array}$

Multiply with 0 and 1

Multiply.

21. $5 \times 0 =$ _____   **22.** $0 \times 9 =$ _____

23. $\begin{array}{r} 4 \\ \times 1 \\ \hline \end{array}$ **24.** $\begin{array}{r} 6 \\ \times 0 \\ \hline \end{array}$ **25.** $\begin{array}{r} 1 \\ \times 8 \\ \hline \end{array}$

Assessment Goal

This two-page assessment covers skills identified as necessary for success in Chapter 7 Division Concepts. The first page assesses the major prerequisite skills for Cluster A. The second page assesses the major prerequisite skills for Cluster B. When the Cluster A and Cluster B prerequisite skills overlap, the skill(s) will be covered in only one section.

Getting Started

- Allow students time to look over the two pages of the assessment. Point out the labels that identify the skills covered.
- Have students find math vocabulary terms used in the assessment. List vocabulary terms on the board as students identify them. If necessary, review the meanings of all essential math vocabulary.

Introducing the Assessment

- Explain to students that these pages will help you know if they are ready to start a new chapter in their math textbooks.
- Students who have transferred from another school may not have been introduced to some of these skills. Encourage students to do their best and assure them you will help them learn any needed skills.

Cluster A Challenge

Those students who demonstrate mastery of the skills on this page will not need to use the reaching worksheets. Instead, these students can do the Cluster A Challenge found on pages 92-93.

Name_____

Equal Groups

Draw each picture. Then write the total amount.

1. 3 groups of 6 squares

2. 7 groups of 5 circles

Total = __18__ squares

Total = __35__ circles

Subtraction

Subtract.

3. 10
$-\ 2$
8

4. 24
$-\ 6$
18

5. 21
$-\ 7$
14

6. $36 - 9 =$ __27__

7. $40 - 5 =$ __35__

Skip Count Backwards

Each pattern is a skip counting pattern. Write the next number in each pattern.

8. 15, 12, 9, 6, __3__

9. 18, 16, 14, 12, __10__

10. 36, 30, 24, 18, __12__

11. 40, 36, 32, 28, __24__

81A Use with Grade 3, Chapter 7, Cluster A

CLUSTER A PREREQUISITE SKILLS

The skills listed in this chart are those identified as major prerequisite skills for students' success in the lessons in Cluster A of the chapter. Each skill is covered by one or more assessment items as shown in the middle column. The right column provides the page number for the lessons in this book that reteach the cluster A prerequisite skills.

Skill Name	Assessment Items	Lesson Pages
Equal Groups	1-2	82-83
Subtraction	3-7	84-85
Skip Count Backwards	8-11	86

Name_____

Missing Factors

Write each missing factor.

12. $2 \times \underline{\ 4\ } = 8$　　　　**13.** $3 \times \underline{\ 6\ } = 18$

14. $5 \times \underline{\ 9\ } = 45$　　　　**15.** $4 \times \underline{\ 8\ } = 32$

Multiplication Facts Through 9

Find each product.

16. $4 \times 7 = \underline{\ 28\ }$　　　　**17.** $6 \times 6 = \underline{\ 36\ }$

18. $\begin{array}{r} 5 \\ \times 8 \\ \hline 40 \end{array}$　　　**19.** $\begin{array}{r} 7 \\ \times 3 \\ \hline 21 \end{array}$　　　**20.** $\begin{array}{r} 8 \\ \times 9 \\ \hline 72 \end{array}$

Multiply with 0 and 1

Multiply.

21. $5 \times 0 = \underline{\ 0\ }$　　　　**22.** $0 \times 9 = \underline{\ 0\ }$

23. $\begin{array}{r} 4 \\ \times 1 \\ \hline 4 \end{array}$　　　**24.** $\begin{array}{r} 6 \\ \times 0 \\ \hline 0 \end{array}$　　　**25.** $\begin{array}{r} 1 \\ \times 8 \\ \hline 8 \end{array}$

© McGraw-Hill School Division

CLUSTER B PREREQUISITE SKILLS

The skills listed in this chart are those identified as major prerequisite skills for students' success in the lessons in Cluster B of the chapter. Each skill is covered by one or more assessment items as shown in the middle column. The right column provides the page numbers for the lessons in this book that reteach the Cluster B prerequisite skills

Skill Name	Assessment Items	Lesson Pages
Missing Factors	12-15	87
Multiplication Facts Through 9	16-20	88-89
Multiply with 0 and 1	21-25	90-91

Alternative Assessment Strategies

- Oral administration of the assessment is appropriate for younger students or those whose native language is not English. Read the skills title and directions one section at a time. Check students' understanding by asking them to tell you how they will do the first exercise in the group.

- For some skill types you may wish to use group administration. In this technique, a small group or pair of students complete the assessment together. Through their discussion, you will be able to decide if supplementary reteaching materials are needed.

Intervention Materials

If students are not successful with the prerequisite skills assessed on these pages, reteaching lessons have been created to help them make the transition into the chapter.

Item correlation charts showing the skills lessons suitable for reteaching the prerequisite skills are found beneath the reproductions of each page of the assessment.

Cluster B Challenge

Those students who demonstrate mastery of the skills on this page will not need to use the reteaching worksheets. Instead, these students can do the Cluster B Challenge found on pages 94-95.

USING THE LESSON

Lesson Goal
- Draw a picture to find the total number of items in a problem with groups of items.

What the Student Needs to Know
- Draw recognizable objects.
- Multiply to find the total number of objects.

Getting Started
- Present students with a picture or a physical group of 20 objects scattered about in no particular order. Then present students with the same 20 objects arranged in groups of 4. Ask:
- *Which (fill in name of object) are easier to count? Why? (Answers may vary.)*
- *Once you have grouped the objects, how could you go about finding the total number? (count by 1s, skip count, multiply)*
- *If I'm going to skip count to find the total number in these groups, by what number should I skip count? (by 4s)*
- *How many times should I skip count by 4s? (5)*
- *This is the same as multiplying what two numbers? (5 x 4)*

What Can I Do?
Read the question and the response. Then discuss the example. Ask:
- *How many pencils are in a box? (6)*
- *How many boxes of pencils are there? (4)*
- *Here is a picture that shows 4 boxes with 6 pencils each.*
- *How shall I find how many pencils I have all together? (count by 1s, skip count, multiply)*
- *How will you skip count? (6 + 6 + 6 + 6)*

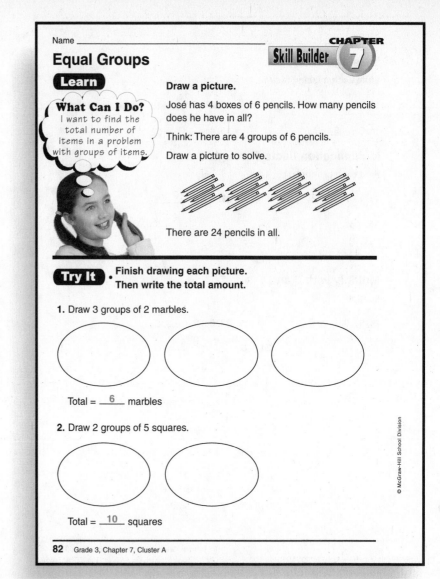

Name _____

Equal Groups

Learn

What Can I Do?
I want to find the total number of items in a problem with groups of items.

Draw a picture.

José has 4 boxes of 6 pencils. How many pencils does he have in all?

Think: There are 4 groups of 6 pencils.

Draw a picture to solve.

There are 24 pencils in all.

Try It · Finish drawing each picture. Then write the total amount.

1. Draw 3 groups of 2 marbles.

Total = ___6___ marbles

2. Draw 2 groups of 5 squares.

Total = ___10___ squares

82 Grade 3, Chapter 7, Cluster A

© McGraw-Hill School Division

WHAT IF THE STUDENT CAN'T

Draw Recognizable Objects
- Have the student make dots, draw small circles, or use counters.
- Have students practice this skill during "free time."

Multiply to Find the Total Number of Objects
- Practice basic multiplication facts for 10 to 15 minutes daily until the student can recall the products for multiplication facts automatically.

Name _____

Power Practice • Draw each picture.
Then write the total amount.

3. 5 groups of 5 flowers

Students should draw
5 groups of 5 flowers.

4. 4 groups of 7 stars

Students should draw
4 groups of 7 stars.

Total = _25_ flowers

Total = _28_ stars

5. 2 groups of 9 circles

Students should draw
2 groups of 9 circles.

6. 6 groups of 3 triangles

Students should draw
6 groups of 3 triangles.

Total = _18_ circles

Total = _18_ triangles

7. 7 groups of 8 balls

Students should draw
7 groups of 8 balls.

8. 9 groups of 4 books

Students should draw
9 groups of 4 books.

Total = _56_ balls

Total = _36_ books

Grade 3, Chapter 7, Cluster A **83**

WHAT IF THE STUDENT CAN'T

Complete the Power Practice
• Discuss each incorrect
answer. Have the student
model any fact he or she
missed, using physical counters rather than drawn ones.

USING THE LESSON

• *How will you show multiplication?*
(4 x 6)
• *What is the total number of pen-*
cils? (24)

Try It
• Have students make their drawings as clear and organized as
possible.
• Check students' drawings for
exercises 1 and 2.
• Have volunteers tell you how
they go from their drawings to
totaling the number of objects.

Power Practice
• For each of the exercises, have
volunteers draw their answers on
the board. Have them tell what
method they use to total the
number of objects.

Lesson Goal
- Use mental math or subtract with regrouping to find the difference between a 1- and a 2-digit number.

What the Student Needs to Know
- Recall subtraction facts through 20.
- Use subtraction fact patterns.
- Understand how to regroup.

Getting Started
Find out what students know about using mental math. Say:
- *In subtracting one number from another, you often find that the number you are subtracting in the ones column is larger than the number you are subtracting from, for example, 11 – 4.*
- *If you don't remember the subtraction fact, how can you find the difference between the numbers using mental math?* (You think of a subtraction fact you know and then add or subtract from there.)
- *For example, if you don't remember 11 – 4, what subtraction fact might you think of?* (possible answer: 14 – 4 = 10).
- *Since 11 is 3 less than 14, the answer will be 3 less than what?* (10)—or in other words—? (7)

What Can I Do?
Read the question and the response. Then discuss the first example. Ask:
- *If you can't remember 12 – 3, what can you do?* (Subtract 13 – 3 and then subtract 1.)

Read the second example. Ask:
- *How would you regroup to solve this problem?* (Think: 7 ones is more than 2 ones, so you have to exchange 1 ten for 10 ones.)

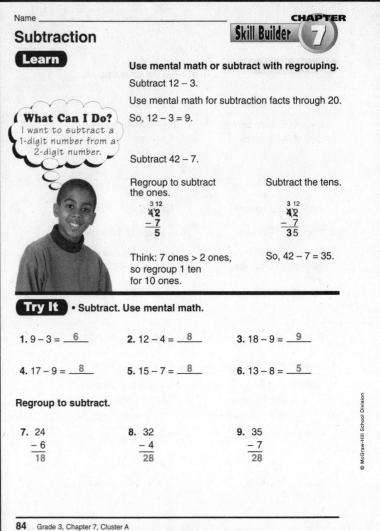

Name _____

Subtraction

Learn

Use mental math or subtract with regrouping.

Subtract 12 – 3.

What Can I Do?
I want to subtract a 1-digit number from a 2-digit number.

Use mental math for subtraction facts through 20.

So, 12 – 3 = 9.

Subtract 42 – 7.

Regroup to subtract the ones.

$$\begin{array}{r} \overset{3\ 12}{\cancel{4}\cancel{2}} \\ -\ 7 \\ \hline 5 \end{array}$$

Subtract the tens.

$$\begin{array}{r} \overset{3\ 12}{\cancel{4}\cancel{2}} \\ -\ 7 \\ \hline 35 \end{array}$$

Think: 7 ones > 2 ones, so regroup 1 ten for 10 ones.

So, 42 – 7 = 35.

Try It • Subtract. Use mental math.

1. 9 – 3 = __6__

2. 12 – 4 = __8__

3. 18 – 9 = __9__

4. 17 – 9 = __8__

5. 15 – 7 = __8__

6. 13 – 8 = __5__

Regroup to subtract.

7.
$$\begin{array}{r} 24 \\ -\ 6 \\ \hline 18 \end{array}$$

8.
$$\begin{array}{r} 32 \\ -\ 4 \\ \hline 28 \end{array}$$

9.
$$\begin{array}{r} 35 \\ -\ 7 \\ \hline 28 \end{array}$$

WHAT IF THE STUDENT CAN'T

Recall Basic Subtraction Facts
- Practice basic subtraction facts through 20 for 10 to 15 minutes daily until the student can recall the differences for the subtraction facts automatically.

Use Subtraction Fact Patterns
- Review how to use mental math. Help students develop proficiency by using subtraction fact patterns, for example: 14 – 6 = 8 so 24 – 6 = 18, 34 – 6 = 28, and so on.

Name _____

Power Practice • Subtract.

10. 8 $\underline{-2}$ 6	**11.** 24 $\underline{-4}$ 20	**12.** 20 $\underline{-5}$ 15	**13.** 27 $\underline{-9}$ 18
14. 56 $\underline{-7}$ 49	**15.** 16 $\underline{-8}$ 8	**16.** 36 $\underline{-9}$ 27	**17.** 54 $\underline{-6}$ 48

18. 14 − 7 = __7__   **19.** 42 − 6 = __36__

20. 81 − 9 = __72__   **21.** 53 − 8 = __45__

22. 75 − 7 = __68__   **23.** 61 − 9 = __52__

24. 14 − 6 = __8__   **25.** 40 − 9 = __31__

26. 57 − 9 = __48__   **27.** 34 − 5 = __29__

28. 22 − 7 = __15__   **29.** 91 − 6 = __85__

Learn with Partners & Parents

Odd Subtraction

You will need two number cubes and a spinner numbered 0–9. Two or more players can play.

• Players take turns. First toss the number cubes. Use numbers to make a 2-digit number. The digits may be in any order.

• Next spin the spinner. Subtract the number on the spinner from the number made with the number cubes.

• If the difference is correct and an even number, the player gets 1 point. If the difference is correct and an odd number, the player gets 2 points. The first player to get 25 points wins.

WHAT IF THE STUDENT CAN'T

Understand How to Regroup

• Use cubes or counters to physically represent the tens and the ones. Show the conversion of 1 ten to 10 ones and back again.

Complete the Power Practice

• Discuss each incorrect answer. Have the student model any fact he or she missed, using cubes or counters along with written numbers.

USING THE LESSON

• *If I add the 10 ones to the number already in the ones column, how many will I have?* (12)

• *If I subtract 7 from 12, how much will be left?* (5)

• *Now what do I have to do?* (Subtract the tens.)

• *How many tens are left after the regrouping?* (3)

• *What is 42 − 7?* (35)

Try It

Have students read each difference aloud and tell how they can use mental math or regrouping to subtract.

Power Practice

Have students complete the practice items. Then review each answer.

Learn with Partners & Parents

You may wish to review these rules with students:

even number − even number = ? (even number)

even number − odd number = ? (odd number)

odd number − odd number = ? (even number)

odd number − even number = ? (odd number)

Familiarity with these rules will allow each player to predict the subtraction result as odd or even. The following variation will introduce an element of strategy to the game. Each player first spins the spinner to find the number that will be subtracted. Then each player rolls the number cubes and forms the 2-digit number.

USING THE LESSON

Lesson Goal
- Use a number line to complete a skip counting pattern backward.

What the Student Needs to Know
- Skip count by numbers from 2 through 9.
- Read a number line.
- Skip count backward to get decreasing numbers.

Getting Started
Review skip counting. Say:
- *Let's skip count to 20 by 2s.* (2, 4, 6, 8, . . .)

Have volunteers skip count by 3s to 30s, 4s to 40, and so on, through 9s to 90.

Tell students that they can also skip count backward.

What Can I Do?
Read the question and the response. Then discuss the example. Ask:
- *What is shown here?* (skip counting backward by 2s)
- *What number comes next?* (6)

Draw a number line on the board.
- *Let's see how we would show this on the number line.* (Draw arrows backward from 14 to 12, and then from 12 to 10. Then have students finish down to 0.)

Try It
Use a large number line on the board or individual number lines from 1 to 20 to complete the skip-counting patterns in exercises 1 and 2.

Power Practice
- Have students complete the practice items. Then review each answer.

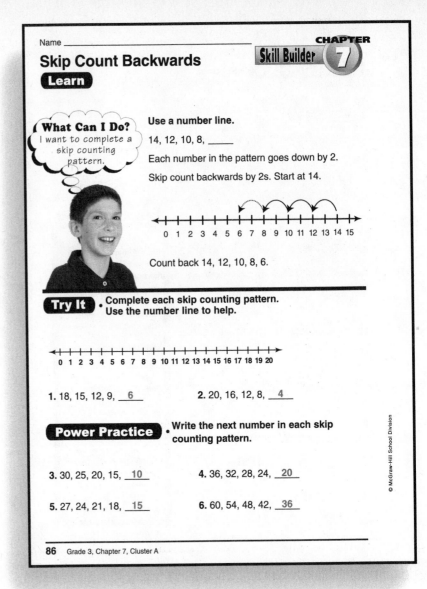

WHAT IF THE STUDENT CAN'T

Read a Number Line
- Review the format of a number line and how it can be used for counting.

Skip Count Forward
- Use counters to form groups for skip counting. Show the student that by gathering the counters into groups of, say, 4, they can count 1-2-3-4, then 5-6-7-8, and so on. The last number in each group of 4 becomes the next number in the skip counting.

Skip Count Backward
- Use the same counters to form groups for skip counting backward. Show students that by gathering the counters into groups of, say, 4, they can start with 20 and remove four counters, one at a time: 20-19-18-17. They have 16 left. Then remove four more counters: 16-15-14-13. There are 12 left. Have students continue until they have only four counters left. Ask: *What is the skip counting pattern?* (20, 16, 12, 8, 4)

Complete the Power Practice
- Discuss each incorrect answer. Help the student see where he or she went wrong.

Missing Factors

Learn

What Can I Do?
I want to find a missing factor.

Use basic multiplication facts.

Write the missing factor.

$2 \times \underline{\ ?\ } = 10$

Think: 2 times what number is equal to 10?

Find the multiplication fact for 2 with a product of 10.

$2 \times 1 = 2$
$2 \times 2 = 4$
$2 \times 3 = 6$
$2 \times 4 = 8$
$\mathbf{2 \times 5 = 10}$

So, 5 is the missing factor.

Try It • Write each product. Then write each missing factor.

1. $3 \times 4 = \underline{\ 12\ }$

   $3 \times \underline{\ 4\ } = 12$

2. $4 \times 5 = \underline{\ 20\ }$

   $4 \times \underline{\ 5\ } = 20$

Power Practice • Write each missing factor.

3. $2 \times \underline{\ 7\ } = 14$

4. $5 \times \underline{\ 3\ } = 15$

5. $4 \times \underline{\ 4\ } = 16$

6. $3 \times \underline{\ 8\ } = 24$

7. $6 \times \underline{\ 4\ } = 24$

8. $4 \times \underline{\ 9\ } = 36$

WHAT IF THE STUDENT CAN'T

Recall Basic Multiplication Facts from 1 to 5

- Have the student use physical counters to make groups of objects.
- Have the student write out lists of multiplication facts and keep them handy to use as a reference.

Complete the Power Practice

- Discuss each incorrect answer. Review how the student can check his or her answers by using counters or lists.

USING THE LESSON

Lesson Goal

- Use basic multiplication facts to find a missing factor.

What the Student Needs to Know

- Recall basic multiplication facts from 1 to 5.

Getting Started

Remind students that they usually multiply two factors to get a product. Here they will have the product and one of the factors and have to find the other factor. Say:

- *Let's see how we can find a missing factor. When I see 2 × ___ = 6, and I immediately recognize a missing factor, that's all there is to the problem. If I don't recognize it immediately, there is a simple method to use.*
- *I can set up a list of facts for 2. I write out 2 × 1 = 2, 2 × 2 = 4, 2 × 3 = 6. So 3 is the missing factor.*

What Can I Do?

Read the question and the response. Then discuss the example. Ask:

- *What do we do if we don't recognize the missing factor in 2 × ___ = 10?* (Make a list of facts for 2.)
- *How far do you have to go to find the factor?* (2 × 5)

Try It

Have students read each of the exercises and use a list of facts, if necessary, to find each of the missing factors.

Power Practice

- Have students complete the practice items. Then review each answer.

Lesson Goal

- Use any multiplication strategy to multiply two numbers through 9.

What the Student Needs to Know

- Double a basic multiplication fact.
- Use repeated addition.
- Skip count by 2s through 9s on a number line.

Getting Started

- Write the multiplication fact 3 × 7 on the chalkboard. Say:
- *Of the three strategies of doubling a known fact, repeated addition, and skip counting on a number line, which ones can be used for this example?* (repeated addition, skip counting on a number line)
- Explain that it is necessary to have one of the factors be an even number to be able to use the doubling method, because you don't get a whole number when you divide an odd number by 2.

What Can I Do?

Read the question and the response. Then discuss the first example. Ask:

- *Can you use the doubling method to find the answer to this example?* (Yes.)
- *What would you double?* (3 × 5 = 15)
- *How would you use repeated addition to solve?* (add 5 six times: 5 + 5 + 5 + 5 + 5 + 5)

Use an existing number line from 1 to 30 or draw a new one. Demonstrate skip counting 6 groups of 5 by drawing arrows that show "jumps" between 0 and 5, 5 and 10, 10 and 15, 15 and 20, 20 and 25, and 25 and 30.

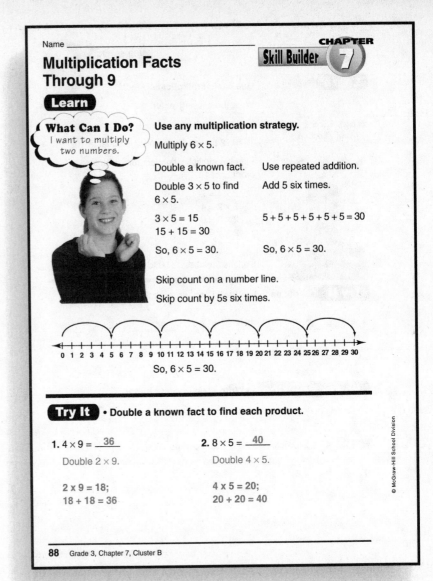

Multiplication Facts Through 9

Learn

What Can I Do?
I want to multiply two numbers.

Use any multiplication strategy.

Multiply 6 × 5.

Double a known fact.   Use repeated addition.

Double 3 × 5 to find   Add 5 six times.
6 × 5.

3 × 5 = 15   5 + 5 + 5 + 5 + 5 + 5 = 30
15 + 15 = 30

So, 6 × 5 = 30.   So, 6 × 5 = 30.

Skip count on a number line.

Skip count by 5s six times.

So, 6 × 5 = 30.

Try It • Double a known fact to find each product.

1. 4 × 9 = __36__   2. 8 × 5 = __40__

Double 2 × 9.   Double 4 × 5.

2 × 9 = 18;   4 × 5 = 20;
18 + 18 = 36   20 + 20 = 40

WHAT IF THE STUDENT CAN'T

Double a Basic Multiplication Fact

- Have the student keep handy a chart of numbers and their doubles (2 × 2 = 4, 2 × 3 = 6, and so on.) to refer to.
- Have the student practice these doubling facts daily until he or she knows them.

Use Repeated Addition

- Practice selected addition facts daily for 5 or 10 minutes: adding equal numbers, such as 4 + 4, then 4 to the sum of that (8 + 4), and so on. Repeat until the student can recall the sums for these addition facts automatically.
- If this is still difficult, have the student use counters to form groups for repeated addition.

Name _____

Use repeated addition to find each product.

3. $3 \times 7 =$ __21__   **4.** $5 \times 5 =$ __25__

Add: __7 + 7 + 7 = 21__   Add: __5 + 5 + 5 + 5 + 5 = 25__

Skip count to find each product.

5. $5 \times 3 =$ __15__   **6.** $4 \times 6 =$ __24__

Count: __3, 6, 9, 12, 15__   Count: __6, 12, 18, 24__

Power Practice • Find each product. Use any method.

7. $2 \times 6 =$ __12__   **8.** $4 \times 4 =$ __16__   **9.** $5 \times 7 =$ __35__

10. $6 \times 7 =$ __42__   **11.** $3 \times 8 =$ __24__   **12.** $9 \times 3 =$ __27__

13. $7 \times 4 =$ __28__   **14.** $8 \times 6 =$ __48__   **15.** $5 \times 8 =$ __40__

16. $\begin{array}{r} 8 \\ \times 2 \\ \hline 16 \end{array}$	**17.** $\begin{array}{r} 3 \\ \times 6 \\ \hline 18 \end{array}$	**18.** $\begin{array}{r} 7 \\ \times 7 \\ \hline 49 \end{array}$	**19.** $\begin{array}{r} 9 \\ \times 3 \\ \hline 27 \end{array}$
20. $\begin{array}{r} 6 \\ \times 6 \\ \hline 36 \end{array}$	**21.** $\begin{array}{r} 9 \\ \times 8 \\ \hline 72 \end{array}$	**22.** $\begin{array}{r} 8 \\ \times 4 \\ \hline 32 \end{array}$	**23.** $\begin{array}{r} 6 \\ \times 9 \\ \hline 54 \end{array}$
24. $\begin{array}{r} 9 \\ \times 4 \\ \hline 36 \end{array}$	**25.** $\begin{array}{r} 7 \\ \times 8 \\ \hline 56 \end{array}$	**26.** $\begin{array}{r} 7 \\ \times 9 \\ \hline 63 \end{array}$	**27.** $\begin{array}{r} 9 \\ \times 9 \\ \hline 81 \end{array}$

Grade 3, Chapter 7, Cluster B   **89**

WHAT IF THE STUDENT CAN'T

Skip Count
• Show the student that by gathering counters into groups of, say, 4, he or she can count 1-2-3-4, then 5-6-7-8, and so on. The last number in each group of 4 becomes the next number in skip counting.

Complete the Power Practice
• Discuss each incorrect answer and review the previous skills if necessary.

USING THE LESSON

• Ask: *Which two methods are most alike?* (repeated addition and skip counting)

Try It
• Have students do exercises 1 and 2 using the doubling method. Check that students understand that they must use the even number as their "double." Ask what would happen if both numbers were even. (They would have a choice of which factor to use as the double.)

• Have students do exercises 3 and 4 using repeated addition. Check to make sure students are clear on which is the number to add and which tells the number of times it gets added.

• Have students do exercises 5 and 6 by skip counting. Check to make sure students are clear on which is the number to skip count and which tells the number of times it gets counted.

Power Practice
• Have students complete the practice items. Then review each answer.

Lesson Goals
- Use properties of multiplication to multiply a number by 0 and 1.

What the Student Needs to Know
- Understand the Identity Property of Multiplication.
- Understand the Zero Property of Multiplication.

Getting Started
Be sure if student know the meaning of *identity*. (it means "the same")

- By placing objects on a table, demonstrate that if you take an object (say, a counter) and place it on the table a number of times (say, 5), you will wind up with a number of objects equal to the number of times you did the placement.
- Demonstrate by holding nothing in your hand that no matter how many times you look at it, you still have nothing. (0)

What Can I Do?
Read the question and the response. Then discuss the examples. Tell students that in using the Identity Property, it does not matter which factor is 1. Ask:

- *What is 4 x 1?* (4) *What is 1 x 4?* (4)

Tell student that in using the Zero Property, it does not matter which factor is 0. Ask?

- *What is 7 x 0?* (0) *What is 0 x 7?* (0)

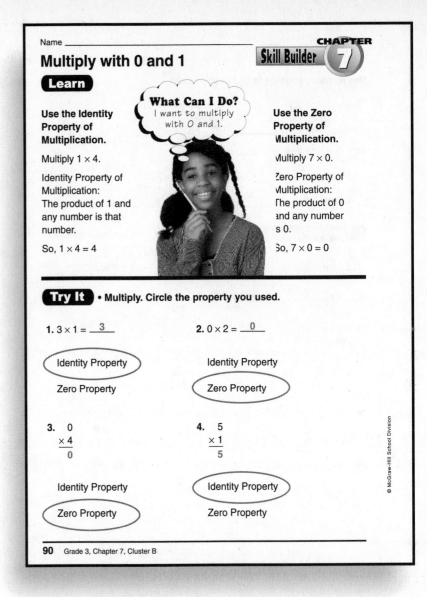

Name _____

Multiply with 0 and 1

Skill Builder CHAPTER **7**

Learn

What Can I Do?
I want to multiply with 0 and 1.

Use the Identity Property of Multiplication.

Multiply 1×4.

Identity Property of Multiplication: The product of 1 and any number is that number.

So, $1 \times 4 = 4$

Use the Zero Property of Multiplication.

Multiply 7×0.

Zero Property of Multiplication: The product of 0 and any number is 0.

So, $7 \times 0 = 0$

Try It • Multiply. Circle the property you used.

1. $3 \times 1 =$ ___3___

    (Identity Property)

    Zero Property

2. $0 \times 2 =$ ___0___

    Identity Property

    (Zero Property)

3.   0
    $\times 4$
    ___0___

    Identity Property

    (Zero Property)

4.   5
    $\times 1$
    ___5___

    (Identity Property)

    Zero Property

90 Grade 3, Chapter 7, Cluster B

© McGraw-Hill School Division

WHAT IF THE STUDENT CAN'T

Remember Which Property Is Which

- Tell the student that if he or she remembers that the Zero Property is for multiplying by 0, the Identity Property has to be for multiplying by 1 or multiplying 1 by another number.

Name _____

Power Practice • Multiply.

5. $2 \times 0 =$ __0__   6. $1 \times 6 =$ __6__   7. $8 \times 1 =$ __8__

8. $0 \times 4 =$ __0__   9. $5 \times 1 =$ __5__   10. $9 \times 0 =$ __0__

11. $7 \times 1 =$ __7__   12. $2 \times 1 =$ __2__   13. $0 \times 8 =$ __0__

14.	15.	16.	17.
0	6	4	8
×3	×1	×1	×0
0	6	4	0

18.	19.	20.	21.
1	3	0	9
×2	×0	×5	×1
2	0	0	9

22.	23.	24.	25.
0	8	0	9
×6	×1	×7	×0
0	8	0	0

26.	27.	28.	29.
0	0	1	0
×0	×1	×1	×8
0	0	1	0

© McGraw-Hill School Division

Grade 3, Chapter 7, Cluster B   **91**

Try It

Have students do exercises 1–4. Ask:

• *How did you decide which property to use?* (If one of the factors is 1, use the Identity Property. If one of the factors is 0, use the Zero Property.)

• *Which property would you use if you multiplied 1 x 0 or 0 x 1.* (It would not matter; you are using both.)

Power Practice

Have students complete the practice items. Then review each answer.

WHAT IF THE STUDENT CAN'T

Complete the Power Practice

• Review missed exercises with the student. Explain again the difference between the Identity Property and the Zero Property.

Lesson Goal

- Complete the division sentence and the related multiplication sentence that can be used to solve each problem.

Introducing the Challenge

- Explore the concept that division and multiplication are opposite operations.
- Demonstrate that if you have 3 numbers that are related as factor–factor–product, they are also related as dividend–divisor– quotient. The opposite is true also.

Say:

- *If you have the numbers 2, 4, and 8, show four ways in which they are related:* (2 x 4 = 8, 4 x 2 = 8, 8 ÷ 4 = 2, 8 ÷ 2 = 4.)

Name _____

Multiplication and Division Sentences

Complete the division sentence that can be used to solve each problem. Complete the related multiplication sentence. Then write the answer.

1. Kathleen had 12 crackers. She put the same number of crackers on 4 plates. How many crackers are on each plate?

   Division Sentence   Multiplication Sentence

   12 ÷ 4 = __3__   4 × __3__ = 12

   Answer: There are 3 crackers on each plate.

2. In Exercise 1, which number is the number of groups? Which number is the number in each group?

   4 is the number of groups; 3 is the number in each group.

   _____

3. Andrew arranged 30 chairs in the cafeteria. He put 5 chairs at each table. How many tables are there in all?

   Division Sentence   Multiplication Sentence

   30 ÷ __6__ = 5   __6__ × 5 = 30

   Answer: There are 6 tables in all.

4. In Exercise 3, which number is the number of groups? Which number is the number in each group?

   6 is the number of groups; 5 is the number in each group.

   _____

Name _____

Write a division sentence and a multiplication sentence that can be used to solve each problem. Write the answer.

5. Mr. Chen gave 8 biscuits to his dogs. He gave each dog 2 biscuits. How many dogs does Mr. Chen have?

Division Sentence	Multiplication Sentence
$8 \div 2 = 4$	$4 \times 2 = 8$

Answer: _Mr. Chen has 4 dogs._

6. Five friends shared 45 crayons equally. How many crayons did each friend get?

Division Sentence	Multiplication Sentence
$45 \div 5 = 9$	$5 \times 9 = 45$

Answer: _Each friend got 9 crayons._

7. Write your own word problem that uses division. Then write a division sentence and a multiplication sentence for that problem.

Answers will vary. Check students' word problems and division

and multiplication sentences.

_____

_____

CHALLENGE

Using the Challenge

Read problem 1.

- Illustrate the problem by using 12 counters (or real crackers).
- Place them one at a time on each of 4 plates until all the items have been used.
- *How many crackers are there on each plate?* (3)
- *Write the division sentence that tells how you divided the crackers?* ($12 \div 4 = 3$)
- Ask students what multiplication sentence is related. ($4 \times 3 = 12$)
- Have students do the rest of the problems. Then review each answer.
- Before students write their own word problems, you might want to model several problems similar to the ones the students have already solved.

CHALLENGE

Lesson Goal
- Use the rules of division to help analyze division problems.

Introducing the Challenge
- Go over the following rules of division with students. Say:
- *If you divide a dividend by each of two divisors, the operation with the larger divisor will result in a smaller quotient.*
- *Demonstrate this, if necessary, by dividing, say, 8 by 4 and 8 by 2. (8 ÷ 4 = 2, which has a larger divisor and a smaller quotient than 8 ÷ 2 = 4)*
- *If you divide any number by itself, you get 1.*
- *If you divide any number by 1, you get that number.*
- *If you divide 0 by any number, you get 0.*
- *You cannot divide a number by 0, because you cannot place a certain number of objects into 0 groups.*

Logical Thinking: Use the Rules!

CHALLENGE CHAPTER **7**

Use rules of division to help you answer each question.

1. Write a division sentence with a dividend of 21 in the space below. Label the dividend, the divisor, and the quotient.

   Possible answer: 21   ÷   3   =   7
                      ↑   ↑   ↑
                   dividend divisor quotient

2. Which has the greater quotient, 12 ÷ 3 or 12 ÷ 4? How do you know?

   12 ÷ 3; Possible answer: 12 ÷ 3 = 4 and 12 ÷ 4 = 3.

   Compare the quotients. 4 > 3.

3. How could you find which has the smaller quotient, 24 ÷ 4 or 24 ÷ 3, **without** dividing? Explain.

   Possible answer: The dividends are the same, so the

   larger the divisor is, the smaller the quotient will be.

   Since 4 > 3, the quotient of 24 ÷ 4 is smaller than the

   quotient of 24 ÷ 3.

4. What is 0 ÷ 499? How do you know?

   0 ÷ 499 = 0; When you divide 0 by any number (except 0),

   the quotient is 0.

Name _____

5. Explain how to find the quotient of, 3,765 ÷ 1.

3,765 ÷ 1 = 3,765; When you divide any number by 1,

the quotient is that number.

6. What is 8,031,603 ÷ 8,031,603? How do you know?

8,031,603 ÷ 8,031,603 = 1: When you divide any number (except 0)

by itself, the quotient is 1.

7. Can 3 be divided by 0? Why or why not?

No, 3 cannot be divided by 0. You cannot divide any number by 0.

It is not possible to put any number of items into 0 groups.

8. Write a word problem that is solved by dividing a number by 1.

Answers will vary. Students' word problems should be solved by

dividing a number by 1.

9. Write a word problem that is solved by dividing a number by itself.

Answers will vary. Students' word problems should be solved by

dividing a number by itself.

Using the Challenge
- Have students do the problems. Then review each answer.
- Students can answer Problem 2 by comparing the quotients to see which is the larger.
- For problem 3, students should see that they can compare divisors. Ask:
- *Which divisor will have the smaller quotient?* (the larger, 4)
- For Problem 4, students should see that the related multiplication sentence will help them: $0 ÷ 499 = 0$ because $0 × 499 = 0$; $3,765 ÷ 1 = 1$ because $1 × 3,765 = 1$
- In connection with Problem 7, tell students that division by 0 is not possible in mathematics.

Name_____

Meaning of Division

Draw each picture. Then tell how many equal groups, or how many are in each group.

1. 24 circles
3 circles in
each group

2. 15 triangles
5 equal groups
of triangles

3. 40 squares
8 squares in
each group

____ groups of
circles

____ triangles in
each group

____ groups of
squares

Skip Count Backward

Complete each skip counting pattern.

4. 56, 49, 42, ___, ___, ___

5. 72, 63, ___, 45, ___

6. 64, 56, ___, 40, ___

7. 42, ___, 30, ___, 18

Function Tables

Complete each table. Then identify the rule.

8.

Input	4	5	7	9
Output	24	30	42	

Rule: _____

9.

Input	3	5	6	8
Output	27	45	54	

Rule: _____

10.

Input	2	5	7	
Output	16	40	56	72

Rule: _____

Multiplication Patterns

Find each product.

11. $7 \times 100 = $ _____   **12.** $4 \times 1{,}000 = $ _____

13. $5 \times 10 = $ _____   **14.** $9 \times 100 = $ _____

Using an Addition Facts Table

Find each sum or difference using the addition facts table.

	0	1	2	3	4	5	6	7	8	9
0	0	1	2	3	4	5	6	7	8	9
1	1	2	3	4	5	6	7	8	9	10
2	2	3	4	5	6	7	8	9	10	11
3	3	4	5	6	7	8	9	10	11	12
4	4	5	6	7	8	9	10	11	12	13
5	5	6	7	8	9	10	11	12	13	14
6	6	7	8	9	10	11	12	13	14	15
7	7	8	9	10	11	12	13	14	15	16
8	8	9	10	11	12	13	14	15	16	17
9	9	10	11	12	13	14	15	16	17	18

15. $8 + 7 = $ _____   **16.** $12 - 3 = $ _____

17. $15 - 9 = $ _____   **18.** $9 + 8 = $ _____

Fact Families

**Write the pair of related subtraction facts
for each pair of addition facts.**

19. $7 + 4 = 11$ **20.** $6 + 9 = 15$
$\quad\ 4 + 7 = 11$ $\quad\ \ 9 + 6 = 15$

_____   _____

_____   _____

CHAPTER 8 PRE-CHAPTER ASSESSMENT

Assessment Goal

This two-page assessment covers skills identified as necessary for success in Chapter 8 Division Facts. The first page assesses the major prerequisite skills for Cluster A. The second page assesses the major prerequisite skills for Cluster B. When the Cluster A and Cluster B prerequisite skills overlap, the skill(s) will be covered in only one section.

Getting Started

- Allow students time to look over the two pages of the assessment. Point out the labels that identify the skills covered.
- Have students find math vocabulary terms used in the assessment. List vocabulary terms on the board as students identify them. If necessary, review the meanings of all essential math vocabulary.

Introducing the Assessment

- Explain to students that these pages will help you know if they are ready to start a new chapter in their math textbooks.
- Students who have transferred from another school may not have been introduced to some of these skills. Encourage students to do their best and assure them you will help them learn any needed skills.

Cluster A Challenge

Those students who demonstrate mastery of the skills on this page will not need to use the reteaching worksheets. Instead, these students can do the Cluster A Challenge found on pages 106-107.

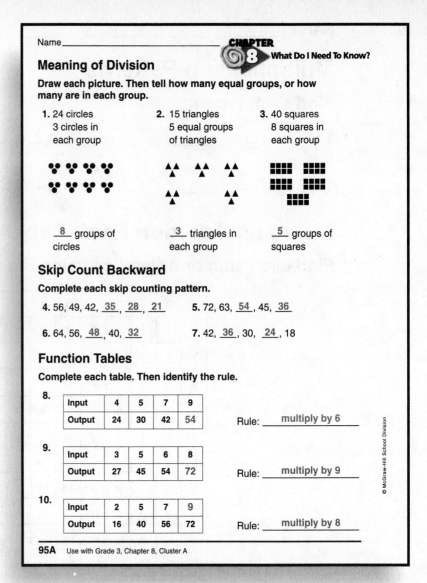

Name_____

Meaning of Division

Draw each picture. Then tell how many equal groups, or how many are in each group.

1. 24 circles
3 circles in each group

___8___ groups of circles

2. 15 triangles
5 equal groups of triangles

___3___ triangles in each group

3. 40 squares
8 squares in each group

___5___ groups of squares

Skip Count Backward

Complete each skip counting pattern.

4. 56, 49, 42, __35__, __28__, __21__

5. 72, 63, __54__, 45, __36__

6. 64, 56, __48__, 40, __32__

7. 42, __36__, 30, __24__, 18

Function Tables

Complete each table. Then identify the rule.

8.

Input	4	5	7	9
Output	24	30	42	54

Rule: _____multiply by 6_____

9.

Input	3	5	6	8
Output	27	45	54	72

Rule: _____multiply by 9_____

10.

Input	2	5	7	9
Output	16	40	56	72

Rule: _____multiply by 8_____

© McGraw-Hill School Division

95A Use with Grade 3, Chapter 8, Cluster A

CLUSTER A PREREQUISITE SKILLS

The skills listed in this chart are those identified as major prerequisite skills for students' success in the lessons in Cluster A of the chapter. Each skill is covered by one or more assessment items as shown in the middle column. The right column provides the page number for the lessons in this book that reteach the cluster A prerequisite skills.

Skill Name	Assessment Items	Lesson Pages
Meaning of Division	1-3	96-97
Skip Count Backward by 6 and 7	4 and 7	98
Skip Count Backward by 8 and 9	5 and 6	99
Function Tables	8-10	100-101

Name_____

Multiplication Patterns

Find each product.

11. $7 \times 100 =$ __700__   **12.** $4 \times 1,000 =$ __4,000__

13. $5 \times 10 =$ __50__   **14.** $9 \times 100 =$ __900__

Using an Addition Facts Table

Find each sum or difference using the addition facts table.

	0	1	2	3	4	5	6	7	8	9
0	0	1	2	3	4	5	6	7	8	9
1	1	2	3	4	5	6	7	8	9	10
2	2	3	4	5	6	7	8	9	10	11
3	3	4	5	6	7	8	9	10	11	12
4	4	5	6	7	8	9	10	11	12	13
5	5	6	7	8	9	10	11	12	13	14
6	6	7	8	9	10	11	12	13	14	15
7	7	8	9	10	11	12	13	14	15	16
8	8	9	10	11	12	13	14	15	16	17
9	9	10	11	12	13	14	15	16	17	18

15. $8 + 7 =$ __15__   **16.** $12 - 3 =$ __9__

17. $15 - 9 =$ __6__   **18.** $9 + 8 =$ __17__

Fact Families

Write the pair of related subtraction facts
for each pair of addition facts.

19. $7 + 4 = 11$ **20.** $6 + 9 = 15$
　　$4 + 7 = 11$ 　　$9 + 6 = 15$

_____$11 - 4 = 7$_____   _____$15 - 9 = 6$_____

_____$11 - 7 = 4$_____   _____$15 - 6 = 9$_____

© McGraw-Hill School Division

Use with Grade 3, Chapter 8, Cluster B   **95B**

CLUSTER B PREREQUISITE SKILLS

The skills listed in this chart are those identified as major prerequisite skills for students' success in the lessons in Cluster B of the chapter. Each skill is covered by one or more assessment items as shown in the middle column. The right column provides the page numbers for the lessons in this book that reteach the Cluster B prerequisite skills

Skill Name	Assessment Items	Lesson Pages
Multiplication Patterns	11-14	102
Using an Adddition Facts Table	15-18	103
Fact Families	19-20	104-105

Alternative Assessment Strategies

• Oral administration of the assessment is appropriate for younger students or those whose native language is not English. Read the skills title and directions one section at a time. Check students' understanding by asking them to tell you how they will do the first exercise in the group.

• For some skill types you may wish to use group administration. In this technique, a small group or pair of students complete the assessment together. Through their discussion, you will be able to decide if supplementary reteaching materials are needed.

Intervention Materials

If students are not successful with the prerequisite skills assessed on these pages, reteaching lessons have been created to help them make the transition into the chapter.

Item correlation charts showing the skills lessons suitable for reteaching the prerequisite skills are found beneath the reproductions of each page of the assessment.

Cluster B Challenge

Those students who demonstrate mastery of the skills on this page will not need to use the reteaching worksheets. Instead, these students can do the Cluster B Challenge found on pages 108-109.

USING THE LESSON

Lesson Goal
- Learn the principle of division.

What the Student Needs to Know
- Understand the idea of dividing a large group of items into equal, smaller groups.
- Add numbers in repetition.

Getting Started
Find out what students know about division. Draw 6 diamonds on the board. Say:

- *There are 6 diamonds on the board. How can you divide the diamonds into 2 equal groups?* (2 equal groups of 3)

What Can I Do?
- Read the question and the response. Then read and discuss the examples. Ask:
- *If you want to draw 12 stars and you know that there are 4 stars in each group, how can you find out how many groups there are?* (Find out how many times you have to add 4 to get 12.)
- *If you want to draw 18 circles and you know that there are 3 equal groups, how can you find out how many circles are in each group?* (Find out how many times you have to add 3 to get 18.)

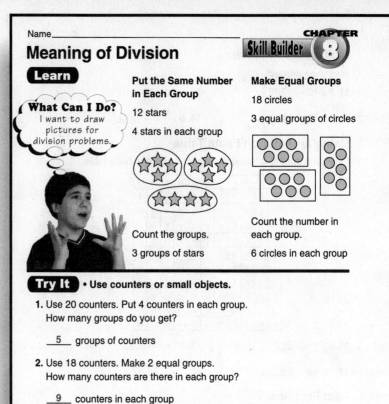

Name_____

Meaning of Division

Learn

What Can I Do? I want to draw pictures for division problems.

Put the Same Number in Each Group

12 stars

4 stars in each group

Count the groups.

3 groups of stars

Make Equal Groups

18 circles

3 equal groups of circles

Count the number in each group.

6 circles in each group

Try It • Use counters or small objects.

1. Use 20 counters. Put 4 counters in each group. How many groups do you get?

   __5__ groups of counters

2. Use 18 counters. Make 2 equal groups. How many counters are there in each group?

   __9__ counters in each group

3. Use 15 counters. Put 3 counters in each group. How many groups do you get?

   __5__ groups of counters

4. Use 24 counters. Make 4 equal groups. How many counters are there in each group?

   __6__ counters in each group

96 Grade 3, Chapter 8, Cluster A

WHAT IF THE STUDENT CAN'T

Understand the Idea of Dividing a Larger Group into Smaller Groups
- Use counters to demonstrate how to divide even numbers into 2 equal parts. Have the student practice doing this with the numbers 2 through 18 until the student can do so easily.

- From here, move on to the idea of 3, 4, 5, 6, 7, 8, and 9 equal groups.
- Demonstrate how repeated addition or multiplication can be used to be sure that a number has been divided correctly.

Name_____

Power Practice . Draw each picture. Then tell how many equal groups, or how many are in each group.

5. 8 squares

4 squares in each group

___2___ groups of squares

6. 10 triangles

2 equal groups of triangles

___5___ triangles in each group

7. 6 stars

3 stars in each group

★ ★ ★   ★ ★ ★

___2___ groups of stars

8. 9 circles

3 equal groups of circles

___3___ circles in each group

9. 16 triangles

8 triangles in each group

___2___ groups of triangles

10. 12 squares

3 equal groups of squares

___4___ squares in each group

© McGraw-Hill School Division

Grade 3, Chapter 8, Cluster A **97**

Try It

Have students look at exercises 1–4. Make sure they understand that the same operation can be used to determine both the number of groups into which a greater number is broken down and to find how many items are in each group.

Power Practice

• Have students complete the practice items. Then review each answer. For any incorrect answers, have students use counters to model the correct number of groups and items.

WHAT IF THE STUDENT CAN'T

Add Numbers in Repetition

• Use counters to demonstrate how a number may be added to itself repeatedly and that the sum increases each time the number is added. For example: $3 + 3 = 6$; $3 + 3 + 3 = 9$; $3 + 3 + 3 + 3 = 12$; and so on.

• Have the student practice adding the numbers 1 through 9 in repetition until the student can do so with ease.

Complete the Power Practice

• Discuss each incorrect answer. Have the student use counting, serial addition, or multiplication to show why the answer is incorrect.

USING THE LESSON

Lesson Goal

- Skip count backwards by 6s and 7s, using only numbers that are products of 6 or 7.

What the Student Needs to Know

- Count forward by 6s and 7s.
- Read a number line.
- Understand the relationship between counting forward and backwards.

Getting Started

Find out what students know about counting by 6s and 7s. Ask:

- As you count forward by 6s, what pattern do you see in the numbers?

If you want to count forward by 7s, how do you do it? (add 7 to each number)

What Can I Do?

- Read the question and the response. Then read and discuss the examples. Ask:
- *As you count backwards by 6s, what pattern do you see in the numbers?* (Each number is 6 less than the number that comes before it.)
- *As you count backwards by 7s, what pattern do you see in the numbers?* (Each number is 7 less than the number that comes before it.)

Try It

Have students complete exercises 1 and 2 by continuing each skip counting sequence and then reading it aloud. Then have them read each sequence backwards.

Power Practice

- Have students complete the practice items. Review each answer. For each incorrect answer, first have students identify the skip counting pattern. Then ask them to correct their counting.

Skip Count Backwards by 6 and 7

Learn

What Can I Do?
I want to count backwards by 6s and 7s.

Use Number Lines

When counting backwards by 6s, start at 60.

0 5 10 15 20 25 30 35 40 45 50 55 60

When counting backwards by 7s, start at 70.

10 15 20 25 30 35 40 45 50 55 60 65 70

Try It • Count forward.

1. Count by 6s up to 60.

   6, __12__, __18__, __24__, 30, __36__, __42__, __48__, __54__, __60__

2. Count by 7s up to 70.

   7, __14__, __21__, __28__, 35, __42__, __49__, __56__, __63__, __70__

Power Practice • Complete each skip counting pattern.

3. 60, 54, __48__, 42, 36, __30__   4. 70, __63__, 56, __49__, 42, 35

5. 42, __36__, 30, __24__, 18, 12   6. 48, 42, __36__, 30, 24, __18__

7. 35, __28__, 21, __14__, 7, 0   8. __30__, 24, 18, __12__, 6, 0

9. __56__, 49, 42, __35__, 28, 21   10. 63, __56__, 49, __42__, 35, 28

WHAT IF THE STUDENT CAN'T

Count Forward By 6s and 7s

- Use drawings or counters to illustrate the numbers that are encountered when counting by 6s and 7s.
- Have the student practice counting by 6s to 60 and 7s to 70 until he or she can do so easily.

Read a Number Line

- Tell the student the number of each mark on a 10-digit section of the number line. Then say a number and have the student point to it. Show how the same principle applies to other sections of the number line.

Understand the Relationship Between Counting Forward and Backwards

- Have the student count from 1 to 20 by ones. Then illustrate how the same thing can be done in reverse, from 20 to 1.
- Have the student practice counting forward and backwards by ones until the student can do it easily.

Complete the Power Practice

- Have the student identify the counting pattern in each exercise. Then guide the student in completing the pattern correctly.

Name_____

Skip Count Backwards by 8 and 9

Skill Builder

What Can I Do?
I want to count backwards by 8s and 9s.

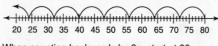
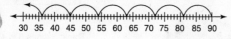

Learn

Use Number Lines

When counting backwards by 8s, start at 80.

20 25 30 35 40 45 50 55 60 65 70 75 80

When counting backwards by 9s, start at 90.

30 35 40 45 50 55 60 65 70 75 80 85 90

Try It • Count forward.

1. Count by 8s up to 80.

8, _16_, _24_, _32_, _40_, _48_, _56_, _64_, _72_, _80_

2. Count by 9s up to 90.

9, _18_, _27_, _36_, _45_, _54_, _63_, _72_, _81_, _90_

Power Practice • Complete each skip counting pattern.

3. 80, _72_, 64, _56_, 48, 40   **4.** _90_, 81, 72, _63_, 54, 45

5. 40, 32, _24_, 16, _8_, 0   **6.** 64, _56_, 48, 40, _32_, 24

7. 54, 45, _36_, _27_, 18, 9   **8.** 45, 36, _27_, 18, 9, _0_

9. _56_, 48, 40, _32_, 24, 16   **10.** 72, 64, _56_, 48, _40_, 32

© McGraw-Hill School Division

Grade 3, Chapter 8, Cluster A   **99**

WHAT IF THE STUDENT CAN'T

Count Forward By 8s and 9s

- Use counters to illustrate the numbers that are encountered when counting by 8s and 9s.
- Practice counting by 8s to 80 and 9s to 90 until the student can do so easily.

Read a Number Line

- Tell the student the number of each mark on a 10-digit section of the number line. Then say a number and have the student point to it. Show how the same principle applies to other sections of the number line.
- Help the student draw a 20-digit section of a number line.

Understand the Relationship Between Counting Forward and Backwards

- Have the student count from 1 to 20 by ones. Then illustrate how the same thing can be done in reverse, from 20 to 1.
- Have the student practice counting forward and backwards by ones until the student can do it easily.

Complete the Power Practice

- Have the student identify the counting pattern in each exercise. Then guide the student in completing the pattern correctly.

USING THE LESSON

- Skip count backwards by 8s and 9s, using only numbers that are products of 8 or 9.

What the Student Needs to Know

- Count forward by 8s and 9s.
- Read a number line.
- Understand the relationship between counting forward and backwards.

Getting Started

Find out what students know about counting by 8s and 9s. Ask:

- *As you count forward by 8s, what pattern do you see in the numbers?* (Each number is 8 greater than the number that comes before it.)
- *As you count forward by 9s, what pattern do you see in the numbers?* (Each number is 9 greater than the number that comes before it.)

What Can I Do?

- Read the question. Then read and discuss the examples. Ask:
- *As you count backwards by 8s, what pattern do you see in the numbers?* (Each number is 8 less that the number that comes before it.)
- *As you count backwards by 9s, what pattern do you see in the numbers?* (Each number is 9 less than the number that comes before it.)

Try It

Have students complete exercises 1 and 2 by completing each skip-counting sequence and then reading it aloud. Then have them read each sequence backwards.

Power Practice

- Have students complete the practice items. Review each answer. For each incorrect answer, first have students identify the skip-counting pattern. Then ask them to correct their counting.

USING THE LESSON

Lesson Goal
- Complete and identify rules for function tables.

What the Student Needs to Know
- Multiply numbers by a given factor.
- Identify the factor by which a number is multiplied.
- Read a function table.

Getting Started
Write the following function table on the board:

Input	Output
1	2
2	4
3	6
4	8

Ask:

- *What is the relationship between the number in the input column and the number in the output column?* (The output number is the input number × 2.)
- *If the number in the input column is 5, what will the number in the output column be?* (10)

What Can I Do?
Read the question and the response. Then discuss the example. Ask:

- *How can you tell what the relationship between the input number and the output number is?* (Use repeated addition or division to determine how many times the input number goes into the output number.)
- *The first input number is 3, and the first output number is 15. How can you be sure that the rule of the table isn't + 12?* (Because the rule doesn't apply to the other numbers.)
- *If the input number is 9, what will the output number be? What if the input number is 7?* (45, 35)

Name_____

Function Tables

Learn

What Can I Do?
I want to find missing numbers in a function table.

Look for the Rule
The input number may be multiplied by some factor. Look at the table to find this factor.

Input	Output
3	15
4	20
6	30
9	?

Think: 3 times 5 is 15.
The rule is "times 5."

Try It • Use the rules to complete the tables.

1. Rule: × 6

Input	Output
3	18
4	24
7	42

2. Rule: × 3

Input	Output
2	6
6	18
9	27

3. Rule: × 4

Input	Output
1	4
5	20
8	32

4. Rule: × 8

Input	Output
3	24
6	48
7	56

5. Rule: × 2

Input	Output
4	8
6	12
8	16

6. Rule: × 7

Input	Output
2	14
4	28
5	35

WHAT IF THE STUDENT CAN'T

Multiply Numbers by a Given Factor

- Use models to illustrate the pattern that develops when consecutive numbers are multiplied by the same factor.
- Use a multiplication table to demonstrate the products that result when different numbers are multiplied by the same factor.

Identify the Factor by Which a Number Is Multiplied

- Use counters to illustrate the way that division and repeated addition can be used to identify the factor by which a number is multiplied. For example, 3 × ____ = 18 can be solved by using counters to determine that 18 can be divided into 6 groups of 3, or that 3 has to be added 6 times to get 18.

Name_____

Power Practice • Complete each table.
Then identify the rule.

7. Rule: $\times 7$

Input	Output
3	21
5	35
7	49
9	63

8. Rule: $\times 3$

Input	Output
1	3
3	9
6	18
7	21

9. Rule: $\times 6$

Input	Output
4	24
5	30
7	42
8	48

10. Rule: $\times 4$

Input	Output
3	12
5	20
6	24
8	32

11. Rule: $\times 5$

Input	Output
4	20
6	30
7	35
9	45

12. Rule: $\times 9$

Input	Output
2	18
4	36
5	45
7	63

13. Rule: $\times 8$

Input	Output
3	24
5	40
7	56
8	64

14. Rule: $\times 2$

Input	Output
2	4
4	8
6	12
9	18

15. Rule: $\times 6$

Input	Output
1	6
3	18
4	24
6	36

© McGraw-Hill School Division

USING THE LESSON

Lesson Goal
- Multiply numbers by 10, 100, and 1,000.

What the Student Needs to Know
- Multiply by one.
- Understand the relationship between 10, 100, and 1,000.

Getting Started
Find out what students know about the relationship between 10, 100, and 1,000. Ask:
- *How many zeros are there in 10? 100? 1,000? (1, 2, 3)*

What Can I Do?
Read the question and the response. Then read and discuss the examples. Ask:
- *What is a simple way of multiplying 4 times 10, 100, or 1,000? (Possible answer: take the number 4 and write 1, 2, or 3 zeros after it.)*

Try It
Have students answer exercises 1 and 2 aloud. Then have students complete exercises 3–6. Ask:
- *As you move from multiplying by 10 to multiplying by 100, then by 1,000, what happens to your products? (They increase by a factor of ten each time.)*

Power Practice
- Have students complete the practice items. Then review each answer.
- Compare any incorrect answers with similar exercises on the page that the student has answered correctly. For example, if the student answers 4 × 100 incorrectly, it can be compared with a correct answer for 4 × 10 or 9 × 100.

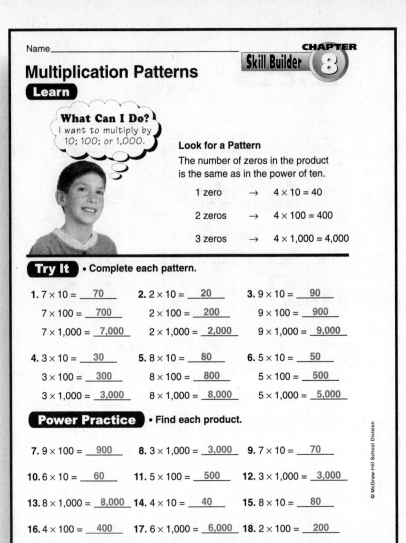

Multiplication Patterns

Learn

What Can I Do?
I want to multiply by 10; 100; or 1,000.

Look for a Pattern
The number of zeros in the product is the same as in the power of ten.

1 zero	→	4 × 10 = 40
2 zeros	→	4 × 100 = 400
3 zeros	→	4 × 1,000 = 4,000

Try It • Complete each pattern.

1. 7 × 10 = __70__   2. 2 × 10 = __20__   3. 9 × 10 = __90__
   7 × 100 = __700__   2 × 100 = __200__   9 × 100 = __900__
   7 × 1,000 = __7,000__ 2 × 1,000 = __2,000__ 9 × 1,000 = __9,000__

4. 3 × 10 = __30__   5. 8 × 10 = __80__   6. 5 × 10 = __50__
   3 × 100 = __300__   8 × 100 = __800__   5 × 100 = __500__
   3 × 1,000 = __3,000__ 8 × 1,000 = __8,000__ 5 × 1,000 = __5,000__

Power Practice • Find each product.

7. 9 × 100 = __900__   8. 3 × 1,000 = __3,000__   9. 7 × 10 = __70__

10. 6 × 10 = __60__   11. 5 × 100 = __500__   12. 3 × 1,000 = __3,000__

13. 8 × 1,000 = __8,000__ 14. 4 × 10 = __40__   15. 8 × 10 = __80__

16. 4 × 100 = __400__   17. 6 × 1,000 = __6,000__   18. 2 × 100 = __200__

102 Grade 3, Chapter 8, Cluster B

WHAT IF THE STUDENT CAN'T

Multiply by One
- Use counters to demonstrate simple multiplication equations, such as 4 × 2 and 4 × 3. Then show how multiplying a number by one results in a product of that number.
- Have the student practice multiplying the numbers 1 through 9 by 1 until the concept is clear.

Understand the Relationships between 10, 100, and 1,000
- Use grid strips and grids to model the relationship between the three numbers.

Demonstrate how it takes 10 strips of 10 grid squares to make 100, and 10 grids of 100 squares to make 1,000.

Complete the Power Practice
- Discuss each incorrect answer. Have the student identify the number of zeros in the second factor. Then have the student write the answer by attaching those zeros to the 1-digit factor.

Using an Addition Facts Table

Learn

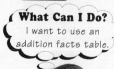

What Can I Do?
I want to use an addition facts table.

To Add

To find 8 + 7, look across the 8 row until you are under the 7. Answer: 15

To Subtract

To find 13 – 5, look across the 5 row until you find 13. Look in the top row for the answer, 8.

+	0	1	2	3	4	5	6	7	8	9	10
0	0	1	2	3	4	5	6	7	8	9	10
1	1	2	3	4	5	6	7	8	9	10	11
2	2	3	4	5	6	7	8	9	10	11	12
3	3	4	5	6	7	8	9	10	11	12	13
4	4	5	6	7	8	9	10	11	12	13	14
5	5	6	7	8	9	10	11	12	13	14	15
6	6	7	8	9	10	11	12	13	14	15	16
7	7	8	9	10	11	12	13	14	15	16	17
8	8	9	10	11	12	13	14	15	16	17	18
9	9	10	11	12	13	14	15	16	17	18	19
10	10	11	12	13	14	15	16	17	18	19	20

Try It • Use the addition facts table.

1. Look in the 7 row. Where is the answer to 7 + 6? <u>underneath the 6</u>
_____

2. Look in the 4 row. Where is the answer to 12 – 4? <u>in the top row,</u>
<u>above the 12</u>

Power Practice • Find each sum or difference using the table.

3. 16 – 9 = <u>7</u>   4. 7 + 6 = <u>13</u>   5. 13 – 8 = <u>5</u>

6. 9 + 5 = <u>14</u>   7. 14 – 8 = <u>6</u>   8. 9 + 6 = <u>15</u>

9. 13 – 6 = <u>7</u>   10. 8 + 6 = <u>14</u>   11. 15 – 6 = <u>9</u>

12. 14 – 9 = <u>5</u>   13. 8 + 4 = <u>12</u>   14. 9 + 8 = <u>17</u>

Grade 3, Chapter 8, Cluster B **103**

WHAT IF THE STUDENT CAN'T

Understand the Relationship between Addition and Subtraction

- Use counters to illustrate addition facts, such as 4 + 9 = 13. Then demonstrate with counters how the same numbers are in the related subtraction fact 13 – 9 = 4.

- Have the student practice by using subtraction facts to write addition facts until the student can do so with ease. For example: 14 – 8 = 6; 6 + 8 = 14.

Complete the Power Practice

- Discuss each incorrect answer. Guide the student in finding the appropriate numbers on the table. Then have the student demonstrate the correct answer to the exercise.

USING THE LESSON

Lesson Goal
- Use an addition facts table to add and subtract.

What the Student Needs to Know
- Understand the relationship between addition and subtraction.

Getting Started
Draw an addition facts table from 0 to 3 on the board. Show how row 1 and column 3 meet at 4, and write 1 + 3 = 4 to represent this fact. Then ask:

- *What are some other addition facts that can be found in this table?* (Possible answers: 2 + 0 = 2; 3 + 3 = 6)

What Can I Do?
Read the question and the response. Then read and discuss the examples. Ask:

- *What is the difference between the way you use the table for addition and for subtraction?* (In addition, you know the row and column, so you look in the table to find the sum where those numbers meet. In subtraction, you know the row and the sum in the table, so you look at the top of the column to find the other numbers.

Try It
Have students demonstrate how they found the answers to exercises 1 and 2. Then have them write each exercise as its own equation.

Power Practice
- Have students complete exercises 3–14. Then review each answer. For each incorrect answer, have students use the table to demonstrate the correct answer for you.

USING THE LESSON

Lesson Goal
- Complete addition/subtraction fact families.

What the Student Needs to Know
- Complete addition and subtraction facts.
- Understand the relationship between addition and subtraction.

Getting Started
Find out what students know about the relationship between addition and subtraction. Write the following addition facts on the board:

$$5 + 7 = 12.$$

Ask:
- *What is a subtraction fact you can write using the same numbers?* (12 − 7 = 5; 12 − 5 = 7)

Have students write another addition fact, along with a related subtraction fact.

What Can I Do?
Read the question and the response. Then read and discuss the examples. Ask:
- *What three numbers appear in each addition and subtraction fact?* (3, 5, 8)
- *Where does 8 appear in the addition facts?* (as the sum or after the equals sign) *Where does 8 appear in the subtraction facts?* (as the first number)
- *How many facts are in the fact family for 3, 5, and 8?* (4) *How many numbers are in each fact?* (3)
- *Do the numbers in a family of facts change from fact to fact, or do they remain the same?* (remain the same)
- *Do any of the facts in a fact family repeat themselves, or are they all different?* (all different)

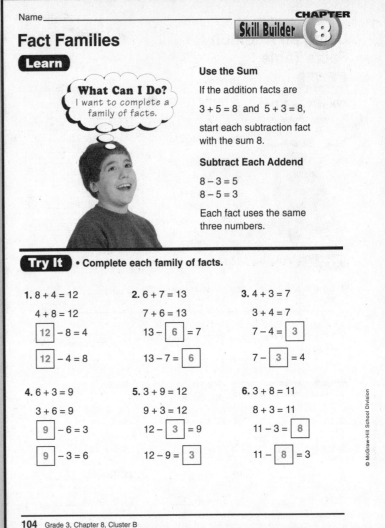

Fact Families

Learn

What Can I Do?
I want to complete a family of facts.

Use the Sum

If the addition facts are

3 + 5 = 8 and 5 + 3 = 8,

start each subtraction fact with the sum 8.

Subtract Each Addend

8 − 3 = 5
8 − 5 = 3

Each fact uses the same three numbers.

Try It • Complete each family of facts.

1. 8 + 4 = 12
   4 + 8 = 12
   12 − 8 = 4
   12 − 4 = 8

2. 6 + 7 = 13
   7 + 6 = 13
   13 − 6 = 7
   13 − 7 = 6

3. 4 + 3 = 7
   3 + 4 = 7
   7 − 4 = 3
   7 − 3 = 4

4. 6 + 3 = 9
   3 + 6 = 9
   9 − 6 = 3
   9 − 3 = 6

5. 3 + 9 = 12
   9 + 3 = 12
   12 − 3 = 9
   12 − 9 = 3

6. 3 + 8 = 11
   8 + 3 = 11
   11 − 3 = 8
   11 − 8 = 3

104 Grade 3, Chapter 8, Cluster B

WHAT IF THE STUDENT CAN'T

Complete Addition and Subtraction Facts
- Use counters to demonstrate the principle of addition. Start with smaller numbers, and work up to showing that 9 + 9 = 18.
- Use counters to demonstrate the principle of subtraction. Start with simple subtraction facts such as 3 − 1 = 2, and work up to show that 18 − 9 = 9.
- Have the student write basic addition and subtraction facts on flash cards. Then have the student practice with flash cards until the facts can be recalled with ease.

Understand the Relationship between Addition and Subtraction
- Use counters to illustrate addition facts, such as 3 + 9 = 12. Then demonstrate with counters how the same numbers are in the related subtraction fact 12 − 9 = 3.
- Have the student practice by using addition facts to write subtraction facts until the student can do so with ease. For example: 8 + 7 = 15; 15 − 7 = 8.

Power Practice • Write the pair of related subtraction facts for each pair of addition facts.

7. $9 + 7 = 16$
$7 + 9 = 16$

____$16 - 9 = 7$____

____$16 - 7 = 9$____

8. $9 + 1 = 10$
$1 + 9 = 10$

____$10 - 9 = 1$____

____$10 - 1 = 9$____

9. $6 + 8 = 14$
$8 + 6 = 14$

____$14 - 6 = 8$____

____$14 - 8 = 6$____

10. $4 + 6 = 10$
$6 + 4 = 10$

____$10 - 4 = 6$____

____$10 - 6 = 4$____

11. $7 + 4 = 11$
$4 + 7 = 11$

____$11 - 7 = 4$____

____$11 - 4 = 7$____

12. $9 + 4 = 13$
$4 + 9 = 13$

____$13 - 9 = 4$____

____$13 - 4 = 9$____

13. $6 + 2 = 8$
$2 + 6 = 8$

____$8 - 6 = 2$____

____$8 - 2 = 6$____

14. $8 + 9 = 17$
$9 + 8 = 17$

____$17 - 8 = 9$____

____$17 - 9 = 8$____

15. $7 + 5 = 12$
$5 + 7 = 12$

____$12 - 7 = 5$____

____$12 - 5 = 7$____

16. $8 + 5 = 13$
$5 + 8 = 13$

____$13 - 8 = 5$____

____$13 - 5 = 8$____

Learn with Partners & Parents

Fact Family Roll

You will need two 1–6 number cubes.

- Roll the cubes to get two numbers to add. If the numbers are the same, roll again.
- The first player to write two addition and two subtraction facts gets one point.
- Play the game until one player has 7 points.

USING THE LESSON

Try It

Have students look at exercises 1 and 2. Ask:

- *How do you know which number to start with in the subtraction facts?* (You start with the number that is the sum of the addition facts.)
- *How do you know which of the lesser numbers is missing from the subtraction facts?* (by comparing the subtraction facts with the addition facts; by solving one of the equations)
- Have students complete exercises 1–6. Check to be sure that students understand that the numbers in a fact family remain consistent.

Power Practice

- Select one of the exercises and have students complete it. Be sure students understand how to convert an addition fact into 2 related subtraction facts.
- Have students complete the remaining practice items. Then review each answer.

WHAT IF THE STUDENT CAN'T

Complete the Power Practice

- Discuss each incorrect answer. Have the student compare each incorrect subtraction fact with a corresponding addition fact. Then have the student use counters to demonstrate the correctness of the revised subtraction fact or facts.

CHALLENGE

Lesson Goal

- Understand how to read and solve division word problems that require that 1 be added to the quotient in order to arrive at the correct answer.

Introducing the Challenge

Find out how familiar students are with division word problems. Have them solve the following word problems:

- *Toby has 15 tennis balls in 5 cans. If each can has the same number of balls, how many balls are in each can?* (3)

- *There are 20 people traveling to a football game. If 4 people go in each car, how many cars are needed?* (5)

Then have students read the introduction to the challenge and the example problem. Draw students' attention to the diagram. Ask:

- *Why is the answer to the problem 5 rather than 4?* (Possible answer: Because Ann starts at the edge of the garden, which means that the first bush is at the zero yard mark. This means that the bush at the 3-yard mark is the second bush, and the bush at the 12-yard mark is the fifth bush.)

Have students solve exercises 1 and 2, using the diagram to demonstrate the correct answer for each problem. Ask:

- *How can each problem be solved by using an equation?* (Divide, then add 1 to the quotient.)

Using the Challenge

- Have students look at exercise 3. Then have them illustrate the problem with a diagram and write an equation to solve it.

Dividing — Plus One

In some kinds of division problems, you need to add 1 to the answer. Read the problem in the box.

> The front side of a garden is 12 yards long. Ann plants a rose bush every 3 yards. How many bushes does she plant?

Although 12 divided by 3 equals 4, the answer is 5 bushes. A diagram helps to show why.

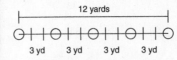

3 yd   3 yd   3 yd   3 yd

Use the diagram to help solve each problem.

1. Judy is nailing up a piece of wood 30 inches long. She puts a nail every 6 inches. How many nails does she use?

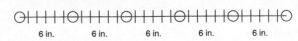

6 in.   6 in.   6 in.   6 in.   6 in.

Judy uses ___6___ nails.

2. A flower bed is 12 feet long. Jake plants tomatoes every 4 feet. How many tomato plants does Jake use?

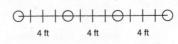

4 ft   4 ft   4 ft

Jake uses ___4___ plants.

© McGraw-Hill School Division

Name _____

Solve each problem.

3. A brick walk is 18 yards long. Hal puts a flower pot every 3 yards. How many flowers pots does he use?

_____7 flower pots_____

4. A clock chimes every 10 minutes. How many times does the clock chime from 8:00 to 9:00?

_____7 times_____

5. For a parade, 30 children get in a line behind a leader. The leader and every 6th child holds a bright yellow flag. How many flags are needed?

_____6 flags_____

6. Potted plants are placed every 3 feet along one edge of a 24-foot long pool. How many potted plants are used?

_____9 potted plants_____

7. Sharon plants a tulip every 2 feet along a wall that is 12 feet long. How many tulips does she use?

_____7 tulips_____

8. Paula digs a hole every 4 feet for a fence. How many holes does she dig if the fence is 24 feet long?

_____7 holes_____

9. A straight road is 32 blocks long. There is a stop sign every 4 blocks. How many stop signs are there along the road?

_____9 stop signs_____

10. A running race is 16 miles long. There is a sign at the beginning, at the end, and every 2 miles in between. How many signs are needed?

_____9 signs_____

CHALLENGE

- Be sure students understand that both the starting point and ending point have to be counted in order to arrive at the correct answer; this means that 1 must be added to the quotient after dividing.
- Have students complete the practice items. Then review each answer.
- For each incorrect answer, have students draw a diagram illustrating the problem. Then have them count out the answer to the problem before writing an equation to solve it.

Have students answer the following word problem:

- *There are 25 cars in a parking lot. Every 5th car is blue. How many blue cars are in the lot?* (5)

Ask:

- *How is this problem different from the problems on the page?* (Possible answer: There isn't a beginning or zero point that has to be included in the count.)

CHALLENGE

Lesson Goal

• Divide numbers in half by breaking them into two parts.

Introducing the Challenge

Find out how comfortable students are in breaking a number down into two addends. Have them break down the following numbers into addends (possible answers are given):

5 (3 + 2)
38 (32 + 6)
24 (20 + 4)
81 (41 + 40)

Then introduce the idea that breaking down a number into addends can make the number easier to work with. Have students read the introduction to the challenge and the two examples. Ask:

• *Why is it helpful to break 56 into 40 + 16?* (because 40 and 16 are easy to divide by 2 and are also easy to add together to get a final answer)

• *Why is it helpful to break 7 into 6 + 1?* (because it simplifies the division process by giving you an even number to divide by 2 and add 1/2 to)

CHALLENGE — CHAPTER 8

Dividing in Half

You can divide a number in half by breaking it into two parts. In the first example, 56 is written as 40 + 16.

Example 1

$$2 \overline{)56} \rightarrow 2 \overline{)40 + 16}^{\,20 + 8}$$

Dividing the whole number 1 in half gives you the fraction $\frac{1}{2}$. When an odd number is divided in half, the answer includes the fraction $\frac{1}{2}$.

Example 2

$$2 \overline{)7} \rightarrow 2 \overline{)6 + 1}^{\,3 + \frac{1}{2}}$$

Complete the steps to divide each number in half.

1. 78 = 60 + 18

   78 ÷ 2 = __30__ + __9__

   78 ÷ 2 = __39__

2. 34 = 20 + 14

   34 ÷ 2 = __10__ + __7__

   34 ÷ 2 = __17__

3. 96 = 80 + 16

   96 ÷ 2 = __40__ + __8__

   96 ÷ 2 = __48__

4. 54 = 40 + 14

   54 ÷ 2 = __20__ + __7__

   54 ÷ 2 = __27__

5. 72 = 60 + 12

   72 ÷ 2 = __30__ + __6__

   72 ÷ 2 = __36__

6. 38 = 20 + 18

   38 ÷ 2 = __10__ + __9__

   38 ÷ 2 = __19__

7. 92 = 80 + 12

   92 ÷ 2 = __40__ + __6__

   92 ÷ 2 = __46__

8. 58 = 40 + 18

   58 ÷ 2 = __20__ + __9__

   58 ÷ 2 = __29__

9. 76 = 60 + 16

   76 ÷ 2 = __30__ + __8__

   76 ÷ 2 = __38__

Name _____

Use an even number to divide an odd number.

10. $8 \div 2 =$ ___4___

$9 \div 2 =$ ___4___ $\frac{1}{2}$

11. $12 \div 2 =$ ___6___

$13 \div 2 =$ ___6___ $\frac{1}{2}$

12. $16 \div 2 =$ ___8___

$17 \div 2 =$ ___8___ $\frac{1}{2}$

13. $4 \div 2 =$ ___2___

$5 \div 2 =$ ___2___ $\frac{1}{2}$

14. $20 \div 2 =$ ___10___

$21 \div 2 =$ ___10___ $\frac{1}{2}$

15. $6 \div 2 =$ ___3___

$7 \div 2 =$ ___3___ $\frac{1}{2}$

16. $18 \div 2 =$ ___9___

$19 \div 2 =$ ___9___ $\frac{1}{2}$

17. $10 \div 2 =$ ___5___

$11 \div 2 =$ ___5___ $\frac{1}{2}$

18. $14 \div 2 =$ ___7___

$15 \div 2 =$ ___7___ $\frac{1}{2}$

Divide each number in half.

19. 84 ___42___

20. 46 ___23___

21. 62 ___31___

22. 42 ___21___

23. 28 ___14___

24. 86 ___43___

25. 52 ___26___

26. 94 ___47___

27. 58 ___29___

28. 36 ___18___

29. 98 ___49___

30. 74 ___37___

31. 27 ___$13\frac{1}{2}$___

32. 19 ___$9\frac{1}{2}$___

33. 25 ___$12\frac{1}{2}$___

34. 21 ___$10\frac{1}{2}$___

35. 35 ___$17\frac{1}{2}$___

36. 17 ___$8\frac{1}{2}$___

CHALLENGE

Using the Challenge

Have students complete exercises 1–9. Review any incorrect answers. Ask:

- *How is each number in these exercises broken down?* (into a multiple of twenty and a number that gives you a one-digit answer when you divide it by 2)

Have students complete exercises 10–18. Review any incorrect answers. Ask:

- *What do these exercises suggest is a good way to break down an odd number that you want to divide by 2?* (Break it down into an even number plus 1; divide the even number below it on the number line and add $\frac{1}{2}$.)

- Have students complete exercises 19–36. Review any incorrect answers. Ask:

- *Why do you think it's possible to divide a number by breaking it down into two parts and dividing them?* (Possible answer: because the two parts still equal the number, and anything you do to the two parts together is the same as doing it to the original number)

Multiplication Facts

Find each product.

1. $7 \times 8 =$ _____   **2.** $6 \times 9 =$ _____   **3.** $5 \times 7 =$ _____   **4.** $9 \times 8 =$ _____

Patterns

Complete each multiplication pattern.

5. 20, 40, 60, 80, _____   **6.** 50, 100, 150, 200, _____

7. 300, 600, 900, 1,200, _____   **8.** 700, 1,400, 2,100, 2,800, _____

Place Value

Write each number.

9.
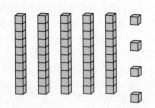

_____

10.
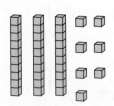

_____

11.
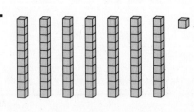

_____

Rounding

Choose the number that correctly completes each sentence.

12. When _____ is rounded to the nearest ten, it rounds to 70.

  57   67   76   79

13. When _____ is rounded to the nearest hundred, it rounds to 400.

  349   286   394   451

14. When _____ is rounded to the nearest thousand, it rounds to 6,000.

  5,137   6,477   4,985   5,324

Name_____

Expanded Form

Write each number in expanded form.

15. $4,512 = 4,000 + $ _____ $ + $ _____ $ + $ _____

16. $7,360 = $ _____ $ + $ _____ $ + $ _____ $ + $ _____

17. $5,063 = $ _____ $ + $ _____ $ + $ _____ $ + $ _____

18. $8,214 = $ _____ $ + $ _____ $ + $ _____ $ + $ _____

Multiplication Properties

Complete by writing the missing number.
Tell which property you used.

19. $4 \times 5 = 5 \times$ _____

_____ Property

20. $7 \times 0 = $ _____

_____ Property

21. $4 \times 12 = (4 \times$ _____ $) + (4 \times$ _____ $)$

_____ Property

Column Addition

Find each sum.

22.	**23.**	**24.**	**25.**
45	173	2,067	4,777
19	452	1,975	264
+ 8	+ 768	+ 4,849	+ 38

Assessment Goal

This two-page assessment covers skills identified as necessary for success in Chapter 9 Multiply by 1-Digit Numbers. The first page assesses the major prerequisite skills for Cluster A. The second page assesses the major prerequisite skills for Cluster B. When the Cluster A and Cluster B prerequisite skills overlap, the skill(s) will be covered in only one section.

Getting Started

- Allow students time to look over the two pages of the assessment. Point out the labels that identify the skills covered.

- Have students find math vocabulary terms used in the assessment. List vocabulary terms on the board as students identify them. If necessary, review the meanings of all essential math vocabulary.

Introducing the Assessment

- Explain to students that these pages will help you know if they are ready to start a new chapter in their math textbooks.

- Students who have transferred from another school may not have been introduced to some of these skills. Encourage students to do their best and assure them you will help them learn any needed skills.

Cluster A Challenge

Those students who demonstrate mastery of the skills on this page will not need to use the reteaching worksheets. Instead, these students can do the Cluster A Challenge found on pages 120-121.

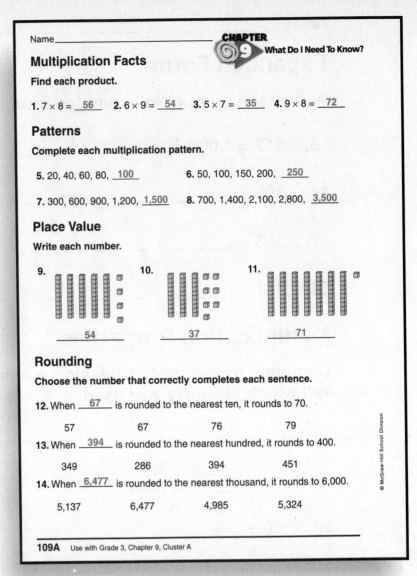

Name_____

CHAPTER 9 · What Do I Need To Know?

Multiplication Facts

Find each product.

1. $7 \times 8 =$ __56__   2. $6 \times 9 =$ __54__   3. $5 \times 7 =$ __35__   4. $9 \times 8 =$ __72__

Patterns

Complete each multiplication pattern.

5. 20, 40, 60, 80, __100__   6. 50, 100, 150, 200, __250__

7. 300, 600, 900, 1,200, __1,500__   8. 700, 1,400, 2,100, 2,800, __3,500__

Place Value

Write each number.

9. ____54____   10. ____37____   11. ____71____

Rounding

Choose the number that correctly completes each sentence.

12. When __67__ is rounded to the nearest ten, it rounds to 70.

   57   67   76   79

13. When __394__ is rounded to the nearest hundred, it rounds to 400.

   349   286   394   451

14. When __6,477__ is rounded to the nearest thousand, it rounds to 6,000.

   5,137   6,477   4,985   5,324

109A Use with Grade 3, Chapter 9, Cluster A

© McGraw-Hill School Division

CLUSTER A PREREQUISITE SKILLS

The skills listed in this chart are those identified as major prerequisite skills for students' success in the lessons in Cluster A of the chapter. Each skill is covered by one or more assessment items as shown in the middle column. The right column provides the page number for the lessons in this book that reteach the cluster A prerequisite skills.

Skill Name	Assessment Items	Lesson Pages
Multiplication Facts	1-4	110
Patterns	5-8	111
Place Value	9-11	112-113
Rounding	12-14	114-115

Name_____

Expanded Form

Write each number in expanded form.

15. $4,512 = 4,000 +$ _500_ $+$ _10_ $+$ _2_

16. $7,360 =$ _7,000_ $+$ _300_ $+$ _60_ $+$ _0_

17. $5,063 =$ _5,000_ $+$ _0_ $+$ _60_ $+$ _3_

18. $8,214 =$ _8,000_ $+$ _200_ $+$ _10_ $+$ _4_

Multiplication Properties

Complete by writing the missing number.
Tell which property you used.

19. $4 \times 5 = 5 \times$ _4_

Commutative Property

20. $7 \times 0 =$ _0_

Zero Property

21. $4 \times 12 = (4 \times \text{\_\_\_\_}) + (4 \times \text{\_\_\_\_})$

Distributive Property   Answers may vary. Possible answers: 10, 2

Column Addition

Find each sum.

22.	**23.**	**24.**	**25.**
45	173	2,067	4,777
19	452	1,975	264
+ 8	+ 768	+ 4,849	+ 38
72	1,393	8,891	5,079

© McGraw-Hill School Division

Use with Grade 3, Chapter 9, Cluster B   **109B**

CLUSTER B PREREQUISITE SKILLS

The skills listed in this chart are those identified as major prerequisite skills for students' success in the lessons in Cluster B of the chapter. Each skill is covered by one or more assessment items as shown in the middle column. The right column provides the page numbers for the lessons in this book that reteach the Cluster B prerequisite skills

Skill Name	Assessment Items	Lesson Pages
Expanded Form	15-18	116
Multiplication Properties	19-21	117
Column Addition	22-25	118-119

Alternative Assessment Strategies

- Oral administration of the assessment is appropriate for younger students or those whose native language is not English. Read the skills title and directions one section at a time. Check students' understanding by asking them to tell you how they will do the first exercise in the group.

- For some skill types you may wish to use group administration. In this technique, a small group or pair of students complete the assessment together. Through their discussion, you will be able to decide if supplementary reteaching materials are needed.

Intervention Materials

If students are not successful with the prerequisite skills assessed on these pages, reteaching lessons have been created to help them make the transition into the chapter.

Item correlation charts showing the skills lessons suitable for reteaching the prerequisite skills are found beneath the reproductions of each page of the assessment.

Cluster B Challenge

Those students who demonstrate mastery of the skills on this page will not need to use the reteaching worksheets. Instead, these students can do the Cluster B Challenge found on pages 122-123.

Lesson Goal

• Multiply using a times table or repeated addition.

What the Student Needs to Know

• Read a table.
• Add numbers in repetition.

Getting Started

Find out what students know about multiplication. Have them solve the following addition sentence: $3 + 3 + 3 + 3 =$ _____ (12). Ask:

• *How can this addition sentence be written as a multiplication fact?* ($4 \times 3 = 12$)

What Can I Do?

• Read the question and the response. Then read and discuss the example. Ask:

• *How can the example be written as a multiplication fact?* ($7 \times 8 = 56$)

• *How is a times table like an addition table? How are the two different?* (Both show you the results of performing an operation with two numbers. A times table shows multiplication, while an addition table shows addition.)

Try It

Have students complete exercises 1–6. Then have them demonstrate on a times table the correct answers to the multiplication sentences.

Power Practice

• Have students complete the practice items. Then review each answer. Be sure that students understand that repeated addition and using the times table should yield the same answer.

Name_____

Multiplication Facts

Learn

What Can I Do?
I want to multiply two numbers.

Use a Times Table
Example: To find 7 times 8, look across the 7 row until you are under the 8. The product is 56.

×	0	1	2	3	4	5	6	7	8	9	10
0	0	0	0	0	0	0	0	0	0	0	0
1	0	1	2	3	4	5	6	7	8	9	10
2	0	2	4	6	8	10	12	14	16	18	20
3	0	3	6	9	12	15	18	21	24	27	30
4	0	4	8	12	16	20	24	28	32	36	40
5	0	5	10	15	20	25	30	35	40	45	50
6	0	6	12	18	24	30	36	42	48	54	60
7	0	7	14	21	28	35	42	49	56	63	70
8	0	8	16	24	32	40	48	56	64	72	80
9	0	9	18	27	36	45	54	63	72	81	90
10	0	10	20	30	40	50	60	70	80	90	100

Try It • Adding can help you multiply. Complete each pair of problems to see how.

1. $5 + 5 + 5 =$ 15
   $3 \times 5 =$ 15

2. $9 + 9 =$ 18
   $2 \times 9 =$ 18

3. $2 + 2 + 2 + 2 =$ 8
   $4 \times 2 =$ 8

4. $6 + 6 + 6 + 6 =$ 24
   $4 \times 6 =$ 24

5. $7 + 7 + 7 =$ 21
   $3 \times 7 =$ 21

6. $8 + 8 =$ 16
   $2 \times 8 =$ 16

Power Practice • Multiply. Add or use the times table.

7. $6 \times 9 =$ 54   8. $7 \times 7 =$ 49   9. $8 \times 6 =$ 48   10. $8 \times 9 =$ 72

11. $4 \times 5 =$ 20   12. $4 \times 6 =$ 24   13. $4 \times 9 =$ 36   14. $7 \times 5 =$ 35

© McGraw-Hill School Division

110 Grade 3, Chapter 9, Cluster A

WHAT IF THE STUDENT CAN'T

Read a Table

• Use an addition table. Show the student how finding the intersection of a column and a row gives the sum of two numbers. Have the student practice writing addition sentences using the table.

• Illustrate how a times table works on the same principle, except that the results shown are based on multiplication instead of addition.

Add Numbers in Repetition

• Use counters to demonstrate repeated addition of a number. Show, for example, that $4 + 4 = 8$, $4 + 4 + 4 = 12$, and so on.

• Show the student how repeated addition can also be written as multiplication, so that $4 + 4 + 4 + 4 + 4 = 20$ becomes $5 \times 4 = 20$. Have the student practice converting examples of repeated addition into multiplication sentences until the student can do so with ease.

Complete the Power Practice

• Discuss each incorrect answer. Have the student show you the correct answer on the times table. Then have the student use repeated addition to demonstrate the correctness of the answer.

Name_____

Patterns

Learn

What Can I Do?
I want to complete a multiplication pattern.

Find the Factor

In this kind of pattern, the numbers 1, 2, 3, and so on are multiplied by the same factor. Find the factor.

60	120	180	240	?
↑	↑	↑	↑	↑
1×60	2×60	3×60	4×60	5×60

The factor is 60.
Since $5 \times 60 = 300$, the ? equals 300.

Try It • Make a pattern starting with each number. Multiply it by 2, 3, 4, 5.

1. 40, __80__, __120__, __160__, __200__   2. 90, __180__, __270__, __360__, __450__

3. 800; __1,600__; __2,400__; __3,200__; __4,000__

Power Practice • Complete each multiplication pattern.

4. 700; 1,400; 2,100; 2,800; __3,500__   5. 30, 60, 90, 120, __150__

6. 900; 1,800; 2,700; 3,600; __4,500__   7. 200, 400, 600, 800, __1,000__

8. 400; 800; 1,200; 1,600; __2,000__   9. 20, 40, 60, 80, __100__

© McGraw-Hill School Division

Grade 3, Chapter 9, Cluster A   **111**

WHAT IF THE STUDENT CAN'T

Multiply a Multiple of 10 or 100 by 2, 3, 4, or 5

- Use tens and hundreds models to show the student what happens when he or she multiplies a multiple of 10 or 100 by 2, 3, 4, or 5. Have the student count the ones in 3 sets of 2 tens models. Point out that he or she can use the basic fact $3 \times 2 = 6$ and write a zero after the 6 to get the same product. Have the student repeat the activity to show the product of 2, 3, 4, or 5 and various other multiples of 10 and 100.

Complete a Multiplication Pattern

- Show the student the following pattern: 2, 4, 6, 8. Explain

that each number in the pattern is a multiple of 2, and that each number is 2 greater than the one before it. Have the student predict the next number in the pattern. Continue with patterns for the numbers 3 through 9 until the concept becomes clear.

- Have the student practice writing multiplication patterns for the numbers 2 through 9.

Complete the Power Practice

- Discuss each incorrect answer. Have the student multiply the factor by 5. Then have the student add the factor to the previous number in the pattern to check that the answer is correct.

Lesson Goal
- Complete multiplication patterns involving multiples of 10 and 100.

What the Student Needs to Know
- Multiply a multiple of 10 and 100 by 2, 3, 4, or 5.
- Complete a multiplication pattern.

Getting Started
Find out what students know about multiplication patterns. Have them complete the following patterns:
4, 8, 12, 16, ____ (20)
3, 6, 9, 12, ____ (15)
7, 14, 21, 28, ____ (35)

What Can I Do?
- Read the question and the response. Then read and discuss the example. Ask:
- *How do you know that the factor is 60?* (Because 60 is the greatest number that each number in the pattern can be divided by evenly. Each number in the pattern is 60 greater than the number before it.)
- *How could you use addition to find 5×60?* ($60 + 60 + 60 + 60 + 60$)

Try It
Have students complete exercises 1–3. Make sure they understand that the numbers in the pattern should increase by the same amount. Ask:
- *If you aren't sure that you have multiplied correctly for a number in the pattern, how can you check it?* (By adding the factor to the number before it in the pattern.)

Power Practice
- Have students complete exercises 4–9. Then review each answer.

Grade 3, Chapter 9, Cluster A   **111**

Lesson Goal

• Write the standard form of a number represented by place-value models.

What the Student Needs to Know

• Recognize tens and ones models.
• Recognize tens and ones digits in 2-digit numbers.

Getting Started

Ask students to think of a 2-digit number. Then ask:

• *How can you break this number into two addends, so that one number is a multiple of ten and the other one is a single digit?* (Possible answer: 53 can be broken down into 50 + 3.)

Have students use place-value models to show the two addends.

What Can I Do?

Read the question and the response. Then read and discuss the example. Ask:

• *How can you write 3 tens as a number?* (30)

• *How can you write 3 tens and 4 ones as an addition sentence?* (30 + 4 = 34)

• *If there were 3 more ones in the model, how would you write the number?* (37) *How many tens would there be?* (3) *How many ones?* (7)

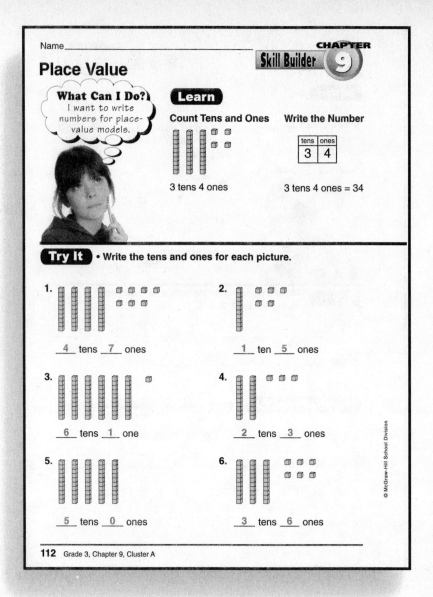

Place Value

What Can I Do? I want to write numbers for place-value models.

Learn

Count Tens and Ones

3 tens 4 ones

Write the Number

tens	ones
3	4

3 tens 4 ones = 34

Try It • Write the tens and ones for each picture.

1. __4__ tens __7__ ones

2. __1__ ten __5__ ones

3. __6__ tens __1__ one

4. __2__ tens __3__ ones

5. __5__ tens __0__ ones

6. __3__ tens __6__ ones

© McGraw-Hill School Division

112 Grade 3, Chapter 9, Cluster A

WHAT IF THE STUDENT CAN'T

Recognize Tens and Ones Models

• Use tens and ones models to illustrate a 2-digit number such as 25. Have the student count the ones and write down the number counted. Point out that the number consists of two numbers written together to show a greater number. Note that the left-hand digit shows how many tens are in the model and that the right-hand digit shows how many ones are used.

• Have the student draw models for 2-digit numbers using tens strips and squares. Each drawing should be labeled with the number, as well as a description of the number of tens and ones in each drawing.

Name_____

Write the tens and ones for each picture.

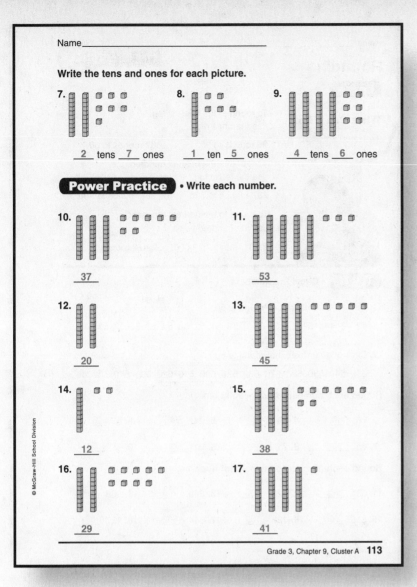

7. __2__ tens __7__ ones   8. __1__ ten __5__ ones   9. __4__ tens __6__ ones

Power Practice • Write each number.

10. __37__

11. __53__

12. __20__

13. __45__

14. __12__

15. __38__

16. __29__

17. __41__

Grade 3, Chapter 9, Cluster A   **113**

© McGraw-Hill School Division

Try It

• Have students look at exercise 1 and tell you the number of tens and ones shown.

• Be sure that students are able to identify the tens and ones in the model. If necessary, have students count out the number of ones in the model to demonstrate the correct answer.

Have students complete exercises 1–9. Ask:

• *Once you find out how many tens and ones are shown in a picture, how can you identify the two-digit number?* (Add the ones to the tens.)

• *If there are no ones in a picture, how do you write the two-digit number?* (Put a zero in the ones place and write the number of tens.)

Power Practice

• Select one of the exercises. Have students write a number sentence, adding the tens to the ones to arrive at the correct two-digit number.

• Have students complete exercises 10–17. Then review each answer.

WHAT IF THE STUDENT CAN'T

Recognize Tens and Ones Digits in 2-Digit Numbers

• Explain that the tens digit in a 2-digit number stands for tens. For example, a 5 in the tens place stands for 5 tens, or 50. Have the student write the standard number for 1 ten, 2 tens, 3 tens, and so on to 9 tens. Then have the student write the standard number for various numbers of tens and ones shown in a place-value chart.

Complete the Power Practice

• Discuss each incorrect answer. Have the student write an addition sentence for the model.

• If the student has difficulty arriving at the correct number of tens, use place-value models to demonstrate the correct answer.

Lesson Goal
- Round numbers to the nearest ten or hundred.

What the Student Needs to Know
- Count by tens.
- Count by hundreds and thousands.
- Understand place value to thousands.

Getting Started
Find out what students know about tens, hundreds, and thousands. Have them count by 10s to 100, 100s to 1,000, and 1,000s to 10,000. Ask:

- *When you count by 10s, 100s, and 1,000s, what happens to the first (left) digit of the numbers as you count?* (It increases by one.)
- *What happens to the other digits in the numbers?* (They remain zero.)

What Can I Do?
Read the question and the response. Then read and discuss the examples. Ask:

- *What does it mean to say that 26 rounds to 30?* (26 is closer to 30 than 20)
- *What does it mean to say that 302 rounds to 300?* (302 is closer to 300 than 400)
- *What does it mean to say that 3,472 rounds to 3,000?* (3,472 is closer to 3,000 than 4,000)
- *When a digit you are rounding is a 5, do you round up or down?* (up)

Name _____

Rounding

Learn

What Can I Do?
I want to round to the nearest ten or hundred.

To round to the nearest ten, use the ones digit.

26 rounds to 30.   32 rounds to 30.

To round to the nearest hundred, use the tens digit.

257 rounds to 300.   302 rounds to 300.

To round to the nearest thousand, use the hundreds digit.

2,901 rounds to 3,000.   3,472 rounds to 3,000.

Try It • Circle the numbers.

1. Circle the numbers that round to 50.

42 43 44 (45 46 47 48 49 50 51 52 53 54) 55 56 57 58

2. Circle the numbers that round to 600.

530 540 (550 560 570 580 590 600 610 620 630 640) 650 660

Round each number to the nearest ten.

3. 76 __80__   **4.** 36 __40__   **5.** 24 __20__   **6.** 57 __60__

7. 85 __90__   **8.** 71 __70__   **9.** 91 __90__   **10.** 65 __70__

Round each number to the nearest hundred.

11. 631 __600__   **12.** 923 __900__   **13.** 349 __300__   **14.** 558 __600__

15. 815 __800__   **16.** 128 __100__   **17.** 644 __600__   **18.** 157 __200__

WHAT IF THE STUDENT CAN'T

Count by Tens
- Have the student use tens models to illustrate the numbers that result when you count by ten. Then have the student write down the sequence of numbers.
- Have the student practice counting by 10s to 100 until it can be done with ease.

Count by Hundreds and Thousands
- Use models to represent hundreds and thousands. Have the student count the models by ones. Then explain what each model represents and have the student count again, this time identifying what is being counted as a hundred or as a thousand.
- Have the student practice counting by hundreds and thousands until it can be done with ease.

Name_____

Round each number to the nearest thousand.

19. 5,847 6,000   20. 9,349 9,000   21. 3,536 4,000

22. 7,518 8,000   23. 1,052 1,000   24. 8,642 9,000

Power Practice • Choose the numbers that correctly complete each sentence.

25. When 27 and 33 are rounded to the nearest ten, they round to 30.

    24   36   27   33

26. When 76 and 84 are rounded to the nearest ten, they round to 80.

    76   89   84   87

27. When 359 and 427 are rounded to the nearest hundred, they round to 400.

    348   359   427   472

28. When 671 and 734 are rounded to the nearest hundred, they round to 700.

    671   734   795   618

29. When 4,830 and 5,361 are rounded to the nearest thousand, they round to 5,000.

    5,912   4,830   4,215   5,361

30. When 1,531 and 2,438 are rounded to the nearest thousand, they round to 2,000.

    1,468   2,438   1,531   2,714

Grade 3, Chapter 9, Cluster A **115**

WHAT IF THE STUDENT CAN'T

Understand Place Value to Thousands

- Use thousands, hundreds, tens, and ones models to illustrate the concept of place value for a variety of numbers. Have the student write down the number of thousands, hundreds, tens, and ones. Then have the student write down the number being modeled.

- Have the student write down a list of 2-digit to 4-digit numbers. Then have the student practice breaking each number down by place value until the procedure becomes familiar.

Complete the Power Practice

- Discuss each incorrect answer. Have the student underline the digit to be used when rounding. Then have the student cross off all digits to the right of that digit.

- Have the student identify how to round each of the numbers in the exercise. Then have the student select the correct answer or answers.

USING THE LESSON

Try It

Have students look at exercises 1 and 2, and circle the appropriate numbers. Ask:

- *How many of the numbers round to 50?* (10) *How many round to 600?* (10)

Be sure students understand that 45 rounds to 50 but 55 does not, and that 550 rounds to 600 but 650 does not.

Select one exercise from exercises 3–10. Have students underline the digit that must be used to round the number, and then round the number. Then have them complete exercises 3–10. Do the same with exercises 11–18 and 19–24. Ask:

- *When you round a number to the nearest ten, hundred, or thousand, which digit do you look at?* (The digit in the place to the right of the place to which you are rounding. To round to the nearest ten, you look at the ones place; to the nearest hundred, the tens place; to the nearest thousand, the hundreds place.)

Power Practice

- Select one of the exercises and have a student explain how the correct answer or answers may be identified and the wrong answers eliminated.

- Have students complete the exercises. Then review each answer.

Lesson Goal

- Write 4-digit numbers in expanded form.

What the Student Needs to Know

- Understand place value through thousands.
- Add 1-digit through 4-digit numbers.

Getting Started

Write the following addition sentence on the board: 4,000 + 300 + 70 + 1 = _____ (4,371)

Have students complete the exercise. Then ask:

- *In your answer, what digit is in the thousands place? hundreds? tens? ones? (4, 3, 7, 1)*

What Can I Do?

- Read the question and the response. Then read and discuss the example. Ask:
- *What does it mean to write the expanded form of a number?* (Possible answer: To write it as an addition, with each addend representing the place value of one digit in the original number.)

Try It

Have the student write each number in expanded form. Ask:

- *What is a rule you can follow when you write the value of any digit in a number?* (Multiply the digit by its place value, so that, for example, a 6 in the hundreds place becomes 600.)

Power Practice

Have students complete the exercises. Then review each answer.

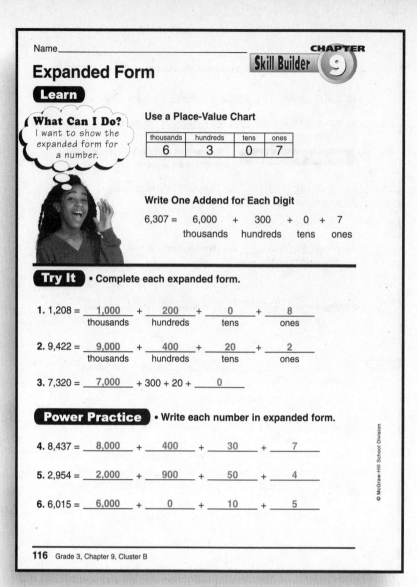

Name_____

Skill Builder CHAPTER 9

Expanded Form

Learn

What Can I Do?
I want to show the expanded form for a number.

Use a Place-Value Chart

thousands	hundreds	tens	ones
6	3	0	7

Write One Addend for Each Digit

6,307 =   6,000   +   300   + 0 + 7
         thousands hundreds tens ones

Try It • Complete each expanded form.

1. 1,208 = _1,000_ + _200_ + _0_ + _8_
         thousands hundreds tens ones

2. 9,422 = _9,000_ + _400_ + _20_ + _2_
         thousands hundreds tens ones

3. 7,320 = _7,000_ + 300 + 20 + _0_

Power Practice • Write each number in expanded form.

4. 8,437 = _8,000_ + _400_ + _30_ + _7_

5. 2,954 = _2,000_ + _900_ + _50_ + _4_

6. 6,015 = _6,000_ + _0_ + _10_ + _5_

116 Grade 3, Chapter 9, Cluster B

WHAT IF THE STUDENT CAN'T

Understand Place Value Through Thousands

- Have the student write the number 2,936 and then read it aloud. Explain that each digit can be seen as one place in a place-value chart. Then have the student tell you how many thousands, hundreds, tens, and ones are in the number. Be sure the student understands that each place can hold only one of the 10 digits 0–9.
- Have the student practice writing 4-digit numbers in a place-value chart until it can be done with ease.

Add 1-Digit through 4-Digit Numbers

- Have the student write and solve the following equation vertically: 5,000 + 800 + 30 + 6. Be sure the student aligns the numbers properly, and adds only the numbers in a given column. Have the student practice addition in both vertical and horizontal formats.

Complete the Power Practice

- For each incorrect part of the expanded form, have the student underline the corresponding digit in the original number and write the place value underneath the blank.

Multiplication Properties

Learn

What Can I Do?
I want to use properties of multiplication.

Property	What It Tells You
Commutative	You can multiply two numbers in either order.
Zero	Any number times zero is zero.
Distributive	You can break a product into the sum of two other products.

Try It • Use the Distributive Property to fill in the blanks.

1. $5 \times 43 = (5 \times 40) + (5 \times \underline{3})$ **2.** $4 \times 31 = (4 \times 30) + (\underline{4} \times 1)$

3. $9 \times 27 = (9 \times \underline{20}) + (9 \times 7)$ **4.** $8 \times 62 = (\underline{8} \times 60) + (8 \times 2)$

Power Practice • Complete by writing the missing number. Tell which property you used.

5. $5 \times 0 = \underline{0}$ _____ $\underline{Zero}$ _____ Property

6. $3 \times 26 = (3 \times \underline{20}) + (\underline{3} \times 6)$ $\underline{Distributive}$ Property

7. $6 \times 7 = 7 \times \underline{6}$ $\underline{Commutative}$ Property

8. $7 \times 18 = (7 \times \underline{10}) + (7 \times \underline{8})$ $\underline{Distributive}$ Property

© McGraw-Hill School Division

Grade 3, Chapter 9, Cluster B **117**

WHAT IF THE STUDENT CAN'T

Multiply a 2-Digit Number by a 1-Digit Number

• Check that students have mastered multiplication facts. Use models to demonstrate finding products of greater numbers. Then have the student do the same. Finally, have the student use the algorithm. Check that the student regroups ones if necessary and remembers to add the regrouped ten(s).

Break a 2-Digit Number Down by Place Value

• Use place-value models to illustrate how a 2-digit number can be seen as the sum of its tens and its ones. For each

number, have the student identify the number of tens and of ones.

• Have the student practice writing 2-digit numbers in expanded form until he or she can do so automatically.

Complete the Power Practice

• For each incorrect property identification, draw the student's attention to the characteristic feature of the mathematics statement: an inversion of order, a zero, or an expansion of the 2-digit number as the sum of two products. Then have the student give a new answer based on this feature.

Lesson Goal

• Understand properties of multiplication.

What the Student Needs to Know

• Multiply a 2-digit number by a 1-digit number.

• Break a 2-digit number down by place value.

Getting Started

Write the following on the board:

$7 \times 6 =$ ____ ; $6 \times 7 =$ ____ (42)

$4 \times 0 =$ ____ ; $9 \times 0 =$ ____ (0)

$3 \times 12 =$ ____ ; $(3 \times 10) + (3 \times 2) =$ ____ (36)

Have students complete the exercises. Ask:

• *What do you notice about each pair of exercises?* (Both have the same answer.)

What Can I Do?

• Read the question. Then introduce the three properties being studied. Relate each property to a pair on the board. Then ask:

• *According to the Commutative Property of Multiplication, $9 \times 4 = 4 \times$ ____ ?* (9)

• *According to the Zero Property of Multiplication, does $2 \times 0 = 7{,}292 \times 0$?* (Yes)

Try It

Have students look at exercises 1 and 2. Ask:

• *According to the Distributive Property, how can you find the number that belongs in the blank in exercise 1?* (Subtract 40 from 43.) *in exercise 2?* (Take the number that 31 is being multiplied by.)

Have students complete exercises 1–4.

Power Practice

• Have students complete the practice items. Then review each answer.

USING THE LESSON

Lesson Goal
- Add three 1-, 2-, 3-, or 4-digit numbers in vertical form.

What the Student Needs to Know
- Add 1-, 2-, 3-, or 4-digit numbers.
- Understand place value through thousands.

Getting Started
- Write the following problem on the board in vertical form: 7 + 4. Have students add. (11) Then write the problem 11 + 3 on the board in vertical form. Have the students add. (14) Ask:
- How could you write these two addition problems as one addition problem? (Students might suggest writing the three addends, 7, 4, and 11, in a column.)
- Write the problem 7 + 4 + 3 on the board in vertical form. Have students add the numbers, two at a time, and compare their result to the sum of 11 + 3. (Both have the same sum, 14.)
- *When you add three numbers, does it make any difference in what order you add them?* (No)

What Can I Do?
Read the question and the response. Then read and discuss the example. Say:
- *If the sum of the first column is 15, what number goes in the ones place?* (5) *What number is added to the tens column?* (1)
- *What is the sum of the tens column?* (10) *How do you write this in the answer?* (Put a zero in the tens place, add one to the hundreds column.)
- *What is the sum of the hundreds column?* (7) *If the sum were 12, how would you write it?* (Put a two in the hundreds place, and create a thousands place to put a one in.)

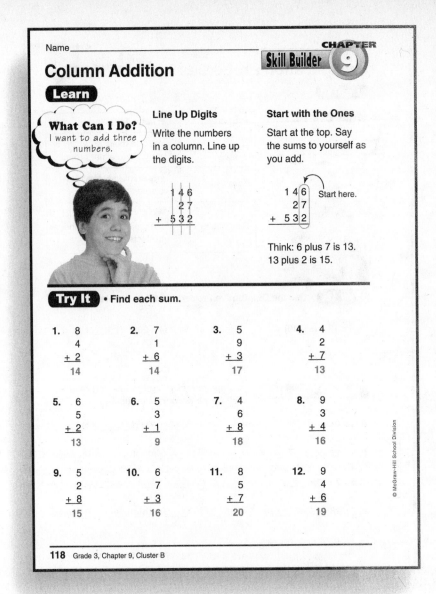

Column Addition

Learn

What Can I Do?
I want to add three numbers.

Line Up Digits
Write the numbers in a column. Line up the digits.

```
  1 4 6
    2 7
+ 5 3 2
```

Start with the Ones
Start at the top. Say the sums to yourself as you add.

```
  1 4 6    Start here.
    2 7
+ 5 3 2
```

Think: 6 plus 7 is 13.
13 plus 2 is 15.

Try It • Find each sum.

1. 8 4 + 2 14	2. 7 1 + 6 14	3. 5 9 + 3 17	4. 4 2 + 7 13
5. 6 5 + 2 13	6. 5 3 + 1 9	7. 4 6 + 8 18	8. 9 3 + 4 16
9. 5 2 + 8 15	10. 6 7 + 3 16	11. 8 5 + 7 20	12. 9 4 + 6 19

© McGraw-Hill School Division

WHAT IF THE STUDENT CAN'T

Add 1-, 2-, 3-, or 4-Digit Numbers
- Use place-value models to illustrate how two 4-digit numbers can be added. Demonstrate regrouping by trading 10 ones for 1 ten, 10 tens for 1 hundred, and 10 hundreds for 1 thousand. Then give the student pairs of 4-digit numbers to add using models.
- Have the student practice adding 4-digit numbers to numbers of 1 to 4 digits until the student can do so with ease.

Understand Place Value Through Thousands
- Have the student write a 4-digit number and read it aloud. Point out that each digit occupies one place in the number. Have the student tell you how many thousands, hundreds, tens, and ones are in the number. If necessary, let the student refer to a place-value chart for help.
- Have the student practice writing 3-digit and 4-digit numbers in a place-value chart until it can be done with ease.

Name_____

The ones are done for you. Finish each problem.

13.	25	14.	59	15.	87	16.	29
	83		43		63		93
	+ 32		+ 72		+ 54		+ 38
	140		174		204		160

17.	56	18.	38	19.	6	20.	15
	17		6		52		87
	+ 4		+ 81		+ 48		+ 6
	77		125		106		108

Power Practice • Find each sum.

21.	58	22.	63
	9		147
	+ 72		+ 41
	139		251

23.	368	24.	413
	210		67
	+ 512		+ 529
	1,090		1,009

25.	2,158	26.	6,215
	1,749		4,670
	+ 5,321		+ 1,912
	9,228		12,797

27.	802	28.	5,106
	157		853
	+ 4,016		+ 29
	4,975		5,988

Learn with Partners & Parents

Three Number Addition

Two or three players can play.

* Take turns. Each player names a three-digit or a four-digit number until three numbers are named.
* Write down each number as it is named. Add the three numbers.
* The first player to get the correct sum wins one point.
* Play until one player has 11 points.

© McGraw-Hill School Division

Grade 3, Chapter 9, Cluster B **119**

USING THE LESSON

Try It

Have students look at exercise 1. Have them write the sum of the first two numbers (12) before adding the third. Have students use counters to illustrate the correct answer. Then have students complete exercises 1–12. For each incorrect answer, have them use counters to demonstrate the correct sum.

Then have students complete exercises 13–20. For each incorrect answer, have them use counters to demonstrate the correct sum of the tens column.

Power Practice

* Select a few of the exercises and have students add the numbers one by one to show the correct answer.
* Have students complete the practice exercises. Then review each answer.

Learn with Partners & Parents

* Players may want to extend the game to adding four numbers that are 3– and 4–digit numbers, or to include 5–digit numbers as well.

WHAT IF THE STUDENT CAN'T

* Have the student write a 3-digit number and a 4-digit number. Ask the student to describe each number in terms of place values. Then have the student write the numbers in a vertical addition problem. Be sure the student understands that each column of number corresponds to a place value.

Complete the Power Practice

* For each incorrect answer, have the student identify each addend in terms of place value. Then have the student add or use counters to arrive at the correct answer one digit at a time.

CHALLENGE

Lesson Goal

- Find the factors of composite numbers and identify prime numbers.

Introducing the Challenge

Introduce students to the following vocabulary.

product: the result you get when you multiply two numbers together

whole number: a number that is not a fraction or a decimal

Find out what students know about multiplication and factors. Write the following on the board:
$6 \times 1 = 6$. Ask:

- *Are there any other whole numbers you can multiply to get 6?* (3 and 2)

Next write the following on the board: $5 \times 1 = 5$. Ask:

- *Are there any other whole numbers you can multiply to get 5?* (No)

Have students read the introduction to the challenge. Then have them identify all the factors of 24. Ask:

- *How do you know that 20 is not a factor of 24?* (Because you can't multiply 20 by another whole number to get 24.)

Factors and Primes

The number 24 can be written as a product of whole numbers in four different ways. The numbers being multiplied are the factors. There are eight different factors of 24.

$24 = 1 \times 24 \qquad 24 = 3 \times 8$
$24 = 2 \times 12 \qquad 24 = 4 \times 6$

Complete to show each number as the product of different factors.

1. $12 = 1 \times \underline{12}$ 2. $18 = 1 \times \underline{18}$ 3. $20 = 1 \times \underline{20}$
  $12 = 2 \times \underline{6}$ $18 = 2 \times \underline{9}$ $20 = 2 \times \underline{10}$
  $12 = 3 \times \underline{4}$ $18 = 3 \times \underline{6}$ $20 = 4 \times \underline{5}$

4. $30 = 1 \times \underline{30}$ 5. $36 = 1 \times \underline{36}$ 6. $40 = 1 \times \underline{40}$
  $30 = 2 \times \underline{15}$ $36 = 2 \times \underline{18}$ $40 = 2 \times \underline{20}$
  $30 = 3 \times \underline{10}$ $36 = 3 \times \underline{12}$ $40 = 4 \times \underline{10}$
  $30 = 5 \times \underline{6}$ $36 = 4 \times \underline{9}$ $40 = 5 \times \underline{8}$
                                     $36 = 6 \times \underline{6}$

Write all the different factors for each number.

7. 12   1, 2, 3, 4, 6, 12   8. 18   1, 2, 3, 6, 9, 18

9. 20   1, 2, 4, 5, 10, 20   10. 30   1, 2, 3, 5, 6, 10, 15, 30

11. 36   1, 2, 3, 4, 6, 9, 12, 18, 36   12. 40   1, 2, 4, 5, 8, 10, 20, 40

Name _____

Sample answers are given for 22, 26, 28, 30, 34, 38, 40, 42.
Try to write each number as two different products.
Circle the numbers for which this is not possible.

13. ③ = __1 × 3__ = _____   14. 4 = __1 × 4__ = __2 × 2__

15. ⑤ = __1 × 5__ = _____   16. 6 = __1 × 6__ = __2 × 3__

17. ⑦ = __1 × 7__ = _____   18. 8 = __1 × 8__ = __2 × 4__

19. 9 = __1 × 9__ = __3 × 3__   20. 10 = __1 × 10__ = __2 × 5__

21. ⑪ = __1 × 11__ = _____   22. 12 = __1 × 12__ = __2 × 6__

23. ⑬ = __1 × 13__ = _____   24. 14 = __1 × 14__ = __2 × 7__

25. 15 = __1 × 15__ = __3 × 5__   26. 16 = __1 × 16__ = __2 × 8__

27. ⑰ = __1 × 17__ = _____   28. 18 = __1 × 18__ = __2 × 9__

29. ⑲ = __1 × 19__ = _____   30. 20 = __1 × 4__ = __2 × 10__

31. 21 = __1 × 21__ = __3 × 7__   32. 22 = __1 × 22__ = __2 × 11__

33. ㉓ = __1 × 23__ = _____   34. 24 = __1 × 24__ = __2 × 12__

35. 25 = __1 × 25__ = __5 × 5__   36. 26 = __1 × 26__ = __2 × 13__

37. 27 = __1 × 27__ = __3 × 9__   38. 28 = __1 × 28__ = __2 × 14__

39. ㉙ = __1 × 29__ = _____   40. 30 = __1 × 30__ = __2 × 15__

41. ㉛ = __1 × 31__ = _____   42. 32 = __1 × 32__ = __2 × 16__

43. The circled numbers are called *prime numbers*. They have
only two factors, themselves and the number 1. What are
the next two prime numbers? __37 and 41__

© McGraw-Hill School Division

CHALLENGE

Using the Challenge

Have students complete exercises 1 through 12. Ask:

- *If you know one factor of a number, how can you find another factor?* (Divide the number by the factor you know.)

- *If one of the factors in a multiplication sentence is 1 and the other factor is not 1, what is the product?* (the other factor)

- *Which of the numbers in exercises 1-6 has the most factors?* (36)

Have students complete exercises 13–42. Ask:

- *What number is a factor of all of these numbers?* (1)

- *What number is a factor of all even numbers?* (2)

- *What number is a factor of all numbers that end in 5 or 0?* (5)

- *Of the numbers you have circled, how many are in the left column?* (10) *How many are in the right column?* (0)

Have students look at exercise 43. Ask:

- *Is it possible for an even number greater than 2 to be a prime number?* (No.) *Why or why not?* (Because an even number greater than 2 will have more than two factors.)

Have students complete the exercise. Then have students explain why the numbers from 33 to 36 and from 38 to 40 are not prime numbers.

CHALLENGE

Lesson Goal
- Square and cube numbers from 1 to 20, and 30.

Introducing the Challenge
Introduce students to the following vocabulary.

square: 1. a geometric figure with four equal sides and four right angles; 2. to multiply a number by itself

cube: 1. a 3-dimensional geometric figure with 6 square faces; 2. to multiply a number by itself three times

Have students read the introduction to the first page of the Challenge. Then read and discuss the example. Ask:

- *What is the area of the square shown?* (25 square units)

Have students complete exercises 1, 2, and 3. Have them draw squares with the dimensions given by each multiplication sentence. Then have students complete exercises 4–6.

Using the Challenge
Have students look at exercise 7. Have them write the exercise out as a multiplication equation before solving it. Then have them go on to complete exercises 8–24. Ask:

- *As the numbers increase, what happens to their squares?* (They also increase.)

- *What is the difference between square of 4 and the square of 3?* (7)

- *What is the difference between the square of 10 and the square of 9?* (19)

Name _____

CHALLENGE CHAPTER **9**

Squares and Cubes

To square a number means to multiply it by itself. The area of a square is a square number.

$5 \times 5 = 25$
25 is a square number.

Find each square.

1. $1 \times 1 =$ __1__   2. $2 \times 2 =$ __4__   3. $3 \times 3 =$ __9__

4. $10 \times 10 =$ __100__   5. $20 \times 20 =$ __400__   6. $30 \times 30 =$ __900__

Square each number.

7. 3 squared __9__   8. 4 squared __16__   9. 5 squared __25__

10. 6 squared __36__   11. 7 squared __49__   12. 8 squared __64__

13. 9 squared __81__   14. 10 squared __100__   15. 11 squared __121__

16. 12 squared __144__   17. 13 squared __169__   18. 14 squared __196__

19. 15 squared __225__   20. 16 squared __256__   21. 17 squared __289__

22. 18 squared __324__   23. 19 squared __361__   24. 20 squared __400__

25. The numbers 3, 4, and 5 are related because 3 squared plus 4 squared equals 5 squared. Find another set of three numbers for which this is true. Prove that your answer is right.

Possible answers: 6, 8, 10; 9, 12,15; 12, 16, 20; 5,12,13

6 x 6 = 36 and 8 x 8 = 64; 64 + 36 = 100 and

10 x 10 = 100. Similar proof may be given

for the other sets of numbers.

122 Grade 3, Chapter 9, Cluster B

Name _____

To cube a number means to multiply it by itself three times. The volume of a cube is a cubic number.

$5 \times 5 \times 5 =$
$25 \times 5 = 125$
125 is a cubic number.

Find each cube.

26. $1 \times 1 \times 1 =$ ___1___   **27.** $2 \times 2 \times 2 =$ ___8___   **28.** $3 \times 3 \times 3 =$ ___27___

Cube each number.

29. 2 cubed ___8___   **30.** 3 cubed ___27___

31. 4 cubed ___64___   **32.** 5 cubed ___125___

33. 6 cubed ___216___   **34.** 7 cubed ___343___

35. 8 cubed ___512___   **36.** 9 cubed ___729___

37. 10 cubed ___1,000___   **38.** 12 cubed ___1,728___

39. 20 cubed ___8,000___   **40.** 30 cubed ___27,000___

41. The number 1 is both a square and a cube. What is the next number for which this is true? Prove that your answer is right.

_____64; It equals 8 squared and 4 cubed._____

_____

_____

CHALLENGE

Have students look at exercise 25. Ask:

- *Will any three numbers in a row yield the same result?* (No.)
- *What is one way of preserving the special relation between these three numbers?* (Possible answer: doubling them)

Next, have students read the introduction to the second page of the challenge. Then read and discuss the example. Ask:

- *What is the volume of the cube shown?* (125 cubic units)
- *What is the relation between 5 squared and 5 cubed?* (5 cubed is 5 times as great as 5 squared)

Have students complete exercises 26–28 by finding the square of each number before going on to find its cube.

Have students look at exercise 29. Have them write it out as a multiplication equation before completing it. Then have students go on to complete exercises 30–40. Ask:

- *What is the difference between the cube of 4 and the cube of 3?* (37)
- *What is the difference between the cube of 10 and the cube of 9?* (271)
- *As the numbers increase, do their cubes increase more rapidly or more slowly than their squares increase?* (more rapidly)

Have the student complete exercise 41. Then review the answer. Ask:

- *Are numbers that are both squares and cubes common or rare?* (rare)

Name_____

Multiplying with Multiples of 10, 100, or 1,000

Find each product.

1.	40	2.	300	3.	6,000	4.	200
	× 6		× 7		× 5		× 9

Division with Remainders

Divide. Write the quotient and remainder.

5. 33 ÷ 8 = ____ R ____   **6.** 27 ÷ 4 = ____ R ____   **7.** 42 ÷ 9 = ____ R ____

 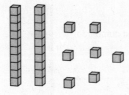

Subtraction

Find each difference.

8.	52	9.	70	10.	41	11.	80
	− 6		− 18		− 39		− 7

Closest Multiple

Find the closest multiple.

12. What multiple of 5 is closest to 21? _____

13. What multiple of 8 is closest to 58? _____

Division Facts

Find each quotient.

14. $63 \div 7 =$ _____   **15.** $81 \div 9 =$ _____

16. $48 \div 6 =$ _____   **17.** $56 \div 8 =$ _____

Multiplying by a 1-Digit Number

Find each product.

18. 46	**19.** 508	**20.** 683	**21.** $\$274$
$\times 2$	$\times 5$	$\times 3$	$\times 8$

22. $4 \times 230 =$ _____   **23.** $7 \times 315 =$ _____

24. $6 \times \$9.34 =$ _____   **25.** $9 \times \$2.70 =$ _____

Assessment Goal

This two-page assessment covers skills identified as necessary for success in Chapter 10 Divide by 1-Digit Numbers. The first page assesses the major prerequisite skills for Cluster A. The second page assesses the major prerequisite skills for Cluster B. When the Cluster A and Cluster B prerequisite skills overlap, the skill(s) will be covered in only one section.

Getting Started

• Allow students time to look over the two pages of the assessment. Point out the labels that identify the skills covered.

• Have students find math vocabulary terms used in the assessment. List vocabulary terms on the board as students identify them. If necessary, review the meanings of all essential math vocabulary.

Introducing the Assessment

• Explain to students that these pages will help you know if they are ready to start a new chapter in their math textbooks.

• Students who have transferred from another school may not have been introduced to some of these skills. Encourage students to do their best and assure them you will help them learn any needed skills.

Cluster A Challenge

Those students who demonstrate mastery of the skills on this page will not need to use the reteaching worksheets. Instead, these students can do the Cluster A Challenge found on pages 136-137.

Name_____

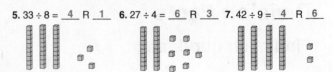
CHAPTER 10 What Do I Need To Know?

Multiplying with Multiples of 10, 100, or 1,000
Find each product.

1.	40	2.	300	3.	6,000	4.	200
	× 6		× 7		× 5		× 9
	240		2,100		30,000		1,800

Division with Remainders
Divide. Write the quotient and remainder.

5. $33 \div 8 =$ __4__ R __1__   6. $27 \div 4 =$ __6__ R __3__   7. $42 \div 9 =$ __4__ R __6__

Subtraction
Find each difference.

8.	52	9.	70	10.	41	11.	80
	− 6		− 18		− 39		− 7
	46		52		2		73

© McGraw-Hill School Division

123A   Use with Grade 3, Chapter 10, Cluster A

CLUSTER A PREREQUISITE SKILLS

The skills listed in this chart are those identified as major prerequisite skills for students' success in the lessons in Cluster A of the chapter. Each skill is covered by one or more assessment items as shown in the middle column. The right column provides the page number for the lessons in this book that reteach the cluster A prerequisite skills.

Skill Name	Assessment Items	Lesson Pages
Multiplying with Multiples of 10, 100, or 1,000	1-4	124-125
Division with Remainders	5-7	126-127
Subtraction	8-11	128

Name_____

Closest Multiple

Find the closest multiple.

12. What multiple of 5 is closest to 21?

13. What multiple of 8 is closest to 58? __56__

Division Facts

Find each quotient.

14. $63 \div 7 =$ __9__   15. $81 \div 9 =$ __9__

16. $48 \div 6 =$ __8__   17. $56 \div 8 =$ __7__

Multiplying by a 1-Digit Number

Find each product.

18.	46	19.	508	20.	683	21.	$274
	$\times 2$		$\times 5$		$\times 3$		$\times 8$
	92		2,540		2,049		$2,192

22. $4 \times 230 =$ __920__   23. $7 \times 315 =$ __2,205__

24. $6 \times \$9.34 =$ __$56.04__   25. $9 \times \$2.70 =$ __$24.30__

Use with Grade 3, Chapter 10, Cluster B   **123B**

CLUSTER B PREREQUISITE SKILLS

The skills listed in this chart are those identified as major prerequisite skills for students' success in the lessons in Cluster B of the chapter. Each skill is covered by one or more assessment items as shown in the middle column. The right column provides the page numbers for the lessons in this book that reteach the Cluster B prerequisite skills

Skill Name	Assessment Items	Lesson Pages
Closest Multiple	12-13	129
Division Facts	14-17	130-131
Multiplying a 2-Digit Number by a 1-Digit Number	18	132-133
Multiplying a 3-Digit Number by a 1-Digit Number	19-25	134-135

Alternative Assessment Strategies

- Oral administration of the assessment is appropriate for younger students or those whose native language is not English. Read the skills title and directions one section at a time. Check students' understanding by asking them to tell you how they will do the first exercise in the group.

- For some skill types you may wish to use group administration. In this technique, a small group or pair of students complete the assessment together. Through their discussion, you will be able to decide if supplementary reteaching materials are needed.

Intervention Materials

If students are not successful with the prerequisite skills assessed on these pages, reteaching lessons have been created to help them make the transition into the chapter.

Item correlation charts showing the skills lessons suitable for reteaching the prerequisite skills are found beneath the reproductions of each page of the assessment.

Cluster B Challenge

Those students who demonstrate mastery of the skills on this page will not need to use the reteaching worksheets. Instead, these students can do the Cluster B Challenge found on pages 138-139.

USING THE LESSON

Lesson Goal
- Multiply with multiples of 10, 100, or 1,000

What the Student Needs to Know
- Recall basic multiplication facts.
- Understand place value up to thousands.
- Multiply by 10, 100, and 1,000.

Getting Started
Have students solve the following two number sentences:

$8 \times 1 =$ ____ (8)

$8 \times 10 =$ ____ (80)

- Ask: *What is the relationship between the first answer and the second answer?* (Possible answers: The second answer is ten times more than the first answer; The second answer is the first answer with a zero attached.)

What Can I Do?
- Read the question and the response. Then read and discuss the example. Ask:
- *Which multiplication fact do you need to know to solve the problem?* ($5 \times 4 = 20$)
- *What do you have to know about place value to solve the problem?* (You have to know that 4,000 is the same as 4 thousands.)
- What would the answer be if the problem were $5 \times 3,000$? (15,000) $5 \times 5,000$? (25,000)

Multiplying with Multiples of 10, 100, or 1,000

Learn

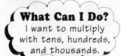

What Can I Do? I want to multiply with tens, hundreds, and thousands.

Use Place Value

$5 \times 4,000$
$= 5 \times 4$ thousands

Use the Basic Fact

5×4 thousands
$= 20$ thousands
$= 20,000$

Try It • Write each number in standard form.

1. 24 tens = __240__   2. 56 hundreds = __5,600__   3. 63 thousands = __63,000__

4. 18 tens = __180__   5. 30 hundreds = __3,000__   6. 12 thousands = __12,000__

7. 35 tens = __350__   8. 14 hundreds = __1,400__   9. 45 thousands = __45,000__

Complete the steps to find each product.

10. 3×80 11. 7×400 12. $6 \times 3,000$

$= 3 \times$ __8__ tens $= 7 \times$ __4__ hundreds $= 6 \times$ __3__ thousands

$=$ __24__ tens $=$ __28__ hundreds $=$ __18__ thousands

$=$ __240__ $=$ __2,800__ $=$ __18,000__

124   Grade 3, Chapter 10, Cluster A

WHAT IF THE STUDENT CAN'T

Recall Basic Multiplication Facts
- Use counters or models to demonstrate the products of multiplying two 1-digit numbers. Then have the student do the same.
- Have the student write multiplication facts on flash cards and practice until they can be recalled with ease.

Understand Place Value through the Thousands
- Have the student practice writing 2-digit through 4-digit numbers in a place value chart and reading them aloud until it can be done

with ease. Be sure the student understands that each place value must have a single digit from 0 to 9.
- Have the student write down the following numbers in place value and standard forms: *3 tens* (30); *4 thousands* (4,000); *7 hundreds* (700); *6 tens* (600); *4 hundreds* (400); *8 thousands* (8,000). Be sure the student understands that a place value that isn't specified can be assumed to have a value of 0.

Use the basic fact to write each product.

13. $4 \times 6 = 24$

$4 \times 60 =$ __240__

14. $7 \times 9 = 63$

$7 \times 900 =$ __6,300__

15. $5 \times 8 = 40$

$5 \times 8,000 =$ __40,000__

16. $3 \times 9 = 27$

$3 \times 90 =$ __270__

17. $6 \times 5 = 30$

$6 \times 500 =$ __3,000__

18. $2 \times 6 = 12$

$2 \times 6,000 =$ __12,000__

19. $6 \times 7 =$ __42__

$6 \times 70 =$ __420__

20. $8 \times 3 =$ __24__

$8 \times 300 =$ __2,400__

21. $4 \times 5 =$ __20__

$4 \times 5,000 =$ __20,000__

22. $5 \times 3 =$ __15__

$5 \times 30 =$ __150__

23. $9 \times 2 =$ __18__

$9 \times 200 =$ __1,800__

24. $8 \times 8 =$ __64__

$8 \times 8,000 =$ __64,000__

Power Practice • Find each product.

25. 800
$\underline{\times\ 9}$
$7,200$

26. 70
$\underline{\times\ 7}$
490

27. $4,000$
$\underline{\times\ 3}$
$12,000$

28. 60
$\underline{\times\ 8}$
480

29. 50
$\underline{\times\ 4}$
200

30. $8,000$
$\underline{\times\ 4}$
$32,000$

31. 600
$\underline{\times\ 6}$
$3,600$

27. $2,000$
$\underline{\times\ 6}$
$12,000$

33. 900
$\underline{\times\ 5}$
$4,500$

34. 30
$\underline{\times\ 4}$
120

35. $7,000$
$\underline{\times\ 8}$
$56,000$

36. 90
$\underline{\times\ 7}$
630

37. $7,000$
$\underline{\times\ 6}$
$42,000$

38. 900
$\underline{\times\ 9}$
$8,100$

39. 50
$\underline{\times\ 2}$
100

40. 500
$\underline{\times\ 6}$
$3,000$

WHAT IF THE STUDENT CAN'T

Multiply by 10, 100, and 1,000

- Use grids, grid strips, and cubes to model multiplication sentences that include these numbers. Show the student how a number may be multiplied by 10, 100, or 1,000 by attaching one, two, or three zeros to the original number. For example, $13 \times 10 = 130$; $13 \times 100 = 1,300$; and $13 \times 1,000 = 13,000$.

- Have the student practice multiplying by 10, 100, and 1,000 until the procedure becomes familiar.

Complete the Power Practice

- Discuss each incorrect answer. Have the student identify the multiplication fact central to the problem. Then have the student describe the first factor in terms of place value. Finally, have the student use words to describe the answer in terms of place value before converting it to standard form.

USING THE LESSON

Try It

Have the students look at exercises 1–3. Make sure students understand that to write each number in standard form, they must multiply the 2-digit number by its place value. For example, 24 tens = 24 × 10 = 240. If students are not comfortable multiplying, have them write the number out in a place-value chart. For example, 24 tens becomes 2 hundreds, 4 tens, and 0 ones, or 240. Then have the students complete the exercises. Ask:

- *What is a quick way to write 27 tens in standard form?* (Add a zero to the end of 27 to get 270.) *27 hundreds in standard form?* (Add two zeros to the end of 27 to get 2,700.) *27 thousands in standard form?* (Add three zeros to the end of 27 to get 27,000.)

Have students look at exercise 10. Be sure they understand how to rewrite 80 as 8 tens to facilitate multiplication. Then have the students complete exercises 10–15.

Have the students look at exercises 16–18. Be sure they understand how to name the second factor in the second number sentence in terms of its place values: 90 = 9 tens; 500 = 5 hundreds; and 6,000 = 6 thousands.

Power Practice

- Have students complete the practice exercises. Then review each answer.

- Select several of the exercises and have students identify the multiplication fact central to each problem.

USING THE LESSON

Lesson Goal
- Divide a 2-digit number by a 1-digit number when the quotient includes a remainder

What the Student Needs to Know
- Recall basic division facts.
- Understand how multiplication and division are related.

Getting Started
Find out what the students know about division. Write the following division sentences on the board:

$8 \div 2$ $9 \div 2$ $10 \div 2$

Ask:
- *Which of these division sentences will give you a whole number as a quotient?* (8 ÷ 2; 10 ÷ 2)
- *Which of these division sentences will not give you a whole number as a quotient?* (9 ÷ 2)
- *What do you call the number that is left after the division?* (the remainder)

What Can I Do?
- Read the question and the response. Then read and discuss the example. Ask:
- *What does "the largest possible quotient" mean?* (It means the greatest number of times that the divisor can go into the number being divided.)
- *How do you know that 7 is the largest possible quotient?* (Because 7 × 6 = 42, which is less than 45, but 8 × 6 = 48, which is greater than 45.)
- *Why do you have to make sure that the remainder is less than the divisor?* (Because if the remainder is greater than the divisor, it means that the divisor can go into the number being divided at least one more time, and that you haven't found the largest possible quotient.)

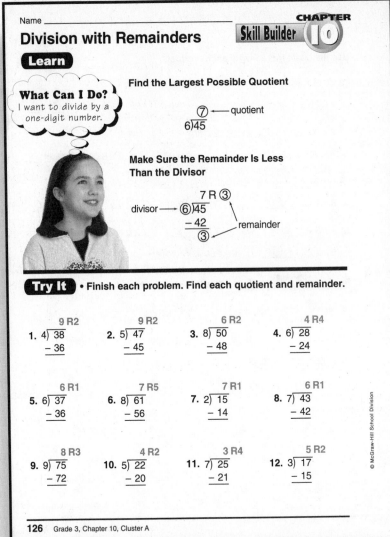

WHAT IF THE STUDENT CAN'T

Recall Basic Division Facts
- Use counters to demonstrate how one number may be divided into equal groups. For example, 14 may be divided into 2 groups of 7, and 20 may be divided into 2 groups of 10 or 4 groups of 5. Then have the student use counters to illustrate the division of other two-digit numbers.
- Have the student practice completing division number sentences with 1-digit divisors until this can be done with ease.

Understand How Multiplication and Division Are Related
- Use counters to demonstrate how multiplication may be used to arrive at a certain product. For example, 6 groups of 7 will give you a product of 42. Then show how this operation may be turned around, so that 42 may be divided into 6 groups of 7.
- Have the student use counters to illustrate multiplication sentences and their division counterparts.
- Have the student practice turning multiplication sen-

Name _____

Power Practice • Write the remainder and the quotient.

13. 37 ÷ 7 = ___5___ R ___2___   **14.** 26 ÷ 3 = ___8___ R ___2___

15. 34 ÷ 5 = ___6___ R ___4___   **16.** 62 ÷ 9 = ___6___ R ___8___

17. 11 ÷ 2 = ___5___ R ___1___

18. 40 ÷ 6 = ___6___ R ___4___

19. 44 ÷ 8 = ___5___ R ___4___

20. 29 ÷ 4 = ___7___ R ___1___

Learn with Partners & Parents

Division Roll

You will need three 1–6 number cubes.

- Roll the cubes. Use the numbers to make two different division problems like this:

☐ ☐ ÷ ☐

- Find the quotient and remainder for each problem you make.

- Roll again. Find the problems with the largest and smallest quotients.

- Roll to get three different digits. Write all six division problems you can make with these digits.

WHAT IF THE STUDENT CAN'T

tences into division sentences, and division sentences into multiplication sentences, until the student can do so with ease.

Complete the Power Practice

- Discuss each incorrect answer. Have the student demonstrate why the quotient given is the largest possible and identify the remainder. Then have the student check the correctness of the remainder by multiplying the divisor by the quotient and adding the remainder to it. The result should be the number being divided.

USING THE LESSON

Try It

- Have the students look at exercise 1. Ask:
- *What should the number be in the quotient?* (9)
- *Why is it the largest possible quotient?* (because 9 × 4 = 36, which is less than 38, but 10 × 4 = 40, which is greater than 38)
- *What is the remainder?* (2)
- *How can you check that this is the correct remainder?* (Check to be sure it is less than the divisor. Then multiply the quotient by the divisor and add the remainder. The number should be equal to the number being divided.)
- Have the students complete the remaining exercises.

Power Practice

- Have a volunteer write exercise 13 on the chalk board as a long division equation. Then have students complete the equation, demonstrating why the quotient is the largest possible and that the remainder is the correct one.
- Have students complete the exercises 14–20. Then review each answer.

Learn with Partners & Parents

- Partners should experiment with many different pairs of numbers for the dividends. If they roll a 3,4, and 7, they should see how many different dividends they can make from any two of the three.
- Ask: *To get a large quotient, what must you have for the divisor?* (a very low divisor) *To get a very low quotient, what must be true of the divisor?* (It must be a very high number.)

Lesson Goal
• Subtract 2-digit whole numbers, regrouping when necessary

What the Student Needs to Know
• Recall basic subtraction facts.
• Understand place value up to tens.

Getting Started
Find out what students know about regrouping. Write the following number in a place value chart on the chalkboard:

tens	ones
7	2

Ask:
• *What number is shown in the place value chart?* (72)
• *If you convert one of the tens to ones, how many ones will there be?* (10 + 2 = 12 ones)

What Can I Do?
• Read the question and the response. Then discuss the example. Ask:
• *Why is the number 53 regrouped as 4 in the tens column and 13 in the ones column?* (Because the top number in the ones column needs to be higher than the bottom number in order to subtract.)
• *When you regroup one of the 5 tens, how many tens are left?* (4)

Try It
Have students look at exercise 1 and tell you what to do to find the answer. Be sure they understand that regrouping means that the tens digit in the first number will be reduced by one. Then have them complete exercises 2–5.

Power Practice
• Have the students complete the practice items. Then review each answer.

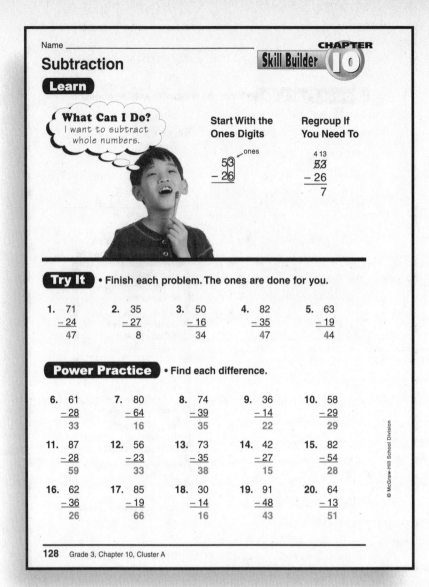

Name _____

Subtraction

Learn

What Can I Do? I want to subtract whole numbers.

Start With the Ones Digits

$$\begin{array}{r} 5\overset{}{3} \\ - 2\overset{}{6} \end{array}$$ ones

Regroup If You Need To

$$\begin{array}{r} {}^{4\ 13} \\ \cancel{5}\cancel{3} \\ - 2\ 6 \\ \hline 7 \end{array}$$

Try It • Finish each problem. The ones are done for you.

1. $\begin{array}{r} 71 \\ -24 \\ \hline 47 \end{array}$ 2. $\begin{array}{r} 35 \\ -27 \\ \hline 8 \end{array}$ 3. $\begin{array}{r} 50 \\ -16 \\ \hline 34 \end{array}$ 4. $\begin{array}{r} 82 \\ -35 \\ \hline 47 \end{array}$ 5. $\begin{array}{r} 63 \\ -19 \\ \hline 44 \end{array}$

Power Practice • Find each difference.

6. $\begin{array}{r} 61 \\ -28 \\ \hline 33 \end{array}$ 7. $\begin{array}{r} 80 \\ -64 \\ \hline 16 \end{array}$ 8. $\begin{array}{r} 74 \\ -39 \\ \hline 35 \end{array}$ 9. $\begin{array}{r} 36 \\ -14 \\ \hline 22 \end{array}$ 10. $\begin{array}{r} 58 \\ -29 \\ \hline 29 \end{array}$

11. $\begin{array}{r} 87 \\ -28 \\ \hline 59 \end{array}$ 12. $\begin{array}{r} 56 \\ -23 \\ \hline 33 \end{array}$ 13. $\begin{array}{r} 73 \\ -35 \\ \hline 38 \end{array}$ 14. $\begin{array}{r} 42 \\ -27 \\ \hline 15 \end{array}$ 15. $\begin{array}{r} 82 \\ -54 \\ \hline 28 \end{array}$

16. $\begin{array}{r} 62 \\ -36 \\ \hline 26 \end{array}$ 17. $\begin{array}{r} 85 \\ -19 \\ \hline 66 \end{array}$ 18. $\begin{array}{r} 30 \\ -14 \\ \hline 16 \end{array}$ 19. $\begin{array}{r} 91 \\ -48 \\ \hline 43 \end{array}$ 20. $\begin{array}{r} 64 \\ -13 \\ \hline 51 \end{array}$

128 Grade 3, Chapter 10, Cluster A

WHAT IF THE STUDENT CAN'T

Recall Basic Subtraction Facts
• Use counters to illustrate subtraction facts. Have the student write a number sentence for each subtraction fact as you demonstrate it.
• Have the student practice completing subtraction sentences using counters and on paper until the student is able to do so with ease.

Understand Place Value up to Tens
• Have the student write a 2-digit number and read it aloud. Explain that each digit can be seen as one place in a place-value chart. Then have the student tell you how many tens and ones are in the number.
• Use grid strips and squares to illustrate how you can regroup in a place-value chart by taking a ten and breaking it into ones. Explain that this kind of regrouping is often necessary in subtracting.

Complete the Power Practice
• Discuss each incorrect answer. Have the student tell you whether regrouping is necessary in the problem. If so, have the student regroup appropriately. Then have the student subtract tens and ones.

Name _____

Closest Multiple

Learn

What Can I Do?
I want to find multiples close to a given number.

Use a List of Multiples

Example: What multiple of 5 is closest to 27?

Multiples of 5: 5, 10, 15, 20, 25, 30, 35, 40, 45, 50

Answer: 25

Try It • List the first ten multiples of each number.

1. 6 __12, 18, 24, 30, 36, 42, 48, 54, 60__

2. 7 __14, 21, 28, 35, 42, 49, 56, 63, 70__

3. 8 __16, 24, 32, 40, 48, 56, 64, 72, 80__

Power Practice • Write a multiple *less than* each number.

What multiple of 6 is closest to each number?

4. 55 __54__   **5.** 20 __18__   **6.** 39 __36__   **7.** 51 __48__   **8.** 25 __24__

What multiple of 7 is closest to each number?

9. 45 __42__   **10.** 30 __28__   **11.** 59 __56__   **12.** 23 __21__   **13.** 50 __49__

What multiple of 8 is closest to each number?

14. 43 __40__   **15.** 66 __64__   **16.** 73 __72__   **17.** 20 __16__   **18.** 35 __32__

© McGraw-Hill School Division

Grade 3, Chapter 10, Cluster B **129**

WHAT IF THE STUDENT CAN'T

Recall Basic Multiplication Facts

• Use counters or models to demonstrate the products of multiplying 6, 7, 8, and 9 by the numbers 1 through 10. Then have the student do the same.

• Have the student write multiplication facts for the numbers 6 through 9 on flash cards. Then have the student practice using the flash cards until the facts can be recalled with ease.

Compare Numbers as Greater Than and Less Than

• Have the student draw a number line from 0 to 10 and point to two numbers. Explain that the number to the right on the line is greater than the one to its left. This means that the number to the left is less than the number to the right.

Complete the Power Practice

• Discuss each incorrect answer with the student, correcting the error.

USING THE LESSON

Lesson Goal

• Find the multiple that is closest to another number

What the Student Needs to Know

• Recall basic multiplication facts.

• Compare numbers as greater than and less than.

Getting Started

Write the numbers from 0 to 20 on the board. Then have students tell you the first 5 multiples of 4 (4, 8, 12, 16, 20). Circle these numbers on the board. Ask:

• *What are the numbers between 0 and 4?* (1, 2, 3) *4 and 8?* (5, 6, 7) *8 and 12?* (9, 10, 11) *12 and 16?* (13, 14, 15) *16 and 20?* (17, 18, 19)

What Can I Do?

Read the question and the response. Then discuss the example. Ask:

• *How do you know that 25 is the multiple of 5 closest to 27?* (Because it is only 2 away from 27, but 30 is 3 away from 27.)

Try It

Look at exercises 1–4 with the students. For each number, have them say the first ten multiples aloud before writing multiples down.

Power Practice

• Be sure students understand that the multiple in each answer must be less than the number given. Then have the students complete the practice items. Review each answer.

Lesson Goal

• Practice division facts

What the Student Needs to Know

• Use a multiplication table.

• Understand how multiplication and division are related.

Getting Started

Find out what students know about the relationship between multiplication and division. Write the following number sentences on the board and have students complete them:

$3 \times 9 =$ _____ (27); $27 \div 3 =$ _____ (9)

$5 \times 4 =$ _____ (20); $20 \div 4 =$ _____ (5)

$8 \times 6 =$ _____ (48); $48 \div 6 =$ _____ (8)

• Say: *Each pair of number sentences uses only 3 numbers. The first number sentence uses the numbers for multiplication and the second uses them for division.*

• Ask: *If you divide the product of a multiplication sentence by one of its factors, what will the quotient be?* (the other factor)

What Can I Do?

• Read the question and the response. Then read and discuss the example. Ask:

• *How do you find the answer to 56 ÷ 8?* (Look across the 8-row until I find 56. Then I look to see the number at the tope of the column containing 56.)

• *How is using a multiplication table to find the answer to a division problem different from using it to find the answer to a multiplication problem?* (In a multiplication problem, you know the row and column and look to see where they meet. In a division problem, you know the row and the number in the table, and look to see what column the number is under.)

Try It

Have the students look at exercise 1. Read the multiplication sentence aloud. Ask:

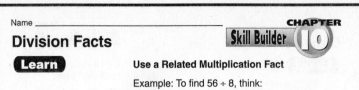

Division Facts

Learn

Use a Related Multiplication Fact

Example: To find 56 ÷ 8, think:
What number times 8 equals 56?

Since 7×8 is 56,
$56 \div 8$ is 7.

Use a Times Table

What Can I Do?
I want to practice the division facts.

×	0	1	2	3	4	5	6	7	8	9	10
0	0	0	0	0	0	0	0	0	0	0	0
1	0	1	2	3	4	5	6	7	8	9	10
2	0	2	4	6	8	10	12	14	16	18	20
3	0	3	6	9	12	15	18	21	24	27	30
4	0	4	8	12	16	20	24	28	32	36	40
5	0	5	10	15	20	25	30	35	40	45	50
6	0	6	12	18	24	30	36	42	48	54	60
7	0	7	14	21	28	35	42	49	56	63	70
8	0	8	16	24	32	40	48	56	64	72	80
9	0	9	18	27	36	45	54	63	72	81	90
10	0	10	20	30	40	50	60	70	80	90	100

Example: To find 56 ÷ 8, look across the 8 row until you get to 56. The answer, 7, is directly above the 56.

Try It • Use the related multiplication fact to write each quotient.

1. $6 \times 8 = 48$

$48 \div 6 =$ __8__

2. $6 \times 9 = 54$

$54 \div 9 =$ __6__

3. $7 \times 7 = 49$

$49 \div 7 =$ __7__

4. $4 \times 8 = 32$

$32 \div 8 =$ __4__

5. $9 \times 8 = 72$

$72 \div 8 =$ __9__

6. $5 \times 9 = 45$

$45 \div 5 =$ __9__

7. $7 \times 9 = 63$

$63 \div 7 =$ __9__

8. $5 \times 7 = 35$

$35 \div 5 =$ __7__

9. $8 \times 8 = 64$

$64 \div 8 =$ __8__

130 Grade 3, Chapter 10, Cluster B

WHAT IF THE STUDENT CAN'T

Use a Multiplication Table

• Have the student write a multiplication fact. On a multiplication table, highlight the two factors in the corresponding row and column. Then illustrate how finding the square where the row and column intersect gives their product.

• Have the student practice writing multiplication sentences using the table until the procedure becomes familiar and the student memorizes multiplication facts.

Understand How Multiplication and Division Are Related

• Use counters to demonstrate how multiplication may be used to arrive at a certain product. For example, 8 groups of 4 will give you a product of 32. Then show how this operation may be turned around, so that 32 may be divided into 8 groups of 4.

• Have the student use counters to illustrate multiplication sentences and their division counterparts.

• Have the student practice turning multiplication sen-

Name _____

Practice dividing by 7. Use the times table if you need help.

10. $49 \div 7 = \underline{7}$ 11. $35 \div 7 = \underline{5}$ 12. $28 \div 7 = \underline{4}$

13. $14 \div 7 = \underline{2}$ 14. $70 \div 7 = \underline{10}$ 15. $56 \div 7 = \underline{8}$

16. $63 \div 7 = \underline{9}$ 17. $21 \div 7 = \underline{3}$ 18. $42 \div 7 = \underline{6}$

Practice dividing by 8. Use the times table if you need help.

19. $72 \div 8 = \underline{9}$ 20. $32 \div 8 = \underline{4}$ 21. $16 \div 8 = \underline{2}$

22. $40 \div 8 = \underline{5}$ 23. $24 \div 8 = \underline{3}$ 24. $56 \div 8 = \underline{7}$

25. $8 \div 8 = \underline{1}$ 26. $64 \div 8 = \underline{8}$ 27. $48 \div 8 = \underline{6}$

Practice dividing by 9. Use the times table if you need help.

28. $45 \div 9 = \underline{5}$ 29. $18 \div 9 = \underline{2}$ 30. $63 \div 9 = \underline{7}$

31. $27 \div 9 = \underline{3}$ 32. $90 \div 9 = \underline{10}$ 33. $72 \div 9 = \underline{8}$

34. $81 \div 9 = \underline{9}$ 35. $54 \div 9 = \underline{6}$ 36. $36 \div 9 = \underline{4}$

Power Practice • Find each quotient.

37. $64 \div 8 = \underline{8}$ 38. $56 \div 7 = \underline{8}$ 39. $24 \div 4 = \underline{6}$

40. $35 \div 5 = \underline{7}$ 41. $32 \div 8 = \underline{4}$ 42. $63 \div 7 = \underline{9}$

43. $21 \div 7 = \underline{3}$ 44. $8 \div 1 = \underline{8}$ 45. $48 \div 8 = \underline{6}$

46. $72 \div 9 = \underline{8}$ 47. $28 \div 4 = \underline{7}$ 48. $24 \div 6 = \underline{4}$

49. $16 \div 2 = \underline{8}$ 50. $36 \div 9 = \underline{4}$ 51. $81 \div 9 = \underline{9}$

© McGraw-Hill School Division

Grade 3, Chapter 10, Cluster B **131**

Lesson Goal

- Multiply 1-digit numbers by 2-digit numbers

What the Student Needs to Know

- Recall multiplication facts.
- Understand place value and regrouping.

Getting Started

Find out what students know about regrouping. Write the following multiplication on the chalk board:

$$\begin{array}{r} 6 \\ \times 2 \\ \hline 12 \end{array}$$

- *Why do you write a 1 in the tens column in the answer?* (because 6 × 2 = 12, which is 1 ten and 2 ones)

Write the following multiplication sentences on the board:

$$\begin{array}{r} 10 \\ \times 6 \\ \hline 60 \end{array} \qquad \begin{array}{r} 12 \\ \times 6 \\ \hline 72 \end{array}$$

- Ask: *What number is in the tens column in the answer to the first problem?* (6) *In the answer to the second problem?* (7) *Why is there a change?* (Because in the second problem, the ones need to be regrouped after you multiply. In the answer, you write a 2 in the ones place, and write 1 ten above the tens column and add it after you multiply the tens.)

What Can I Do?

- Read the question and the response. Then read and discuss the example. Ask:
- *In what order do you multiply the digits of a two-digit number?* (Start with the ones, then multiply the tens.)
- *When do you need to regroup to the next place value in a multiplication problem?* (when the number in a place value is more than 9)
- *How do you regroup?* (After multiplying, write down the digit in the ones place in the product and add the digit in the tens

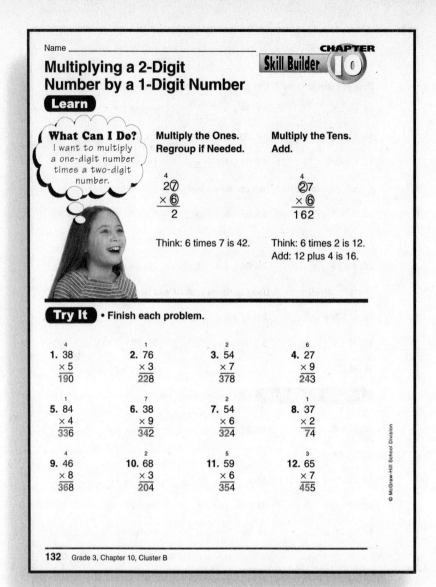

WHAT IF THE STUDENT CAN'T

Recall Basic Multiplication Facts

- Use counters or models to demonstrate the products of multiplying two 1-digit numbers. Then have the student do the same.
- Have the student write out a multiplication table for the numbers 0 through 9.
- Have the student write multiplication facts on flash cards and practice until they can be recalled with ease.

Understand Place Value and Regrouping

- Have the student write a two-digit number and read it aloud. Then have the student tell you how many tens and ones are in the number.
- Have the student practice writing 2-digit numbers in a place-value chart until it can be done with ease.

Name _____

Find each product. These problems have no regrouping.

13. 32 × 4 —— 128	14. 73 × 3 —— 219	15. 51 × 7 —— 357	16. 43 × 2 —— 86
17. 91 × 5 —— 455	18. 62 × 2 —— 124	19. 72 × 3 —— 216	20. 34 × 2 —— 68

Power Practice • Find each product.

21. 32 × 6 —— 192	22. 68 × 2 —— 136	23. 24 × 7 —— 168	24. 69 × 4 —— 276
25. 24 × 9 —— 216	26. 53 × 7 —— 371	27. 78 × 3 —— 234	28. 46 × 8 —— 368
29. 88 × 3 —— 264	30. 39 × 5 —— 195		
31. 26 × 8 —— 208	32. 57 × 6 —— 342		
33. 47 × 2 —— 94	34. 83 × 4 —— 332		
35. 65 × 5 —— 325	36. 45 × 9 —— 405		

Learn with Partners & Parents

Greatest Product Game

You will need one set of 0 to 9 digit cards.

• Turn the cards over and mix them up. Each player draws three cards.

• Make a problem like this:

☐ × ☐ ☐

Find your product.

• The player with the greater product gets one point. Play until one player has 7 points.

© McGraw-Hill School Division

Grade 3, Chapter 10, Cluster B **133**

WHAT IF THE STUDENT CAN'T

• Use grid strips and squares to illustrate a situation where regrouping is required. For example: 1 ten, 7 ones (17) + 2 tens, 8 ones (28) = 3 tens, 15 ones. Since a number in a place value may only be 9 or less, the ones must be regrouped. To get the answer of 45, 10 of the ones are converted to 1 ten, making a total of 4. The 5 ones remain in the ones column.

Complete the Power Practice

• Discuss each incorrect answer. Have the student write out the multiplication of the ones column as a multiplication fact. Then have the student write down the ones digit and regroup the tens. Finally, have the student multiply the tens column and add the results of the regrouping.

• Have the student use the distributive property of multiplication to check the correctness of each revised answer. For example, 32 × 6 = 192 can be broken into (30 × 6) + (2 × 6) = 180 + 12 = 192.

place to the product of the next column.)

Try It

Look at exercise 1 with students. Ask:

• *How can you complete this problem?* (Multiply 5 by 3, then add 4.)

Be sure students understand that they should first multiply the tens column, and then add any numbers resulting from regrouping. Then have them complete exercises 1–12.

Have the students look at exercise 13. Check to be sure they understand the order in which they should multiply the digits of the two-digit number. Ask:

• *How can you find the answer to this problem?* (Multiply 4 by 2 to get 8, then write this in the ones column. Multiply 4 by 3 to get 12, then write a 1 in the hundreds column and a 2 in the tens column.)

Have the students complete exercises 13–20.

Power Practice

• Have students complete the practice items. Then review each answer.

• Select a few of the exercises. Have volunteers demonstrate how to get at the correct answer by regrouping.

Learn with Partners & Parents

• Ask: *To get a high product, what kind of number should you have as the tens digit of the 2-digit number?* (a number greater than 5)

• *What other number should be 5 or greater?* (the 1-digit factor)

• Players may enjoy playing a reverse game where they try to get products that are low.

Grade 3, Chapter 10, Cluster B **133**

USING THE LESSON

Lesson Goal
- Multiply 3-digit numbers by 1-digit numbers

What the Student Needs to Know
- Recall basic multiplication facts.
- Understand place value and regrouping.

Getting Started
Find out what students know about regrouping. Write the following multiplications on the board and have students solve:

$$\begin{array}{r} 43 \\ \times 2 \\ \hline 86 \end{array} \qquad \begin{array}{r} 43 \\ \times 4 \\ \hline 172 \end{array}$$

Ask:

- *Is regrouping required in the first problem?* (No) *Why or why not?* (Because the value of the ones place after multiplying is 6, which is not greater than 9.)

- *Why is regrouping required in the second problem?* (Because the value of the ones place after multiplying is 12, which is greater than 9.)

- *How do you regroup?* (You write down the digit in the ones place in the answer. Then you write the digit in the tens place above the tens column and add it after you multiply the column.)

What Can I Do?
- Read the question and the response. Then read and discuss the example. Ask:

- *In what order do you multiply the digits of a three-digit number?* (Start with the ones, then move on to the tens, and then on to the hundreds.)

- *How do you regroup tens to hundreds when multiplying tens?* (Write the ones digit in the tens place of the product. Then write the tens digit of your product above the hundreds column and add it to the product of that column.)

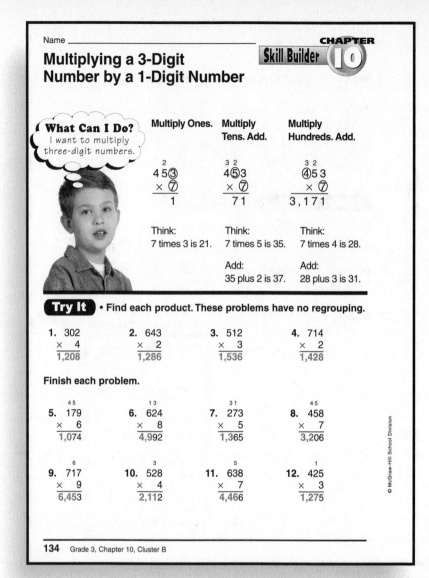

Name _____

Multiplying a 3-Digit Number by a 1-Digit Number

Skill Builder CHAPTER 10

What Can I Do? I want to multiply three-digit numbers.

Multiply Ones.	Multiply Tens. Add.	Multiply Hundreds. Add.
$\begin{array}{r} \overset{2}{} \\ 45\textcircled{3} \\ \times \textcircled{7} \\ \hline 1 \end{array}$	$\begin{array}{r} \overset{32}{} \\ 4\textcircled{5}3 \\ \times \textcircled{7} \\ \hline 71 \end{array}$	$\begin{array}{r} \overset{32}{} \\ \textcircled{4}53 \\ \times \textcircled{7} \\ \hline 3,171 \end{array}$
Think: 7 times 3 is 21.	Think: 7 times 5 is 35. Add: 35 plus 2 is 37.	Think: 7 times 4 is 28. Add: 28 plus 3 is 31.

Try It • Find each product. These problems have no regrouping.

| **1.** $\begin{array}{r} 302 \\ \times 4 \\ \hline 1,208 \end{array}$ | **2.** $\begin{array}{r} 643 \\ \times 2 \\ \hline 1,286 \end{array}$ | **3.** $\begin{array}{r} 512 \\ \times 3 \\ \hline 1,536 \end{array}$ | **4.** $\begin{array}{r} 714 \\ \times 2 \\ \hline 1,428 \end{array}$ |

Finish each problem.

| **5.** $\begin{array}{r} \overset{45}{} \\ 179 \\ \times 6 \\ \hline 1,074 \end{array}$ | **6.** $\begin{array}{r} \overset{13}{} \\ 624 \\ \times 8 \\ \hline 4,992 \end{array}$ | **7.** $\begin{array}{r} \overset{31}{} \\ 273 \\ \times 5 \\ \hline 1,365 \end{array}$ | **8.** $\begin{array}{r} \overset{45}{} \\ 458 \\ \times 7 \\ \hline 3,206 \end{array}$ |
| **9.** $\begin{array}{r} \overset{6}{} \\ 717 \\ \times 9 \\ \hline 6,453 \end{array}$ | **10.** $\begin{array}{r} \overset{3}{} \\ 528 \\ \times 4 \\ \hline 2,112 \end{array}$ | **11.** $\begin{array}{r} \overset{5}{} \\ 638 \\ \times 7 \\ \hline 4,466 \end{array}$ | **12.** $\begin{array}{r} \overset{1}{} \\ 425 \\ \times 3 \\ \hline 1,275 \end{array}$ |

134 Grade 3, Chapter 10, Cluster B

WHAT IF THE STUDENT CAN'T

Recall Basic Multiplication Facts

- Use counters or models to demonstrate the products of multiplying two 1-digit numbers. Then have the student do the same.

- Have the student write out a multiplication table for the numbers 0 through 9.

- Have the student write multiplication facts on flash cards and practice until they can be recalled with ease.

Understand Place Value and Regrouping

- Have the student write a three-digit number and read

it aloud. Then have the student tell you how many hundreds, tens, and ones are in the number.

- Have the student practice writing 3-digit numbers in a place-value chart until it can be done with ease.

- Use grids, grid strips and squares to illustrate multiplication with regrouping. For example: 2 hundreds, 8 tens, and 5 ones (285) + 4 hundreds, 5 tens, and 2 ones

© McGraw-Hill School Division

Name _____

Find each product. Use a dollar sign and decimal point in each answer.

13. $3.52	14. $1.76	15. $8.04	16. $4.63
× 6	× 5	× 8	× 2
$21.12	$8.80	$64.32	$9.26

Power Practice • Find each product.

17. 314	18. 261	19. 585	20. 193
× 7	× 3	× 4	× 7
2,198	783	2,340	1,351

21. 426	22. 619	23. 758	24. 294
× 2	× 9	× 5	× 8
852	5,571	3,790	2,352

25. $7.24	26. $5.81	27. $2.90	28. $6.35
× 5	× 6	× 4	× 2
$36.20	$34.86	$11.60	$12.70

29. $8 \times 341 =$ __2,728__   30. $3 \times 826 =$ __2,478__   31. $7 \times 684 =$ __4,788__

32. $7 \times 684 =$ __4,788__   33. $5 \times 489 =$ __2,445__   34. $9 \times 327 =$ __2,943__

35. $8 \times 295 =$ __2,360__   36. $6 \times 372 =$ __2,232__   37. $3 \times 898 =$ __2,694__

38. $5 \times \$2.43 =$ __$12.15__   39. $9 \times \$7.56 =$ __$68.04__   40. $6 \times \$4.07 =$ __$24.42__

41. $6 \times \$7.15 =$ __$42.90__   42. $5 \times \$9.49 =$ __$47.45__   43. $8 \times \$3.89 =$ __$31.12__

44. $7 \times \$4.78 =$ __$33.46__   45. $9 \times \$6.85 =$ __$61.65__   46. $4 \times \$7.79 =$ __$31.16__

© McGraw-Hill School Division

Grade 3, Chapter 10, Cluster B   **135**

WHAT IF THE STUDENT CAN'T

(452) = 7 hundreds, 13 tens, and 7 ones. Since a place value may only be 9 or less, the tens column must be regrouped. To get the answer of 737, 10 of the tens are regrouped as 1 hundred, making a total of 7 hundreds. 3 tens remain in the tens column, and there are 7 ones.

Complete the Power Practice

• Discuss each incorrect answer. Have the student write out the multiplication in each place-value column as a multiplication fact, including the addition of any regrouped numbers.

• Have the student use the distributive property of multiplication to check the correctness of each revised answer. For example, $314 \times 7 = 2,198$ can be broken into $(300 \times 7) + (10 \times 7) + (4 \times 7) = 2,100 + 70 + 28 = 2,198$.

USING THE LESSON

Try It

Have the students look at exercise 2. Check to be sure they understand the order in which they should multiply the digits of the three-digit number. Ask:

• *Which digit should you multiply first?* (3, or the ones) *second?* (4, or the tens) *third?* (6, or the hundreds)

Then have students complete exercises 1–4.

Have students look at exercise 6. Be sure students understand that any numbers that result from regrouping should only be added after the column has been multiplied. Ask:

• *What is the final step in the multiplication?* (Multiply 6 hundreds by 8, then add 1 hundred.)

Then have students complete exercises 5–8.

Have students look at exercise 9. Ask:

• *How many times in all do you have to regroup in this problem?* (2)

• *After you regroup the tens column, how many hundreds will you need to add to the hundreds column?* (1)

Then have students complete exercises 9–16.

Power Practice

• Have students complete exercises 17–46. Then review each answer.

• Select a few of the exercises. Have volunteers demonstrate how to arrive at the correct answer by regrouping.

CHALLENGE

Lesson Goal

- Learn how the use of parentheses changes the order of operations and the value of a number sentence.

Introducing the Challenge

Write the following number sentence on the board:

$7 \times 4 + 6$

Ask:

- *If you do the multiplication part of the number sentence first, what is your final answer? (34)*
- *If you do the addition part of the number sentence first, what is your final answer? (70)*

Write the following number sentence on the board:

$28 \div 4 - 2$

Ask:

- *If you do the division part of the number sentence first, what is your final answer? (5)*
- *If you solve the subtraction part of the number sentence first, what is your final answer? (14)*

Have students read the introduction to the Challenge. Then look at the two example problems. Make it clear that both problems include the same numbers in the same order. Say:

- *Simplify both problems by doing the operation in parentheses first. What operation must still be done in each sentence? (12 + 2; 3 × 6)*

Using Parentheses

Parentheses show what operation to do first.
In $(3 \times 4) + 2$, you multiply and then add.
In $3 \times (4 + 2)$, you add and then multiply.

Use two steps to solve each problem.

1. $(5 \times 2) + 1 =$

___10___ $+ 1 =$

___11___

2. $3 \times (8 \div 2) =$

$3 \times$ ___4___ $=$

___12___

3. $(12 \div 2) - 4 =$

___6___ $- 4 =$

___2___

4. $5 + (12 \div 3) =$

$5 +$ ___4___ $=$

___9___

5. $(9 - 2) \times 3 =$

___7___ $\times 3 =$

___21___

6. $11 - (4 \times 2) =$

$11 -$ ___8___ $=$

___3___

Use parentheses to make two different problems.

7. $(3 \times 4) + 2 =$ __14__

$3 \times (4 + 2) =$ __18__

8. $(15 \div 5) - 2 =$ __1__

$15 \div (5 - 2) =$ __5__

9. $(12 - 8) + 1 =$ __5__

$12 - (8 + 1) =$ __3__

10. $(9 - 3) \times 2 =$ __12__

$9 - (3 \times 2) =$ __3__

11. $(6 \times 10) - 2 =$ __58__

$6 \times (10 - 2) =$ __48__

12. $(8 + 6) \div 2 =$ __7__

$8 + (6 \div 2) =$ __11__

13. $(18 \div 2) + 4 =$ __13__

$18 \div (2 + 4) =$ __3__

14. $(15 - 5) \times 2 =$ __20__

$15 - (5 \times 2) =$ __5__

15. $(3 \times 8) - 1 =$ __23__

$3 \times (8 - 1) =$ __21__

16. $(6 + 9) \div 3 =$ __5__

$6 + (9 \div 3) =$ __9__

17. $(30 - 5) \times 2 =$ __50__

$30 - (5 \times 2) =$ __20__

18. $(24 \div 4) + 2 =$ __8__

$24 \div (4 + 2) =$ __4__

Name _____

Here are some different numbers you can make using four 3s.

19. $(3 \div 3) \times (3 \div 3) =$

$\underline{\ 1\ } \times \underline{\ 1\ } = \underline{\ 1\ }$

20. $(3 \div 3) + (3 \div 3) =$

$\underline{\ 1\ } + \underline{\ 1\ } = \underline{\ 2\ }$

21. $(3 \times 3) - (3 + 3) =$

$\underline{\ 9\ } - \underline{\ 6\ } = \underline{\ 3\ }$

22. $(3 + 3) - (3 \div 3) =$

$\underline{\ 6\ } - \underline{\ 1\ } = \underline{\ 5\ }$

23. $(3 + 3) + (3 - 3) =$

$\underline{\ 6\ } + \underline{\ 0\ } = \underline{\ 6\ }$

24. $(3 + 3) + (3 \div 3) =$

$\underline{\ 6\ } + \underline{\ 1\ } = \underline{\ 7\ }$

25. $(3 \times 3) - (3 \div 3) =$

$\underline{\ 9\ } - \underline{\ 1\ } = \underline{\ 8\ }$

26. $(3 \times 3) - (3 - 3) =$

$\underline{\ 9\ } - \underline{\ 0\ } = \underline{\ 9\ }$

Now make some different numbers using four 4s.
Possible answers are given.

27. $(4 - 4) + (4 - 4) =$

$\underline{\ 0\ } + \underline{\ 0\ } = \underline{\ 0\ }$

28. $(4 - 4) + (4 \div 4) =$

$\underline{\ 0\ } + \underline{\ 1\ } = \underline{\ 1\ }$

29. $(4 \div 4) + (4 \div 4) =$

$\underline{\ 1\ } + \underline{\ 1\ } = \underline{\ 2\ }$

30. $(4 + 4) - (4 \div 4) =$

$\underline{\ 8\ } - \underline{\ 1\ } = \underline{\ 7\ }$

31. $(4 + 4) + (4 - 4) =$

$\underline{\ 8\ } + \underline{\ 0\ } = \underline{\ 8\ }$

32. $(4 + 4) + (4 \div 4) =$

$\underline{\ 8\ } + \underline{\ 1\ } = \underline{\ 9\ }$

Grade 3, Chapter 10, Cluster A **137**

CHALLENGE

Using the Challenge

Have students complete exercises 1–6. Review each answer. Then select one exercise 2 or 5, and move the parentheses from one pair of numbers to the other. Have a volunteer solve the new problem and compare the two answers.

Have students complete exercises 7–18. Ask:

- *Do any of the exercises give you the same answer for both problems?* (No)

Have students look at exercise 19. Ask:

- *In what order should you solve the parts of this problem?* (Solve both parts in the parentheses first, and then multiply the two parts.)

Then have students complete exercises 19–32. Ask:

- *How could you use four threes to get 10?* $((3 \times 3) + (3 \div 3) = 10)$

Have students complete exercises 27–32. Ask:

- *In these exercises, which answer will give you the highest number?* $(4 \times 4) \times (4 \times 4) = 256)$ *Does it matter in what order you solve the parts of this problem?* (No) *Why or why not?* (Because it's a multiplication problem, and the commutative rule of multiplication applies.)

CHALLENGE

Lesson Goal
- Use division to find and apply speed and work rates.

Introducing the Challenge
Find out what students know about rates. Have them solve the following word problems:

- *Roberto works 4 hours for a neighbor and earns $20. How many dollars does he earn for each hour he works? ($5)*
- *Kyra drives 150 miles. Her car uses 5 gallons of gas. How many miles does Kyra get out of each gallon of gas? (30 miles)*

Explain that the answers to both problems may be written as rates. Rates use the word *per*, which means "for each." So Roberto earns $5 per hour, and Kyra's car gets 30 miles per gallon.

Have students read the introduction to the first page of the Challenge. Explain that speed is a kind of rate, because it tells you how much distance is traveled in a unit of time--for example, how many miles are traveled in one hour. Ask:

- *If a car travels at a speed of 47 miles per hour, how many miles will it travel in 1 hour? (47)*

Have students read the introduction to the second page of the Challenge. Explain that work rates tell you how much work can be done in a unit of time. Ask:

- *If Jack can wash 4 plates in a minute, what is his rate of work? (4 plates per minute)*

Using the Challenge
Have the students look at exercise 1. Ask:

- *How can you find how many hours it will take to travel 240 miles at this speed? (Divide 240 by 30 to get 8.)*

Then have students look at exercise 5. Ask:

- *How can you find the speed needed to travel 360 miles in this time? (Divide 360 by 12 to get 30 miles per hour.)*

Name _____

Distance, Speed, and Time

Distance equals speed times the time traveled. If you are given the distance and the speed, divide to find the time. If you are given the distance and the time, divide to find the speed.

A car travels 240 miles. Find the time it takes at each of these speeds.

1. 30 miles per hour

___8___ hours

2. 60 miles per hour

___4___ hours

3. 40 miles per hour

___6___ hours

A car travels 360 miles. Find the speed needed to complete the trip in each of these times.

4. 6 hours

___60___ miles per hour

5. 12 hours

___30___ miles per hour

6. 9 hours

___40___ miles per hour

Solve each problem.

7. A person walks 8 miles per hour. How long will it take the person to walk 40 miles?

___5 hours___

8. A boat goes 58 miles in 2 hours. What is the boat's average speed?

___29 miles per hour___

9. A family drives 400 miles in 8 hours. What is their average speed for this trip?

___50 miles per hour___

10. A plant grows 8 millimeters per day. At this rate, how long will it take the plant to grow 4 centimeters?

___5 days___

© McGraw-Hill School Division

Name _____

Work, Rate, and Time

The work completed equals the rate times the time at work. If you are given the work completed and the rate, divide to find the time. If you are given the work completed and the time, divide to find the rate.

A student needs to read 400 pages. Find the time it will take at each rate.

11. 20 pages per day   12. 2 pages per minute   13. 50 pages per hour

   _20_ days   _200_ minutes   _8_ hours

A factory is filling 800 jars with juice. Find the rate needed to finish the job in each of these times.

14. 100 seconds   15. 5 hours   16. 40 minutes

  _8_ jars per second   _160_ jars per hour   _20_ jars per minute

Solve each problem.

17. If you can pick 2 apples per minute, how long will it take to pick 100 apples?

          50 minutes

18. Some students are raking leaves. At what rate must they work to fill 20 bags in 5 hours?

          4 bags per hour

19. A machine prints 50 pages per minute. How long will it take this machine to print 600 pages?

          12 minutes

20. Some students are washing cars. How fast must they work to wash a dozen cars in 60 minutes?

          1 car per 5 minutes

CHALLENGE

Have students complete exercises 1–10. Review each answer.

Have students look at exercise 11. Ask:

- *Which operation will you use to find the correct number of days?* (division)

Then have students look at exercise 14. Ask:

- *Which operation will you use to find the correct rate of jars per second?* (division)

Have students complete exercises 11–20. Review each answer.

Conclude by asking:

- *When would you use multiplication when working with rates?* (When you know the time and the rate, and are trying to find out a distance traveled, or an amount of work done.)

Measuring Length

How many paper clips long is each object?

1.

_____ paper clips

2.

_____ paper clips

3. Crayon

_____ paper clips

4.

_____ paper clips

Ordering Whole Numbers

Order from greatest to least.

5. 45, 54, 14, 19, 41 _____

6. 456, 389, 309, 512, 498 _____

Multiplication and Division Facts
Multiply.

7.   6
  $\times\,4$

8.   9
  $\times\,3$

9.   8
  $\times\,1$

Divide.

10. $5\overline{)25}$

11. $6\overline{)42}$

12. $7\overline{)56}$

Name _____

Capacity

Underline the object that holds more liquid when completely filled.

13.

14.

15.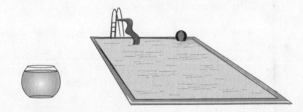

16.

Multiply and Divide by 10, 100, and 1,000

Find each product.

17. $6 \times 100 =$ _____

18. $10 \times 8 =$ _____

19. $7 \times 1,000 =$ _____

20. $40 \div 10 =$ _____

21. $800 \div 100 =$ _____

22. $5,000 \div 1,000 =$ _____

Comparing Numbers

Use the number line to compare each pair of numbers.
Write > or <.

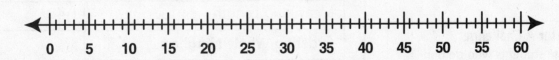

23. 47 ____ 39   **24.** 15 ____ 51   **25.** 32 ____ 36

Assessment Goal

This two-page assessment covers skills identified as necessary for success in Chapter 11 Measurement. The first page assesses the major prerequisite skills for Cluster A. The second page assesses the major prerequisite skills for Cluster B. When the Cluster A and Cluster B prerequisite skills overlap, the skill(s) will be covered in only one section.

Getting Started

- Allow students time to look over the two pages of the assessment. Point out the labels that identify the skills covered.

- Have students find math vocabulary terms used in the assessment. List vocabulary terms on the board as students identify them. If necessary, review the meanings of all essential math vocabulary.

Introducing the Assessment

- Explain to students that these pages will help you know if they are ready to start a new chapter in their math textbooks.

- Students who have transferred from another school may not have been introduced to some of these skills. Encourage students to do their best and assure them you will help them learn any needed skills.

Name _____

Measuring Length

How many paper clips long is each object?

1. _____3_____ paper clips

2. _____5_____ paper clips

3. Crayon   _____4_____ paper clips

4. _____8_____ paper clips

Ordering Whole Numbers

Order from greatest to least.

5. 45, 54, 14, 19, 41   _____54, 45, 41, 19, 14_____

6. 456, 389, 309, 512, 498   _____512, 498, 456, 389, 309_____

Multiplication and Division Facts

Multiply.

7. $\begin{array}{r} 6 \\ \times\,4 \\ \hline 24 \end{array}$ 8. $\begin{array}{r} 9 \\ \times\,3 \\ \hline 27 \end{array}$ 9. $\begin{array}{r} 8 \\ \times\,1 \\ \hline 8 \end{array}$

Divide.

10. $5\overline{)25}$ remainder 5 11. $6\overline{)42}$ remainder 7 12. $7\overline{)56}$ remainder 8

139A   Use with Grade 3, Chapter 11, Cluster A

CLUSTER A PREREQUISITE SKILLS

The skills listed in this chart are those identified as major prerequisite skills for students' success in the lessons in Cluster A of the chapter. Each skill is covered by one or more assessment items as shown in the middle column. The right column provides the page number for the lessons in this book that reteach the cluster A prerequisite skills.

Skill Name	Assessment Items	Lesson Pages
Measuring Length	1-4	140-141
Ordering Whole Numbers	5-6	142-143
Multiplication and Division Facts	7-12	144-145

Cluster A Challenge

Those students who demonstrate mastery of the skills on this page will not need to use the reteaching worksheets. Instead, these students can do the Cluster A Challenge found on pages 152-153.

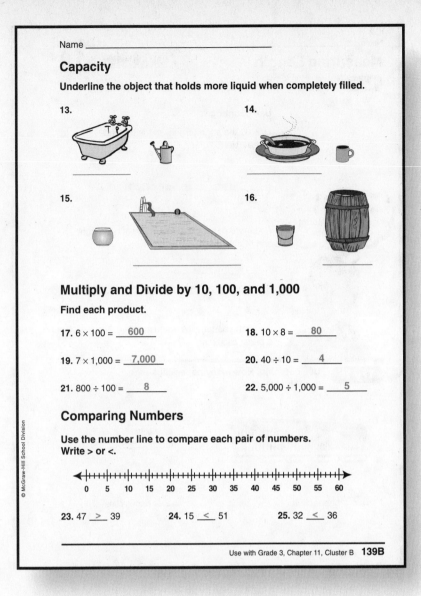

Name _____

Capacity

Underline the object that holds more liquid when completely filled.

13.

14.

15.

16.

Multiply and Divide by 10, 100, and 1,000

Find each product.

17. $6 \times 100 =$ ___600___   **18.** $10 \times 8 =$ ___80___

19. $7 \times 1,000 =$ ___7,000___   **20.** $40 \div 10 =$ ___4___

21. $800 \div 100 =$ ___8___   **22.** $5,000 \div 1,000 =$ ___5___

Comparing Numbers

Use the number line to compare each pair of numbers.
Write > or <.

```
◄─┼┼┼┼┼┼┼┼┼┼┼┼┼┼┼┼┼┼┼┼┼┼┼┼┼┼┼┼┼┼┼┼┼┼┼┼►
  0   5   10  15  20  25  30  35  40  45  50  55  60
```

23. 47 ___>___ 39 **24.** 15 ___<___ 51 **25.** 32 ___<___ 36

Use with Grade 3, Chapter 11, Cluster B **139B**

© McGraw-Hill School Division

CLUSTER B PREREQUISITE SKILLS

The skills listed in this chart are those identified as major prerequisite skills for students' success in the lessons in Cluster B of the chapter. Each skill is covered by one or more assessment items as shown in the middle column. The right column provides the page numbers for the lessons in this book that reteach the Cluster B prerequisite skills

Skill Name	Assessment Items	Lesson Pages
Capacity	13-16	146-147
Multiply and Divide by 10, 100, and 1,000	17-22	148-149
Comparing Numbers	23-25	150-151

Alternative Assessment Strategies

- Oral administration of the assessment is appropriate for younger students or those whose native language is not English. Read the skills title and directions one section at a time. Check students' understanding by asking them to tell you how they will do the first exercise in the group.

- For some skill types you may wish to use group administration. In this technique, a small group or pair of students complete the assessment together. Through their discussion, you will be able to decide if supplementary reteaching materials are needed.

Intervention Materials

If students are not successful with the prerequisite skills assessed on these pages, reteaching lessons have been created to help them make the transition into the chapter.

Item correlation charts showing the skills lessons suitable for reteaching the prerequisite skills are found beneath the reproductions of each page of the assessment.

Cluster B Challenge

Those students who demonstrate mastery of the skills on this page will not need to use the reteaching worksheets. Instead, these students can do the Cluster B Challenge found on pages 154-155.

USING THE LESSON

Lesson Goal
• Measure length using paper clips.

What the Student Needs to Know
• Understand length.
• Understand the concept of a unit of measurement.

Getting Started
Draw a line segment on the board. Ask:

• *If I measure this line segment from beginning to end, what am I measuring?* (its length)

Then draw a triangle on the chalkboard. The sides of the triangle should each have a different measure. Point to the side of the triangle. Ask:

• *If you measure this side of the triangle, what are you measuring?* (the length of the side)

Do the same for each of the other sides of the triangle.

What Can I Do?
• Read the question and the response. Then read and discuss the example. Ask:

• *What is the unit of measurement used in the example?* (paper clip)

• *Is each paper clip in the example the same length?* (Yes)

• *In measuring, can there be any space between paper clips, or do they need to be end to end to give an accurate answer?* (They should be end to end.)

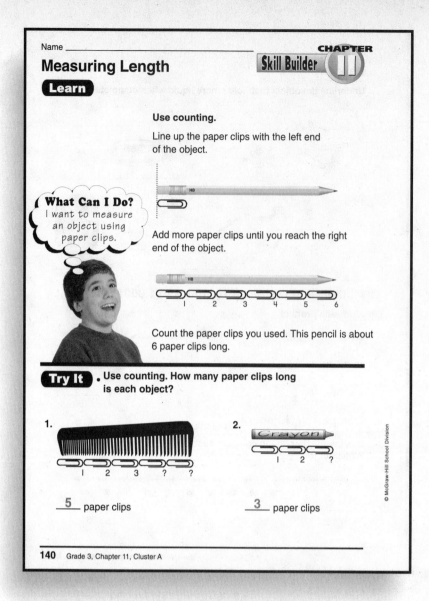

Name _____

Measuring Length

Learn

Use counting.

Line up the paper clips with the left end of the object.

What Can I Do?
I want to measure an object using paper clips.

Add more paper clips until you reach the right end of the object.

1 2 3 4 5 6

Count the paper clips you used. This pencil is about 6 paper clips long.

Try It • Use counting. How many paper clips long is each object?

1.
1 2 3 ? ?

__5__ paper clips

2.
1 2 ?

__3__ paper clips

© McGraw-Hill School Division

140   Grade 3, Chapter 11, Cluster A

WHAT IF THE STUDENT CAN'T

Understand Length
• Draw a line segment on the chalkboard. Explain that the length of the segment tells how far it runs from beginning to end. Note that different segments will have different lengths.

• Explain that, just as a line segment can be measured for length, shapes and objects may be measured for length. Have the student draw various shapes and objects, drawing a line for each one that represents the length of the figure.

Understand the Concept of a Unit of Measurement
• Explain that to measure the length of something, you need to have a unit of measurement. A unit of measurement can be an agreed-upon length, such as a foot or a meter. In addition, a unit of measurement can be an object such as a paper clip or eraser.

• Use an object in the classroom to demonstrate how different units of measurement can be used to measure the same object. For

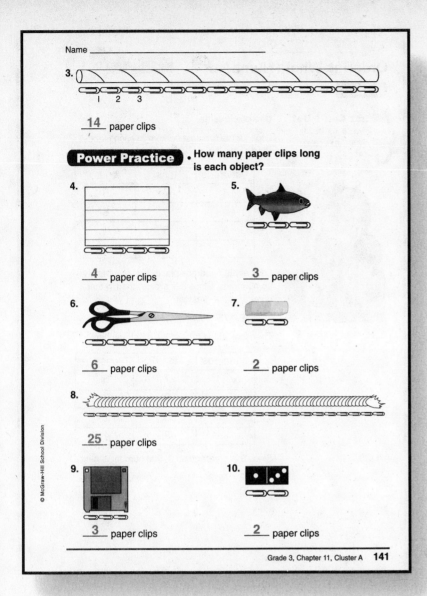

Name _____

3.

___14___ paper clips

Power Practice • How many paper clips long is each object?

4.

___4___ paper clips

5.

___3___ paper clips

6.

___6___ paper clips

7.

___2___ paper clips

8.

___25___ paper clips

9.

___3___ paper clips

10.

___2___ paper clips

© McGraw-Hill School Division

WHAT IF THE STUDENT CAN'T

example, a stapler can be measured in inches, centimeters, or paper clips. Then have the student use various units of measurement to measure other items.

Complete the Power Practice
• Discuss each incorrect answer. Have the student count off the paper clips to arrive at the correct answer.

Try It
Look at exercises 1–3. Have students count off the number of paper clips in each exercise. Ask:

• *Why should you mark the number at the end of each paper clip instead of at the beginning?* (Because until you reach the end of the paper clip, you haven't reached that number of paper clips in length.)

Power Practice
• Have students complete the practice items. Then review each answer.

USING THE LESSON

Lesson Goal
- Order whole numbers from greatest to least.

What the Student Needs to Know
- Understand place value through hundreds.
- Order numbers from 0 to 9.

Getting Started
Find out what students know about ordering whole numbers. Write the following numbers on the board.

429, 16, 95, 3, 700

Ask:
- *Which of these numbers is the greatest?* (700)
- *Which of these numbers is the least?* (3)
- *Which number is greater, 95 or 16?* (95)
- *Which number is less, 95 or 429?* (95)
- *How do you know that one number is greater than another?* (Possible answer: The number that is farther along on a number line is greater.)

What Can I Do?
Read the question and the response. Then read and discuss the example. Ask:
- *Why do you start at the left and work to the right?* (Because the values at the left have the greatest place value, and the place values get less as you move to the right. For example, a hundred is greater than a ten, which is greater than a one.)
- *How do you know that the two numbers that have a value in the hundreds place are greater than the two numbers that don't?* (Because the numbers that don't have a value written in the hundreds place have 0 hundreds, and 0 is less than 1 and less than 3.)

Ordering Whole Numbers

Learn

What Can I Do?
I want to order whole numbers from greatest to least.

Use place value.

Look for the greatest number in each place. Start at the left.

hundreds	tens	ones
1	7	5
	9	8
3	5	2
	3	4

Look at the hundreds place. Two numbers have no hundreds. Since 3 is greater than 1, that number is the greatest.

352, 175, _____, _____

Then look at the tens of the other numbers.

hundreds	tens	ones
✓ 1	7	5
	9	8
✓ 3	5	2
	3	4

Since 9 is greater than 3, that number is next.

352, 175, 98, 34

WHAT IF THE STUDENT CAN'T

Understand Place Value Through Hundreds
- Have the student write a 3-digit number and read it aloud. Explain that each digit can be seen as one place in a place-value chart. Then have the student tell you how many hundreds, tens, and ones are in the number.
- Have the student practice writing 2-digit and 3-digit numbers in a place-value chart until it can be done with ease.

Order Numbers from 0 to 9
- Have the student draw a number line from 0 to 9. Explain that as you move to the right on the line, the numbers are greater. At the same time, as you move left on the number line, the numbers are lesser. Have the student practice finding pairs of numbers on the line and identifying the greater and lesser of each pair.

Name_____

Try It • Use place value. Order from greatest to least.

1. 6̲5, 2̲8, 7̲6, 8̲2, 13 _____ 82, 76, 65, 28, 13 _____

2. 1̲16, 1̲93, 1̲27, 1̲88, 1̲00 _____ 193, 188, 127, 116, 100 _____

Power Practice • Order from greatest to least.

3. 73, 88, 79, 94, 65 _____ 94, 88, 79, 73, 65 _____

4. 315, 195, 327, 255, 97 _____ 327, 315, 255, 195, 97 _____

5. 56, 38, 60, 154, 75 _____ 154, 75, 60, 56, 38 _____

6. 465, 856, 246, 365, 754 _____ 856, 754, 465, 365, 246 _____

7. 38, 47, 42, 29, 37 _____ 47, 42, 38, 37, 29 _____

8. 118, 87, 93, 104, 90 _____ 118, 104, 93, 90, 87 _____

9. 159, 167, 219, 178, 146 _____ 219, 178, 167, 159, 146 _____

10. 68, 73, 69, 61, 75 _____ 75, 73, 69, 68, 61 _____

Grade 3, Chapter 11, Cluster A **143**

WHAT IF THE STUDENT CAN'T

- Give the student sets of three numbers from 0 to 9. Have the student order each set from greatest to least. The student should continue practicing until the procedure can be done with ease.

Complete the Power Practice

- Discuss each incorrect answer. Have the student write each number in the exercise in a place-value chart. Then have the student order the numbers by comparing digits beginning in the hundreds column and moving right to the next place value or values as needed.

USING THE LESSON

- *The number 98 has 9 tens, while 175 has only 7 tens. When you order from greatest to least, which number comes first, 98 or 175?* (175 because it has 1 hundred and 98 has 0 hundreds.)

Try It
Look at exercise 1. Have students write each number in a place-value chart before ordering them from greatest to least. Ask:

- *What is the greatest value in the tens place?* (8) *What is the least value in the tens place?* (1)

- *What is the greatest value in the ones place?* (8) *Which number has this value?* (28) *Where in the order of numbers does 28 fall?* (It is the second-least number.)

Look at exercise 2. Have students write each number in a place-value chart before ordering them from greatest to least. Ask:

- *Which place value should you use to order the numbers?* (tens place) *Why?* (Because all the numbers have the same value in the hundreds place.)

Power Practice

- Have students complete the practice items. Then review each answer.

- Select a few of the exercises and have students use place value to demonstrate how to order them from greatest to least.

Lesson Goal
- Recall multiplication and division facts with the aid of arrays.

What the Student Needs to Know
- Make an array.
- Understand multiplication.
- Understand division.

Getting Started
Find out what students know about arrays. Draw an array of 3 rows of 7 counters on the board. Ask:
- *How many counters are in this figure?* (21)
- *How can you tell how many counters are in the figure without counting each one or using addition?* (Multiply the number of rows by the number of counters in each row.)
- *What multiplication fact does this figure illustrate?* ($3 \times 7 = 21$)

What Can I Do?
- Read the question and the response. Then read and discuss the first example. Ask:
- *If there were one less row, what multiplication fact would the array show?* ($3 \times 6 = 18$)
- *If there were one less counter in each row, but the number of rows remained the same, what multiplication fact would the array show?* ($4 \times 5 = 20$)
- Read and discuss the second example. Ask:
- *If the problem asked you to solve $24 \div 6$, how many counters would you put in each group in the array?* (6)
- *When you use an array to show a division fact, how can you check to be sure the array is correct?* (Multiply the number of groups in the array by the number of counters in each group.)

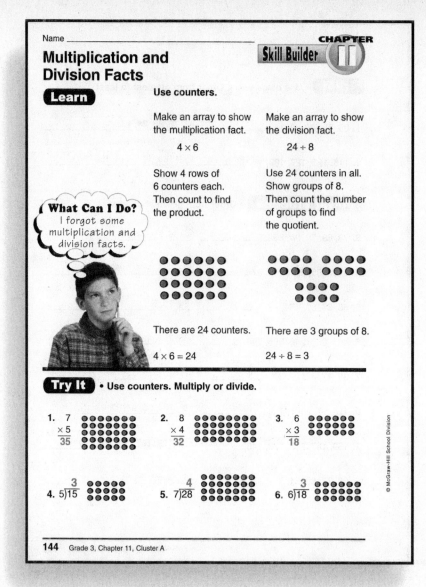

Name _____

Multiplication and Division Facts

Learn

What Can I Do? I forgot some multiplication and division facts.

Use counters.

Make an array to show the multiplication fact.

4×6

Show 4 rows of 6 counters each. Then count to find the product.

There are 24 counters.

$4 \times 6 = 24$

Make an array to show the division fact.

$24 \div 8$

Use 24 counters in all. Show groups of 8. Then count the number of groups to find the quotient.

There are 3 groups of 8.

$24 \div 8 = 3$

Try It • Use counters. Multiply or divide.

1. $\begin{array}{r} 7 \\ \times 5 \\ \hline 35 \end{array}$

2. $\begin{array}{r} 8 \\ \times 4 \\ \hline 32 \end{array}$

3. $\begin{array}{r} 6 \\ \times 3 \\ \hline 18 \end{array}$

4. $5\overline{)15}$ → 3

5. $7\overline{)28}$ → 4

6. $6\overline{)18}$ → 3

© McGraw-Hill School Division

144 Grade 3, Chapter 11, Cluster A

WHAT IF THE STUDENT CAN'T

Make an Array
- Draw a 3×4 array. Have the student write down how many rows are in the array (3), how many counters are in each row (4), and how many counters there are in all (12). Then explain to the student that the array represents the multiplication fact $3 \times 4 = 12$. Point out that the number of rows is one factor, and the number of counters in each row is the other factor.
- Using the same array, explain how it also represents the division fact $12 \div 4 = 3$. Point out that the number of counters in each row is the divisor, and that the number of rows is the quotient.
- Have the student practice drawing arrays for multiplication and division facts until he or she can do so easily.

Understand Multiplication
- Have the student complete the following number sentence: $8 + 8 + 8 =$ _____ (24). Explain that this sentence can also be written 3×8, where the first number (3) tells you how many times you need to add the second number (8).
- Have the student convert multiplication facts into addition sentences and vice versa until the concept of multiplication becomes clear.

Name_____

Power Practice • Multiply or divide.

7. $\begin{array}{r} 3 \\ \times 2 \\ \hline 6 \end{array}$	8. $\begin{array}{r} 4 \\ \times 6 \\ \hline 24 \end{array}$	9. $\begin{array}{r} 2 \\ \times 7 \\ \hline 14 \end{array}$	10. $\begin{array}{r} 0 \\ \times 4 \\ \hline 0 \end{array}$
11. $6\overline{)30}$ quotient 5	12. $3\overline{)27}$ quotient 9	13. $7\overline{)42}$ quotient 6	14. $9\overline{)36}$ quotient 4
15. $\begin{array}{r} 9 \\ \times 4 \\ \hline 36 \end{array}$	16. $\begin{array}{r} 8 \\ \times 8 \\ \hline 64 \end{array}$	17. $\begin{array}{r} 7 \\ \times 5 \\ \hline 35 \end{array}$	18. $\begin{array}{r} 2 \\ \times 9 \\ \hline 18 \end{array}$
19. $5\overline{)40}$ quotient 8	20. $1\overline{)6}$ quotient 6	21. $4\overline{)8}$ quotient 2	22. $7\overline{)56}$ quotient 8
23. $\begin{array}{r} 8 \\ \times 0 \\ \hline 0 \end{array}$	24. $\begin{array}{r} 7 \\ \times 9 \\ \hline 63 \end{array}$	25. $\begin{array}{r} 4 \\ \times 4 \\ \hline 16 \end{array}$	26. $\begin{array}{r} 7 \\ \times 2 \\ \hline 14 \end{array}$
27. $8\overline{)72}$ quotient 9	28. $9\overline{)54}$ quotient 6	29. $9\overline{)72}$ quotient 8	30. $5\overline{)20}$ quotient 4
31. $\begin{array}{r} 9 \\ \times 9 \\ \hline 81 \end{array}$	32. $\begin{array}{r} 1 \\ \times 3 \\ \hline 3 \end{array}$	33. $\begin{array}{r} 7 \\ \times 8 \\ \hline 56 \end{array}$	34. $\begin{array}{r} 9 \\ \times 3 \\ \hline 27 \end{array}$
35. $8\overline{)48}$ quotient 6	36. $2\overline{)16}$ quotient 8	37. $5\overline{)45}$ quotient 9	38. $4\overline{)32}$ quotient 8

USING THE LESSON

Try It

Have students look at exercise 1. Ask:

- *How many rows will be in your array?* (5) *How many counters will be in each row?* (7)

Then have students complete exercises 1–3.

Have students look at exercise 4. Ask:

- *How many counters in all will be in your array?* (15) *How many will be in each group?* (5)

Then have students complete exercises 4–6.

Power Practice

- Have students complete the practice items. Then review each answer.

WHAT IF THE STUDENT CAN'T

Understand Division

- Use counters to illustrate how a larger number may be broken down into a smaller number of equal groups. Write the relevant division fact. For example, 15 may be broken into 3 groups of 5, and labeled 15 ÷ 5 = 3. Explain that the first number is the number being divided, that the second number tells how many will be in each group, and the third tells how many groups there will be.

- Have the student practice writing and illustrating division sentences until it can be done with ease.

Complete the Power Practice

- For each incorrect multiplication fact, have the student circle how many rows should be in the array, and underline how many counters should be in each row. Then have the student draw the array, and count or use repeated addition to arrive at the correct answer.

- For each incorrect division fact, have the student circle how many counters should be in the array in all, and underline how many counters should be in each group. Then have the student draw an array and count groups to arrive at the correct answer.

USING THE LESSON

Lesson Goal
• Compare the capacity of objects.

What the Student Needs to Know
• Compare the size of real-life objects based on non-scale drawings.

Getting Started
Find out what students know about capacity. Ask:
• *What are some objects that can hold a tiny amount of liquid?* (Possible answers: an eyedropper, a teaspoon, a thimble)
• *What are some objects that can hold a huge amount of liquid?* (Possible answers: a water tower, a swimming pool, an oil tanker)
• *Of two objects of different size, which can usually hold more liquid—the larger object or the smaller object?* (the larger object)

What Can I Do?
• Read the question and the response. Then read and discuss the example. Ask:
• *If the drawing of the drinking glass were larger than the drawing of the pool, what would the correct answer to the problem be?* (It would still be the pool.) *Why?* (Because it is the size of the object in real life that matters, not how large it is drawn.)

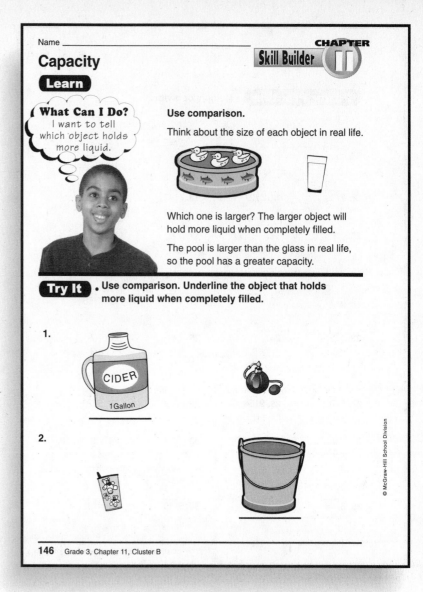

WHAT IF THE STUDENT CAN'T

Compare the Size of Real-Life Objects Based on Non-Scale Drawings
• Draw a truck and a television so that both drawings are about the same size. Ask the student to identify both drawings. Explain that the drawings don't really show how big the objects are compared to one another. Make it clear that the student has to form a picture of how big both objects are in real life.

• Encourage the student to draw the objects as they might look if they were sitting next to each other. Be sure the student is able to draw one object as noticeably larger than the other.

• Explain that another way of testing which of two objects is larger is to figure out whether one object will fit into another. For example, a television can fit into a truck, but a truck can't fit into a television set.

Name_____

Power Practice • Underline the object that holds more liquid when completely filled.

3.

4.   FIDO

5.

6.

7.

8.   Cola

9.   MILK   Pint

10.

WHAT IF THE STUDENT CAN'T

- Have the student practice comparing the sizes of objects represented in words or pictures until it can be done easily.

Complete the Power Practice

- Discuss each incorrect answer. Have the student identify both objects in the exercise. Ask the student to envision both objects next to one another, and to tell you which is larger and able to hold more liquid.

- If the student is unable to visualize the correct answer, have the student draw both objects as they might appear sitting side by side. Then have the student identify which object is able to hold more liquid.

USING THE LESSON

Try It

Have students look at exercises 1 and 2. Be sure it is clear to students what each object is. Then have students complete the exercises. Review the answers. Have volunteers describe how one object is larger than the other.

Power Practice

- Have students complete the practice items. Then review each answer.
- Select a few of the exercises and have a volunteer identify both objects. Then have the volunteer describe the relative sizes of both objects.

Lesson Goal
- Multiply and divide by 10, 100, and 1,000.

What the Student Needs to Know
- Multiply by 1.
- Divide by 1.
- Understand the relationship between 10, 100, and 1,000.

Getting Started
Find out what students know about multiplication facts involving 1. Write the following multiplication sentence on the board and have students solve:

4 × 1 = ___ (4)

Ask:

- *If you change the first factor to 5, what is the answer? (5) What is the answer if you change the first factor to 23? (23)*

- *If you multiply any number by 1, what will the product be?* (the number you are multiplying)

Write the following division sentence on the board and have students solve:

4 ÷ 1 = ___ (4)

Ask:

- *If you change the number being divided to 9, what will the quotient be? (9) What is the quotient if you change the number being divided to 41? (41)*

- *If you divide any number by one, what will the quotient be?* (the number you are dividing)

What Can I Do?
- Read the question and the response. Then read and discuss the multiplication sentences. Ask:

- *What multiplication fact do you need to know to solve these problems? (7 × 1 = 7)*

Name _____

Multiply and Divide by 10, 100, and 1,000

Learn

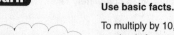

What Can I Do?
I want to multiply and divide by 10 and 1,000.

Use basic facts.

To multiply by 10, 100, or 1,000, use basic facts to write the first digit.

7 × 10 = ?
7 × 100 = ?
7 × 1,000 = ?

Use the basic fact 7 × 1 = 7.

Then count the number of zeros in 10, 100, or 1,000. Write the number of zeros in the product.

10 has 1 zero, so 7 × **10 = 70**.
100 has 2 zeros, so 7 × **100 = 700**.
1,000 ha : zeros, so 7 × **1,000 = 7,000**.

Use multiplication to divide.

To divide by 10, 100, or 1,000, use what you know about multiplication.

60 ÷ 10 = ?

600 ÷ 100 = ?

6,000 ÷ 1,000 = ?

You know that multiplication and division are related operations.

6 × 10 = 60,
so 60 ÷ 10 = 6.

6 × 100 = 600,
so 600 ÷ 100 = 6.

6 × 1,000 = 6,000,
so 6,000 ÷ 1,000 = 6

WHAT IF THE STUDENT CAN'T

Multiply by 1
- Use counters to illustrate multiplication facts involving the numbers 2 through 9. Then introduce facts for multiplying by 1. Demonstrate that, just as 2 × 5 is represented by 2 groups of 5, 1 × 5 is represented by 1 group of 5. Be sure the student understands that any number multiplied by 1 is equal to itself.

- Have the student use counters to illustrate and solve the multiplication facts for 1 until he or she can do so with ease.

Divide by 1
- Use counters to illustrate division facts for the number 1. Explain that in each fact, the original number is broken down into "groups" of 1, and that this means the quotient will be equal to the number being divided.

- Have the student use counters to illustrate and solve the division facts for 1 until he or she can do so with ease.

Name_____

Try It • Use basic facts. Find each product.

1. $10 \times 9 =$ ___90___   2. $8 \times 100 =$ ___800___   3. $4 \times 1,000 =$ ___4,000___

Use multiplication to complete each division sentence.

4. $4 \times 100 = 400$ so $400 \div 100 =$ ___4___

5. $1,000 \times 8 = 8,000$ so $8,000 \div 1,000 =$ ___8___

6. $7 \times 10 = 70$ so $70 \div 10 =$ ___7___

Power Practice • Find each product or quotient.

7. $1,000 \times 5 =$ ___5,000___   8. $400 \div 100 =$ ___4___

9. $7,000 \div 1,000 =$ ___7___   10. $2 \times 100 =$ ___200___

11. $30 \div 10 =$ ___3___   12. $100 \times 8 =$ ___800___

13. $\begin{array}{r} 1,000 \\ \times\ 2 \\ \hline 2,000 \end{array}$ 14. $100\overline{)800}$ (8)   15. $\begin{array}{r} 100 \\ \times 3 \\ \hline 300 \end{array}$ 16. $1,000\overline{)9,000}$ (9)

17. $\begin{array}{r} 1,000 \\ \times\ 3 \\ \hline 3,000 \end{array}$ 18. $1,000\overline{)4,000}$ (4)   19. $\begin{array}{r} 1,000 \\ \times\ 5 \\ \hline 5,000 \end{array}$ 20. $10\overline{)90}$ (9)

21. $1,000 \times 3 =$ ___3,000___   22. $6,000 \div 1,000 =$ ___6___

23. $50 \div 10 =$ ___5___   24. $100 \times 4 =$ ___400___

25. $1,000 \times 8 =$ ___8,000___   26. $40 \div 10 =$ ___4___

© McGraw-Hill School Division

WHAT IF THE STUDENT CAN'T

Understand the Relationship Between 10, 100, and 1,000

- Use grid strips and grids to model the relationship between the three numbers. Demonstrate how it takes 10 strips of 10 grid squares to make 100, and 10 grids of 100 squares to make 1,000.
- Have the student practice regrouping tens into hundreds and hundreds into thousands, as well as thousands into hundreds and hundreds into tens, until it can be done with ease.

Complete the Power Practice

- For each incorrect multiplication exercise, have the student identify the multiplication fact relevant to the problem. Then have the student explain how many zeros should be added to the product to arrive at the correct answer.
- For each incorrect division exercise, have the student write a related multiplication sentence. Then have the student identify the number in the multiplication sentence that is the quotient of the division sentence.

USING THE LESSON

- *If you multiply by 10, how many zeros do you write in the product? (1) If you multiply by 100? (2) If you multiply by 1,000? (3)*
- Read and discuss the division sentences. Ask:
- *How do you use multiplication sentences to solve these problems?* (You figure out what number $\times$ 10 = 60, what number $\times$ 100 = 600, and what number $\times$ 1,000 = 6,000. The missing factor in the multiplication sentence is the quotient in the division sentence.)
- *What division fact will also help you solve these problems?* ($6 \div 1 = 6$)
- *If you divide by 10, how many zeros do you take off the number being divided to get the quotient? (1) If you divide by 100? (2) If you divide by 1,000? (3)*

Try It

Have students look at exercise 1. Ask:

- *What multiplication fact do you need to know to solve this problem?* ($1 \times 9 = 9$)
- *How many zeros will you write at the end of the product?* (1)

Then have students complete exercises 1–3.

Have students look at exercise 4. Ask:

- *Which number in the multiplication sentence is the quotient for the division sentence?* (the first factor, 4)

Then have students complete exercises 4–6.

Power Practice

- Have students complete the practice items. Then review each answer.

Lesson Goal
- Compare two numbers.

What the Student Needs to Know
- Read a number line.
- Use the > and < signs.

Getting Started
Find out what students know about comparing numbers. Write the numbers 16 and 83 on the board. Ask:

- *When you count from 1 to 100, which of these numbers do you come to first?* (16)

Find out what students know about number lines. Draw a number line from 1 to 10 on the board. Ask:

- *In which direction do the numbers on the number line increase or become greater?* (from left to right)

- *In which direction do the numbers decrease?* (from right to left)

What Can I Do?
- Read the question and the response. Then read and discuss the example. Ask:

- *How can you tell that 43 is greater than 34 using the number line?* (43 is to the right of 34 on the number line, and the number to the right is always greater.)

- *How can you use place value to check your answer?* (Check the numbers in the tens place of both numbers. 43 has a 4 in the tens place, and 34 has a 3 in the tens place. Since 4 is greater than 3, you know that 43 is greater than 34.)

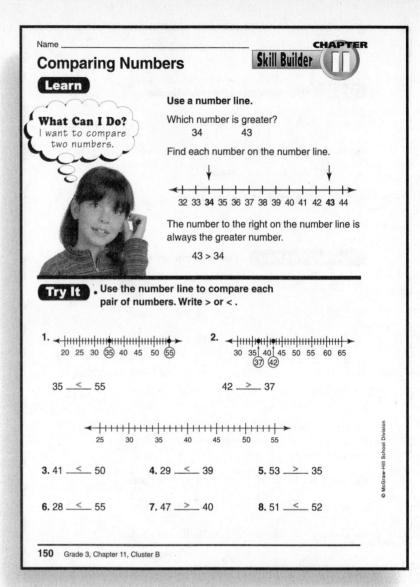

Name _____

Comparing Numbers

Learn

What Can I Do? I want to compare two numbers.

Use a number line.

Which number is greater?
34   43

Find each number on the number line.

32 33 **34** 35 36 37 38 39 40 41 42 **43** 44

The number to the right on the number line is always the greater number.

43 > 34

Try It . Use the number line to compare each pair of numbers. Write > or < .

1.
20 25 30 ㉟ 40 45 50 ㊺

35 __<__ 55

2.
30 35 40 45 50 55 60 65
㊲ ㊷

42 __>__ 37

25 30 35 40 45 50 55

3. 41 __<__ 50   4. 29 __<__ 39   5. 53 __>__ 35

6. 28 __<__ 55   7. 47 __>__ 40   8. 51 __<__ 52

© McGraw-Hill School Division

150   Grade 3, Chapter 11, Cluster B

WHAT IF THE STUDENT CAN'T

Read a Number Line
- Draw a number line from 10 to 30 and read the numbers aloud. Then have the student do so. Point to numbers on the line and have the student identify them. Be sure the student understands that the numbers increase as you move from left to right
- Have the student draw a number line from 40 to 60, labeling each number.

Use the > and < Signs
- Explain that these signs are used to compare two numbers. In a comparison like 9 > 2, the > sign means that 9 is greater than 2. The comparison can also be written 2 < 9, where the < sign means that 2 is less than 9.

Name_____

Power Practice • Use the number lines to compare each pair of numbers. Write > or < .

```
←┼┼┼┼┼┼┼┼┼┼┼┼┼┼┼┼┼┼┼┼┼┼┼┼┼┼┼┼┼┼┼┼┼┼┼┼┼┼┼┼┼┼┼┼┼┼→
   50    55    60    65    70    75    80    85    90    95
```

9. 57 _<_ 75   10. 66 _>_ 56   11. 73 _<_ 83

12. 79 _>_ 59   13. 60 _<_ 81   14. 77 _>_ 57

15. 82 _>_ 79   16. 90 _>_ 59   17. 74 _>_ 73

```
←┼┼┼┼┼┼┼┼┼┼┼┼┼┼┼┼┼┼┼┼┼┼┼┼┼┼┼┼┼┼┼┼┼┼┼┼┼┼┼┼┼┼┼┼┼┼→
  100   105   110   115   120   125   130   135   140   145
```

18. 111 _<_ 117

19. 134 _>_ 128

20. 130 _<_ 138

21. 107 _<_ 113

22. 128 _<_ 132

23. 106 _<_ 119

24. 137 _>_ 131

25. 127 _>_ 107

Learn with Partners & Parents

One More, One Less

Any number of people can play.

• Choose a number from 50 to 59 and write it down. Then look for numbers that are one more than your number and one less than your number. Look in the grocery store, at home, or on license plates and billboards.

• When you look for numbers, you must find the exact number. If you are looking for 54, then you must find 54. The digits cannot be part of another number, such as 8,542.

• When you find both these numbers, start looking for numbers that are two more and two less than your number. Keep playing until you are looking for zero.

• The person who has found more numbers wins.

© McGraw-Hill School Division

Grade 3, Chapter 11, Cluster B **151**

WHAT IF THE STUDENT CAN'T

• If the student has difficulty writing the signs correctly, mention that the opening in the sign should be toward the greater number. So, if you compare 8 and 4, the open end of the sign will face the 8, and the comparison will either read 8 > 4 or 4 < 8.

• Have the student practice comparing single-digit numbers until the concept becomes clear.

Complete the Power Practice

• Have the student label both number lines by writing "less" on the left side of the line and "greater" on the right side.

• Discuss each incorrect answer. Have the student find both numbers on the number line and identify which is less and which is greater. Then have the student complete the exercise correctly.

USING THE LESSON

Try It

Have students look at exercise 1. Ask:

• *Which number is farther to the right?* (55) *farther to the left?* (35)

Then have the students complete exercises 1 and 2.

Have students look at exercise 3. Have a volunteer find both numbers on the number line and identify which is farther right. Then have students complete exercises 3–8.

Power Practice

• Have students complete the practice items in both sets. Then review each answer.

• Select a few of the exercises from both sets. Have a volunteer find both numbers on the appropriate number line and compare them to one another.

Learning with Partners & Parents

• Suggest that students work in pairs and play the game for a week. Students should also look in text books, newspapers or magazines.

• Have students keep track of the numbers they start with and of those that they find in order to calculate their score after a week.

Grade 3, Chapter 11, Cluster B **151**

CHALLENGE

Lesson Goal
• Use addition sums to reveal riddle answers written in code.

Introducing the Challenge
Find out what students know about codes. Write the following code on the board:

62 = A; 5 = T; 19 = R

To the side, write:

62   19   5

Explain that these numbers are actually a word written in code, and that the code can be broken using the key on the board. Point to each number and have students identify which letter it represents. Write each letter above its number, and have students identify the code word (ART). Explain that there are many different codes that can be used to write words.

Read the introduction to the Challenge. Ask:

• *What is the first step you will need to take to break the code?* (Find the sum for each exercise.)

• *What should your second step be?* (Use the sums to match each exercise number with a letter in the code.)

• *What will your final step be?* (Write each letter in the blank above its exercise number.)

Addition Riddles
Find each sum. Then you'll be ready to solve the riddles on the next page.

1. 52 + 87 139	**2.** 91 + 35 126	**3.** 84 + 57 141	**4.** 65 + 48 113
5. 77 + 88 165	**6.** 62 + 59 121	**7.** 25 + 63 88	**8.** 40 + 32 72
9. 94 + 63 157	**10.** 51 + 78 129	**11.** 39 + 43 82	**12.** 82 + 66 148
13. 61 + 65 126	**14.** 74 + 45 119	**15.** 89 + 64 153	**16.** 26 + 99 125
17. 38 + 27 65	**18.** 97 + 74 171	**19.** 68 + 84 152	**20.** 74 + 57 131
21. 76 + 62 138	**22.** 49 + 39 88	**23.** 41 + 84 125	**24.** 49 + 97 146

Name _____

In the riddles below, the number under each blank is the number of an exercise on page 86. Find the answer for that exercise in the bottom row of one of these charts.

Above each answer is the letter it stands for. Write the letters on the blanks to solve the riddles.

A	B	C	D	E	F	G	H	I	J	K	L	M
88	139	141	113	125	152	99	146	138	129	87	171	119

N	O	P	Q	R	S	T	U	V	W	X	Y	Z
131	82	121	72	165	126	157	153	144	148	178	65	100

25. Why did the student take his math book to the school nurse?

B E C A U S E   I T   H A D
1 23 3 22 15 2 23   21 9   24 22 4

S O   M A N Y   P R O B L E M S .
13 11   14 22 20 17   6 5 11 1 18 23 14 2

26. Why is a dollar smarter than a quarter?

B E C A U S E   I T   H A S
1 23 3 7 15 2 23   21 9   24 22 2

M O R E   C E N T S .
14 11 5 16   3 23 20 9 13

27. Why does a math student love a calculator?

B E C A U S E   O N E   C A N
1 23 3 7 15 2 23   11 20 16   3 7 20

A L W A Y S   C O U N T   O N   I T .
7 18 12 7 17 2   3 11 15 20 9   11 20   21 9

Grade 3, Chapter 11, Cluster A **153**

Using the Challenge

Have students complete the Challenge. Review the answers to the riddles. Ask:

• *In breaking the code, did you notice any words that repeated themselves? Which ones?* (Possible answers: *because, it*)

• *What are some ways you can check to be sure you have broken the code correctly?* (See if the answer to the riddle makes sense; see if any words are misspelled; be sure that every sum and exercise matches up with a letter.)

• *Suppose that your answer to number 2 reads "because it has more dents." How would you go back and try to find the correct answer?* (Possible answer: start by figuring out which word doesn't make sense. Then go through and check your math for the exercises underneath each of the letters in the word.)

CHALLENGE

Lesson Goal

- Use scale drawing and the answers to subtraction problems to reveal a hidden message.

Introducing the Challenge

Find out what students know about scale drawings. On the board, draw 2 squares, one small and one large. In the small square, draw the following figure:

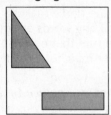

Explain to students that you want to reproduce the same shapes in the larger square. Ask:

- *How can I be sure that the rectangle will stay the same size compared to the larger square?* (Possible answer: See how many times larger the second square is, and draw the new rectangle as that many times larger than the first one.)

- *How can I make the new shapes the right size without using a ruler?* (Possible answer: As you draw the new square, compare it with the original. Be sure the part of the square taken up by the shapes is the same.)

Subtraction Puzzle

Find each difference. Then match the difference to the numbers in the squares on the next page. Trace the square exactly like the small square below the exercise. When you finish, you will see an important message.

1.	2.	3.	4.
84 − 19 65	75 − 57 18	60 − 39 21	59 − 26 33

5.	6.	7.	8.
77 − 46 31	80 − 52 28	91 − 49 42	63 − 27 36

9.	10.	11.	12.
52 − 18 34	79 − 38 41	63 − 56 7	71 − 68 3

13.	14.	15.	16.
82 − 37 45	47 − 25 22	90 − 63 27	76 − 38 38

Name _____

3	7	18	21
22	2_	2_	31
33	34	36	38
41	4_		65

Make up your own subtraction puzzle for your friends.
Decide what your secret message will be and make
up subtraction exercises for each square.

© McGraw-Hill School Division

CHALLENGE

Have students read the introduction to the Challenge. Explain that what they will be doing is similar to solving a code, except that the numbers correspond to parts of a picture instead of letters.

Using the Challenge

Have students complete the exercises and check to see that each difference matches up with a square on page 155. Ask:

- *As you draw each square, should its sides match up with the sides of the squares around it?* (yes)

Have students fill in the puzzle on page 155. Check to be sure that the message "you win" is visible to all students. Ask:

- *How many squares did it you have to draw to find the hidden message?* (16)

- *If you wrote this message in a code where each letter is replaced by a number, how many numbers would you have to write?* (6)

- *Which of these two ways is a better way of putting a message in code? Why?* (Possible answers: A drawing code, because it's easier to keep the message from people you don't want to see it; a number code, because there's less chance that something will go wrong when you try to decode it.)

Classify Objects

Tell what is common about each group.

1. book
magazine
newspaper

2. chair
sofa
stool

3. brown
green
orange

4. swordfish
tuna
trout

_____ _____ _____ _____

Identify Sides and Angles

Write the number of sides and angles for each figure.

5.

_____ sides

_____ angles

6.

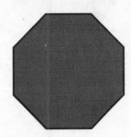

_____ sides

_____ angles

7.

_____ sides

_____ angles

8.

_____ sides

_____ angles

9.

_____ sides

_____ angles

10.

_____ sides

_____ angles

Name _____

Comparing Angles

Compare each pair of angles. Write > or <.

11.

12.

13.

A ___ B   C ___ D   F ___ G

Measuring Line Segments

Measure the length of each line segment to the nearest $\frac{1}{2}$ inch.

Length

14. _____   _____

15. _____   _____

16. _____   _____

Add 3 or More Addends

Find each sum.

17. $8 + 15 + 8 + 15 =$ _____

18. $16 + 16 + 16 + 16 =$ _____

19. $45 + 25 + 45 + 25 + 45 =$ _____

20. $300 + 600 + 300 + 500 + 200 =$ _____

CHAPTER 12 PRE-CHAPTER ASSESSMENT

Assessment Goal

This two-page assessment covers skills identified as necessary for success in Chapter 12 Geometry. The first page assesses the major prerequisite skills for Cluster A. The second page assesses the major prerequisite skills for Cluster B. When the Cluster A and Cluster B prerequisite skills overlap, the skill(s) will be covered in only one section.

Getting Started

• Allow students time to look over the two pages of the assessment. Point out the labels that identify the skills covered.

• Have students find math vocabulary terms used in the assessment. List vocabulary terms on the board as students identify them. If necessary, review the meanings of all essential math vocabulary.

Introducing the Assessment

• Explain to students that these pages will help you know if they are ready to start a new chapter in their math textbooks.

• Students who have transferred from another school may not have been introduced to some of these skills. Encourage students to do their best and assure them you will help them learn any needed skills.

Cluster A Challenge

Those students who demonstrate mastery of the skills on this page will not need to use the reteaching worksheets. Instead, these students can do the Cluster A Challenge found on pages 166-167.

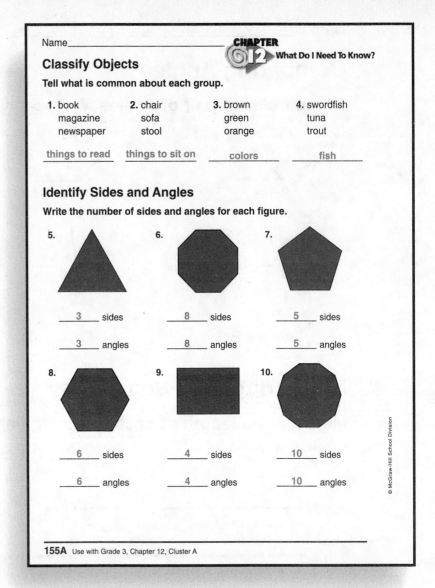

Name_____

Classify Objects

Tell what is common about each group.

| 1. book magazine newspaper | 2. chair sofa stool | 3. brown green orange | 4. swordfish tuna trout |

things to read   things to sit on   colors   fish

Identify Sides and Angles

Write the number of sides and angles for each figure.

5. 3 sides 3 angles

6. 8 sides 8 angles

7. 5 sides 5 angles

8. 6 sides 6 angles

9. 4 sides 4 angles

10. 10 sides 10 angles

© McGraw-Hill School Division

155A Use with Grade 3, Chapter 12, Cluster A

CLUSTER A PREREQUISITE SKILLS

The skills listed in this chart are those identified as major prerequisite skills for students' success in the lessons in Cluster A of the chapter. Each skill is covered by one or more assessment items as shown in the middle column. The right column provides the page number for the lessons in this book that reteach the cluster A prerequisite skills.

Skill Name	Assessment Items	Lesson Pages
Classify Objects	1-4	156-157
Identify Sides and Angles	5-10	158-159

Name _____

Comparing Angles

Compare each pair of angles. Write > or <.

11.
12.
13.

A

C

F

B

D

G

A $\leq$ B   C $\geq$ D   F $\leq$ G

Measuring Line Segments

Measure the length of each line segment to the nearest $\frac{1}{2}$ inch.

		Length
14. _____		$2\frac{1}{2}$ in.
15. _____		4 in.
16. _____		$1\frac{1}{2}$ in.

Add 3 or More Addends

Find each sum.

17. $8 + 15 + 8 + 15 =$ ___46___

18. $16 + 16 + 16 + 16 =$ ___64___

19. $45 + 25 + 45 + 25 + 45 =$ ___185___

20. $300 + 600 + 300 + 500 + 200 =$ ___1,900___

Use with Grade 3, Chapter 12, Cluster B **155B**

Alternative Assessment Strategies

- Oral administration of the assessment is appropriate for younger students or those whose native language is not English. Read the skills title and directions one section at a time. Check students' understanding by asking them to tell you how they will do the first exercise in the group.

- For some skill types you may wish to use group administration. In this technique, a small group or pair of students complete the assessment together. Through their discussion, you will be able to decide if supplementary reteaching materials are needed.

Intervention Materials

If students are not successful with the prerequisite skills assessed on these pages, reteaching lessons have been created to help them make the transition into the chapter.

Item correlation charts showing the skills lessons suitable for reteaching the prerequisite skills are found beneath the reproductions of each page of the assessment.

CLUSTER B PREREQUISITE SKILLS

The skills listed in this chart are those identified as major prerequisite skills for students' success in the lessons in Cluster B of the chapter. Each skill is covered by one or more assessment items as shown in the middle column. The right column provides the page numbers for the lessons in this book that reteach the Cluster B prerequisite skills

Skill Name	Assessment Items	Lesson Pages
Comparing Angles	11-13	160-161
Measuring Line Segments	14-16	162-163
Add 3 or More Addends	17-20	164-165

Cluster B Challenge

Those students who demonstrate mastery of the skills on this page will not need to use the reteaching worksheets. Instead, these students can do the Cluster B Challenge found on pages 168-169.

Lesson Goal
- Identify what a group of objects has in common.

What the Student Needs to Know
- Make a list.
- Describe an object.

Getting Started
Find out what students know about classifying objects. Write "dog" on the board and underline it. Have students suggest words that describe a dog, and write each word under the heading. Then write "elephant" on the board and have students offer words that describe an elephant.

Point out that some of the things named in describing the two animals are different. For example, an elephant has a trunk, but a dog does not.

Have students check to see if any descriptions are in both lists. If not, point out that although the two animals seem quite different, dogs and elephants have many things in common; for example, they both have tails, they both walk on four legs, and so on. Most important, both creatures belong to a group we call animals.

What Can I Do?
- Read the question and the response. Then read and discuss the example. Ask:
- *Each object is described by its color: yellow is under banana, orange is under orange, and red is under apple. What are some other kinds of descriptions used for the objects?* (Possible answers: how it tastes, what type of object it is, what it's like to bite into.)
- *What is the name of the group to which each object belongs?* (fruit)

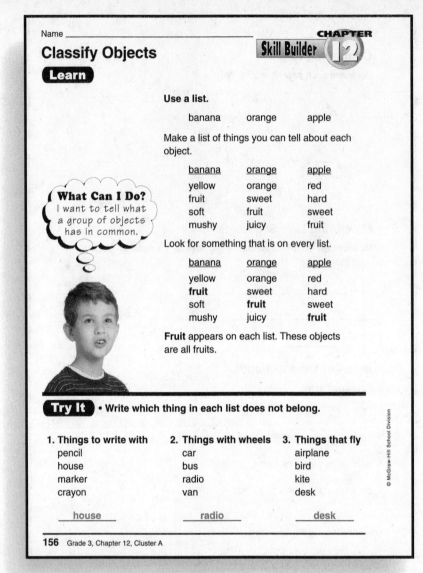

Classify Objects
Learn

Use a list.

   banana   orange   apple

Make a list of things you can tell about each object.

banana	orange	apple
yellow	orange	red
fruit	sweet	hard
soft	fruit	sweet
mushy	juicy	fruit

Look for something that is on every list.

banana	orange	apple
yellow	orange	red
fruit	sweet	hard
soft	**fruit**	sweet
mushy	juicy	**fruit**

Fruit appears on each list. These objects are all fruits.

What Can I Do?
I want to tell what a group of objects has in common.

Try It • Write which thing in each list does not belong.

1. Things to write with	2. Things with wheels	3. Things that fly
pencil	car	airplane
house	bus	bird
marker	radio	kite
crayon	van	desk
house	_radio_	_desk_

156   Grade 3, Chapter 12, Cluster A

© McGraw-Hill School Division

WHAT IF THE STUDENT CAN'T

Make a List
- Have the student assist you in writing out a list of several kinds of fruit underneath the heading "Fruit." Explain that a list helps you organize words or ideas so that they're easier to understand. Be sure the student understands that the heading of a list tells you what the list is about, and each of the items on a list relates to the heading.
- Have the student practice writing lists for various headings until the concept becomes clear.

Describe an Object
- Explain that describing an object is a way of answering certain questions about the object. Have the student describe a basketball for you by writing the answers to questions. For example: What color is it? (orange) What do you do with it? (you dribble it) What shape is it? (round)
- Have the student practice writing descriptions for objects until it can be done with ease.

Power Practice • Tell what is common about each group.

Answers may vary. Possible answers are given.

4. rose
   daffodil
   daisy

   _____ flowers _____

5. pine
   oak
   maple

   _____ trees _____

6. elephant
   hyena
   zebra

   _____ [wild] animals _____

7. milk
   juice
   water

   _____ things you drink _____

8. red
   blue
   yellow

   _____ colors _____

9. stream
   river
   creek

   _____ things with [flowing] water _____

10. snow
    rain
    sleet

    _____ wet weather _____

11. hammer
    wrench
    saw

    _____ tools _____

12. tree
    grass
    flower

    _____ things that grow _____

13. quarter
    dime
    nickel

    _____ money _____

14. skirt
    socks
    jacket

    _____ clothes _____

15. ice cube
    snow
    refrigerator

    _____ cold things _____

16. Alaska
    California
    Texas

    _____ states _____

17. uncle
    cousin
    sister

    _____ relatives _____

18. candle
    sun
    lamp

    _____ things that give light _____

© McGraw-Hill School Division

Grade 3, Chapter 12, Cluster A **157**

USING THE LESSON

Try It

Have students look at exercise 1. Ask:

- *Which of the objects does not belong?* (house) *Why not?* (You can't write with a house.)
- *Would a ball-point pen belong in this list?* (yes) *Would a banana belong?* (no)

Have students complete exercises 2 and 3. For each exercise, have volunteers name other objects that belong in the group and then give examples of objects that do not belong.

Power Practice

- Have students complete the practice exercises. Review each answer.
- Select several of the exercises. Have volunteers give lists of descriptors for each of the objects in each exercise. Circle the descriptors that all three objects have in common.

WHAT IF THE STUDENT CAN'T

Complete the Power Practice

- Discuss each incorrect answer. For each object, have the student write a list of words or phrases that describe it. Then have the student cross out any words that do not appear in more than one list.
- If a description appears under more than one object, ask the student whether the description also applies to the third object. If it doesn't, then have the student move on to another description and ask the same question.

- If the student is unable to identify qualities that apply to more than just one object, suggest asking questions that apply to all three objects. For example: How does it feel? What do you do with it? What does it look like? Then have the student use the answers to the questions to arrive at the correct answer.

USING THE LESSON

Lesson Goal
- Identify the number of sides and angles of a figure.

What the Student Needs to Know
- Identify a line segment.
- Identify an angle.

Getting Started
Find out whether students can recognize the sides and angles in a closed plane figure. Draw a triangle on the board. Ask:
- *How many sides does this figure have?* (3)
- *How many corners does this figure have?* (3)

What Can I Do?
- Read the question and the response. Then read and discuss the example. Be sure students understand that "angle" is the word used in mathematics for a corner. Ask:
- *Is the number of sides the same as the number of angles?* (Yes.)
- *Do you have to know the name of the figure to tell how many sides and angles it has?* (No.)

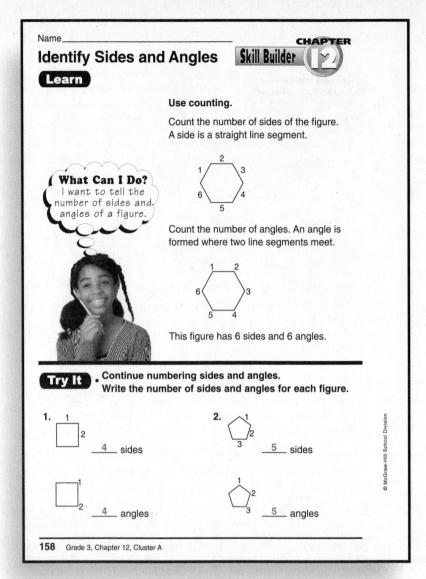

Learn

Use counting.

Count the number of sides of the figure. A side is a straight line segment.

What Can I Do? I want to tell the number of sides and angles of a figure.

Count the number of angles. An angle is formed where two line segments meet.

This figure has 6 sides and 6 angles.

Try It • Continue numbering sides and angles. Write the number of sides and angles for each figure.

1. ___4___ sides

___4___ angles

2. ___5___ sides

___5___ angles

158   Grade 3, Chapter 12, Cluster A

WHAT IF THE STUDENT CAN'T

Identify a Line Segment
- Explain that a line segment is part of a straight line. On the board, illustrate that a line segment can stand on its own, or it can join with other line segments to form a closed figure.
- Be sure that the student understands that a line segment must be straight, and that a curved line is not a line segment.
- Have the student use a ruler to practice drawing closed figures with line segments.

Identify an Angle
- Explain that an angle is formed where the ends of two line segments meet. Draw several examples of line segments that meet to form different-sized angles.
- Then draw several closed figures, such as triangles, rectangles, and parallelograms. Ask students to identify the points at which the sides meet to form an angle.

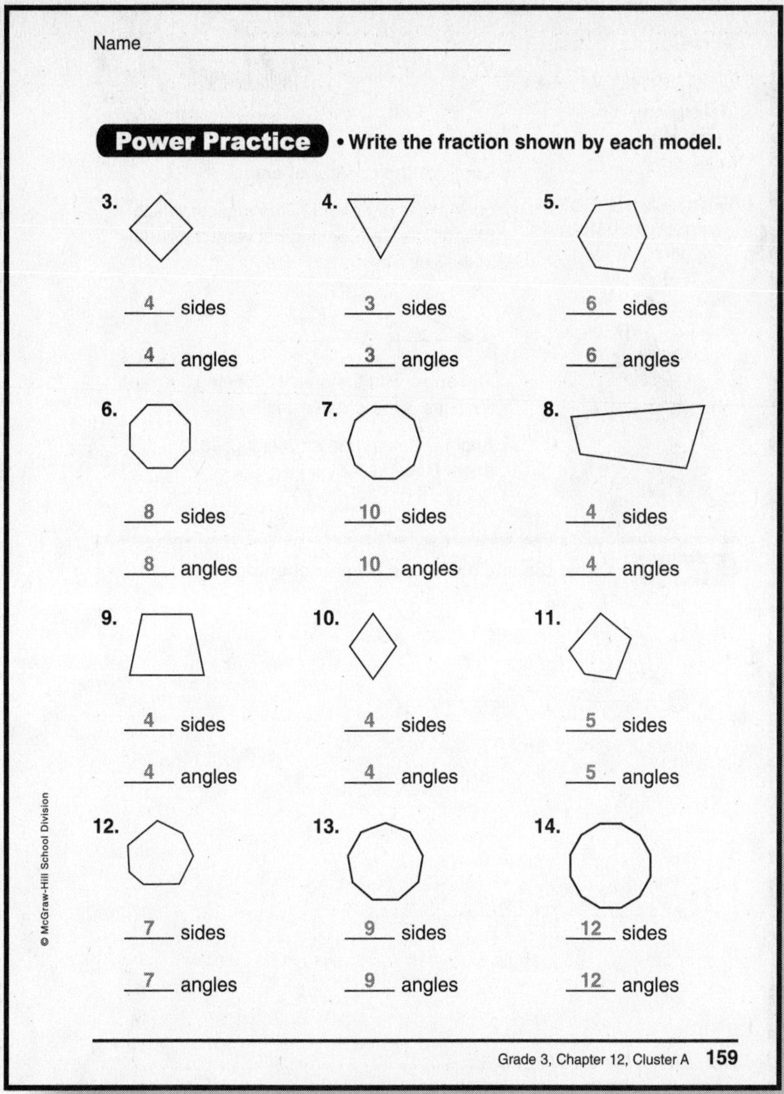

Name_____

Power Practice • Write the fraction shown by each model.

3.

___4___ sides

___4___ angles

4.

___3___ sides

___3___ angles

5.

___6___ sides

___6___ angles

6.

___8___ sides

___8___ angles

7.

___10___ sides

___10___ angles

8.

___4___ sides

___4___ angles

9.

___4___ sides

___4___ angles

10.

___4___ sides

___4___ angles

11.

___5___ sides

___5___ angles

12.

___7___ sides

___7___ angles

13.

___9___ sides

___9___ angles

14.

___12___ sides

___12___ angles

© McGraw-Hill School Division

Grade 3, Chapter 12, Cluster A **159**

WHAT IF THE STUDENT CAN'T

Complete the Power Practice
• Discuss each incorrect answer. Have the student number each side of the figure. Then have the student predict the number of angles in the figure before numbering them. Then have the student identify the correct answer.

Try It
Have students look at exercise 1. Ask:
• *How many sides does the figure have?* (4)
• *How many angles does it have?* (4)

Then have students complete exercise 2.

Power Practice
• Have students complete the practice items. Then review each answer. Students should discover that the number of sides in a figure will always be the same as the number of angles.

Lesson Goal
- Compare the width of angles.

What the Student Needs to Know
- Recognize an angle.
- Use the > and < signs.

Getting Started
Find out what students know about comparing. Write the following problem on the board:

32 _____ 67

Ask:
- *Which of these two numbers is greater?* (67)
- *Which sign should go in the blank?* (the "less than" sign, or <)

Then write the following problem on the board.

93 _____ 74

Ask:
- *What should go in the blank?* (the "greater than" sign, or >)

What Can I Do?
Read the question and the response. Then read and discuss the example. Explain that, just as you can compare two numbers, you can compare two angles. Ask:
- *How can you compare angle A and angle B using the "less than" sign?* (angle A < angle B)

Draw the following angles on the board:

C   D

- *Which angle has the greater opening, angle C or angle D?* (angle C)
- *How would you use a symbol to show the relationship between the two angles?* (angle C > angle D; angle D < angle C)

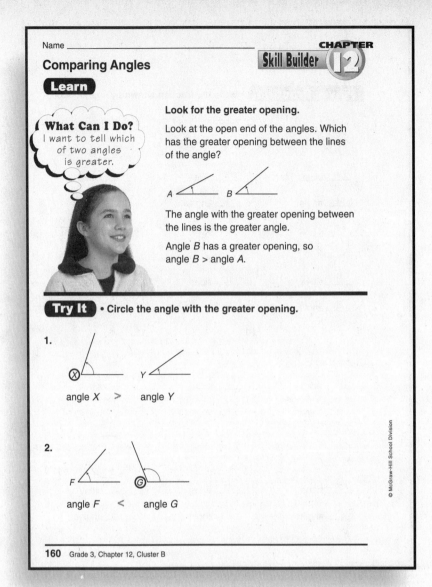

Name _____

Learn

What Can I Do?
I want to tell which of two angles is greater.

Look for the greater opening.

Look at the open end of the angles. Which has the greater opening between the lines of the angle?

A   B

The angle with the greater opening between the lines is the greater angle.

Angle B has a greater opening, so angle B > angle A.

Try It • Circle the angle with the greater opening.

1.
X   Y

angle X   >   angle Y

2.
F   G

angle F   <   angle G

© McGraw-Hill School Division

WHAT IF THE STUDENT CAN'T

Recognize an Angle
- Explain that an angle is created where two lines or line segments meet. Illustrate how the size of the angle depends on the directions in which the lines run. Show several examples of angles on the board, such as a 20° angle, a 60° angle, a 90° angle, and a 100° angle. Have the student tell you which angle has the smallest opening and which has the greatest.
- Have the student use a ruler to practice drawing angles until the concept becomes clear.

Use the > and < Signs
- Explain that these signs are used to compare two numbers or figures. In a comparison like 9 > 2, the > sign means that 9 is greater than 2. The comparison can also be written 2 < 9, where the < sign means that 2 is less than 9.
- If the student has difficulty writing the signs correctly, mention that the opening in the sign should point to the greater of the two numbers or figures. For example, angle F in Try It is less than angle G. So the open end of the sign will face angle G, and the comparison will either read

Name _____

Compare each pair of angles. Circle the angle with the greater opening. Write > or <.

3.

angle P __>__ angle Q

4.

angle S __<__ angle T

Power Practice • Compare each set of angles. Write > or <.

5.

angle J __>__ angle K

6.

angle C __<__ angle D

7.

angle A __>__ angle B

8.

angle N __>__ angle O

9.

angle R __<__ angle S

10.

angle V __>__ angle W

Try It

Have students complete exercises 1 and 2. Ask:

- *Which of the four angles appears to have the greatest opening?* (angle G)
- *Which of the four angles appears to have the smallest opening?* (angle Y)

Power Practice

- Be sure students understand how to use the > and < signs. Have them complete the practice exercises. Then review each answer.

WHAT IF THE STUDENT CAN'T

angle G > angle F or angle F < angle G.

- Have the student practice using the < and > signs to compare single-digit numbers until the concept becomes clear.

Complete the Power Practice

- Discuss each incorrect answer. Have the student look at each angle in the exercise, and identify which has a greater opening. Then have the student use the > and < signs to write two comparisons of the angles.

- If the student is unable to identify the opening of one angle as being larger than the other, have the student use a ruler to turn both angles into triangles by drawing lines across the openings. Then have the student estimate or measure the length of the lines to identify the greater angle.

Lesson Goal

- Measure line segments to the nearest $\frac{1}{2}$-inch.

What the Student Needs to Know

- Read a ruler.
- Round a measurement to the nearest half-inch.

Getting Started

Find out how familiar students are with using rulers. Ask:

- *What does each number on an inch ruler stand for?* (the number of inches from 0 at the left of the ruler to that point on the ruler.)

- *How do you use a ruler to measure an object?* (Possible answer: You line up one end of the object with the beginning of the ruler. Then you check to see the measure on the ruler at the point where the end of the object is.)

- What are the little marks on the ruler for? (they mark $\frac{1}{2}$-inches, $\frac{1}{4}$-inches, $\frac{1}{8}$-inches, and $\frac{1}{16}$-inches on the ruler.)

What Can I Do?

- Read the question and the response. Then read and discuss the example. Ask:

- *If you don't line up the left end of the line segment with the edge of the ruler, will your measurement still be correct?* (No) *Why or why not?* (The measurement won't start from zero.)

- *Why was the measurement rounded to $2\frac{1}{2}$ inches instead of 2 inches?* (Because it was only $\frac{1}{8}$ of an inch to $2\frac{1}{2}$ inches, but $\frac{3}{8}$ of an inch to 2 inches.)

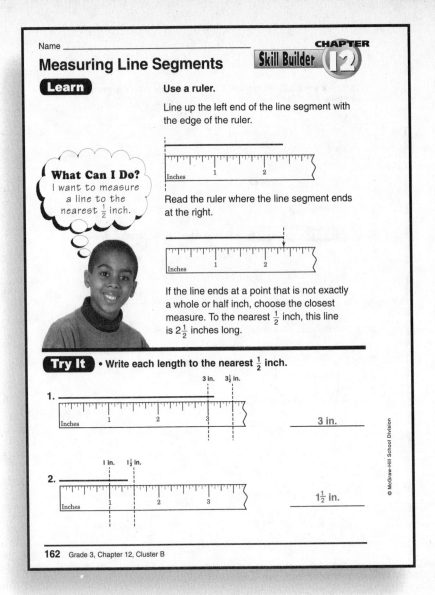

Name _____

Measuring Line Segments

Skill Builder CHAPTER **12**

Learn

Use a ruler.

Line up the left end of the line segment with the edge of the ruler.

What Can I Do?
I want to measure a line to the nearest $\frac{1}{2}$ inch.

Read the ruler where the line segment ends at the right.

If the line ends at a point that is not exactly a whole or half inch, choose the closest measure. To the nearest $\frac{1}{2}$ inch, this line is $2\frac{1}{2}$ inches long.

Try It • Write each length to the nearest $\frac{1}{2}$ inch.

1.
3 in.

2.
$1\frac{1}{2}$ in.

© McGraw-Hill School Division

162 Grade 3, Chapter 12, Cluster B

WHAT IF THE STUDENT CAN'T

Read a Ruler

- Draw a simplified ruler, using the numbers 1 through 5. Explain to the student that each of the large marks next to the numbers represents 1 inch. Then add half-inch marks to the ruler. Explain to the student that even though the half-inch marks don't have a number next to them, you can tell what they represent by going back to the last number and adding $\frac{1}{2}$.

- Have the student look at a ruler and identify the inch marks and half-inch marks. Then give the student several line segments to measure. Be sure that each line segment ends exactly at an inch or half-inch mark.

Round a Measurement to the Nearest Half-inch

- Have the student use a ruler to count from 0 inches to 10 inches by $\frac{1}{2}$s (0, $\frac{1}{2}$, 1, $1\frac{1}{2}$ ...). Explain that when you round a measurement to the nearest half-inch, you can round it to any number that you can reach by counting by $\frac{1}{2}$s.

- Have the student measure a line segment that measures somewhere between $3\frac{1}{2}$ and 4 inches. Explain that when a measurement doesn't come

Name _____

Power Practice Use an inch ruler. Measure the length of each line segment to the nearest $\frac{1}{2}$ inch.

3. _____ 4 in.

4. _____ $4\frac{1}{2}$ in.

5. _____ 4 in.

6. _____

7. _____ $1\frac{1}{2}$ in.

8. _____ $2\frac{1}{2}$ in.

9. _____ 4 in.

10. _____ $3\frac{1}{2}$ in.

11. _____ 2 in.

© McGraw-Hill School Division

Grade 3, Chapter 12, Cluster B **163**

Try It

Have students look at exercises 1 and 2. Be sure that they are able to distinguish between an inch mark and a half-inch mark on the rulers. Ask:

• *How can you use the smaller marks between the inch mark and the half-inch mark to round to the nearest measure?* (Possible answer: Find the mark where the segment ends. Then count the small marks back to the previous inch and forward to the next inch. Compare to see which inch is closer to the end of the segment. Round up or down to that inch.)

Then have students complete the exercises.

Power Practice

• Have the students complete the practice items. Then review each answer.

WHAT IF THE STUDENT CAN'T

out exactly at an inch or half-inch mark, you can round the measurement to the nearest half-inch. Mention that if you can't tell which is closer just by looking, you can use the smaller marks on the ruler to count which is closer. Then have the student round the measurement of the line segment to the closest measure.

Complete the Power Practice

• Discuss each incorrect answer. Have the student carefully line up the edge of the ruler with the left end of the line segment. Then have the student measure the segment, using a piece of tape to mark the end of the segment on the ruler. The student should then round to the nearest measure to arrive at the correct answer.

Lesson Goal

- Add more than two 2-digit or 3-digit numbers

What the Student Needs to Know

- Recall basic addition facts.
- Add more than two 1-digit numbers.
- Understand place value through hundreds and regrouping.

Getting Started

Find out what students know about adding more than two numbers. Write the following addition sentence on the board:

2 + 9 + 5 = _____ (16)

Ask:

- *How can you find the sum of these three numbers?* (Add two of the numbers together, then add the third number to the sum of the first two.)
- *Does it matter in which order you add the numbers?* (No.)
- *What is the sum of the numbers?* (16)

Then write the following addition sentence on the board:

4 + 1 + 9 + 8 = _____ (22)

Ask:

- *What are some ways you can find the sum of these four numbers?* (Possible answers: Find the sum of the first two and the last two, then add them together; Add the first two numbers, add the third to that sum, and add the fourth to that sum to get the answer.)

Have volunteers demonstrate different methods of solving the problem. Be sure students understand that each method should result in the same answer (22).

What Can I Do?

- Read the question and the response. Then read and discuss the example. Ask:
- *In which order should you add the columns?* (Start with the ones, then add the tens.)

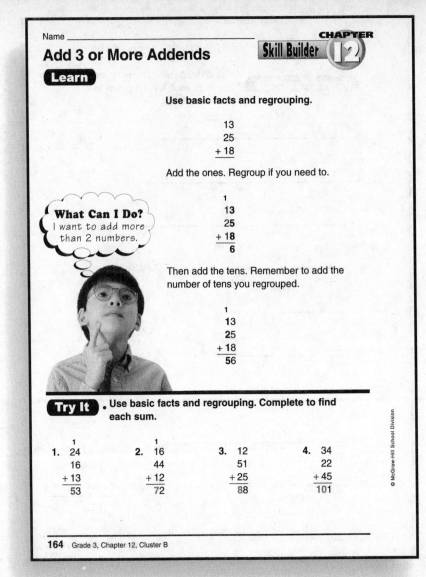

Add 3 or More Addends

Learn

Use basic facts and regrouping.

13
25
+ 18

Add the ones. Regroup if you need to.

1
13
25
+ 18
——
6

Then add the tens. Remember to add the number of tens you regrouped.

1
13
25
+ 18
——
56

What Can I Do?
I want to add more than 2 numbers.

Try It . Use basic facts and regrouping. Complete to find each sum.

1. 1 24 16 + 13 —— 53	2. 1 16 44 + 12 —— 72	3. 12 51 + 25 —— 88	4. 34 22 + 45 —— 101

164 Grade 3, Chapter 12, Cluster B

© McGraw-Hill School Division

WHAT IF THE STUDENT CAN'T

Recall Basic Addition Facts

- Practice addition facts for 10 to 15 minutes daily until the student can recall the sums for the addition facts easily.

Add More than Two 1-Digit Numbers

- Have the student write out the following addition sentence:

5 + 2 + 9 = _____

Use counters to illustrate how you can solve an addition sentence of three or more numbers by adding the numbers in order. Have the student write the sum of the first two numbers in the number

sentence (7). Then have the student add this number to the last number of the sentence to arrive at the correct answer (16).

- Have the student practice solving addition sentences of three or more 1-digit numbers until it can be done with ease.

Understand Place Value Through Hundreds and Regrouping

- Have the student write a 3-digit number and read it aloud. Explain that each digit can be seen as one place in a place-value chart. Then have the student tell you how

Name _____

Power Practice • Find each sum.

5. 15
    15
    + 15
    ‾‾‾‾
    45

6. 12
    24
    + 36
    ‾‾‾‾
    72

7. 34
    26
    + 31
    ‾‾‾‾
    91

8. 23
    33
    + 43
    ‾‾‾‾
    99

9. 44
    55
    + 66
    ‾‾‾‾
    165

10. 27
    23
    + 38
    ‾‾‾‾
    88

11. 84
    23
    + 16
    ‾‾‾‾
    123

12. 123
    123
    + 123
    ‾‾‾‾‾
    369

13. 200
    500
    + 300
    ‾‾‾‾‾
    1,000

14. 34
    34
    + 34
    ‾‾‾‾
    102

15. 47
    48
    + 49
    ‾‾‾‾
    144

16. 400
    300
    + 700
    ‾‾‾‾‾
    1,400

17. 25 + 42 + 19 = __86__

18. 113 + 243 + 115 = __471__

19. 19 + 19 + 19 = __57__

20. 300 + 400 + 200 = __900__

21. 18 + 52 + 18 + 52 = __140__

22. 900 + 800 + 700 = __2,400__

23. 400 + 600 + 300 = __1,300__

24. 24 + 35 + 46 + 57 = __162__

© McGraw-Hill School Division

Learn with Partners & Parents

Exercise Exchange

• Working by yourself, write six exercises. Three of the exercises should involve adding four 2-digit numbers. The other exercises should involve adding four 3-digit numbers.

• Create an answer key for your exercises.

• Then exchange exercises with your partner. Find the answers to your partner's exercises.

• For any answers that disagree, work with your partner to determine the correct sum.

Grade 3, Chapter 12, Cluster B **165**

• *What is the sum of the ones column?* (16) *What do you do with the 6?* (Write it underneath the ones column.) *What do you do with the 1?* (Add it to the tens column.)

• *What happens if you forget to add the tens you regroup when you add the tens column?* (You will get the wrong digit in the tens place of your sum.)

Try It

Have students look at exercise 1. Ask:

• *What is the sum of the numbers in the ones column?* (13)

• *What is the sum of the numbers in the tens column?* (4 tens + 1 ten = 5 tens)

Then have students complete exercises 1–4.

Power Practice

Have the students look at exercise 9. Ask:

• *What is the sum of the tens column?* (15 tens + 1 ten from the grouping = 16 tens) *How do you write this sum in the answer?* (Write the 6 in the tens place of the answer, and create a hundreds place to write the 1 in.)

• Have students write exercises 17–24 in vertical form before they find the sum.

• Have students complete the practice items. Then review each answer.

• Select several of the problems. Have volunteers come up to the board and demonstrate how they arrived at the correct answer.

Learn with Partners & Parents

• After students exchange their exercises and do the problems they were given, they should give the exercises back to their partners. Partners should circle the answers and the addition to be sure that their partners added correctly.

WHAT IF THE STUDENT CAN'T

many hundreds, tens, and ones are in the number.

• Have the student practice writing 2-digit and 3-digit numbers in a place-value chart until it can be done with ease.

• Use grid strips and squares to illustrate a situation where regrouping is required. For example, show the student how 6 ones + 7 ones = 13 ones. Since a place value needs to be 9 or less, 10 of the ones are regrouped, giving you 1 ten and 3 ones.

• Have the student practice regrouping ones into tens until it can be done with ease.

Complete the Power Practice

• Discuss each incorrect answer. Have the student write out an addition sentence for each column, including regrouping. As the student finds the sum of each column, have him or her write a digit in the answer to the exercise. When all columns have been added, have the student read off the answer.

• If the student has difficulty adding the numbers correctly, have him or her use counters for assistance.

Grade 3, Chapter 12, Cluster B **165**

CHALLENGE

Lesson Goal
- Complete a math circle by using addition, subtraction, multiplication, and division.

Introducing the Challenge
Find out how comfortable students are using addition, subtraction, multiplication, and division in sequence. Write the following number sentence on the board:

$$12 + 11 = \underline{\quad} \text{ (23)}$$

Have students solve. Then write the following immediately to the right of the sum:

$$- 7 = \underline{\quad} \text{ (16)}$$

Have the students subtract. Then write the following to the right of the difference:

$$\div 4 = \underline{\quad} \text{ (4)}$$

Have the students divide. Then write the following to the right of the quotient and have students solve:

$$\times 3 = \underline{\quad} \text{ (12)}$$

Ask:
- *What number did we begin with?* (12) *What number did we end with?* (12)
- *If we had made a mistake in solving any of these problems, would we still have ended up at 12?* (No.)

Using the Challenge
Have students read the introduction to the Challenge. Ask:
- *What number should go in the first empty space?* (8)

Then have students complete the circle. Encourage them to write out any problems that they find difficult.

After students have had time to complete the circle, review the answers to each problem. Have volunteers write out each step on the board. Have students follow along by checking off each correct answer, and circling each incorrect answer. Ask:

Circle Math

Begin at the top of each circle. Go clockwise around the circle. Add, subtract, multiply, or divide, starting with the answer of the previous problem.

When you have made it all around the circle, you should have the same number you started with.

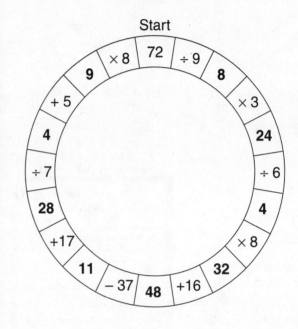

Name _____

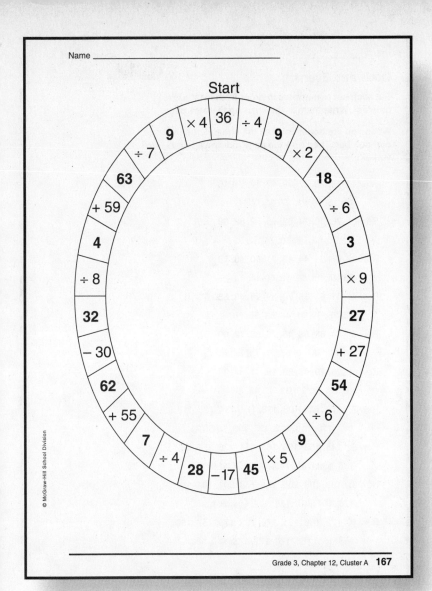

Start

CHALLENGE

- *If you end up at the wrong number, how can you find where you went wrong.* (Possible answer: Start at the beginning and double-check each step until you find one that you did incorrectly. Then use the correct answer as a starting point for completing the rest of the steps correctly.)

- *If you want to start at the top and work counterclockwise, what do you need to do to each problem?* (Reverse the operations: Change addition signs to subtraction signs and vice versa; reverse multiplication signs to division signs and vice versa.)

Have students look at the second circle. Ask:

- *If you start at the top and go clockwise, what number should go in the first empty space?* (9)

- *If you go counterclockwise, what number should go in the first empty space?* (9) *Why?* (Because the multiplication sign in front of the 4 should be reversed to a division sign, and 36 ÷ 4 = 9.)

Then have the students complete the circle. Summarize by asking:

- *Can you use any number to start a math circle?* (Yes.) *Why?* (Possible answer: Because any number can be the beginning of one number sentence and the answer to another number sentence.)

CHALLENGE

Lesson Goal

• Order numbers on a chart, shading the odd numbers to reveal a hidden message.

Introducing the Challenge

Find out what students know about ordering numbers. Write the following numbers in a column: 76, 4, 19, 6, 205

Ask:

• *Which of these numbers is least?* (4)

Write this number next to the column. Then ask:

• *Which of these numbers is the greatest?* (205)

Write this number to the right of the 4, leaving enough space for the other 3 numbers. Then have students place the remaining numbers in order from least to greatest (6, 19, 76). Write these numbers in the space between 4 and 205.

Use this series of numbers to find out what students know about even and odd numbers. Ask:

• *If a number can be divided by 2 and the quotient is a whole, is it even or odd?* (even)

• *If a whole number results in a fraction when you divide it by 2, is it odd or even?* (odd)

• *When you count, do you ever count two odd or two even numbers in a row?* (No)

Ask students to identify the odd numbers in the series on the board (19, 205). Circle these numbers. Then have students identify the even numbers (4, 6, 76). Be sure that students understand that each number must be classified as either odd or even.

Odds and Evens

Put each set of numbers in order from least to greatest. Write them in the chart on the next page.

When you are done, color all the squares that have an odd number. Then turn the page sideways to see how you did.

Row 1: 19, 23, 27, 39, 42, 14, 31, 15
        14, 15, 19, 23, 27, 31, 39, 42

Row 2: 70, 56, 74, 53, 95, 62, 82, 68
        53, 56, 62, 68, 70, 74, 82, 95

Row 3: 66, 54, 44, 43, 71, 60, 48, 58
        43, 44, 48, 54, 58, 60, 66, 71

Row 4: 41, 53, 35, 70, 39, 28, 49, 65
        28, 35, 39, 41, 49, 53, 65, 70

Row 5: 74, 66, 58, 46, 78, 52, 72, 60
        46, 52, 58, 60, 66, 72, 74, 78

Row 6: 23, 29, 43, 33, 19, 47, 37, 27
        19, 23, 27, 29, 33, 37, 43, 47

Row 7: 112, 122, 128, 138, 116, 134, 125, 118
        112, 116, 118, 122, 125, 128, 134, 138

Row 8: 145, 153, 138, 160, 144, 136, 158, 152
        136, 138, 144, 145, 152, 153, 158, 160

Row 9: 188, 198, 206, 184, 178, 201, 187, 192
        178, 184, 187, 188, 192, 198, 201, 206

Row 10: 172, 166, 161, 178, 183, 170, 157, 180
        157, 161, 166, 170, 172, 178, 180, 183

Name _____

1.	14	15	19	23	27	31	39	42
2.	53	56	62	68	70	74	82	95
3.	43	44	48	54	58	60	66	71
4.	28	35	39	41	49	53	65	70
5.	46	52	58	60	66	72	74	78
6.	19	23	27	29	33	37	43	47
7.	112	116	118	122	125	128	134	138
8.	136	138	144	145	152	153	158	160
9.	178	184	187	188	192	198	201	206
10.	157	161	166	170	172	178	180	183

© McGraw-Hill School Division

Grade 3, Chapter 12, Cluster B **169**

Using the Challenge

Have students read the introduction to the Challenge. Then look at Row 1. Ask:

- *Which of these numbers is the least?* (14) *Which is the greatest?* (42)
- *What is the order of these numbers from least to greatest?* (14, 15, 19, 23 , 27, 31, 39, 42)
- *Which of the numbers are odd?* (15, 19, 23, 27, 31, 39)
- *Which of the numbers are even?* (14, 42)

Then have students complete the Challenge. Be sure students are able to decipher the word "OK" on the chart. Ask:

- *Which row has only even numbers?* (5)
- *Which row has only odd numbers?* (6)
- *If you don't have the numbers in the correct order, what happens to the chart?* (The wrong squares on the chart get shaded, which keeps the word from being clear.)
- *If you shade the even numbers instead of the odd numbers, what happens to the chart?* (OK is spelled out in white squares against a shaded background.)

Identify Equal Parts

Circle the figures that show equal parts.

1.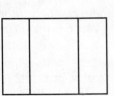

2.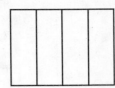

3.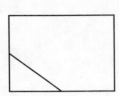

4.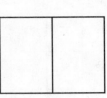

Patterns

Draw what the next figure in the pattern could be.

5. 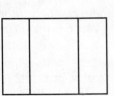 , , ,

_____

6. ▲▲▲▲▲▲▲△ , ▲▲▲▲▲▲△△ , ▲▲▲▲▲△△△ ,

_____

Equivalent Names

Match a number in Column A with a number in Column B
that names the same number.

Column A

7. 2,509 _____

8. 259 _____

9. 2,059 _____

10. 2,590 _____

Column B

a. 25 hundreds 9 tens

b. 2 thousands 5 tens 9 ones

c. 25 hundreds 9 ones

d. 200 + 50 + 9

e. 2 thousands 5 hundreds 9 tens

Addition and Subtraction Facts

Find each sum or difference.

11. $6 + 9 =$ _____   **12.** $15 - 9 =$ _____

13. $14 - 7 =$ _____   **14.** $5 + 8 =$ _____

15. $8 + 4 =$ _____   **16.** $17 - 8 =$ _____

17. $7 + 6 =$ _____

Frequency Tables

Complete the table.

Students Who Attend Special Assembly

Class	Tally	Number
3-1	卌 II	7
3-2	卌 卌 I	**18.** _____
3-3	III	**19.** _____
3-4	卌 卌 卌 I	**20.** _____

Assessment Goal

This two-page assessment covers skills identified as necessary for success in Chapter 13 Fractions and Probability. The first page assesses the major prerequisite skills for Cluster A. The second page assesses the major prerequisite skills for Cluster B. When the Cluster A and Cluster B prerequisite skills overlap, the skill(s) will be covered in only one section.

Getting Started

- Allow students time to look over the two pages of the assessment. Point out the labels that identify the skills covered.

- Have students find math vocabulary terms used in the assessment. List vocabulary terms on the board as students identify them. If necessary, review the meanings of all essential math vocabulary.

Introducing the Assessment

- Explain to students that these pages will help you know if they are ready to start a new chapter in their math textbooks.

- Students who have transferred from another school may not have been introduced to some of these skills. Encourage students to do their best and assure them you will help them learn any needed skills.

Cluster A Challenge

Those students who demonstrate mastery of the skills on this page will not need to use the reteaching worksheets. Instead, these students can do the Cluster A Challenge found on pages 180-181.

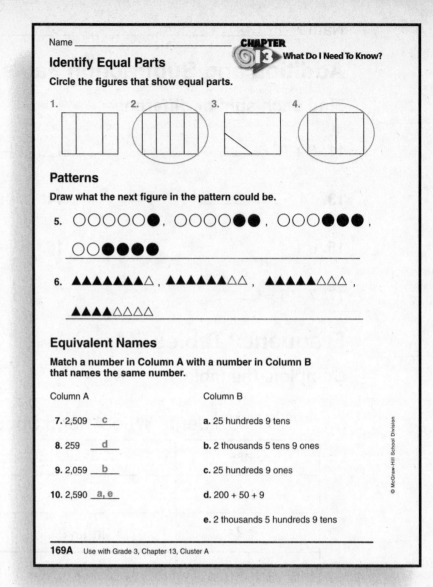

Name _____

CHAPTER 13 What Do I Need To Know?

Identify Equal Parts

Circle the figures that show equal parts.

1.   2.   3.   4.

Patterns

Draw what the next figure in the pattern could be.

5. ○○○○○●, ○○○○●●, ○○○●●●,

○○●●●●

6. ▲▲▲▲▲▲▲△, ▲▲▲▲▲▲△△, ▲▲▲▲▲△△△,

▲▲▲▲△△△△

Equivalent Names

Match a number in Column A with a number in Column B that names the same number.

Column A	Column B
7. 2,509 _c_	**a.** 25 hundreds 9 tens
8. 259 _d_	**b.** 2 thousands 5 tens 9 ones
9. 2,059 _b_	**c.** 25 hundreds 9 ones
10. 2,590 _a, e_	**d.** 200 + 50 + 9
	e. 2 thousands 5 hundreds 9 tens

© McGraw-Hill School Division

169A   Use with Grade 3, Chapter 13, Cluster A

CLUSTER A PREREQUISITE SKILLS

The skills listed in this chart are those identified as major prerequisite skills for students' success in the lessons in Cluster A of the chapter. Each skill is covered by one or more assessment items as shown in the middle column. The right column provides the page numbers for the lessons in this book that reteach the Cluster A prerequisite skills.

Skill Name	Assessment Items	Lesson Pages
Identify Equal Parts	1-4	170-171
Patterns	5-6	172-173
Equivalent Names	7-10	174-175

Name _____

Addition and Subtraction Facts

Find each sum or difference.

11. $6 + 9 =$ ___15___   **12.** $15 - 9 =$ ___6___

13. $14 - 7 =$ ___7___   **14.** $5 + 8 =$ ___13___

15. $8 + 4 =$ ___12___   **16.** $17 - 8 =$ ___9___

17. $7 + 6 =$ ___13___

Frequency Tables

Complete the table.

Students Who Attend Special Assembly

Class	Tally	Number
3-1	꒞꒞꒞ ꒞꒞	7
3-2	꒞꒞꒞ ꒞꒞꒞ ꒞	**18.** ___11___
3-3	꒞꒞꒞	**19.** ___3___
3-4	꒞꒞꒞ ꒞꒞꒞ ꒞꒞꒞ ꒞	**20.** ___16___

CLUSTER B PREREQUISITE SKILLS

The skills listed in this chart are those identified as major prerequisite skills for students' success in the lessons in Cluster B of the chapter. Each skill is covered by one or more assessment items as shown in the middle column. The right column provides the page numbers for the lessons in this book that reteach the Cluster B prerequisite skills

Skill Name	Assessment Items	Lesson Pages
Addition and Subtraction Facts	11-17	176-177
Frequency Tables	18-20	178-179

Alternative Assessment Strategies

- Oral administration of the assessment is appropriate for younger students or those whose native language is not English. Read the skills title and directions one section at a time. Check students' understanding by asking them to tell you how they will do the first exercise in the group.

- For some skill types you may wish to use group administration. In this technique, a small group or pair of students complete the assessment together. Through their discussion, you will be able to decide if supplementary reteaching materials are needed.

Intervention Materials

If students are not successful with the prerequisite skills assessed on these pages, reteaching lessons have been created to help them make the transition into the chapter.

Item correlation charts showing the skills lessons suitable for reteaching the prerequisite skills are found beneath the reproductions of each page of the assessment.

Cluster B Challenge
Those students who demonstrate mastery of the skills on this page will not need to use the reteaching worksheets. Instead, these students can do the Cluster B Challenge found on pages 182-183.

Lesson Goal

- Identify equal and unequal fractional parts.

What the Student Needs to Know

- Compare shapes.
- Compare sizes.
- Understand the terms *equal* and *not equal.*

Getting Started

Draw a square on the board. Tell students that it shows a sandwich. *Suppose you were sharing this sandwich with a friend. How could you cut it into two equal parts?* (Students might describe cutting it in half with a horizontal or vertical line or cutting it in half with a diagonal line.)

- To review the terms *equal* and *not equal,* ask: *What does it mean if two numbers are equal?* (They are the same amount.) *Write 2 and 2 on the chalkboard. Are these numbers equal?* (Yes.) *Erase one 2 and change it to a 6. Are these numbers equal?* (No.)

- *Draw two squares that are the same size. Are these squares equal?* (Yes.) *How do you know?* (They are the same size and shape.) *Erase one and draw another square that is much larger or smaller. Are these squares equal?* (No.) *Why not?* (They are not the same size.)

What Can I Do?

- Read the question and the response. Then review the examples with the students.

Have students look at the circle on the left. Ask: *How many parts are in the circle?* (3) *Are they all the same size and shape?* (No.) *Are the three parts equal?* (No.)

- Next look at the second circle. *Imagine this circle is a pizza four friends are sharing. Are the slices equal?* (Yes.) *Is this a fair way to share the pizza for 4 people?* (Yes.)

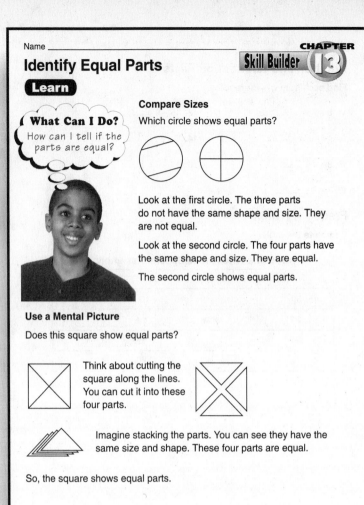

Name _____

Identify Equal Parts

Skill Builder

CHAPTER 13

Learn

What Can I Do?
How can I tell if the parts are equal?

Compare Sizes

Which circle shows equal parts?

Look at the first circle. The three parts do not have the same shape and size. They are not equal.

Look at the second circle. The four parts have the same shape and size. They are equal.

The second circle shows equal parts.

Use a Mental Picture

Does this square show equal parts?

Think about cutting the square along the lines. You can cut it into these four parts.

Imagine stacking the parts. You can see they have the same size and shape. These four parts are equal.

So, the square shows equal parts.

© McGraw-Hill School Division

170 Grade 3, Chapter 13, Cluster A

WHAT IF THE STUDENT CAN'T

Name Equal Shapes

- Review the shapes rectangle, square, and triangle. Remind the student that rectangles can look very different from one another. Draw three or four different rectangles, very wide or very tall. Help the student recognize that they are all rectangles, but they are not equal. Then draw two equal rectangles. Repeat with squares and triangles.

Compare Sizes Mentally

- Have the student use construction paper and safety scissors to model the drawings shown in the exercises. Remind the student that the models may not be exactly the same as the drawings, but can help in finding an answer. Demonstrate by copying exercise 5 on paper and cutting it out. Show that the three rectangles are not the same size. They do not form an equal stack. The parts shown are not equal.

Name _____

Tell whether or not each rectangle shows equal parts.
• Write *equal* or *not equal*. Use the drawings to help you compare parts.

1. not equal

2. equal

3. equal

Power Practice • Tell whether or not each shape shows equal parts. Write *equal* or *not equal*.

4. equal

5. not equal

6. equal

7. not equal

8. not equal

9. equal

10. not equal

11. equal

12. equal

13. equal

14. not equal

15. equal

16. equal

17. not equal

18. equal

19. not equal

© McGraw-Hill School Division

Grade 3, Chapter 13, Cluster A   **171**

USING THE LESSON

- Draw students' attention to the divided square. Ask: *What is a mental picture?* (a picture in your mind) *How does thinking of cutting this square help you decide if the pieces are equal?* (Answers will vary.)

- Students might practice identifying equal parts by copying drawings from the lesson, cutting the parts, and trying to stack them, as shown in "Use a Mental Picture."

Try It

- For exercises 1–3, have students tell how many parts are in each drawing. Then have them compare the sizes and shapes of the parts to see if they are equal.

- Encourage students to use the drawings showing the parts separated. Ask: *In exercise 1, what do the two drawings show?* (The first drawing shows a rectangle divided by a line; the second drawing shows the two parts separated.) *Are the two parts the same size and shape?* (No.) *What is the answer for exercise 1?* (not equal)

Power Practice

- You may wish to allow partners to work together to solve exercises 4–19. Suggest that students start each exercise by counting the number of parts. Then have them look at each part to see whether or not they are equal.

- When students find a shape that shows equal parts, have students describe both the shape and the part.

- After students have finished the exercises, ask these questions to help them review their work: *Which drawing shows a rectangle divided into equal squares?* (15) *Which drawing shows a rectangle divided into equal triangles?* (13)

WHAT IF THE STUDENT CAN'T

Use the Terms Equal and Not Equal

- Allow partners to practice the words *equal* and *not equal* in a brief activity. First, have students create note cards that read *equal* and *not equal*. To begin, one student writes a number or draws a shape. The other student mixes up the two note cards and draws one. If the card says equal, the student writes an equal number or draws an equal shape. If the cards says not equal, the student writes a number or draws a shape that is not equal.

Complete the Power Practice

- Discuss each incorrect answer. Have the student count the number of parts shown and talk about their sizes and shapes.

Lesson Goal
• Identify and continue number and shape patterns.

What the Student Needs to Know
• Understand that patterns follow rules.
• Recognize squares, triangles, and circles.
• Recognize number patterns.

Getting Started
• Write the word patterns on the board and ask: *What is a pattern?* Allow students to share their ideas. Explain: *In mathematics, a pattern is something that repeats in a special way. Patterns can include shapes or numbers. If you know how a pattern repeats, you can find the next shape or number in the pattern.*

• Write this series of numbers on the board: 1, 2, 3, 4, 5, 6, 7. Ask: *What number could come next?* (8). *Why?* (It is 1 higher than 7.)

• Write this series of shapes on the board: circle, square, square, circle, square, square, circle. *What shape could come next?* (square) *Why?* (Because each circle is followed by two squares.)

What Can I Do?
• Read the question and the response. Then read and discuss the examples. Draw students' attention to the shape pattern under "Look for Changes." Point out that this pattern goes from top to bottom. The first figure shows four squares and one triangle. The second figure shows three squares and two triangles.

• Ask: *How many shapes are in the first line?* (5) *How many shapes are in the second line?* (5) *In the third line?* (5) *How many shapes do you think will be in the fourth line?* (5) *Why?* (The number of shapes stays the same.) *What changes?* (the number of squares and triangles)

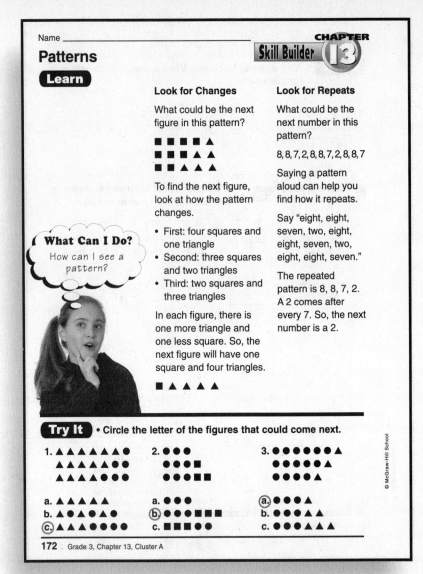

WHAT IF THE STUDENT CAN'T

Recognize Shape Patterns
• Encourage the student to use construction paper cut-outs to model the figures. After reproducing the patterns shown, the student can use the manipulative shapes to find the next figure in the pattern. You may wish to help the student by providing the correct shapes. For example, to solve exercise 7, the student should first recreate the series shown. Then give him or her four circles and two squares with the request to find the correct order.

Recognize Number Patterns
• Point out to the student that the number patterns in this lesson go from left to right. Encourage the student to read each series of numbers aloud to hear the repeating pattern. The student can also use the pitch of the voice to accentuate patterns. For example, to read the pattern in exercise 16, the student might use a high pitch for every 5, a low pitch for every 9, and a medium pitch for every 3.

Name _____

Write the repeating pattern.

4. 9, 9, 3, 2, 9, 9, 9, 3, 2, 9, 9, 9, 3, 2, 9, 9, 9, 3, 2   <u>9</u> <u>9</u> <u>3</u> <u>2</u>

5. 6, 7, 1, 5, 6, 7, 1, 5, 6, 7, 1, 5, 6, 7, 1, 5   <u>6</u> <u>7</u> <u>1</u> <u>5</u>

Power Practice • Draw the figure that could come next.

6. 7. 8.

9. 10. 11.

Write what the next number in each pattern could be.

12. 5, 9, 3, 5, 9, 3, 5, 9, 3, 5, <u>9</u>

13. 8, 2, 1, 0, 8, 2, 1, 0, 8, 2, 1, <u>0</u>

14. 3, 3, 4, 9, 3, 3, 4, 9, 3, 3, 4, 9, <u>3</u>

15. 8, 2, 9, 7, 7, 8, 2, 9, 7, 7, 8, 2, 9, 7, <u>7</u>

16. 6, 0, 3, 1, 3, 6, 0, 3, 1, 3, 6, 0, 3, <u>1</u>

17. 1, 1, 2, 2, 3, 3, 4, 4, 5, 5, 6, <u>6</u>

18. 1, 3, 5, 7, 9, 11, 13, 15, 17, 19, <u>21</u>

Learn with Partners & Parents

Secret Patterns

One player writes down a secret pattern using these shapes: ▲ ■ ●

The other player asks yes or no questions to guess the pattern. For example: Does the first shape have straight sides? Are there four figures in the pattern?

When you think you know the pattern, write it down. Find out if your guess is correct. Then switch roles and play again.

Grade 3, Chapter 13, Cluster A   **173**

WHAT IF THE STUDENT CAN'T

Understand that Patterns Follow Rules

- Have the student practice identifying the rules that produce familiar patterns, such as the following:

  1, 3, 5, 7, 9, 11

  2, 4, 6, 8, 10, 12

  5, 10, 15, 20, 25, 30, 35

  Have the student name the rule that each pattern follows.

Recognize Squares, Triangles, and Circles

- Allow the student to create flash cards to review these shapes. Encourage the student to draw circles and squares of different sizes and triangles of different sizes and shapes. Partners can use the cards to practice using the terms *square, triangle,* and *circle.*

USING THE LESSON

- After finding the fourth figure in the pattern, students can continue the pattern to find the fifth figure. *How many triangles will there be?* (5) *How many squares?* (0)

- Have students look at the number pattern under Look for Repeats. Have students read the numbers aloud. The rhythm of reading the pattern will often help students identify the repeating pattern.

- Ask: *What number always comes after a 2?* (8) *Could this pattern continue forever?* (Yes.) *How?* (You could keep repeating 8, 8, 7, 2 endlessly.)

Try It

- Explain that the patterns in exercises 1-3 all go from top to bottom. Ask: *How many shapes are in the first row of exercise 1?* (7) *In the second row?* (7) *In the third row?* (7) *How many shapes will be in the fourth row?* (7)

Power Practice

- You may wish to select examples from exercises 6–18 to complete as a class. Assign remaining exercises for individual practice.

- Remind students that the patterns in exercises 6–11 go from top to bottom. Encourage them to begin by counting how many shapes are in each row.

- After completing the activities, suggest that students work together to review one another's work. Encourage students to describe each pattern and the rules it follows.

Learn with Partners & Parents

- Tell students to begin by choosing secret patterns that use circles, squares, and triangles. After several rounds, they can change to number patterns.

USING THE LESSON

Lesson Goal
- Compare numbers written in standard and expanded form.

What the Student Needs to Know
- Recognize place value in numbers written in standard form.
- Write a number in expanded form.
- Use a place-value chart.

Getting Started
Remind students that the same number can be written in different ways. For example, 30 and 3 tens are different names for the same number. You may wish to introduce the term equivalent. Say: *Two names are equivalent if they name the same number.*

- Write the numbers 23, 538, 7,399, and 3,687 on the board. Have students identify the 3 in each number. Ask: *Which number shows 3 ones?* (23) *Which number shows 3 thousands* (3,687). *What does the 3 in 538 show?* (3 tens or 30) *What does the 3 in 7,399 show?* (3 hundreds or 300)

- Write "2 hundreds and 5 ones" on the board. Then write 250 and 205. Ask: *Which number matches "2 hundreds and 5 ones"?* (205)

What Can I Do?
- Read the question and the response. Then read and discuss the examples. Have students read the labels on the place-value chart. Then ask:
- *What does the 5 in 5,428 show?* (5 thousands; 5,000) *What does the 4 show?* (4 hundreds, 400) *What does the 2 show?* (2 tens; 20) *What does the 8 show?* (8 ones; 8)
- Help students relate numbers in expanded form with numbers written in a place-value chart. After students read the expanded form for 9,366, have them write the number in a place-value chart.

Equivalent Names

Learn

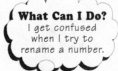

What Can I Do?
I get confused when I try to rename a number.

Use a Place-Value Chart

Is 5,428 equal to 5 thousands, 4 hundreds, 2 tens, and 8 ones? Write 5,428 in a place-value chart.

thousands	hundreds	tens	ones
5	4	2	8

Read the numbers and their place value.

5 thousands 4 hundreds 2 tens 8 ones

Yes, 5,428 is equal to 5 thousands, 4 hundreds, 2 tens, and 8 ones.

Is 5,428 equal to 54 hundreds, 2 tens, and 8 ones? Read the place-value chart.

Think: 5 thousands 4 hundreds is the same as 54 hundreds.

So 5,428 is also equal to 54 hundreds, 2 tens, and 8 ones.

Write a Number in Expanded Form

Write 9,366 in expanded form.

First, write the thousands.	9,000
Then, write the hundreds.	300
Then, write the tens.	60
Then, write the ones.	6

Add the numbers together.

$9,366 = 9,000 + 300 + 60 + 6$

Is 5,612 equal to $5,000 + 100 + 60 + 2$?

To answer, combine the expanded number.

$$
\begin{array}{r}
5,000 \\
100 \\
60 \\
+\quad 2 \\
\hline
5,162
\end{array}
$$

5,162 is not equal to 5,612.

So, 5,612 is not equal to $5,000 + 100 + 60 + 2$.

© McGraw-Hill School Division

WHAT IF THE STUDENT CAN'T

Recognize Place Value in Numbers Written in Standard Form
- Have the student use place-value charts to complete each activity. Review the organization of the chart, reinforcing the fact that each place value is ten times greater than the place value to its right.
- Encourage the student to add labels to several numbers written in standard form. Write 4,572 and then have the student label each digit with its correct place value.

Write a Number in Expanded Form
- Have the student look at numbers written in expanded form and look for patterns. The student should notice that each number usually has one less zero than the number to its left. Have the student add several numbers in expanded form to find the equivalent number in standard form. Then demonstrate how to do the same steps "backwards" to rewrite the standard number in expanded form.

Name _____

Try It • Use the place-value chart to help you answer each question.

1. Is 6,938 equal to 6 thousands, 3 hundreds, 9 tens, and 8 ones?

thousands	hundreds	tens	ones

_____ not equal _____

Complete each expanded form.

2. 1,502 = __1,000__ + 500 + __2__

3. 9,911 = 9,000 + __900__ + __10__ + __1__

4. 8,067 = __8,000__ + __60__ + __7__

5. 2,821 = __2,000__ + __800__ + __20__ + __1__

Power Practice • Circle the numbers in each row that are equal.

6. (668) (6 hundreds 6 tens 8 ones)   600 + 80 + 6

7. (7,283) 7 thousands 2 tens 3 ones   (7,000 + 200 + 80 + 3)

8. (6,594) (65 hundreds 9 tens 4 ones)   6,000 + 5,000 + 9,000 + 4,000

Write the number in the box that is equal to each number below.

628	6,208	6,882

9. 600 + 20 + 8   10. 6,000 + 800 + 80 + 2   11. 62 hundreds 8 ones

____628____   ____6,882____   ____6,208____

© McGraw-Hill School Division

Grade 3, Chapter 13, Cluster A **175**

WHAT IF THE STUDENT CAN'T

Use a Place-Value Chart
- Allow the student to use manipulatives to model numbers in the lesson. Review the terms thousands, hundreds, tens, and ones to make sure the student is comfortable with place-value vocabulary.

Complete the Power Practice
- Review incorrect answers. Have the student vocalize the thinking processes to identify errors in logic. Encourage the student to read confusing numbers aloud. Point out that when you read a number, such as 6,882, you are using place-value words (6 thousand, 8 hundred, eighty-two).

USING THE LESSON

- When students identify two numbers that are not equal, such as 5,612 and 5,162, ask them to identify which number is greater than the other. Reinforce the understanding of equivalence by pointing out that if one number is larger than another number, the two numbers are not equal.

Try It
- Help students complete the place-value chart. Remind students that only one digit can go in each square of the place-value chart. In exercise 1, students might try to write 69 in the hundreds column. Help them understand that only the 9 goes in the hundreds column; the 6 should be written in the thousands column.

- To complete exercises 2–5, have students begin by counting the number of digits in each number. Explain: *If there are four digits in a number, the expanded number will usually have four addends. Why are there only three addends in exercises 2 and 4?* (Because one of the digits in each number is a zero.)

Power Practice
- Students can compare numbers by writing them all in the same form. Suggest that students use place-value charts to help them compare the numbers.

- For exercises 9–11, remind students that numbers in the box may look similar even if they are not equal. Have them read each of the numbers in the box to help them understand why each number is different from the others.

USING THE LESSON

Lesson Goal
- Complete addition and subtraction facts.

What the Student Needs to Know
- Add two 1-digit numbers.
- Subtract 1-digit numbers.
- Use addition to check subtraction.
- Recognize the relationship between addition and subtraction.

Getting Started
- Write $2 + 4 = 6$ on the board. Say: *This is an addition fact. It is always true.* Then write $6 - 1 = 5$ on the board. Say: *This is a subtraction fact. It is always true.*
- Remind students that they use addition and subtraction facts when they solve many different kinds of problems. Some facts, such as $2 + 2 = 4$, are easy to remember. But sometimes you might forget an addition or subtraction fact. This lesson will help them review ways they can find an answer when they forget a fact.

What Can I Do?
- Read the question and the response. Then read and discuss the examples. Begin with the example under "Rearrange and Count On." Use models to demonstrate $3 + 8$. Then switch the order of the groups to show $8 + 3$. Ask: *Have I changed the number of things?* (No.) So $3 + 8$ is always equal to $8 + 3$.
- Point out that counting on is useful when you are adding a small number, such as 1, 2, 3, or 4. Counting on can be confusing if you are adding on a larger number, such as 8 or 9.
- Next, discuss how counting back can help you subtract. You may wish to use models to demonstrate $12 - 3$. Ask: *How could you count back to find the answer to $14 - 5$?* (Start at 14 and then count back five numbers: 14, 13, 12, 11, 10, 9.)

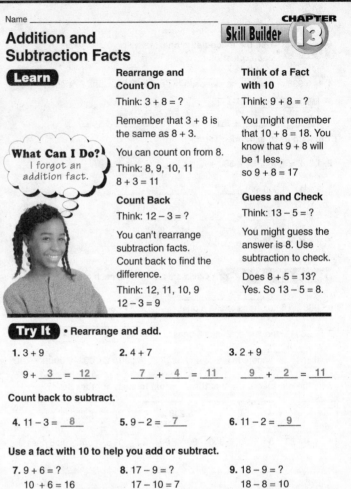

CHAPTER
Skill Builder **13**

Addition and Subtraction Facts

Learn

What Can I Do?
I forgot an addition fact.

Rearrange and Count On
Think: $3 + 8 = ?$

Remember that $3 + 8$ is the same as $8 + 3$.

You can count on from 8.

Think: 8, 9, 10, 11
$8 + 3 = 11$

Count Back
Think: $12 - 3 = ?$

You can't rearrange subtraction facts. Count back to find the difference.

Think: 12, 11, 10, 9
$12 - 3 = 9$

Think of a Fact with 10
Think: $9 + 8 = ?$

You might remember that $10 + 8 = 18$. You know that $9 + 8$ will be 1 less, so $9 + 8 = 17$

Guess and Check
Think: $13 - 5 = ?$

You might guess the answer is 8. Use subtraction to check.

Does $8 + 5 = 13$?
Yes. So $13 - 5 = 8.$

Try It • Rearrange and add.

1. $3 + 9$

$9 + \underline{\ 3\ } = \underline{\ 12\ }$

2. $4 + 7$

$\underline{\ 7\ } + \underline{\ 4\ } = \underline{\ 11\ }$

3. $2 + 9$

$\underline{\ 9\ } + \underline{\ 2\ } = \underline{\ 11\ }$

Count back to subtract.

4. $11 - 3 = \underline{\ 8\ }$

5. $9 - 2 = \underline{\ 7\ }$

6. $11 - 2 = \underline{\ 9\ }$

Use a fact with 10 to help you add or subtract.

7. $9 + 6 = ?$
$10 + 6 = 16$
So, $9 + 6 = \underline{\ 15\ }$.

8. $17 - 9 = ?$
$17 - 10 = 7$
So, $17 - 9 = \underline{\ 8\ }$.

9. $18 - 9 = ?$
$18 - 8 = 10$
So, $18 - 9 = \underline{\ 9\ }$.

WHAT IF THE STUDENT CAN'T

Add Two 1-Digit Numbers
- Have the student use manipulatives to model each fact. Using manipulatives for addition can help with understanding why groups can be re-ordered without changing the total amount ($4 + 8 = 8 + 4$).
- Have the student create addition fact flash cards to practice learning common facts.

Subtract Two 1-Digit Numbers
- Have the student use manipulatives to model each fact. Using manipulatives for subtraction can help with understanding the meaning of subtraction. Remind the student that subtracting refers to taking some away.

Name _____

Add or subtract. Then check your answer.

10. 8 + 7 = __15__   **11.** 14 − 8 = __6__   **12.** 12 + 6 = __18__

__15__ − 7 = 8   __6__ + 8 = 14   __18__ − 6 = 12

Power Practice • Add or subtract.

13. 6 + 9 = __15__   **14.** 15 − 8 = __7__

15. 9 + 7 = __16__   **16.** 19 − 9 = __10__

17. 16 − 7 = __9__   **18.** 13 − 5 = __8__

19. 9 + 3 = __12__   **20.** 11 − 9 = __2__

21. 12 − 5 = __7__   **22.** 14 − 6 = __8__

23. 4 + 8 = __12__   **24.** 8 + 3 = __11__

25. 8 + 1 = __9__   **26.** 16 − 9 = __7__

27. 17 − 9 = __8__   **28.** 14 − 8 = __6__

Learn with Partners & Parents

The Answer Is...

This game can help you remember addition and subtraction facts. Try this game with 2 to 4 players.

- Write the numbers 10 to 20 on index cards and mix them.
- Turn one card over. Players take turns writing addition or subtraction expressions that have the answer shown.
- If a player writes an incorrect expression or cannot think of another expression to add to the list, he or she is out for the round.
- Keep playing until no one can add another expression. The last player to add an expression gets to keep the card.
- Turn the next card over to begin the next round. The player with more cards at the end of the game is the winner.

© McGraw-Hill School Division

Grade 3, Chapter 13, Cluster B   **177**

USING THE LESSON

- Next, point out that facts with 10 can be easy to remember. Thinking of a fact with 10 can help you remember a forgotten fact.
- Finally, explain that guessing and checking can be helpful . Students can use models to help them check their answers.

Try It

- Have students complete exercises 1-12 to help them practice the four strategies for finding addition and subtraction facts. Encourage students to talk about how they solved each exercise.

Power Practice

- Have partners check one another's answers. Guide students to use one of the strategies for adding or subtracting when they do not know the answer.
- Partners can work together on exercises 13–28. Each partner finds one answer and then they compare their numbers to see if they are equal or not equal. Review the terms *equal* and *not equal* before students begin these activities.

Learn with Partners & Parents

- Model the activity by writing 11 on the board. Say: *Suppose you pick the 11 card. What addition facts might your write?* (1 + 10; 2 + 9; 3 + 8; 4 + 7; 5 + 6) *What subtraction problems have an answer of 11?* (12 − 1, 13 − 2, 14 − 3, and so on)
- You may wish to have students begin using only addition facts. After one or two rounds, students can add subtraction facts to the game.

WHAT IF THE STUDENT CAN'T

Use Addition to Check Subtraction

- Have the student write an addition fact, such as 5 + 3 = 8. Then have him or her write two subtraction facts that use the same numbers. (8 − 5 = 3; 8 − 3 = 5) Then have the student solve a subtraction fact, such as 12 − 7 = 5.

Explain that the student can use addition to make sure the answer is correct by adding the two smaller numbers to see if they equal the largest number (5 + 7 = 12). Encourage the student to use manipulatives to demonstrate each subtraction problem and then "undo" the subtraction using addition.

Lesson Goal
• Create and read tally charts.

What the Student Needs to Know
• Mark tallies in groups of five.
• Read chart labels.
• Compare quantities in charts.

Getting Started
• Ask the class a question, such as: *How many of you have a cat at home?* or *How many of you are wearing blue today?* Count raised hands and mark a tally for each student. Mark each fifth tally as a slanting horizontal line over four vertical lines.

• After tallying the answer, count the number of tallies. Demonstrate how you can use skip counting to count groups of fives.

What Can I Do?
• Read the question and the response. Then read and discuss the example. Ask: *What do the numbers in the box show?* (test scores for one class) *What does the tally chart show?* (How many of the scores are below 80, between 80 and 90, and above 90.) *If there was one more test score and it was 73, where would you mark a tally?* (under Below 80)

• *How does the tally chart help you compare the test scores?* (Answers include the fact that the tally chart groups test scores together; students may find it less confusing than the large list of numbers.)

• *How does skip counting help you count tallies?* (You can skip count by fives and then count on to find the total.) *How would you write tallies for the number 28?* (You would mark five groups of five and three ones.) *If a chart shows 6 groups of 5 and 2 ones, what is the number shown?* (32)

Name _____

Frequency Tables

Learn

Make a Tally Chart
This box shows the test scores for one class.

87	76	91	92	95	87	96	68	87	89	97	76	69	70
82	93	65	91	80	79	86	75	82	95	90	91	89	82

Are more test scores below 80 or above 90?

What Can I Do? I want to organize a lot of information.

Use a chart to keep track. Add one tally mark for each test score. Cross off the scores you have tallied.

Below 80	80 to 90	Above 90
‖‖ ‖‖‖	‖‖‖ ‖‖‖ ‖	‖‖‖ ‖‖‖‖

Count and compare to answer the question. There are 8 scores below 80 and 9 scores above 90.

There are more test scores above 90.

Try It • Complete the tally chart to count the marbles. The white marbles are already tallied and crossed off.

White	Black	Dots	Stripes
‖‖‖ ‖‖‖ ‖‖‖‖	**1.** ‖‖‖ ‖‖‖ ‖	**2.** ‖‖‖ ‖	**3.** ‖‖‖ ‖‖‖‖

© McGraw-Hill School Division

WHAT IF THE STUDENT CAN'T

Mark Tallies Consistently
• Have students practice writing tallies with a partner. Students can count books on a bookshelf, windows in a classroom, or groups of manipulatives. Reinforce the fact that every fifth line goes diagonally across four vertical tallies.

• Allow students to practice writing tallies for any number and then have a partner count the number of tallies. Partners should check to make sure that each group of tallies contains five lines.

Read Chart Labels
• Review the importance of reading chart labels by reproducing one of the lesson charts on the board, but without the labels. Point out that without labels, you do not know what the information in the chart means. Add the labels and have the student explain how these help in reading the information in the chart.

Name _____

Use the tally chart to answer these questions.

4. How many white marbles are there? _____14_____

5. How many black marbles are there? _____11_____

6. How many marbles with dots are there? _____6_____

7. How many marbles with stripes are there? _____9_____

8. Arrange the marble patterns in order from fewest to most.

_____dots_____ _____stripes_____ _____black_____ _____white_____

Power Practice • Complete the tally chart. Then answer the questions.

This box shows the average temperatures for one month.

| 72° 71° 68° 75° 65° 68° 72° 77° 78° 80° 82° 81° 81° 79° 78° |
| 75° 72° 69° 68° 70° 71° 74° 76° 80° 81° 82° 71° 69° 74° 73° |

60° to 69°	70° to 79°	80° to 89°
9. ‖‖‖ I	10. ‖‖‖ ‖‖‖ ‖‖‖ II	11. ‖‖‖ II

12. For how many days was the average temperature between 60° and 69°? _____6_____

13. For how many days was the average temperature between 70° and 79°? _____17_____

14. For how many days was the average temperature between 80° and 89°? _____7_____

USING THE LESSON

Try It

• Exercises 1-3 help students practice marking tallies and using tallies to keep track. Encourage students to use an organized method so that they do not count any marbles twice and do not leave any out. Suggest that they count one color at a time. First cross off a marble and then add a tally in the correct chart box. Repeat until all marbles are crossed off.

Power Practice

• Have students follow an organized method to complete the tally chart for exercises 9-14. Encourage them to cross off a number and then mark a tally in the correct chart box. Have volunteers answer the questions in exercises 12-14 aloud.

WHAT IF THE STUDENT CAN'T

Compare Quantities in Charts

• Point out that the student can use tallies to compare amounts. Help the student recognize why the tally for 8 is clearly greater than the tally for 6. Even without doing an exact count, you can see that one number is greater.

As the student completes the exercises, encourage him or her to decide whether or not an exact count is needed to answer the question. For example, in exercise 13, the student will probably be able to find the highest tally in the chart without counting.

CHALLENGE

Lesson Goal
- Use color patterns to show equal parts.

Introducing the Challenge
- Ask students to describe a quilt. Explain that quilts are sewn together from different fabrics. A quilt can use many different colors or only a few. Quilt patterns can be very simple or very detailed.

- You may wish to point out that most traditional quilts are made up of blocks, which are squares. Each square shows a pattern. In this lesson, students will explore coloring quilt patterns.

- Draw a square on the board. Ask: *How could you color this square half blue and half white?* (Answers will vary. Allow students to demonstrate different methods of coloring the square.)

- Ask a volunteer to read aloud the introduction. Ask: *How can you tell that the two patterns have the same shapes?* (They are both made up of triangles.) *What is the difference between the two patterns?* (They are colored differently.)

- Look at the pattern on the left. *How many triangles are in the pattern?* (18) *How many of the triangles are white?* (9)

- Look at the pattern on the right. *How many triangles are in the pattern?* (18) *How many of the triangles are white?* (6)

Quilt Patterns

Adam examines his grandmother's quilt. He notices two patterns. They have the same shapes but different colors.

This pattern is equal parts blue and white.

This pattern is equal parts blue, white, and black.

You can tell the parts are equal by counting. There are 9 blue triangles and 9 white triangles. They are all the same size.

There are 6 blue triangles, 6 white triangles, and 6 black triangles.

Find a color pattern that matches each description.

1. Equal parts blue and white.

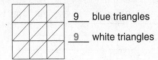

   9   blue triangles
   9   white triangles

2. Equal parts blue, white, and black.

   6   blue triangles
   6   white triangles
   6   black triangles

3. Equal parts green, white, and red.

   3   green squares
   3   white squares
   3   red squares

4. Equal parts green and white.

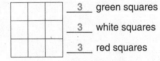

   2   green squares
   2   white squares
   5   green triangles
   5   white triangles

© McGraw-Hill School Division

Name _____

5. Equal parts blue, white, red, and black.

__4__ blue squares

__4__ white squares

__4__ red squares

__4__ black squares

6. Equal parts blue, white, red, and black.

__8__ blue triangles

__8__ white triangles

__8__ red triangles

__8__ black triangles

7. Can this pattern be colored in equal parts red and black? Explain your answer.

No; nine squares cannot be evenly colored in two colors

unless one square is divided into two equal parts.

8. Can this pattern be colored in equal parts red, white, green, and yellow? Explain your answer.

Yes; the pattern can be colored in four equal colors.

Each color should include 1 square and 6 triangles.

CHALLENGE

Using the Challenge

- Have students read the directions carefully. Explain that there are many different coloring patterns for each exercise, but the numbers that fill in the blanks will be the same for every pattern.

- Suggest that students begin by counting the shapes in a pattern. Students then count the total number of colors.

- Point out the missing numbers in each exercise. Explain that each number needs to be equal for the patterns to show equal parts. For example, in exercise 2, students will add 6 triangles in each color.

- Students may wish to copy the patterns and cut them out to help them find the equal groups.

- To answer question 7, help students understand that 9 squares cannot be divided evenly in half. To color the pattern in equal parts red and black, one of the squares would have to be divided into two equal parts so that there could be $4\frac{1}{2}$ squares in each color.

- To answer question 8, students should first count the number of squares and the number of triangles. They can then decide how many of each shape would be each of the four colors (1 square and 6 triangles in each color).

- After students finish their coloring patterns, have teams of 3 or 4 compare their results. Discuss how two different patterns can show the same equal parts.

- Students can continue the exploration by creating their own quilt patterns. Have partners consider whether or not each pattern shows equal parts.

CHALLENGE

Lesson Goal

- Use a tally chart to record and interpret the results of a probability experiment.

Introducing the Challenge

- Hand a volunteer a group of 20 coins. Ask: *If you toss all of the coins, how many do you think will land heads up?* (Predictions will vary.) Have the volunteer toss the coins (one or two at a time). Then ask the volunteer to call out the results while you tally them at the board. Compare students' predictions with the actual results. Ask: *If we repeated the experiment, would you change your prediction? Why or why not?*

- Tell students that they will conduct a series of coin tossing experiments. The results of each experiment may help them predict what will happen in the next experiment.

Using the Challenge

- Have students read the introduction and describe the tally chart. Provide students with play money or pennies to conduct the experiments.

- You may wish to have students work with a partner. One partner can toss the coin or coins; the other can record the results. Encourage students to swap roles after each experiment.

- After students complete exercises 1-3, have them pause and discuss the results. Ask them to predict what would happen if they tossed the coin 20 or 30 times.

- Draw students' attention to the chart for the next experiment. Ask: *What does HH stand for?* (Heads, Heads; both coins land heads up.) *What does HT stand for?* (Heads, Tails; one coin lands heads up; one lands tails up.)

Name _____

Coin Tosses

One Coin

This tally chart shows the results of ten coin tosses.
H stands for heads up.
T stands for tails up.

H	T

Toss a coin ten more times. Add your results to the chart above.

1. How many tallies are there for heads now? <u>Answers will vary.</u>

2. How many tallies are there for tails now? <u>Answers will vary.</u>

3. How many tallies are there in all? <u>20</u>

Two Coins

Try this experiment with two coins. Toss the coins 20 times. Use this chart to keep track of the results.

HH	HT	T T

4. How many times did both coins land heads up? <u>Answers will vary.</u>

5. How many times did both coins land tails up? <u>Answers will vary.</u>

6. How many times was one coin heads up and one coin tails up? <u>Answers will vary.</u>

7. If you repeated the experiment, do you think you would get the same results? Why or why not?

   <u>Students should explain that the exact numbers may be different,</u>

   <u>but it is likely that the coins will land HT more often than HH or TT.</u>

Name _____

Three Coins

This chart shows the possible results when you toss three coins.

HHH	HHT	HTT	TTT

Before you begin, make some predictions. You will toss the coins 30 times.
Answers will vary.

8. I think all three coins will land heads up _____ times.

9. I think all three coins will land tails up _____ times.

10. I think two coins will land heads up and one coin will land tails up _____ times.

11. I think one coin will land heads up and two coins will land tails up _____ times.

Now toss the coins 30 times. Tally your results in the chart.
Answers will vary.

12. How many times did all three coins land heads up? _____

13. How many times did all three coins land tails up? _____

14. How many times did two coins land heads up and one land tails up? _____

15. How many times did one coin land heads up and two land tails up? _____

16. How are your results for three coins similar to your results for two coins?
   Students should notice that the outcomes with mixed heads and
   tails are more frequent than those with only heads or only tails.

CHALLENGE

Why isn't there a column for TH? (That result is the same as HT; For this experiment, the order of the coins doesn't matter.)

- Make sure that students take time to answer the question in exercise 7 thoroughly. You may wish to have a brief group or class discussion to help students analyze their results and make predictions.

- Discuss the chart labeled "Three Coins." Make sure that students understand the chart headings.

- The exercises guide students through the process of making and testing a prediction. Encourage students to compare their predictions and their results.

- Ask: *If I toss four coins, do you think they are more likely to land all heads or two heads and two tails? Why?* (Answers will vary. Most students will agree that two heads and two tails are more likely. Their experiments will probably have indicated that all heads or all tails will be the least likely outcomes when tossing four coins.)

Name _____

Meaning of Fractions

Show a fraction.

1. Shade $\frac{3}{4}$ of the rectangle.

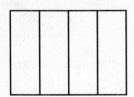

2. Shade $\frac{5}{16}$ of the square.

3. Shade $\frac{7}{8}$ of the circle.

4. Shade $\frac{2}{3}$ of the square.

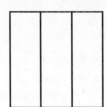

Money Amounts

Tell how much money is shown.

5.  _____

6.  _____

7.  _____

8.  _____

Mixed Numbers

Write each mixed number.

9.  _____

10.   _____

Name_____

Addition

Find each sum.

11.   56
     + 19

12.   148
     + 209

13. $3.67
     + 1.93

14. $45 + 38 = $ _____

15. $\$6.13 + \$1.97 + \$0.67 = $ _____

Subtraction

Find each difference.

16.   51
     − 14

17. 321
     − 162

18. $8.04
     − 5.36

19. $80 − 65 = $ _____

20. $\$5.49 − \$0.89 = $_____

Assessment Goal

This two-page assessment covers skills identified as necessary for success in Chapter 14 Relate Fractions and Decimals. The first page assesses the major prerequisite skills for Cluster A. The second page assesses the major prerequisite skills for Cluster B. When the Cluster A and Cluster B prerequisite skills overlap, the skill(s) will be covered in only one section.

Getting Started

- Allow students time to look over the two pages of the assessment. Point out the labels that identify the skills covered.

- Have students find math vocabulary terms used in the assessment. List vocabulary terms on the board as students identify them. If necessary, review the meanings of all essential math vocabulary.

Introducing the Assessment

- Explain to students that these pages will help you know if they are ready to start a new chapter in their math textbooks.

- Students who have transferred from another school may not have been introduced to some of these skills. Encourage students to do their best and assure them you will help them learn any needed skills.

Cluster A Challenge

Those students who demonstrate mastery of the skills on this page will not need to use the reteaching worksheets. Instead, these students can do the Cluster A Challenge found on pages 194–195.

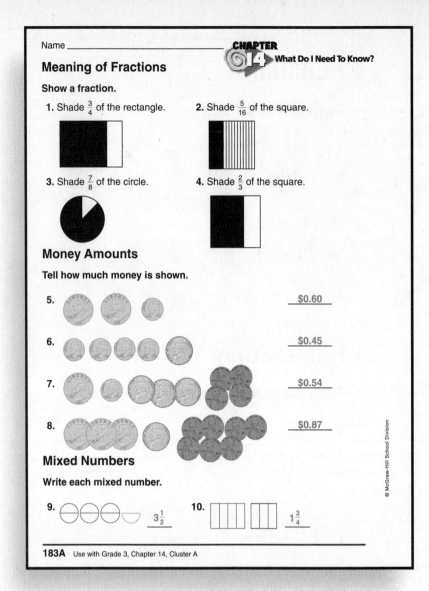

Name _____

Meaning of Fractions

Show a fraction.

1. Shade $\frac{3}{4}$ of the rectangle.

2. Shade $\frac{5}{16}$ of the square.

3. Shade $\frac{7}{8}$ of the circle.

4. Shade $\frac{2}{3}$ of the square.

Money Amounts

Tell how much money is shown.

5. _____ $0.60

6. _____ $0.45

7. _____ $0.54

8. _____ $0.87

Mixed Numbers

Write each mixed number.

9. _____ $3\frac{1}{2}$

10. _____ $1\frac{3}{4}$

183A Use with Grade 3, Chapter 14, Cluster A

CLUSTER A PREREQUISITE SKILLS

The skills listed in this chart are those identified as major prerequisite skills for students' success in the lessons in Cluster A of the chapter. Each skill is covered by one or more assessment items as shown in the middle column. The right column provides the page numbers for the lessons in this book that reteach the Cluster A prerequisite skills.

Skill Name	Assessment Items	Lesson Pages
Meaning of Fractions	1-4	184-185
Money Amounts	5-8	186-187
Mixed Numbers	9-10	188-189

Name_____

Addition

Find each sum.

11.	56 + 19 75	12.	148 + 209 357	13.	$3.67 + 1.93 $5.60

14. $45 + 38 =$ ___83___

15. $6.13 + $1.97 + $0.67 =$ ___$8.77___

Subtraction

Find each difference.

16.	51 − 14 37	17.	321 − 162 159	18.	$8.04 − 5.36 $2.68

19. $80 − 65 =$ ___15___

20. $5.49 − $0.89 =$ ___$4.60___

Use with Grade 3, Chapter 14, Cluster B **183B**

CLUSTER B PREREQUISITE SKILLS

The skills listed in this chart are those identified as major prerequisite skills for students' success in the lessons in Cluster B of the chapter. Each skill is covered by one or more assessment items as shown in the middle column. The right column provides the page numbers for the lessons in this book that reteach the Cluster B prerequisite skills

Skill Name	Assessment Items	Lesson Pages
Addition	11-15	190-191
Subtraction	16-20	192-193

Alternative Assessment Strategies

• Oral administration of the assessment is appropriate for younger students or those whose native language is not English. Read the skills title and directions one section at a time. Check students' understanding by asking them to tell you how they will do the first exercise in the group.

• For some skill types you may wish to use group administration. In this technique, a small group or pair of students complete the assessment together. Through their discussion, you will be able to decide if supplementary reteaching materials are needed.

Intervention Materials

If students are not successful with the prerequisite skills assessed on these pages, reteaching lessons have been created to help them make the transition into the chapter.

Item correlation charts showing the skills lessons suitable for reteaching the prerequisite skills are found beneath the reproductions of each page of the assessment.

Cluster B Challenge
Those students who demonstrate mastery of the skills on this page will not need to use the reteaching worksheets. Instead, these students can do the Cluster B Challenge found on pages 196-197.

Lesson Goal

• Represent fractions as parts of a whole.

What the Student Needs to Know

• Identify numerators and denominators.

• Model fractions as parts of a whole.

• Understand different models of the same fraction.

Getting Started

• Write 1, 2, and $\frac{1}{2}$ on the board. Ask: *Which of these numbers is a fraction?* $\frac{1}{2}$ *How do you know?* (It has two numbers, stacked one on top of the other, with a horizontal line between them.) Have students write other fractions on the board. Discuss what all fractions have in common (two numbers and a horizontal line.)

• Draw a circle or square on the chalkboard. Ask a volunteer to divide the drawing in half. After the student correctly divides the shape, label it with $\frac{1}{2}$. Tell students that they can use drawings to show many different fractions.

What Can I Do?

Read the question and the response. Then read and discuss the examples. Ask:

• *What is the number above the line in a fraction called?* (the numerator) *What is the number below the line called?* (the denominator)

• Have students count the number of parts in the rectangle (8). Explain that the rectangle is divided into eighths. After exploring $\frac{7}{8}$ on the page, you may wish to have students model $\frac{1}{8}$, $\frac{4}{8}$, $\frac{5}{8}$, and $\frac{8}{8}$. Point out that to model $\frac{8}{8}$ you need to color the entire rectangle. Write: $\frac{8}{8} = 1$.

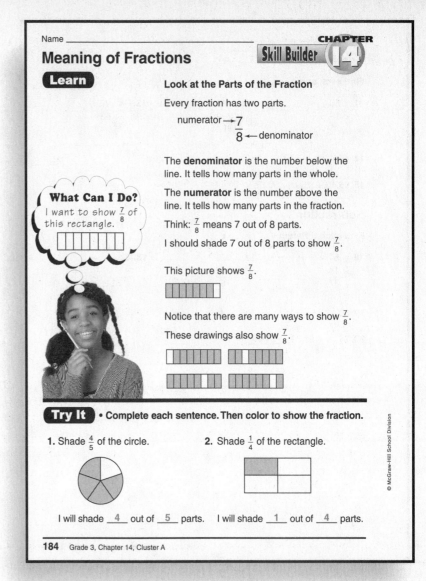

WHAT IF THE STUDENT CAN'T

Identify Numerators and Denominators

• If the student gets confused when using unfamiliar fractions, remind him or her it really helps to draw a quick sketch of a familiar fraction, such as $\frac{1}{2}$ or $\frac{3}{4}$. Looking at the sketch can help the student remember that the numerator is the number of parts in the fraction and the denominator is the number of parts in the whole.

• You may wish to help the student remember the terms "numerator" and "denominator" by pointing out that both "denominator" and "down" begin with the letter *d*. This fact can help the student remember which number is which in a fraction.

Model Fractions as Parts of a Whole

• Suggest that the student use fraction manipulatives to practice modeling fractions. Encourage the student to write down each fraction he or she models.

Understand Different Models of the Same Fraction

• Draw a circle divided into thirds and color in one third. Ask: *How many parts does this*

Name _____

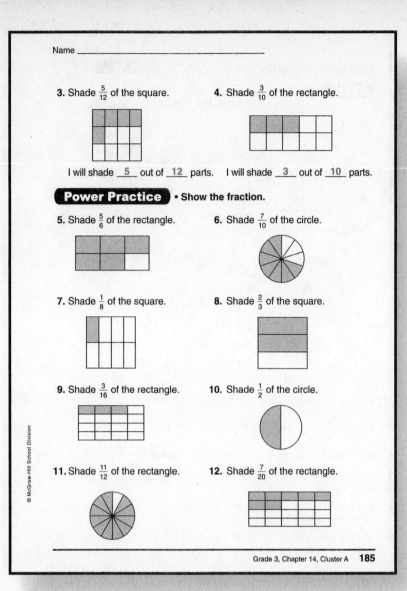

3. Shade $\frac{5}{12}$ of the square.

I will shade __5__ out of __12__ parts.

4. Shade $\frac{3}{10}$ of the rectangle.

I will shade __3__ out of __10__ parts.

Power Practice • Show the fraction.

5. Shade $\frac{5}{6}$ of the rectangle.

6. Shade $\frac{7}{10}$ of the circle.

7. Shade $\frac{1}{8}$ of the square.

8. Shade $\frac{2}{3}$ of the square.

9. Shade $\frac{3}{16}$ of the rectangle.

10. Shade $\frac{1}{2}$ of the circle.

11. Shade $\frac{11}{12}$ of the rectangle.

12. Shade $\frac{7}{20}$ of the rectangle.

© McGraw-Hill School Division

Grade 3, Chapter 14, Cluster A **185**

WHAT IF THE STUDENT CAN'T

circle have? (3) *How many parts are shaded?* (1) *What fraction does this circle show?* ($\frac{1}{3}$) Draw another circle divided into thirds. Shade a different third. *How are these two models different?* (Different parts are shaded.) *How are they the same?* (They both show $\frac{1}{3}$.) Show students additional examples of fraction models that are shaded differently but show the same fraction.

Complete the Power Practice

• Have the student work with a partner to complete each drawing. Encourage partners to take turns shading in the

drawings. Suggest that students begin by saying: *"I will shade ___ out of ___ parts,"* substituting the correct numbers from the fraction they are planning to show.

• Students may want to find all of the possible models for $\frac{7}{8}$. Explain that there are 8 different ways to color in the rectangle to show $\frac{7}{8}$. In each, one part out of the eight equal parts in each drawing is left unshaded.

• For each fraction model, emphasize that there is more than one correct model.

Try It

• Have students read each fraction aloud to solve exercises 1–4. Help them understand that to complete each sentence, they can write the numerator in the first blank and the denominator in the second blank. Then they can follow the directions to decide how to color the drawing.

• Allow students to compare their drawings. Remind students that different drawings can represent the same fraction.

Power Practice

• You may wish to allow students to use colored pencils or crayons to complete the exercises.

• Remind students that if they get confused, they can fill in a sentence like the ones in exercises 1–4: "I will shade ___ out of ___ parts."

Lesson Goal
- Count money amounts.

What the Student Needs to Know
- Add more than two addends.
- Recognize that addends can be rearranged.
- Skip count by 5s, 10s, and 25s.

Getting Started
- Give each student a small handful of play money. Ask students to describe how they can count how much money they have. Encourage them to share their own counting strategies.
- Tell students that this lesson will review two strategies they can use to add money amounts.
- Review the words *penny, nickel, dime,* and *quarter.* Have students say and spell each word and tell how many cents each coin is worth.
- Review skip counting. Have students practice skip counting by 5s, 10s, and 25s.

What Can I Do?
Read the question and the response. Then read and discuss the examples. You may wish to use play money to model the amounts shown on the page. Say:
- *Name each coin in the first group.* (dime, quarter, penny, quarter, dime) *If I move the penny to the beginning, have I changed the amount of money?* (No.) Help students understand that rearranging coins in a set does not change the value of the set.
- Tell students that rearranging coins can often help them add. It is usually easier to add coins that are the same first. To add a large group of coins, begin by sorting them into groups of the same kind of coins.

Name _____

Money Amounts

Skill Builder

Learn

Arrange and Add

How much money is shown here?

What Can I Do?
I want to find how much money is shown.

It can be easier to add when coins are in order. Put the coins in order from most to least valuable. You can use your imagination or play money.

Add the amounts.
Think: 25¢ + 25¢ = 50¢
50¢ + 10¢ = 60¢
60¢ + 10¢ = 70¢
70¢ + 1¢ = 71¢

The coins show 71¢.

Skip Count and Add

How much money is shown here?

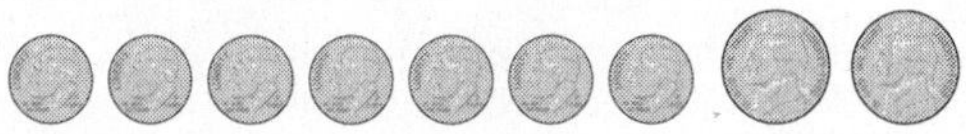

If there are a lot of one kind of coin, try skip counting.

To count dimes, skip count by 10s.

Think: 10, 20, 30, 40, 50, 60, 70
Then add the value of two nickels.
Think: 70 + 5 + 5 = 80

The coins show 80¢.

186   Grade 3, Chapter 14, Cluster A

© McGraw-Hill School Division

WHAT IF THE STUDENT CAN'T

Add More Than Two Addends
- Break the addition into a series of smaller, one-step problems. Have the student find totals one step at a time. First, the student can add the values of two coins together. Next, he or she adds the value of one coin to that result. The students keeps adding until he or she has added all of the coins.

Recognize That Addends Can Be Rearranged
- Encourage the student to work with concrete models, such as play money. Have the student find the total value of a set of coins. Write an addition sentence showing the order in which the coins were added. Then rearrange the coins and have them find the total value again. Write another addition sentence showing the new order of addition. Emphasize the fact that the total value does not change, no matter what order you add the coins.

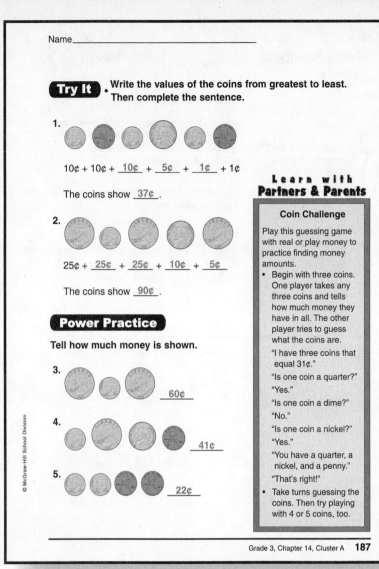

Name _____

Try It • Write the values of the coins from greatest to least.
Then complete the sentence.

1.

10¢ + 10¢ + _10¢_ + _5¢_ + _1¢_ + 1¢

The coins show _37¢_ .

2.

25¢ + _25¢_ + _25¢_ + _10¢_ + _5¢_

The coins show _90¢_ .

Power Practice

Tell how much money is shown.

3.
_60¢_

4.
_41¢_

5.
_22¢_

**Learn with
Partners & Parents**

Coin Challenge

Play this guessing game with real or play money to practice finding money amounts.

• Begin with three coins. One player takes any three coins and tells how much money they have in all. The other player tries to guess what the coins are.

"I have three coins that equal 31¢."

"Is one coin a quarter?"

"Yes."

"Is one coin a dime?"

"No."

"Is one coin a nickel?"

"Yes."

"You have a quarter, a nickel, and a penny."

"That's right!"

• Take turns guessing the coins. Then try playing with 4 or 5 coins, too.

Grade 3, Chapter 14, Cluster A **187**

WHAT IF THE STUDENT CAN'T

Skip Count by 5s, 10s, and 25s

• Have students write the counting series for skip counting by 5s, 10s, and 25s up to 50 and to 100. Have partners take turns counting by these numbers. If they get stuck or disagree, partners can refer to the counting sheets.

Complete the Power Practice

• If the student has trouble deciding how to rearrange the coins, have him or her practice with different numbers of quarters, dimes, nickels, and pennies of play money. Draw several combinations on the board and ask

the student to group the coins to make adding or multiplying easier.

• Go over the exercises with the student. Ask him or her which problems could be solved by skip counting. Have the student skip count aloud so you can determine if he or she is counting correctly.

• Allow the student to use paper and pencil to help them keep track of larger money amounts. Encourage the student to develop mental math skills by answering the question and then using paper and pencil to check the answers.

• After students read the first example, have them practice using small handfuls of play money.

• Read the second example. Ask: *Why is skip counting useful for counting this set of coins?* (There are a lot of dimes, so you can skip count by 10s to find how much they are worth.) *What if the two nickels were at the beginning of the set. How would you count then?* (Answers vary. Students might rearrange the set and count the dimes first, or they might add the nickels together to get 10 and then skip count on by 10s from 10.)

Try It

• Allow students to use play money to model each set on coins shown. Concrete models can be particularly helpful for exercises 1–4, in which students practice rearranging addends.

Power Practice

• Have students tell whether they will rearrange coins or skip count to solve each exercise.

Learn with Partners & Parents

• Have students play several rounds of this guessing game to help them practice evaluating coin amounts.

• After students have played several rounds with three coins, ask: *What is the greatest amount of money you can have with three coins?* (75¢ if quarters are the largest available coin; $1.50 with half dollars and $3 with dollar coins) *What is the least amount you can have with three coins?* (3¢)

Lesson Goal

- Model and write mixed numbers.

What the Student Needs to Know

- Model whole numbers and fractions.

- Understand that mixed numbers combine a whole number and a fraction.

Getting Started

- Review fractions with students. Draw a square on the board and divide it into four equal parts. Write $\frac{3}{4}$ on the board. Ask: *How can I shade $\frac{3}{4}$ of this square?* (Shade 3 out of the 4 parts.) *Is $\frac{3}{4}$ more or less than 1?* (less) *Is $\frac{3}{4}$ more or less than 0?* (more)

- Draw a number line on the board. Label 0, 1, 2, 3, and 4. Ask: *Where do you think $2\frac{1}{2}$ is on this number line?* (Students should indicate halfway between 2 and 3.) *Where is $3\frac{1}{2}$?* (halfway between 3 and 4)

What Can I Do?

Read the question and the response. Then read and discuss the example. Ask:

- *What is a mixed number?* (A mixed number is a number that includes a whole number and a fraction.) *Are all mixed numbers greater than 1?* (Yes.) *Why?* (Because they all have a whole number, which is 1 or greater, plus a fraction.)

- Have students look at the model of $2\frac{1}{4}$. *How does this model show the whole number 2?* (Two whole rectangles are shaded.) *How does the model show the fraction $\frac{1}{4}$?* (One quarter, or one fourth, of the third rectangle is shaded.)

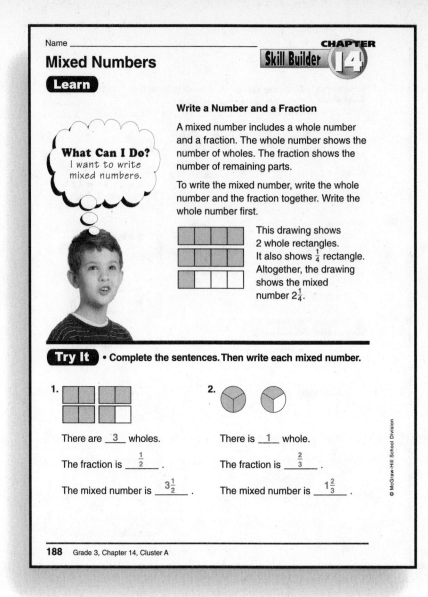

Name _____

Mixed Numbers

Learn

What Can I Do?
I want to write mixed numbers.

Write a Number and a Fraction

A mixed number includes a whole number and a fraction. The whole number shows the number of wholes. The fraction shows the number of remaining parts.

To write the mixed number, write the whole number and the fraction together. Write the whole number first.

This drawing shows 2 whole rectangles. It also shows $\frac{1}{4}$ rectangle. Altogether, the drawing shows the mixed number $2\frac{1}{4}$.

Try It • Complete the sentences. Then write each mixed number.

1.

There are ___3___ wholes.

The fraction is ___$\frac{1}{2}$___ .

The mixed number is ___$3\frac{1}{2}$___ .

2.

There is ___1___ whole.

The fraction is ___$\frac{2}{3}$___ .

The mixed number is ___$1\frac{2}{3}$___ .

© McGraw-Hill School Division

188 Grade 3, Chapter 14, Cluster A

WHAT IF THE STUDENT CAN'T

Model Whole Numbers and Fractions

- Have the student practice modeling whole numbers. Write the fraction $\frac{4}{4}$ on the board and draw a circle divided into four parts. Ask: *How can you shade this circle to show $\frac{4}{4}$?* (Color all four parts.)

Write $\frac{4}{4} = 1$ on the board. Explain that when you shade an entire shape, it can represent one whole number. Add another circle divided into four parts and shade all four parts. Ask: *What whole number do these circles show?* (2) Repeat with other whole num-

bers, such as $\frac{5}{5}$, $\frac{3}{3}$, and $\frac{8}{8}$.

- Review modeling fractions. Write these fractions on the board: $\frac{1}{2}$, $\frac{3}{5}$, $\frac{5}{8}$, $\frac{3}{10}$ and have the student describe how to show each fraction. Remind the student that the denominator of a fraction tells how many parts are in the whole. The numerator tells how many of the parts are in the fraction.

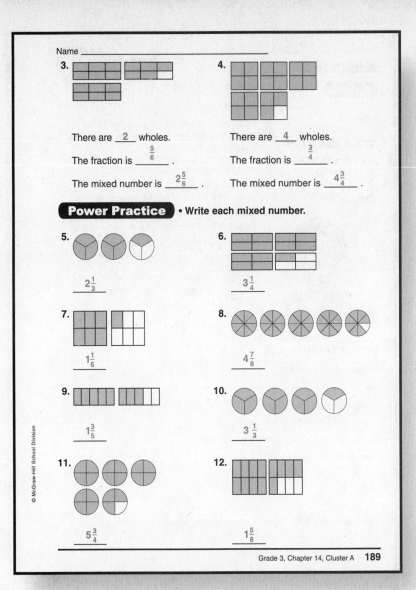

Name _____

3. There are __2__ wholes.

The fraction is __5/6__ .

The mixed number is __2 5/6__ .

4. There are __4__ wholes.

The fraction is __3/4__ .

The mixed number is __4 3/4__ .

Power Practice • Write each mixed number.

5. $2\frac{1}{3}$

6. $3\frac{1}{4}$

7. $1\frac{1}{6}$

8. $4\frac{7}{8}$

9. $1\frac{3}{5}$

10. $3\frac{1}{3}$

11. $5\frac{3}{4}$

12. $1\frac{5}{8}$

USING THE LESSON

- Review the meaning of mixed numbers by writing these numbers on the board: 5, $4\frac{1}{2}$, 6, and $3\frac{5}{6}$. Have students identify the mixed numbers ($4\frac{1}{2}$, $3\frac{5}{6}$) and explain why they are mixed numbers.

Try It •   Ask a volunteer to read each exercise aloud and complete the sentences below the models.

- You may wish to have students use fraction manipulatives to model each mixed number in exercises 1–4.

Power Practice

- Help students answer exercises 5–12 by following this strategy. First, count the number of wholes shown. Write that number as the first part of the mixed number. Then, look at the shape that is only partly shaded. Write the fraction that names the shaded area. Put the whole number and the fraction together to write the answer.

WHAT IF THE STUDENT CAN'T

Understand That Mixed Numbers Combine a Whole Number and a Fraction

- Help the student visualize mixed numbers by creating concrete models. Cut three identical squares out of construction paper. Ask: *How many squares do I have?* (3) Fold one square in half and cut along the fold. Discard one half and show the remaining half with the other squares. *How many squares do I have now?* ($2\frac{1}{2}$) Have students name the parts of the mixed number. (the whole number 2 and the fraction $\frac{1}{2}$) Have students create

paper models to show and write other mixed numbers.

Complete the Power Practice

- Encourage the student to use fraction manipulatives to model the mixed numbers in the exercises.

- Emphasize that different models can show the same mixed number. Have the student draw four circles divided into quarters and four squares divided into quarters. Ask him or her to shade $3\frac{1}{4}$ of the circles. Then have the student draw four more circles and shade $3\frac{1}{4}$ of the squares in a different way.

Lesson Goal
- Add 3-digit numbers

What the Student Needs to Know
- Add numbers without regrouping.
- Add numbers with regrouping.
- Estimate sums.

Getting Started
- Have students review basic addition facts using flash cards or number cards. Have students describe strategies for remembering addition facts.
- Write 62 + 35 on the board. Have students explain how they can find the sum. Students may want to write a stacked addition problem to help them add. Ask: *What numbers are in the ones place?* (2 and 5) *What is 2 + 5?* (7) *What numbers are in the tens place?* (6 and 3) *What is 6 tens + 3 tens?* (9) *What is the total?* (97)
- Write 28 + 37 on the board. Have a volunteer write the problem as a stacked addition problem. Make sure students align the ones and tens. Ask: *What numbers are in the ones place?* (8 and 7) *What is 8 + 7?* (15) *What numbers are in the tens place?* (2 and 3) *What is 2 tens + 3 tens?* (5 tens) *What is 5 tens + 15?* (65)

What Can I Do?
Read the question and the response. Then read and discuss the examples.
- Tell students that they will follow the same steps to add 3-digit numbers as they used for 2-digit numbers.
- Help students understand how to rewrite addition problems by stacking the numbers. Explain that stacking can help line up the ones, tens, and hundreds. Write 578 + 98 on the board. Ask: *How many ones are in each number?* (8 and 8) *What is 8 + 8?* (16)

Name _____

Addition

Skill Builder **Learn**

CHAPTER 14

What Can I Do?
I want to add three-digit numbers.

Rewrite the Problem

What is 578 + 98?

Write this problem by stacking the numbers. Remember to stack the numbers so that the ones are above the ones.

To add, start with the ones.

Think: 8 + 8 = 16
Write the 6 and regroup the 10 ones as 1 ten

Think: 1 ten + 7 tens + 9 tens = 17 tens.
Write the 7 and rename 10 tens as 1 hundred.

Think: 1 hundred + 5 hundreds = 6 hundreds.
Write the 6.

$$
\begin{array}{r} 578 \\ + 98 \\ \hline \end{array}
\qquad
\begin{array}{r} \overset{1}{5}78 \\ + 98 \\ \hline 6 \end{array}
\qquad
\begin{array}{r} \overset{1\ 1}{5}78 \\ + 98 \\ \hline 76 \end{array}
\qquad
\begin{array}{r} \overset{1\ 1}{5}78 \\ + 98 \\ \hline 676 \end{array}
$$

So, 578 + 98 = 676.

Estimate Before You Add

What is $3.85 + $5.17?

Round each amount to the nearest dollar.

Think: $3.85 is close to $4.
   $5.17 is close to $5.

So, the answer will be close to $4 + $5, or $9.

Rewrite the problem to add.

$$
\begin{array}{r} \$3.85 \\ + \ 5.17 \\ \hline \$9.02 \end{array}
$$

The answer is $9.02. It is close to your estimate of $9.

WHAT IF THE STUDENT CAN'T

Add Numbers Without Regrouping
- Have the student practice addition facts to 18. Give the student number cards from 1 to 9 and have him or her practice selecting two cards and finding the sum. A partner can evaluate the responses.
- Make sure that the student aligns numbers accurately before adding. The student might use a place-value chart to help with the alignment of ones, tens, and hundreds.

Add Numbers With Regrouping
- Have the student use place-value manipulatives to practice renaming 10 ones as 1 ten and 10 tens as 1 hundred. The student can model each of the exercises to help with the visualization of the addition.
- Make sure the student remembers to write down the 1 or other number when he or she regroups. Check the student's work to see that he or she is using accurate annotations to keep track of regrouping.

Name _____

1. 226 + 367

```
    2   2   6
+   3   6   7
    5   9   3
```

2. $7.35 + $1.19

```
$   7  .  3   5
+   1  .  1   9
$   8  .  5   4
```

3. 820 + 451

```
    8   2   0
+   4   5   1
  1,2   7   1
```

Estimate. Then find the exact sum. Use your estimate to check your answer.

4. $6.08 + $5.89

$6.08 is close to $6 .
$5.89 is close to $6 .

The answer will be close to $12 .
Exact sum = $11.97

5. 717 + 825

717 is close to 700 .
825 is close to 800 .

The answer will be close to 1,500 .
Exact sum = 1,542

Power Practice • Find each sum.

6.
```
    484
+   273
    757
```

7.
```
    704
+   609
  1,313
```

8.
```
  $9.32
+  5.12
 $14.44
```

9.
```
  $3.89
+  8.02
 $11.91
```

10.
```
    649
+   886
  1,535
```

11.
```
  $8.02
   2.20
+  0.79
 $11.01
```

12. 532 + 126 = _658_   **13.** 625 + 104 = _729_   **14.** $5.12 + $2.95 = _$8.07_

15. 410 + 327 = _737_   **16.** 742 + 327 = _1,069_   **17.** $3.89 + $3.99 = _$7.88_

© McGraw-Hill School Division

Grade 3, Chapter 14, Cluster B **191**

WHAT IF THE STUDENT CAN'T

Estimate Sums

- Allow the student to practice estimating. The student can estimate using rounding or front-end estimation. Write several 3-digit numbers, such as 213, 877, 692, 541, and 368 and have the student round each to the nearest hundred. Then repeat with 3-digit money amounts, asking the student to round to the nearest dollar.

Complete the Power Practice

- Have the student work with a partner to complete the activities. Suggest that partners take turns finding sums and then checking the sum to make sure it is accurate.

USING THE LESSON

- *How can you rename the 1 in 16?* (the 1 equals 1 ten) Follow the rest of the addition as described.

- In the second example, have students discuss how estimating can help you check your answers. Remind students that they might round to the nearest dollar or the nearest hundred.

Try It

- Students practice writing stacked addition problems in exercises 1–3. Remind students to line up ones, tens, and hundreds.

- Students practice estimating and finding exact sums in exercises 4–5. Have students compare their estimates and their exact answers.

Power Practice

- Encourage students to estimate each sum before adding. Remind students to show renaming. Before students begin an exercise, they can also predict whether or not they will need to rename ones or tens to solve the exercise.

- Allow students to use a second piece of paper to write stacked addition problems to solve exercises 12–17.

- If students are confused by the decimal points in problems dealing with money, help them see that they can simply add the numbers as though they were hundreds and then add the decimal point in the sum. Estimating should help students decide where to place the decimal point.

USING THE LESSON

Lesson Goal
- Subtract 3-digit numbers.

What the Student Needs to Know
- Subtract without regrouping.
- Subtract with regrouping.

Getting Started
- Write 28 – 13 on the board. Ask a volunteer to write the problem as a stacked problem. Make sure the student aligns ones and tens. Ask: *Do you need to regroup to find the answer?* (No.) *Why not?* (Because you can take 3 from 8 without regrouping and 1 from 2 without regrouping.) *What is the difference?* (15)
- Write 51 – 18 on the board. Ask: *Can you subtract 8 from 1?* (No.) *How can regrouping help you find the difference?* (You can regroup 1 ten as 10 ones.) Have a volunteer continue the subtraction. *What is the difference?* (33)

What Can I Do?
Read the question and the response. Then read and discuss the example. Have a volunteer read the reasoning strategy aloud. Ask:

- *How do you know you can subtract 187 from 462?* (Because 187 is less than 482.) *Why do you need to regroup to find this difference?* (Because you cannot subtract 7 from 2 and you cannot subtract 8 tens from 5 tens.)

- Have students discuss why addition helps them check their answer. Ask: *What if you add your answer to the number you are subtracting and you do not get the third number in the problem?* (Your answer is probably incorrect.)

- You may wish to model additional subtraction problems that require no regrouping (854 – 623); regrouping only tens (352 – 249); regrouping only hundreds (702 – 611); or regrouping tens and hundreds (428 – 379).

Subtraction

Learn

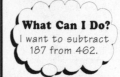

What Can I Do?
I want to subtract 187 from 462.

Regroup Tens and Hundreds

Write the subtraction problem.

$$\begin{array}{r} 462 \\ -\,187 \end{array}$$

Think: I can't subtract 7 from 2 because 7 is greater than 2. I need to regroup.

Look at the tens column.

The 6 in the tens column equals 6 tens. It can also equal 5 tens plus 10 ones. Regroup 1 ten as 10 ones.

$$\begin{array}{r} {}^{5\,12} \\ 46\!\!\!/2 \\ -\,187 \\ \hline 5 \end{array}$$

Think: 12 – 7 = 5

You can't subtract 8 tens from 5 tens. Look at the hundreds column. The 4 in the hundreds column equals 4 hundreds. It can also equal 3 hundreds and 10 tens. Regroup 1 hundred as 10 tens.

$$\begin{array}{r} {}^{15} \\ {}^{3\,5\,12} \\ 46\!\!\!/2 \\ -\,187 \\ \hline 75 \end{array}$$

Think: 15 tens – 8 tens = 7 tens

Finally, subtract 100 from 300.

$$\begin{array}{r} {}^{15} \\ {}^{3\,5\,12} \\ 46\!\!\!/2 \\ -\,187 \\ \hline 275 \end{array}$$

Check your answer with addition.

275 + 187 = 462

© McGraw-Hill School Division

WHAT IF THE STUDENT CAN'T

Subtract Without Regrouping
- Have the student create flash cards to help him or her remember basic subtraction facts. Allow partners to quiz one another on these facts.
- Make sure the student is aligning subtraction problems accurately. Suggest that the student use place-value charts to help with the alignment ones, tens, and hundreds.

Subtract With Regrouping
- Have the student use place-value manipulatives to help with regrouping for subtraction. Partners can model each exercise and then check their answers by adding.

Name _____

Try It . Tell whether or not you need to regroup to subtract.
Write *yes* or *no*.

1. 685
   − 222   no

2. 712
   − 431   yes

3. $2.99
   − 1.57   no

4. 902
   − 374   yes

5. 843
   − 255   yes

6. $1.28
   − 0.97   yes

Complete.

7. 8 tens = 7 tens and ___10___ tens

8. 6 hundreds = 5 hundreds and ___10___ tens

9. 9 tens = ___8___ tens and 10 ones

10. 4 hundreds = ___3___ hundreds and 10 tens

Power Practice • Find each difference.

11. $9.57
    − 7.23
    $2.34

12. 843
    − 757
    86

13. 736
    − 98
    638

14. 406
    − 389
    17

15. 600
    − 217
    383

16. $7.04
    − 0.88
    $6.16

17. 837 − 225 = ___612___

18. 756 − 657 = ___99___

19. $5.62 − $3.79 = ___$1.83___

20. 336 − 63 = ___273___

21. 400 − 282 = ___118___

22. $772 − $108 = ___$664___

23. $7.83 − $6.94 = ___$0.89___

24. 405 − 317 = ___88___

© McGraw-Hill School Division

Grade 3, Chapter 14, Cluster B **193**

Try It

- Deciding whether or not regrouping will be necessary can help students choose subtraction strategies. After students answer exercises 1–6, you may wish to have them check the subtractions by adding.

- The number sentences in exercises 7–10 will give students practice in regrouping. Students can use place-value manipulatives to model each equation.

Power Practice

- Encourage students to decide whether or not they will need to regroup to solve each exercise. Students may also wish to estimate before subtracting.

- Students can check their answers by adding.

WHAT IF THE STUDENT CAN'T

Complete the Power Practice

- Have the student read several subtraction problems and answers aloud. Then have the student practice writing and reading the related addition problem. For example: 837 minus 225 equals 612. 612 plus 225 equals 837.

- If the student forgets how to form the related addition sentence, encourage him or her to recall a simpler subtraction fact: 8 − 2 = 6; 6 + 2 = 8.

- For exercises that have money amounts, remind the student to ignore the dollar sign and decimal point and subtract following the same

steps as for other numbers. Then after subtracting, the student can place the decimal point two places from the right. Encourage the students to work with a partner who can estimate to help with the placement of the decimal point.

CHALLENGE

Lesson Goal
- Evaluate the relationship between digits in mixed numbers.

Introducing the Challenge
- Remind students that mixed numbers include a whole number and a fraction. Tell them that they will play a game in which they draw number cards to build a mixed number.

- Have students prepare number cards for the numbers 2, 3, 4, 6, and 8. Students will also need paper for scoring and construction paper or cardboard for each game board.

Using the Challenge
- Have a volunteer read the game rules on page 194. You may wish to model one round of the game. Make sure that students understand that each player draws his or her own game board. Explain that if both players create the same mixed number, nobody scores for that round.

- Ask: *What is the goal of the game?* (to build the greatest mixed number)

- Draw students' attention to the fraction diagrams. Ask: *Is $\frac{1}{2}$ greater or less than $\frac{1}{3}$?* (greater) *How do you know?* (The diagrams show that $\frac{1}{2}$ is larger than $\frac{1}{3}$) *Is $\frac{1}{4}$ greater or less than $\frac{1}{3}$?* (less)

- After students have played several rounds, ask: *What are the possible fractions in the mixed number?* ($\frac{1}{2}$, $\frac{1}{3}$, $\frac{1}{4}$) *Which fraction greatest?* ($\frac{1}{2}$)

- Exercises 1–4 help students analyze their results.

Name _____

Game of Mixed Numbers

Try this number game.

Create three number cards.   **Each partner draws this play board.**

$\boxed{}\ \dfrac{1}{\boxed{}}$

Follow these rules to create a mixed number:

- Shuffle the cards.
- Take turns picking 1 card.
- Write the number in one rectangle on your game board.
- Put the card back. Shuffle again.
- Pick again to complete your mixed number.

The player with the greatest number wins.

Use the diagram at the right to help you compare fractions.

1. What is the greatest possible mixed number you can get in this game? How do you know?
   $4\frac{1}{2}$; The greatest mixed number would have the greatest whole number (4) and the largest possible fraction ($\frac{1}{2}$).

2. What is the smallest possible mixed number you can get in this game? How do you know?
   $2\frac{1}{4}$; The smallest mixed number would have the smallest whole number (2) and the smallest possible fraction ($\frac{1}{4}$).

3. If you draw a 2 on your first turn, where will you write it? Why?
   Players should write the 2 in the denominator of the fraction because $\frac{1}{2}$ is the greatest possible fraction.

4. If you draw a 4 on your first turn, where will you write it? Why?
   Players should write the 4 in the whole number space of the mixed number because 4 is the greatest possible whole number.

194   Grade 3, Chapter 14, Cluster A

Name _____

Try the game with these cards and this game board.

3 4 6 8

$\dfrac{\boxed{}\ 2}{\boxed{}}$

Follow the same rules, except the player with the smallest number wins. Use the diagram at the right to help you compare fractions.

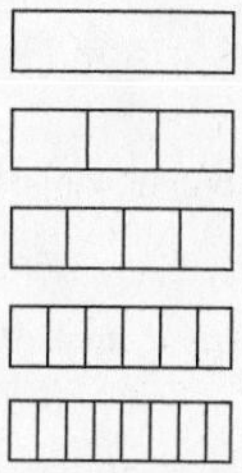

5. What mixed number will always win (or at least tie)? How do you know?
$3\frac{2}{8}$; The smallest possible number will always win or tie. The smallest possible mixed number includes the smallest possible whole number (3) and the smallest possible fraction ($\frac{2}{8}$).

6. What is the greatest possible mixed number you can get in this game? How do you know?
$8\frac{2}{3}$; The greatest mixed number would have the greatest whole number (8) and the largest possible fraction ($\frac{2}{3}$).

7. If you draw an 8 on your first turn, where will you write it? Why?
Players should write the 8 in the denominator of the fraction because $\frac{2}{8}$ is the smallest possible fraction.

8. If you draw a 3 on your first turn, where will you write it? Why?
Players should write the 3 in the whole number space of the mixed number because 3 is the smallest possible whole number.

CHALLENGE

- Discuss the game variation on page 195. Ask: *How is this game different from the first version?* (The number cards are different, the fraction has a 2 in the numerator, and the goal is to build the least number, not the greatest.)

- Draw students' attention to the fraction diagrams. Ask: *Is $\frac{2}{4}$ greater or less than $\frac{2}{6}$?* (greater) *How do you know?* (The diagrams show that $\frac{2}{4}$ is larger than $\frac{2}{6}$.) *Is $\frac{2}{3}$ greater or less than $\frac{2}{8}$?* (greater)

- After students have played several rounds, ask: *What are the possible fractions in the mixed number?* ($\frac{2}{3}, \frac{2}{4}, \frac{2}{6}, \frac{2}{8}$) *Which fraction is least?* ($\frac{2}{8}$)

CHALLENGE

Lesson Goal
- Complete input and output tables that follow addition and subtraction rules.

Introducing the Challenge
- Write 12 + ? = 19 on the board. Ask: *What is the missing number?* (7) *How did you find an answer?* (Answers will vary. Some students will use guessing and checking. Others will subtract 12 from 19.)
- Tell students that input/output tables contain missing numbers like the addition sentence. In this activity, students will learn how to complete these tables, using a rule.

Using the Challenge
- Ask a volunteer to read the definition and instruction at the top of the page. Say: *Each input and output table follows one set rule. The rule can be applied to any number, which is called the* input. *The result after the rule is applied is called the* output.
- Draw students' attention to the example at the top of the page. Ask: *What is the rule for this input and output table?* (Add 105.) *What output would you get for an input of 1?* (106) *How do you know?* (1 + 105 = 106) *If you get an output of 110, what was the input number?* (5) *How do you know?* (5 + 105 = 110)
- Have volunteers name additional input numbers for the first input and output table. Then have others name the correct output number.
- Have students work with a partner to solve the exercises. Encourage partners to begin by saying what is missing in each table. Partners can ask questions to help them find each missing number. For example, in exercise 1, they might ask "What happens to 657 when you add 172" and "What number plus 172 equals 999?"

Input/Output Tables

An input and output table shows how numbers change when you follow a rule.

Rule: Add 105

Input	80	90	95	203	?
Output	185	195	200	?	847

To find a missing output, think: What happens to 203 when you add 105?
203 + 105 = 308

To find a missing input, think: What number plus 105 would equal 847?
? + 105 = 847

You can subtract to find an answer: 847 − 105 = 742

Find the missing input, output, or rule.

1. Rule: Add 172

Input	12	134	548	657	827
Output	184	306	720	829	999

2. Rule: Subtract 268

Input	874	846	818	971	451
Output	606	578	550	703	183

3. Rule: Add 101

Input	78	283	366	871	453
Output	179	384	467	972	554

4. Rule: Subtract 97

Input	323	804	223	478	97
Output	226	707	126	381	0

5. Rule: Subtract 225

Input	389	650	226	780	250
Output	164	425	1	555	25

6. Rule: Add 390

Input	5	60	112	250	313
Output	395	450	502	640	703

Name _____

Use the numbers in the box to complete each input and output table.

7. | 76 255 256 435 |

Rule: Add 180

Input	76	255
Output	256	435

8. | 49 111 326 388 |

Rule: Subtract 277

Input	326	388
Output	49	111

9. | 1 55 56 200 255 |

Rule: Add 55

Input	1	200
Output	56	255

10. | 10 125 135 775 900 |

Rule: Subtract 125

Input	135	900
Output	10	775

11. | 5 6 248 253 254 |

Rule: Add 248

Input	5	6
Output	253	254

12. | 999 700 687 312 13 |

Rule: Subtract 687

Input	700	999
Output	13	312

13. | 110 111 221 222 333 |

Rule: Add 111

Input	110	222
Output	221	333

14. | 305 300 605 615 915 |

Rule: Subtract 300

Input	605	915
Output	305	615

© McGraw-Hill School Division

- Students can guess and check to find missing numbers, or use addition and subtraction.

- Encourage students to look for helpful clues in the existing table data. For example, in exercise 4, the rule is missing. Students can look at the final column of the table. They will notice that when 97 is input, the output is 0. This data gives a clue that the rule is "subtract 97." Students can test this rule on other input/output pairs to make sure it is the correct rule.

- For Exercises 7–14, students use numbers from a box to complete input and output tables. You may wish to model exercise 7 as a class model. Explain: *The rule is "Add 180." So each input number plus 180 will equal an output number. Let's start with 76. 76 plus 180 is 256, so 76 and 256 are an input/output pair.*

- Encourage students to look for clues that will help them find missing rules. For example, in exercise 9, students might notice that 55 and 56 are 1 apart, and 1 is a number in the box. They might try "Add 1" as the rule, but they will notice that although 55 and 56 work, 200 and 255 do not. They can then try "Add 55" as the rule and will discover the correct input/output pairs of 1, 56 and 200, 255.

- Note that the order of input/output pairs may vary in correct answers.